WhiteBlaze Pages
2018

A Complete Appalachian Trail Guidebook

Rick "Attroll" Towle

One Blaze · at a Time · Appalachian · Trail · WhiteBlaze.net

web site

email

WhiteBlaze Pages
www.whiteblazepages.com
attroll@whiteblazepages.com

Contents

© WhiteBlaze Pages 2018

Trail Updates from the Appalachian Trail Conservancy (ATC)

Keep an eye out here for the most up to date trail information or changes.

www.appalachiantrail.org/home/explore-the-trail/trail-updates

Preface

WhiteBlaze Pages is intended for thru hikers, long distance hikers, and section hikers on the Appalachian Trail. Its intent is to help you know where you are and what is around you at any given time, and to find services when you leave the trail for rest and resupply in nearby towns.

With help from the Appalachian Trail Conservancy (ATC), I have made every effort to make this as up to date as possible; however the trail and its surroundings are constantly changing. If you find any inaccurate or wrong information in this book, I would greatly appreciate it if you would write through the web site or the email listed in this book.

This book was done by hands on research and data collection. The establishments in this book do not pay to be listed. I receive no funding to produce this book. I currently do not pay anyone for furnishing information.

HELP ME KEEP THIS GUIDE UP TO DATE
I am requesting feedback. Corrections, suggestions, comments, and any information for improving this book for next year's edition can be sent to:

WhiteBlaze Pages
www.whiteblazepages.com
attroll@whiteblazepages.com

Printed in the United States of America
First Printing, 2017
978-0-9984562-1-8
WhiteBlaze Publishing
Denmark, ME 04022

WhiteBlaze Publishing
www.whiteblazepublishing.com

Updates and correction information

There are sometimes updates and corrections that come out after the book has been received from the printers. You can find this information at the following web address below.
www.whiteblazepages.com/updates/2018/

Acknowledgments

Credits for data collection and inputs to WhiteBlaze Pages are as follows, by name or trail name.
Appalachian Trail Conservancy (ATC)
Alpha-Gal
Richard Anderson
Chris Chambers
Bob "couscous" Geiser
Vic Hasler
Stewart Holt
Mrs Joy
Richard Ketelle of the Smoky Mountains Hiking Club.
LittleRock
Margaret Mills
Sue (Mama Liption) Spring
Ratman & Tumbler
Jeff Taussig

I would also like to thank the WhiteBlaze members for their help in contributing to this.

It's yours for the taking.
All you have to do is put one foot in front of the other.
Your the only one that can make it happen.
Hike Your Own Hike

Common reoccurring Appalachian Trail questions

What is the Appalachian Trail?
The Appalachian Trail also known as the "AT" is a National Scenic Trail extending from Springer Mountain, Georgia, to Mount Katahdin, Maine.

How long is the Appalachian Trail?
The trail measured 2,190.9 miles in 2018. The total distance changes slightly every year as the trail gets rerouted as needed.

How long does it take to thru-hike the entire trail?
If trying to complete the entire trail in one calendar year, it takes between five to seven months to complete. The success rate is, about 20 percent of hikers who begin the trail will complete it.

What is a thru hiker?
A thru hiker is someone who is attempting to complete the entire Trail in once calendar year. It does not have to be in one continuous direction, just completing the whole trail.

How much does a thru-hike cost?
The average cost to hike the entire Appalachian Trail as a thru-hike is approximately $3,000, which is about $1.50 per mile. This is just the spending money for hiking the trail. This does not include your gear.

What direction should you hike for a thru-hike, from GA to ME or ME to GA?
You can pick any direction you want.

The direction depends on the hiker and the start date. If you can start in early spring it is better to start in Georgia because the mountains in New England are still very cold and snowy. Most hike northbound, beginning in Georgia anytime from March to April. Southbound hikers generally start in Maine from late May to July.

Some hikers start down south and then realize they will not make it to Mount Katahdin before Baxter State Park closes on mid-Oct. Once they realize this they often jump ahead to Mount Katahdin, and then hike south to where they got off the trail. This is called Flip-Flopping.

Where do thru-hikers stay at night?
Most hikers stay at the many shelters and tent sites along the trail. There is always a shelter or a tent site within a day's walk.

How easy it is to get to a town?
The trail usually crosses a road about every five miles but this does not mean a trail town is close by. In this guidebook the access points to get to the trail towns are marked at road crossings along with the distance to them.

Where do thru-hikers get food and other supplies?
They get them by going into a trail town to grocery stores or whatever else is available. Another option is to set up a series of mail drops. This is having packages sent to you in trail towns along the trail. Some hikers do this to make sure they have food and supplies to last until the next town. See "Mail drop information" in this guide.

They say there are bears, wild boars and poisonous snakes?
There is no real need to fear bears, snakes, and wild boars. As long as you keep your eyes open and stay clear. The most important thing a hiker can do is to hanging their food in bear bags or bear boxes in known bear activity areas.

Appalachian Trail

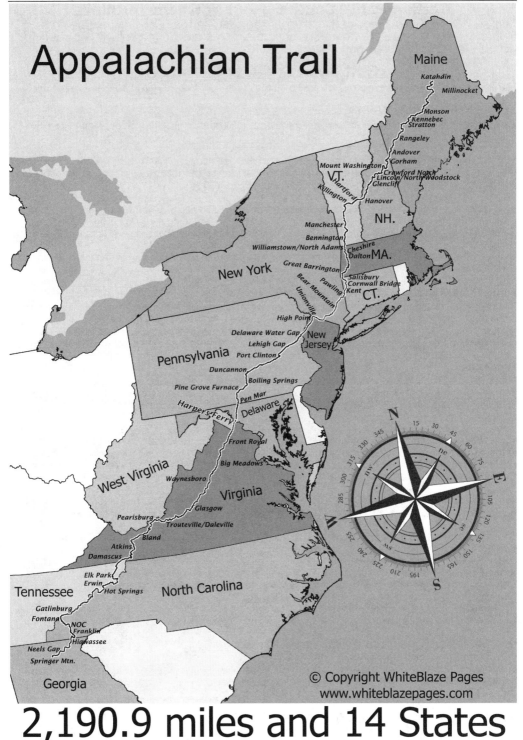

© Copyright WhiteBlaze Pages
www.whiteblazepages.com

2,190.9 miles and 14 States

Make a copy of this map and share it with family and friends.
They can track the progress of your hike.

Getting to the Southern and Northern Termini's

This section provides suggested instructions for getting to Springer Mountain and Mount Katahdin. There are numerous shuttle services mentioned below that will help get you to these locations and other trail heads.

Getting to Springer Mountain

The southern terminus of the Appalachian Trail is on top of Springer Mountain, and is accessible only by foot.

Starting at Amicalola Falls or Big Stamp Gap

There are two factors to consider as to whether you want to start your hike at Big Stamp Gap/USFS 42 or at Amicalola Falls State Park.

1. If starting at Amicalola Falls State Park, you have to hike the Approach Trail that leads to the AT. The Approach Trail is 8.8 miles. The start of the Approach Trail is a staircase of 604 steps. Do you want to add another 8.8 miles onto your already planned 2,000 plus mile hike?

2. If you start at Big Stamp Gap, you are 1.0 miles north on the AT already. If you want to get to Springer Mountain (the actual beginning of the AT) you will have to hike south on the AT for 1.0 miles and then retrace your steps back. This is a very easy hike in and back out. Cost comparisons and time are the factors to consider here. Spending a day traveling from Atlanta to Amicalola Falls and another day to hike up the approach trail, vs. going direct to the AT from the airport and hiking northbound on the AT in about 4 hours after your plane lands.

Springer Mountain, Amicalola Falls State Park, Georgia

The closest major city to the southern terminus of the AT is Atlanta, GA, 103 miles from Big Stamp Gap and the nearest point to get on the AT. It is 82 miles from Amicalola Falls State Park, if you want to hike the Approach Trail. Some shuttle services will pick you up in Atlanta, but it is more economical to take Greyhound or AMTRAK to Gainesville to go 42 miles to Big Stamp Gap or 38 miles from the Amicalola Falls State Park.

Suggestions:

Hikers will likely find information directing them from the Atlanta airport to take public transportation (Marta) from the airport to North Springs Marta station and find a ride to the AT from there. Some have found an Uber ride to Amicalola Falls Park where they climb the 8 mile approach trail to the AT.

However shuttle drivers like to avoid the very heavy traffic around North Springs, where snarled traffic often adds 2-3 hours to a trip leaving other hikers waiting. It is much faster to ride directly from the Atlanta airport to the top of Springer Mountain by a route that avoids the GA Hwy 400 traffic. By doing this you will avoid a ride around Atlanta to North Springs and then finding a ride to Amicalola paying for a campsite or a room at the lodge and spending a day hiking the Approach Trail. Unless you want to hike the approach trail.

Going directly to Springer Mountain can save a hiker at least one and a half days by avoiding the Approach Trail out of Amicalola Falls State Park, but costing perhaps $30 more than the North Springs route.

Driving directions to Springer Mountain from Amicalola Falls State Park

Turn right when leaving Highway 52 for 7.8 miles.
Follow Southern Road for 7.8 miles.
Turn right onto Roy Road for 5.0 miles.
Turn right onto Doublehead Road for 2.1 miles until you see Mt. Pleasant Church on your left.
Turn right onto dirt road (Forest Service Road 42 is unsigned).
You should see a large sign indicating that this is the entrance to the Blue Ridge Wildlife Management Area. There should also be a small brown sign saying : "Springer Mt. 6.5 miles".

Driving directions from points in GA
Geeting to Springer from points in northern GA
Get on US 76 in northern GA
Follow US 76 east until you get to Ellijay.
Once in Ellijay, follow the direction I mentioned below for Ellijay.

Getting to Springer from Elligay, GA (from western GA)
From Ellijay get on GA 52 East for about 5.3 miles.
Turn left onto Big Creek Road, which will turn into Douublehead Road. Stay on these roads for 12.6 miles.
Turn right onto dirt road (Forest Service Road 42 is unsigned).
You should see a large sign indicating that this is the entrance to the Blue Ridge Wildlife Management Area. There should also be a small brown sign saying : "Springer Mt. 6.5 miles".

Getting to Springer from Dahlonega, GA (from eastern GA)
Follow GA-52 West about 8.9 miles.
Turn right onto Nimblewill Church Road for 2.3 miles.
Turn right onto Forest Service 28-1/FS 28-1 Rd for 2.0 miles.
Turn left on Winding Stair Gap road/FS-77 for 5.0 miles.
Turn left on Forest Service Road for 2.6 miles to Springer Mountain parking lot.

Getting to Springer from southern, GA
The best bet for doing this is the find your way to either Ellijay or Dahlonega and follow those drirections as mentioned above.

Shuttles to Springer Mountain/Amicalola Falls State Park:

🚐**Richard Anderson** 706-276-2520(home) 404-408-2524(cell)
richardjanderson@etcmail.com. Based in Ellijay. Hiker Rides from Atlanta Airport or Bus Station; from Gainesville Amtrak or Greyhound station, to Springer and all points on the AT in Georgia, NC, up to Fontana. Section hiker rides from any trailhead to another, prompt "rescue" rides if your plans change. 10+ years' Experience, reliable, friendly, and on time.
🚐◈**Appalachian Adventure Company** - Tom Bazemore
706-265-9454, 865-456-7677 thomasbazemore@icloud.com
AT Passport location.
Based in Blairsville,GA. Shuttles range Atlanta, Asheville, Knoxville airports & bus stations and Gainesville, GA Amtrak & bus stations, and along AT.
Anywhere from Amicalola Falls S.P. and Springer Mtn. GA through Great Smoky Mountains National Park.
Can shuttle up to 10 people, can go as far north as Damascus, VA for a large enough group. Will also stop at outfitters or grocery stores along the way.
🚐◈**Ron Brown** 706-669-0919(cell) 706-636-2825(home) hikershuttles@outlook.com
Please leave a message with your phone number if you get voice mail.
Flat rate for shuttles to or from any part of the AT from Atlanta to Fontana and nearby towns, as well as Amicalola Falls S.P., Atlanta airport, and Gainesville, GA.
Dogs welcome; extra stops OK. Fuel on request.
🚐**Sam Duke** 706-994-6633. Shuttles from Atlanta to Fontana. Based out of Blairsville.
🚐**Marty Rogers** 678-576-6315(cell) mr814kw@hotmail.com, Based in Atlanta. Shuttles range Atlanta airport, train and bus stations to Amicalola or Springer. Can stop at REI outfitters in-route.
🚐**Roadrunner Driving Services** 828-524-3265, 706-201-7719 or email where2@mac.com. Based in Franklin, NC. Shuttles range Atlanta to Damascus.

Getting to Mount Katahdin

The northern terminus of the Appalachian Trail is on top of Mount Katahdin, and is accessible only by foot.
Mount Katahdin, Baxter State Park, Maine:
Most routes to Mount Katahdin lead through Bangor, Maine, a town with an airport, bus terminal and train station. Bangor is approximately 91 miles from Baxter State Park. Some shuttle services will pick you up in Bangor, but it is more economical to take Cyr Bus Lines to Medway, 31 miles from Baxter State Park.

Driving direction to Baxter State Park/Mount Katahdin

From I-95, take exit 244 onto ME 157 heading to Millinocket.
Stay on ME 157 for 11.1 miles, will change into Central Street at the end.
Turn right onto Katahdin Ave for 0.2 miles.
Turn left onto Bates Street/Millinocket Road for 8.4 miles.
You will reach the store North Woods Trading Post on your right.
Stay to the right on Baxter Park Road for 8.8 miles.
You will reach Baxter State Park gate.
After going through the gate you will go to the left for 7.8 mile to Katahdin Stream Campground and The Birches Lean-to and campground, follow the signs.

Getting to Medway and Millinocket area:

🚐**Cyr Bus Lines Station**, 153 Gilman Falls Ave, Old Town, ME 04468
800-244-2335, 207-827-2335, 207-827-2010 (www.cyrbustours.com)
Depart Bangor 6pm - arrive Medway 7:40pm, fare $10.50
Depart Medway 9:30am - arrive Bangor 11:10am
🚐**Shaw's Lodging** 207-997-7069, Monson, ME, shuttles covering all of Maine.

Shuttles and Taxis to Baxter State Park from the Medway Millinocket area:

🚐**Town Taxi** 207-723-2000, 207-447-3474 Rides from Medway to Millinocket $12, from Millinocket to Abol Bridge $45, Millinocket to Katahdin Stream/The Birches $55.

🚐**Katahdin B&B** 207-723-5220, Millinocket, ME, shuttles from/to bus station also between Monson and Millinocket or Bangor airport by arrangement.

🚐**Maine Quest Adventures** 207-746-9615, 207-746-9615 (www.mainequestadventures.com) Medway, ME, will pick up at Medway bus station and drop off at Katahdin Stream or Abol Bridge $50, if late in the afternoon, stay at base camp and tent on lawn for free, access to bathroom (no shower), shuttles to Monson and parts of 100 Mile Wilderness, phone off late fall until spring.

🚐**The Appalachian Trail Lodge** 207-723-4321 (www.appalachiantraillodge.com) Millinocket, ME, shuttles within 150 miles.

Friends and family joining you in Baxter State Park

If you are planning on having family or friends join you at Baxter Stat©e Park to hike, you will need to contact Baxter State Park Headquarters at 207-723-5140 well in advance. You need to do this to check on regulations, parks visitor and day use fees, reservations, availability of camping at campgrounds in the park. Reservations improve a little after Labor Day weekend.

Trail Tidbits

Dryer use for laundry - The dryers you will use on the trail are mostly gas. They can get very hot. Synthetics (poly/plastic things) will usually do OK for one cycle. Keep an eye out regardless. The second cycle will definitely melt some sock liners, stiffeners in certain hats, sleeping bags (yikes) etc.

Pictures - Start early. Take lots of pics of people. Lots of pics of shelter life, the woods, etc. but be sure and start early on people and write their names down. You will thank very thankful of this later. It's better to take to many pictures then a few more.

Chaffing - Many have this problem early.
All the creams and ointments in the world are great for AFTER the fact.
Even not wearing underwear under your shorts or pants does not work all the time as the salt builds up on your pants and chafes you anyway. Spandex does the job for some. With spandex there is no rubbing. They are light, durable, good support and dried pretty well (overnight in the sleeping bag when damp). Others wear a kilt with nothing underneath.

Do your business before you head into a town - In town you can't just relieve yourself anywhere, like you are used to doing on the trail. Before you go into town, especially if you are hitching. Take out your money holder/wallet whatever you're using and put it on your person, this way if you get separated from your pack for any reason you will still have your I.D. etc.

Trail and shelter registers - Read them, many tidbits of info can sometimes be found here. Write in them, if anyone is trying to get hold of you this will help a lot. It is a good security measure as it narrows down the search area significantly.

Caffeine - Be careful. Your body is not used to high doses (daily coffee drinkers ignore) of caffeine and drinking a lot in town WILL keep you up all night.
Be advised that iced-tea in the south is real tea and has caffeine.

The Four W's - Water, Weather, Weight and Where is the next blaze. Order varies with mood of hiker.

~ Walking Home ~

Abbreviations

AT or A.T. - Appalachian Trail
ATC – Appalachian Trail Conservancy
AMC – Appalachian Mountain Club
AYCE – All You Can Eat
AYH - American Youth Hostels
BMT - Benton MacKaye Trail
BRP - Blue Ridge Parkway
BSP - Baxter State Park
B/L/D - Breakfast/lunch/dinner
DOC – Dartmouth Outing Club
EAP – Each addition person
FedEx - Federal Express
GMC – Green Mountain Club
HYOH - Hike Your Own Hike
KSC - Katahdin Stream Campground
LT – Long Trail
LNT – Leave No Trace
MATC - Maine Appalachian Trail Club
MP - Mile Point or Mile Post
NHP - National Historical Park
NOC - Nantahala Outdoor Center
NPS – National Park Service
PATC - Potomac Appalachian Trail Club
PP – Per Person
SDMP - Skyline Drive Milepost
SMNP - Smoky Mountain National Park
SNP - Shenandoah National Park
USFS - United States Forest Service
USGS - United States Geological Survey
USP - United Parcel Service
USPS - U.S. Postal Service

Directions and mileages as mentioned in this book

When referring to North on the Appalachian Trail, it will always be the direction that leads to Mount Katahdin.

When physically on the Appalachian Trail
For North bound hikers: West is Left and East is Right.
For South bound hikers: West is Right and East is Left.

When stepping off the Appalachian Trail
When off the AT on a side trail or anything other than being on the AT, all directions will be either left or right. This applies the same to North bound and Soutbound hikers.

Mileages
Mileages are in miles and tenths. If you see something like (1.3), this means 1.3 miles. If you see something like (1.3W), this means 1.3 to the west. (1.3E) would meant 1.3 to the east.

Notes, information, and warnings

Springs and water sources - The purity of springs and water along the Appalachian Trail from natural sources cannot be guaranteed. All water should be treated before use.

Pet owners - Carry a vaccine history with you and make sure your pets are on monthly heartworm (from mosquitoes) and flea & tick prevention year around due to the high risk especially tick borne diseases.

Parking coordinates - The parking coordinates are not always 100% accurate but should get you within eyesight of the parking area. Always do your research ahead of time on the parking area to make sure there are no issues with using the parking area.

Hammocks and hammock camping - When the hammock icon is displayed it means that there are possibilities for hammocks in that area. In some cases you may have to branch out up to 100 feet or so beyond the area to find good trees. Hanging also varies from season to season due to the growth of the underbrush.
When using a hammock, please use Leave No Trace (LNT) procedures.

White Mountains - The AMC maintains campsites one the Appalachian Trail in the White Mountains from Eliza Brook south of South Kinsman in Franconia Notch to Speck Pond in Maine, including Hermit Lakes shelter in Tuckerman racvine and 4 sites along the Grafton loop trail in Grafton Notch in Maine. Every one of these sites has space for hammocks. The caretakers usually have a place in mind not over platforms (need that space for tents) somewhere within the site, usually 3 or 4 sites known for hammocks.

There is no camping of any kind within the Forest Protection Area (FPA) at every hut in the White Mountain, this includes hammocks. The FPA is a quarter mile circle around the hut. Every hut has an FPA. This is a U.S. Forest Service law, not an AMC rule.

Establishment prices - The data and prices for establishments were collected by calling around, usually in the winter before this book went to the printers. This means the establishment owners or propietors gave the prices for the upcoming year. Sometimes these prices were estimates. They are not obligated to maintain these prices.

Mail drop Packaging Guidelines

▶ Use your real name (not a trail name), and include an ETA on your mail drops.
▶ Be prepared to show an ID when you retrieve your mail.
▶ Only send "General Delivery" mail to a Post office.
▶ If you are unsure of your need for an item (eg: a winter bag), consider using Priority Mail; unopened Priority Mail may be forwarded.
▶ The "C/O" name is essential when sending your mail drop to a business's PO Box; without it, they may not be able to retrieve your mail.
▶ Do not send mail drops to a lodging facility unless you plan to stay with them. If your plans change, offer to pay for the service of holding your mail.

Packages sent to post offices:

```
John Doe
C/O General Delivery
Trail Town, VA 12345

Please hold for AT hiker
ETA May 16, 2009
```

Packages sent to businesses:

```
John Doe
C/O Hiker Hostel
2176 Appalachian Way
Trail Town, VA 12345
Please hold for AT hiker
ETA May 16, 2009
```

Data explanation

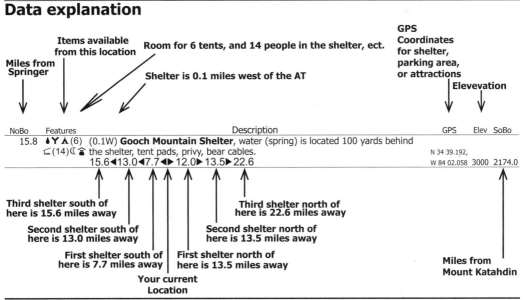

AT Passports

For centuries hikers of the Camino de Santiago Trail in Spain required a "passport" to stay in some municipal and parish Albergues. The passport has spaces for stamps, this proved that you have walked that day and are entitled to stay in an Albergue, (pilgrims only hostels), if there is space, they are valid for walkers and cyclist.

The AT Passport is a little different, as a passport is not requirement to stay at hostels. There are a lot more than just hostels on the AT Passport. The intention of the passport is to document your journey. At designated locations along the trail and in trail towns. These are establishments with stamps that hikers can collect.

The passport often ends up being a treasured possession as it is a great reminder of all the places you have stopped at or stayed overnight. The stamps are all different, no two stamps are alike.

We have extra pages in the back of the book for personal notes or AT Passport stamp collecting, if you are wishing to collect these stamps for memory or keepsake.

Trail Names and how they are derived

A trail name is a name that you can either give to yourself or someone will give you. Often times you are given a name from another hiker for an event or something that you did.

An example of this is a person named Giggles. They received there trail name because they giggled a lot. There was another person that I know with the trail name of Nature's Own. They received the trail name because they used the plastic bags from the bread Nature's Own for boot liners when hiking in snow.

Be aware... if someone gives you a trail name, and you answer to it, even once, there is a very strong possibility that you will get stuck with it.

Icons Descriptions

★★★★★	See notes and establishments listed below this entry.
♦	Source of drinking water. Water is always listed first
◊	Seasonal water source, not always reliable (unreliable)
Y	Intersection, junction, side trail, connecting trail or adjoining trail.
⌒	Footbridge or any other bridge
⊤	Power line or electrical wires
⌣	Possibilities for hammocks available. In some cases you may have to expand up to 100 feet beyond the area to find trees but you can hang. Availability of hanging also depends on the growth of the underbrush. When using a hammock, please use LNT procedures.
Λ	(x) Tent sites, may sometimes be listed with (capacity) or tent platforms
⊏	(x) AT Shelter and (capacity)
ℭ	Privy
🐻	Bear cables or bear box available for food bags
◉	●●◐ Cell phone signal strength, based on a nice clear day.
$	Overnight/caretaker fee. On town maps it represents a bank.
▲	Summit or crest
◀▶	Direction and miles to next shelter South or North. This does not include the mileage distance the shelter is off the trail.
📷	Views, overlooks or photo opportunities
🗼	Lookout, fire tower or observation tower
⚓	Water falls
◉	Attractions, important or historical features, other photo opportunities
▲	Road, gravel road, logging road, woods road, or any other road
P	(x) Parking. Vehicle capacity, and fee inside parenthesis. If there is a fee there will be a "$". Coordinates should get you within eyesight of parking area. Always check ahead for parking safety.
✕	Railroad crossing, tracks
🏊	Swimming possibilities
⛱	Picnic Table or picnic area
🗑	Trash can usually available
🚣	Boating or boats available for use
📪	Post Office
⌂	Hostel
🛏	Lodging. Do not deoend on the prices to include tax.
◈	AT Passport location. Get your book stamp here. (www.atpassport.com). When icon is on maps, it referres to the Appalachian Trail.
⊗	No Pets
👤	Work For Stay (WFS)
⚗	Fuel for stove
△	Laundry
💻	Computer available for use
📶	WiFi available
🚿	Shower available to use with out stay
🎒	Slackpacking may be available
🚗	Shuttle, Bus or Taxi
✉	Mail drop location
🏧	ATM
🛒	Long term resupply
🏪	Short term resupply
✕	Anywhere that serves food for a fee
☎	Pay phone or public phone
🏃	Outfitter
✗	Hardware store
🚻	Public Restroom
💊	Pharmacy
⚕	First Aid, doctor, hospital or urgent care
🐕	Vet or Kennel
✂	Barber
ⓘ	Information Area
🍸	Purchase or serves alcohol
🎬	Movie Theater
■	Not categorized
✈	Airport or airfield
🚌	Bus or bus station
🚂	Train or train station

NoBo	Features	Description	GPS	Elev	SoBo
0.0	Y▲O	**Springer Mountain**, rock overlook at summit. AT bronze plaque located here and register located in rock. Blue blaze trail is the Approach Trail from Amicalola Falls. **Don't forget your starting photo and to sign the register**	N 34 37.603, W 84 11.633	3782	2190.9
0.2	◊Y▲(18) ⊏(12) ⌣((☂(2)	(0.2E) **Springer Mountain Shelter**, water (spring) 80 yards on a blue blazed trail in front of the shelter but is known to go dry, tenting, privy, 2 bear boxes. Benton MacKaye Trail (southern terminus) is located 50 yards north on the AT. ◀▶2.6▶7.9▶15.5	N 34 37.760, W 84 11.565	3730	2190.7
1.0	▲P(25)	Cross **USFS 42**, Big Stamp Gap. Information board. Parking fee.	N 34 38.240, W 84 11.709	3350	2189.9
1.3	Y	Junction with Benton MacKaye Trail.		3430	2189.6
1.6	◊	Cross Davis Creek and small tributary		3235	2189.3
1.9	Y	Rich Mountain ridge crest. Benton MacKaye trail junction east.		3303	2189.0
2.6	◊	Cross Stover Creek		2993	2188.3
2.8	◊Y▲(3) ⊏(16) ⌣((☂	(0.1E) **Stover Creek Shelter**, water behind shelter is often dry but good water can be found where trail crosses Stover Creek 100 yards north of shelter, tent pads, privy, bear cables. ◀2.6◀▶5.3▶12.9▶24.7	N 34 39.017, W 84 11.832		2188.1
2.9	◊	Cross Stover Creek			2188.0
3.8	◊	Cross Stover Creek		2660	2187.1
4.2	Y	Junction with Benton MacKaye to the east, Duncan Ridge Trail to west		2580	2186.7
4.3	◊▲⌣▲ P(5-6)	Cross **USFS 58**, Three Forks. Stover Creek, Chester Creek, and Long Creek all converge here. Parking.	N 34 39.809, W 84 11.037	2530	2186.6
5.2	◊Y⚒	Trail junctions to Long Creek Falls, Benton MacKaye and Duncan Ridge Trails. BMT is marked with white diamonds, Duncan Ridge is marked with blue blazes to the west, Long Creek is also blue blazed.		2800	2185.7
6.2	▲⛺ P(6-8)	Cross **USFS 251**, Hickory Flats, picnic pavilion, Hickory Flats cemetery is located (0.1) west		3000	2184.7
7.4	◊▲(30) ⌣	Ridgecrest below Hawk Mountain, campsite, tent pads.		3250	2183.5
8.0	◊	Cross Stream, skirts the side of Hawk Mountain		3191	2182.9
8.1	◊Y▲ ⊏(12) ⌣((☂	(0.2W) **Hawk Mountain Shelter**, water is located 400 yards on a blue blazed trail behind the shelter, tent pads, privy, bear cables. ◀7.9◀5.3◀▶7.6▶19.4▶20.6	N 34 39.965, W 84 08.183	3194	2182.8
8.6	▲P(8)	Cross **USFS 42/69**, Hightower Gap, parking.	N 34 39.818, W 84 07.786	2854	2182.3
10.5	▲P(6-8)	Cross Horse Gap. USFS 42 is visible to the west.	N 34 39.344, W 84 06.348	2673	2180.4
11.5	▲	Sassafras Mountain, summit		3336	2179.4
12.2	▲P(6)	Cross **USFS 42/80**, Cooper Gap, parking	N 34 39.183, W 84 05.070	2800	2178.7
13.5	▲	Cross logging road		3024	2177.3
14.2	◊	Cross Justus Creek		2564	2176.7
14.4	Y◊▲	Trail to the west to tent pads. Water source is Justus Creek		2626	2176.5
14.9	◊	Cross Small stream		2605	2176.0

NoBo	Features	Description	GPS	Elev	SoBo
15.3	♦	Cross Blackwell Creek		2601	2175.6
15.7	♦Υ⅄(12) ⊏(14) ⤳(⊂⛺	(0.1W) Gooch Mountain Shelter, water (spring) is located 100 yards behind the shelter, tent pads that can accommodate two tents each, privy, bear box. 15.5◄12.9◄7.6◄► 11.8► 13.0► 22.1	N 34 39.192, W 84 02.058	3000	2175.2
16.9	♦▲P	Cross USFS 42. Gooch Gap, Water is located north 100 yards north and east 200 yards on a blue blazed trail.	N 34 39.126, W 84 01.938	2821	2174.0
17.0	♦	Marked trail to water 230 yards east on old road.		2804	2173.9
17.9	▲	Cross abandon road		2955	2173.0
18.2		Liss Gap		3032	2172.7
18.8		Jacks Gap		3045	2172.1
19.0	📷	Follow crest of Ramrock Mountain, rock outcropping, views to south.		3260	2171.9
19.5		Tritt Gap		3031	2171.4
20.5	♦▲⛺♦♦ ⇌P(40) ★★★★★	Cross GA. 60, Woody Gap, picnic area, water (spring) is located (0.1) west of the AT on northern side of the gap.	N 34 40.659, W 83 59.987	3198	2170.4
	⌂⇌ ◈♨⛺ ⊚⛟◱	(6.0E) Barefoot Hills (previously Hiker Hostel) 770-312-7342. reservations@barefoothills.com (www.barefoothills.com/) AT Passport location. Open year round. $42+ Bunks. $100+ Private room for two. $130+ Private Cabin for two. Stay includes breakfast, bed linens, towel and shower. Canister fuel and limited gear, FOR REGISTERED HOTEL GUESTS ONLY. Mail drops: (USPS) PO Box 802 or (FedEx/UPS) 7693 Hwy 19N, Dahlonega, GA 30533. **Deals/Specials**: (Feb 1-Apr 30): $210 pickup from Atlanta North Springs MARTA Station with overnight stay in bunk, breakfast, and shuttle to Amicalola or Springer. Upgraded rooms available. Feb 1 thru Apr 30: 5pm free daily pickup at Woody Gap FOR REGISTERED HOTEL GUESTS ONLY.			

Suches, GA (2.0W)

	⌂ ◈⛺ ⛺⊚◱	**Wolfpen Gap Country Store** 706-747-2271. AT Passport location. **Store:** M–Th 8am–8pm, F 8am-9pm, Sa 9am–9pm, Su 9am–7pm. Coleman by the ounce & canisters. Full menu, with hamburgers, chicken, philly cheese steaks, etc served Thursday - Sunday. **Hostel:** Bunks $20. Laundry $5 per load. Non guest shower $5. Free pickup for overnight guests at Woody or Gooch Gap. Accepts all major credit cards. Shuttles for a fee to all Georgia Trail heads. Also a designated Post Office. Mail drops: 41 Wolf Pen Gap Rd, Suches, GA 30572.			
	⌂⇌⅄ ⛺⊚	(0.7 west of Post Office) **High Valley Resort** 404-720-0087. (www.highvalleyresort.com) Open Apr-Oct. Camping $15PP, bunkhouse $55PP. Includes access to bathhouse, showers and lodge with satellite TV. Cabins $125 and up, some sleep 4, some sleep up to 8. Wifi available.			
	⇌⌂⅄✕ ⛺	(7W) **Wildcat Lodge and Campground** 706-973-0321. Open year round. $15 bunkroom, $15 camping. Lodge room sleeps 8 $100, $25EAP. Camp store has Coleman and canister fuel. Diner serves Breakfast and lunch.			
	■	**Jim and Ruth Ann Miner** 706-747-5434. Lives in town and are available if you need help.			
	🚗	**Wes Wisson** 706-747-2671, 706-781-4333. dwisson@windstream.net. Shuttles range from Gap to Gap only. Any other information call.			
	🚗	**Suches Hiker Shuttles** 678-967-9510, texting works best in the mountains. Murris Miller, ask for Murris. 24/7 emergency service . To and from any location in GA or Western NC, Dogs OK. Based out of Suches, GA.			
21.5	📷	Rocky face of Big Cedar Mountain, Preaching Rock, rock outcrop just south of summit.	N 34 41.231, W 83 59.644	3737	2169.4
22.0	♦	Small spring to west in Augerhole Gap		3624	2168.9
22.7	♦	Cross small stream on east slop of ridge.		3310	2168.2
22.8		Dan Gap		3261	2168.1
23.4	♦ΥP	Miller Gap. Cross Dockery Lake Trail. Spring about 100 yards east on Dockery Lake Trail. Dockery Lake Trail leads (3.5) east top Dockery Lake Recreation area.		3050	2167.5
23.7	♦⅄(4)⤳	Lance Creek, tent pads are located 100 yards north on the creek.		2880	2167.2
25.6		Flat area known as Burnett Field Mountain		3480	2165.3
26.0	◊	Water (spring) unreliable		3330	2164.9
26.1	♦Υ▲ ★★★★★	Jarrard Gap, USFS, water (stream) is located (0.3) west. Jarrard Gap Trail (1.0) west to Lake Winfield Scott.		3250	2164.8
	⅄⛺♦♦	(1.0W) on the Jarrad Gap Trail (blue blazed) to **Lake Winfield Scott Recreation Area** (www.cfaia.org/lake-winfield-scott-recreation-area-campgrounds-in-georgia) Tent sites for 5 persons and two vehicles $18, showers and bathrooms. Coordinates N 34 44.420, W 83 53.520.			
26.5	📷	Reach shoulder of Gaddis Mountain.		3536	2164.4

NoBo		Features / Description	GPS	Elev	SoBo
27.5	◊ ⲩ ⲗ ⊏(7) ⌣ ⲥ ⲅ	Bird Gap (0.4W) **Woods Hole Shelter**, water (stream) on trail to shelter is unreliable in dry months, privy, tenting, bear cables. 24.7◀19.4◀11.8◀▶ 1.2▶ 10.3▶ 15.1 Bird Gap, Freeman Trail just east bypasses Blood Mtn. and rejoins AT at Flatrock Gap	N 34 44.228, W 83 57.300	3650	2163.4
27.8	◊ⲩP	Slaughter Creek Trail at Slaughter Creek Gap, water is unreliable.	N 34 44.239, W 83 58.416	3790	2163.1
27.9	ⲗ(8)	Slaughter Creek campsite to the west, tent pads. **Fires are not permitted**.		3800	2163.0
28.7	⊏(8) ⲥ ⲗ ⲓⲟ	Blood Mountain, open rocky summit. **Blood Mountain Shelter**, is located south of summit, no water at shelter, privy, view. **Fires are not permitted**. 20.6 ◀3.0◀1.2◀▶ 9.1▶ 13.9▶ 21.2	N 34 44.399, W 83 56.243	4461	2162.2
29.3	ⲓⲟ	Trail follows steep rock slope with views		4334	2161.6

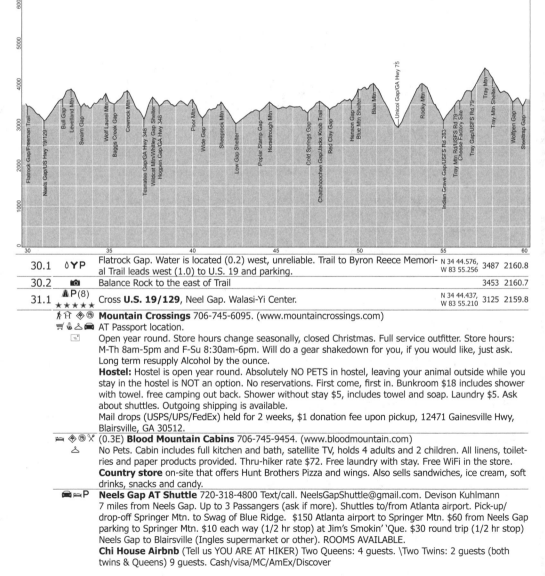

30.1	◊ⲩP	Flatrock Gap. Water is located (0.2) west, unreliable. Trail to Byron Reece Memorial Trail leads west (1.0) to U.S. 19 and parking.	N 34 44.576, W 83 55.256	3487	2160.8
30.2	ⲓⲟ	Balance Rock to the east of Trail		3453	2160.7
31.1	ⲗP(8) ★★★★★	Cross **U.S. 19/129**, Neel Gap. Walasi-Yi Center.	N 34 44.437, W 83 55.210	3125	2159.8

ⲭ ⲏ ◈ ⓢ **Mountain Crossings** 706-745-6095. (www.mountaincrossings.com)
ⲙ ⳑ ⳛ Ⳝ AT Passport location.
ⲱ Open year round. Store hours change seasonally, closed Christmas. Full service outfitter. Store hours: M-Th 8am-5pm and F-Su 8:30am-6pm. Will do a gear shakedown for you, if you would like, just ask. Long term resupply Alcohol by the ounce.
Hostel: Hostel is open year round. Absolutely NO PETS in hostel, leaving your animal outside while you stay in the hostel is NOT an option. No reservations. First come, first in. Bunkroom $18 includes shower with towel. free camping out back. Shower without stay $5, includes towel and soap. Laundry $5. Ask about shuttles. Outgoing shipping is available.
Mail drops (USPS/UPS/FedEx) held for 2 weeks, $1 donation fee upon pickup, 12471 Gainesville Hwy, Blairsville, GA 30512.

ⲙ ◈ ⓢ ⲭ (0.3E) **Blood Mountain Cabins** 706-745-9454. (www.bloodmountain.com)
ⳛ No Pets. Cabin includes full kitchen and bath, satellite TV, holds 4 adults and 2 children. All linens, toiletries and paper products provided. Thru-hiker rate $72. Free laundry with stay. Free WiFi in the store.
Country store on-site that offers Hunt Brothers Pizza and wings. Also sells sandwiches, ice cream, soft drinks, snacks and candy.

ⲙ ⲙ P **Neels Gap AT Shuttle** 720-318-4800 Text/call. NeelsGapShuttle@gmail.com. Devison Kuhlmann 7 miles from Neels Gap. Up to 3 Passangers (ask if more). Shuttles to/from Atlanta airport. Pick-up/drop-off Springer Mtn. to Swag of Blue Ridge. $150 Atlanta airport to Springer Mtn. $60 from Neels Gap parking to Springer Mtn. $10 each way (1/2 hr stop) at Jim's Smokin' 'Que. $30 round trip (1/2 hr stop) Neels Gap to Blairsville (Ingles supermarket or other). ROOMS AVAILABLE.
Chi House Airbnb (Tell us YOU ARE AT HIKER) Two Queens: 4 guests. \Two Twins: 2 guests (both twins & Queens) 9 guests. Cash/visa/MC/AmEx/Discover

Blairsville, GA 30514 (14W) All major services.

Misty Mountain Inn & Cottages 706-745-4786. (www.mistymountainproperties.com)
New owners in 2016, Craig Griffiths.
B&B rooms without breakfast $108, additional $10 includes breakfast. 6 Cottages available in sizes range for 1 to 6 people, price range from $105 to $125. Full kitchen and bath. Laundsry, free WiFi. Shuttles: Free pickup and return from Neel Gap, Tesnatee and Hogpen Gap. Slackpacking included with multi night stay.
Shuttle Services: Year round

Jim's Smokin' Que (BBQ) 706-835-7427 (jimssmokinque.com) M-W closed, Th-Sa 11am-8pm, Sun closed. Mini golf available.

Blairsville Bikes and Hikes 706-745-8141.
M-F 10am-5:30pm, Sat 10am-3pm, Sun closed. Fuel and hiker food available "Hiking essentials".

The Further Shuttle Appalachian 772-321-0905, 706-400-9105.
(www.thefurthershuttleappalachian.com)
24/7 service year round. Based out of Blairsville, GA. Donald Ballard.
Shuttles from Atlanta, GA to Davenport Gap, TN, will discuss anything further. Parking available at house for section hikers. Pets are welcome.

Dahlonega, GA 30597(17E) All major services.

NoBo		Description	GPS	Elev	SoBo
32.2	♦▲	Bull Gap, water (spring) on blue blazed trail to the west downhill 200 yards.		3644	2158.7
32.6	▲	Levelland Mountain, wooded summit		3942	2158.3
32.8	📷	Crest of Levelland Mountain, open rocky area, view.		3668	2158.1
33.3		Swaim Gap		3450	2157.6
34.1	♦	Pass west of Rock Spring Top, water (spring) is located to the west of the trail.		3520	2156.8
34.8	📷	Wolf Laurel Top, open rock face east of the trail offers views.		3766	2156.1
35.3	♦▲⌣	Baggs Creek Gap, not an obvious gap. Water (spring) is located down and overgrown road to the west, not an ATC approved camping spot.		3591	2155.6
36.1	▲📷	Cowrock Mountain, summit offers good views of the valley below.		3842	2154.8
37.1	▲ P(10-12)	Cross **GA. 348**, Tesnatee Gap and Russell Scenic Highway.	N 34 43.576, W 83 50.862	3138	2153.8
37.6	📷	Rock cliff with views of Cowrock Mountain and gorge of Town Creek.		3614	2153.3
37.8	♦Y▲ ▲(3)⌁(7) ⌣☾☎📷	Crest Wildcat Mountain. (1.2E) **Whitley Gap Shelter**, water (spring) located (0.2) beyond shelter, privy, (0.1E) beyond shelter to tent sites, bear cables, view. 22.1◄10.3◄9.1◄►4.8►12.1►20.2	N 34 42.743, W 83 50.064	3370	2153.1
38.0	♦○ ▲ P(10-12) ★★★★★	Cross **GA. 348**, Hogpen Gap, water (spring) south side of road on a blue blazed trail. **AT plaque on rock.**	N 34 43.554, W 83 50.393	3450	2152.9

Blairsville, GA 30514 (14.0W) All major services. See Notes at mile 31.1

NoBo		Description	GPS	Elev	SoBo
38.9		White Oak Stamp, ridge crest.		3470	2152.0
40.0	▲	Poor Mountain, summit.		3650	2150.9
40.6		Wide Gap.		3169	2150.3
41.8	▲	Sheep Rock Top, rocky summit.		3600	2149.1
42.6	♦▲(4) ⌁(7) ⌣☾☎	Blue blaze 190 yards east to **Low Gap Shelter**, water located 30 yards in front of shelter, tenting, privy, bear cables. 15.1◄13.9◄4.8◄►7.3►15.4►22.8	N 34 46.576, W 83 49.470	3050	2148.3
44.0	♦▲	Poplar Stamp Gap, water (stream) is located several feet east down an old road bed.		3330	2146.9
46.4		Cold Springs Gap, pay no attention to the name you will not find a spring.		3300	2144.5
47.6	♦YP(7)	Chattahoochee Gap, Jack's Gap Trail west (2.4) to GA. 180 and parking. Water (spring) is located 200 yards east on a steep blue blazed trail.	N 34 50.872, W 83 47.924	3500	2143.3
48.3	Y	Red Clay Gap		3485	2142.6
49.0	▲	Campsites to west of tail.		3600	2141.9
49.2	♦Y	Spring is located several yards to the west on a trail down a rocky slope.		3500	2141.7
49.4	♦	Flat area known as Rocky Knob. Water is about 150 yards west down rocky slope.		3629	2141.5
49.5		Henson Gap		3580	2141.4
49.8	♦	Spring on west side trail. This is the water for Blue Mountain Shelter.		3890	2141.1
49.9	♦▲(4) ⌁(7) ⌣☾☎	**Blue Mountain Shelter** (no potable water) at shelter, water (spring) located (0.1) south of shelter on AT, tenting, privy, bear cables. 21.2◄12.1◄7.3◄►8.1►15.5►23.6	N 34 49.033, W 83 46.004	3900	2141.0
50.8	▲	Blue Mountain, summit		4025	2140.1
52.3	▲○ P(14) ★★★★★	Cross **GA. 75**, Unicoi Gap, **AT plaque placed in a rock on north side of road.**	N 34 48.107, W 83 44.569	2949	2138.6

Helen, GA 30545 (9.0E) See map of Helen, GA.

PO M–F 9am–12:30pm and 1:30pm-4pm, Sa 9am-12pm. 706-878-2422.

Best Western Motel Riverpark Inn 706-878-2111.
Open year round. Rates between Mid-Mar thru end of Apr are $55 for single and $5 for each additional person, limit 4 people, includes breakfast buffet during festivals. Microwave, fridge, Computer available for use, free WiFi. Ride to and from trail weekdays only when staff is available.

Helendorf River Inn 800-445-2271. (www.helendorf.com)
Rates range from $45-$85, $10EAP depending on season. Weekend rates are higher. Pets $20. Includes continental breakfast. Laundry, free WiFi. Visa/MC/Disc accepted.

Super 8 Motel 706-878-2191, 706-878-2191. Open year round. No Pets. Offers a hiker room with two bed for two people $55, EAP $5 with a maximum of 4 people, offer is good for M-Th, microwave, fridge. Indoor pool. Free WiFi.

Econo Lodge 706-878-8000.
Open year round. Weekday rates $68, weekend rates are higher, includes continental breakfast, microwave, fridge, free WiFi. Accepts only pets under 20 pounds with pet fee $20.

Country Inn and Suites 706-878-9000.
Open year round. Call for rates, stay includes hot breakfast, indoor pool and whirl pool, laundry, Computer available to use, free WiFi.

Betty's Country Store (IGA) 706-878-2617. (bettysinhelen.com) M-Th 7am-8pm, F-Sa 7am-9pm Su 7am-8pm.

Laundromat 706-779-2066.

White County Library 706-878-2438. M-F 9am-6pm, Sa-Su closed.

Hiawassee, GA 30546 (12E) See Hiawassee and map at mile 69.0

Helen, GA

Mile		Description	GPS	Elev	SoBo
52.9	♦	Cross Stream		3504	2138.0
53.2	Y	Rocky Mountain Trail leads (0.1) west to USFS 283.		3702	2137.7
53.7	⛰▲📷	Rocky Mountain, summit		4017	2137.2
53.9	📷	Rock ledges with good views.		3965	2137.0
55.0	Y▲P	Cross **USFS 283**, Indian Grave Gap. Blue blaze trail leads (1.9) east to Andrews Cove Campground.	N 34 47.562, W 83 42.858	3113	2135.9
55.7	▲	Cross **USFS 79**, Tray Mountain Road		3580	2135.2
56.0	♦▲⌣	Cheese Factory Site, water (spring) is located 50 yards west. There is no cheese factory here. There is nothing here now that would make you even think there was one located here. However in the 1800's there was once one here. Now it is a good flat area for a picnic or camping.		3590	2134.9
56.5	📷	Rocky cliff with small overlook.		3853	2134.4
56.7	▲P(6)	Cross **USFS 79/698**, Tray Mountain Road, Tray Gap	N 34 47.963, W 83 41.460	3847	2134.2

NoBo	Features	Description	GPS	Elev	SoBo
57.5	▲ ◙ ☕	Tray Mountain, small rocky summit, views in all directions.		4430	2133.4
58.0	♦ Y ⅄(3) ⊏(7) ↝ ⟨ ☎	Blue blaze trail 150 yards to **Tray Mountain Shelter**, water (spring) located 250 yards behind shelter, tenting, privy, bear cables. 20.2◄15.4◄8.1◄▶7.4▶15.5▶22.8	N 34 48.238, W 83 40.614	4200	2132.9
59.2		Wolfpen Gap		3600	2131.7
59.8	♦ Y	Steeltrap Gap, water (spring) is located 280 yards east down blue blaze trail.		3490	2131.1

NoBo	Features	Description	GPS	Elev	SoBo
60.3		West side of Young Lick Knob.		3800	2130.6
61.6		Cross Swag of the Blue Ridge		3400	2129.3
62.7	♦ ⅄ ↝	Sassafras Gap, camp sites, water (spring) is located 150 yards downhill to the east.		3500	2128.2
63.6	♦ ⅄ ↝ ▲ P	Addis Gap, old fire road leads (0.5) east to campsite and water and eventually to **USFS 26-2**. During Turkey hunting season the locals like to use this campsite because they can drive into it. Old fire road leads (8.0) east to GA. 197.		3304	2127.3
64.6	Y	Trail to Kelly Knob (0.2) west		4276	2126.3
65.4	♦ Y ⅄(4) ⊏(12) ↝ ⟨ ☎	(0.3E) **Deep Gap Shelter**, water (spring) is located (0.1) south on the trail to the shelter, tenting, privy, bear cables. 22.8◄15.5◄7.4◄▶8.1▶15.4▶20.3	N 34 52.941, W 83 38.772	3550	2125.5
66.4	Y ⅄ ◙	Blue blaze trail east leads several yards to campsites and view, **no water**.		3827	2124.5
66.6	⅄	McClure Gap		2121	2124.3
66.8	▲	Powell Mountain, summit		3850	2124.1
67.8		Moreland Gap. An old overgrown roadbed leads west.		3050	2123.1
68.4	♦	Several streams in this area.		2650	2122.5
69.0	♦ ▲ ♨ P(12) ★★★★★	Cross **U.S. 76**, Dicks Creek Gap, picnic area, water is located (0.5W). **See Map of Dicks Creek Gap.**	N 34 54.739, W 83 37.131	2675	2121.9

⌂ ⅄ ◈ ☕ (0.5W) **Top of Georgia Hiking Center** 706-982-3252 (www.topofgeorgiahikingcenter.org)
⌂ ▭ ◕ ⚲ AT Passport location.
◉ ▥ P ▣ Open year-round 7-7. No alcohol or drugs.
Street sign with arrow marks the easy half mile downhill road walk to TOG from gap (NoBo hikers head left, SoBo hikers head right). Pet friendly. Bunk and shower $30 and private 2 bed cabins $70. Both include free continental breakfast and use of full hostel kitchen with your stay. Separate suite for hikers with pets. Advance reservations available but not required. Laundry $5/load (we do it for you) with free hospital scrubs provided. Computer, free Wi-Fi. Pizza & snacks available. Full resupply. Discount outfitter on site specializes in thru-hiker gear. Free shuttles year-round to Hiawassee, Dicks Creek Gap and Unicoi Gap daily for overnight guests. TOG shuttles travel as far south as Atlanta Marta North Springs Station and north to Fontana for a fee. Offers slackpacking options (whole state of GA and up to NOC). Print your Smoky Mtn Permits here. Fun morning seminar "10 Keys for a Successful Thru-Hike". Pack shakedowns by proprietor, Triple Crowner and guide Bob "Sir-Packs-Alot" Gabrielsen. Parking available. Mail drops: ($2 fee) held for 21 days. ID required to pick up packages: 7675 US Hwy 76 E., Hiawassee GA 30546.

(5.0W) **Henson Cove B&B** 800-714-5542. (www.hensoncoveplace.com).
Only small well behaved pets. B&B rooms $125 and up, breakfast included. Breakfast an addition-
al $8 per person. Free laundry, computer available for use, no downloads, free WiFi. Stay includes
free ride to and from Dick's Creek Gap or Unicoi Gap and for resupplying in town. Shuttles and
parking available for section hikers. Accepts Credit Cards.
Mail drops for guest only: 1137 Car Miles Rd, Hiawassee, GA 30546.

Hiawassee, GA 30546 (11.0W). See map of Hiawassee, GA.

PO M-F 8:30am-5pm, Sa 8:30am-12pm. 706-896-4173.

Hiawassee Budget Inn
706-896-4121. (www.hiawasseebudgetinn.com)
AT Passport location.
Open year round. $39.99 per person, limited to four per room, $5 for each additional person. $50 pet
deposit. Rooms include cable TV, refrigerators, microwaves. Coin laundry. Computer available for use.
Free Wifi. Free Shuttles for guests to and from Dick's Creek Gap and Unicoi Gap, leaves at 9 and 11 am
for the months of March thru April. There is a fee for Non guest.
Mail drops for guests: 193 S Main Street - Hiawassee, Georgia. 30546

Three Eagles Outfitters, Satellite store in Franklin, the Satellite in Hiawassee is Mtn Crossings.
Open from March to the first week of May. Hours are 8:15 am to 2 pm, 7 days during season. It is
Located at the Budget Inn, jam packed with all a hiker could need Fuel by the ounce. Offers free bumps
to our main store in Franklin, and if product is not there it can be brought next day if we are out of
something you need.

Mull's Inn 706-896-4195.
No pets. Call for pricing, free WiFi. Shuttles by arrangement
Mail drops for guests: 213 N Main St, Hiawassee, GA 30546.

Holiday Inn Express 706-896-8884.
No pets. $79 and up, includes continental breakfast, laundry. Indoor pool and hot tub. Computer availa-
ble for use, free WiFi. Accepts Credit Cards.
Mail drops for guests: 300 Big Sky Drive, Hiawassee, GA 30546.

Lake Chatuge Lodge 706-896-5253. (www.lakechatugelodge.com)
Rates stating at $90 but can be more depending on month and higher on weekends, includes continen-
tal breakfast, laundry, computer available for use, free WiFi.

Mountain Roots Outfitters 706-896-1873.
M-Sa 11am-5:30pm, Sun closed. Canister fuel, freeze dried meals, small gear items

Ingles 706-896-8312. (www.ingles-markets.com) Deli, bakery, salad bar. M-Su 7am-10pm. Pharmacy; M-F 9am-9pm, Sa-Su 9am-6pm.

Freds 706-896-4302. M-Sa 8am-9pm, Su 9am-8pm; Pharmacy 706-896-1774. M-F 9am-7pm, Sa 9am-
4pm, Su closed.

Bear Meadows Grill 706-896-0520. (www.bearmeadowsgrill.net) M - closed, Tu 11 am-8 pm, W 11
am-2:30 pm, Th-F 11 am-8:30 pm, Sa closed.

Georgia Mountain Restaurant 706-896-3430. Serves breakfast, lunch and dinner. M-Su 6am-
7:30pm.

Rib Country BBQ 706-970-3615. M-Su 11am-8pm.

Daniels Steak House 706-896-8008. All you can eat lunch and dinner. M-Su 11am-8:30pm.

Big Al's Pizza 706-896-1970. They also deliver. M-Sa 11:30am-8pm, Su 12pm-7pm.

Chatuge Regional Hospital 706-896-2222. M-Su 24 hours.

The Medicine Shoppe 706-896-4686. M-F 9am-5pm, Sa-Su closed.

Wash Tub Coin Laundry 706-896-4441.

Hiawassee Animal Hospital 706-896-4173. (www.hiawasseeanimalhospital.com) M-F 8:30am-
5:30pm, Sa 8:30am-1pm, Su closed.

Goin' Postal 706-896-1844. (www.goinpostalhiawassee.com)
M-F 10am-5pm Sa-Su closed. FedEx and UPS shipping, also offer DHL and USPS services.

Hiawassee, GA

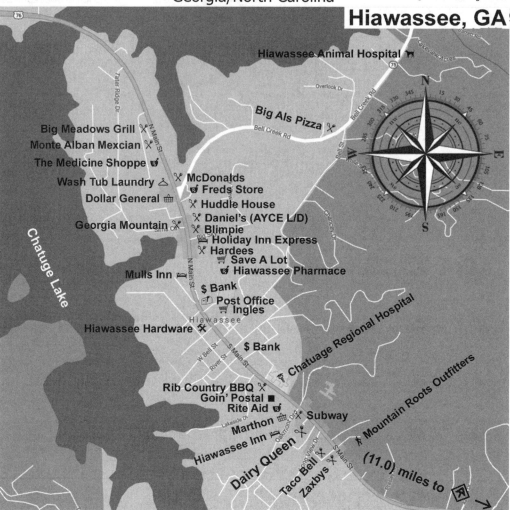

Hiawassee Animal Hospital

Big Als Pizza

Big Meadows Grill
Monte Alban Mexcian
The Medicine Shoppe
Wash Tub Laundry
Dollar General
McDonalds
Freds Store
Huddle House
Daniel's (AYCE L/D)
Georgia Mountain
Blimpie
Holiday Inn Express
Hardees
Save A Lot
Hiawassee Pharmace
Mulls Inn
Bank
Post Office
Ingles
Hiawassee
Hiawassee Hardware

Chatuge Lake

Chatuage Regional Hospital

Bank

Rib Country BBQ
Goin' Postal
Rite Aid
Marthon
Subway
Hiawassee Inn
Dairy Queen
Taco Bell
Zaxbys

Mountain Roots Outfitters

(11.0) miles to

70.1	◊⚑	Campsite east of trail, water.		3150	2120.8
70.8		Cowart Gap, tall pines.		2900	2120.1
71.9	📷	Good views from Buzzard Knob when the leaves are not on trees.		3675	2119.0
72.3		Bull Gap		3550	2118.6
73.5	◊⚑⚑(6) ⊏(14) ⌣☾☂	Plumarchard Gap. (0.2E) **Plumarchard Gap Shelter**, water located 200 yards west on AT beyond shelter, tenting, privy, bear cables. Caution the stump in front of the shelter has been home to copperhead snakes. Creek on trail to shelter and spring (0.1W) of AT. 23.6◄15.5◄8.1◄►7.3►12.2►19.8	N 34 56.762, W 83 35.298	3050	2117.4
74.2		As Knob, crosses high point below summit.		3460	2116.7
74.8	⚑	Blue Ridge Gap, cross dirt road **USFS 72**.		3020	2116.1
75.8	◊⚑	Campsite, water		3500	2115.1
76.0		Rich Cove Gap		3390	2114.9
77.4	📷	Small knob west of trail with good views.		3695	2113.5
77.9	State Line	Georgia–North Carolina State Line, register in tree.		3825	2113.0
78.0	◊⚑⌣●	Bly Gap, water (spring) is located east of the trail and 250 feet south of the gap. Gnarly twisted oak tree located here. **Often photographed tree.**		3840	2112.9
78.7	📷	Sharp Top, shirts the summit, vista		4300	2112.2
79.1	📷	View of Shooting Creek Valley.		4521	2111.8
79.9		Sassafras Gap		4300	2111.0
80.5	◊	Cross stream		4549	2110.4
80.7	📷	Viewpoint to the west.		4627	2110.2

North Carolina

NoBo	Features	Description	GPS	Elev	SoBo
80.8	♦Y⅄ ⊏(8)〰《	Blue blaze 100 feet east to **Muskrat Creek Shelter**, water (spring) is located behind shelter, tenting, privy. 22.8◄15.4◄7.3◄►4.9►12.5►21.2	N 35 01.232, W 83 34.896	4600	2110.1
81.6	♦Y⅄	Edge of White Oak Stamp, water (spring) is located to the east. Tent sites to west and east. Camp out of site of the trail to the west or east.		4620	2109.3
81.8	Y	Chunky Gal Trail to the west (5.5) to U.S. 64.		4700	2109.1
82.7		Water Oak Gap, small clearing.		4490	2108.2
83.7	📷	View.		4737	2107.2
84.8	♦Y⅄ P(8-10) ★★★★★	Cross **USFS 71**, Deep Gap, Kimsey Creek Trail leads (3.7W) to USFS **Standing Indian Campground. See notes at NOBO mile 105.5.**	N 35 02.376, W 83 33.150	4341	2106.1
85.7	♦⅄⊏(8) 〰《	Blue blaze 250 feet east to **Standing Indian Shelter**, water (creek) located 70 yards downhill from shelter, tenting, privy. 20.3◄12.2◄4.9◄►7.6►16.3►19.7	N 35 02.520, W 83 32.884	4760	2105.2
87.2	Y⅄📷	Lower Ridge Trail junction, east leads 600 feet to Standing Indian Mountain summit. West leads (4.2) to Standing Indian Campground.		5498	2103.7

NoBo	Features	Description	GPS	Elev	SoBo
90.1	◊Y⅄	Beech Gap, water (spring) is located 100 feet to the east but is unreliable. Beech Gap Trail leads (2.8) west to USFS 67 parking area.		4460	2100.8
91.9		Coleman Gap, dense rhododendron thicket.		4200	2099.0
92.9	YP(3)	Timber Ridge Trail leads (2.3) west to USFS 67 parking area.	N 35 1.323, W 83 30.218	4700	2098.0
93.3	♦⅄⊏(8) 〰《	Blue blaze 100 feet east to **Carter Gap Shelter**, water (spring) is located 200 yards west on blue blaze trail, tenting, privy. 19.8◄12.5◄7.6◄►8.7►12.1►19.6	N 34 59.939, W 83 29.648	4540	2097.6
94.7	📷	North side of Ridgepole Mountain		4990	2096.2
95.0	Y📷	Unmarked trail leads 25 feet east to Little Ridgepole vista of Pickens Nose.		4749	2095.9
97.0	♦⅄〰	Betty Creek Gap, water (spring) is located to the east.		4300	2093.9
97.9	⅄P(1-2)	Cross **USFS 83**, Mooney Gap. Road closed mid-Dec thru first of Apr.	N 35 02.129, W 83 28.211	4400	2093.0
98.2	♦	Log steps, spring		4500	2092.7
98.8	⅄	Bearpen Gap		4700	2092.1
99.2	Y	Two blue blazed trails intersect here. Bearpen Trail (2.6) west to USFS 67, gravel. The other blue blaze trail is the Albert Mountain bypass trail that reconnects with the AT at mile 100.		4790	2091.7
99.5	⅄📷𝕀 P(7)	Albert Mountain summit, fire tower	N 35 03.154, W 83 28.651	5250	2091.4
99.7		Albert Mountain bypass trail leads west (0.8) to reconnect with the AT at mile 99.2 northbound.		5035	2091.2
100.1		Big Spring Gap.		4954	2090.8
102.0	♦Y⅄(5) ⊏(16) 〰《	(0.1W) **Long Branch Shelter**, water, tent sites, privy. 21.2◄16.3◄8.7◄►3.4►10.9►18.2	N 35 04.198, W 83 29.889	4932	2088.9
102.1	♦	Cross stream		4930	2088.8
102.9	Y	Glassmine Gap, Long Branch Trail (2.0) west to USFS 67		4130	2088.0

NoBo	Features	Description	GPS	Elev	SoBo
103.9	◊	Unreliable spring below trail. Several seasonal water sources are one mile in either direction.		4363	2087.0
105.4	◊Υ⊏(8) ⌣⊄	Blue blaze 300 feet west to **Rock Gap Shelter**, water (spring) is known to go dry, privy. 19.7◄12.1◄3.4◄►7.5►14.8►19.6	N 35 05.486, W 83 31.386	3760	2085.5
105.5	◊Υ▲ P(6-7) ★★★★★	Rock Gap, (0.7E) to water. (1.5W) **Standing Indian Campground**.	N 35 05.644, W 83 31.350	3750	2085.4
	▲⛺♦♦ ♨⊞P	(1.5W) **Standing Indian Campground** 828-524-6441. Campsites $16, open Apr 1 - Nov 30. Showers, camp store, pay phone. Pets must be leashed. Parking is permitted year round.			
106.1	▲	Cross **Old U.S. 64**, Wallace Gap		3738	2084.8
106.2	◊	Cross stream.		3745	2084.7
108.5	◊	Cross Stream.		3797	2082.4
109.2	◊▲ P(15-20) ★★★★★	Cross **U.S. 64**, Winding Stair Gap, piped spring.	N 35 07.185, W 83 32.891	3770	2081.7

Franklin, NC 28734 (10E) (all major services) See map of Franklin north side and south side.

⌂ PO M-F 8:30am-5pm, Sa 9am-12pm. 828-524-3219

⌂⇌♦ **Budget Inn** 828-524-4403. (www.budgetinnoffranklin.com)
△⛺⊕🚗 AT Passport location. Open year round. $39.99 per person, limited to four per room, $5 for each addi-
☞ tional person. $50 pet deposit. Rooms include cable TV, refrigerators and microwaves, free WiFi

⌂△♨ **Jack Tarlin Hostel** 828-524-2064. (www.baltimorejacksplace.com)
🖳⊕☞ On site outfitter - Satellite of Three Eagles Outfitter. Bunk room $20 per person, 10 bunks on hand. ri-
vate rooms single $39.99 plus $5 for each extra person per room. Shower without stay $5. Coin laundry,
computer available for use, free WiFi. Smoky Mountain permits for free here. Shuttle runs at 9 and 11
am for the months of March thru April to and from Rock Gap, Wallace Gap and Winding Stair Gap. Motel
guests may call for free pickup. 4 pm shuttle around town for errands for guests.
Mail drops for guest: 433 East Palmer Street, Franklin, NC 28734.

⌂▲♦ **Gooder Grove Hostel** 828-332-0228.
△⊕♦🚗 Located in the heart of downtown Franklin, a short walk from Main Street breweries, restaurants and
P☞ shops. Daily shuttles to local outfitters stores.
AT Passport location. Open Year Round. May be closed September 10 — October 1, please call ahead.
Call for a shuttle or reservations. Bunk: $23 per person, includes fresh linens Private room: $43. Tent
or hammock: $13 per person. Laundry is $5. Free Wifi. Shuttle from Winding Stair Gap or Rock Gap at
9:30, 12:30, and 3:30 daily, end of February through April. Pet friendly, with fenced dog lot and kennel.
Parking for section hikers. Shuttles for slackpacking and guided hikes available.
Mail drops: 130 Hayes Circle, Franklin, NC 28734

⇌♦⊕ **Sapphire Inn** 828-524-4406. (www.sapphireinnfranklin.com)
☞ AT Passport location. Room $50 and up. Pet fee $15, free WiFi
Mail drops for guests: 761 East Main Street, Business 441, Franklin, NC 28734.

⇌🖳⊕☞ **Microtel Inn & Suites by Wyndham Franklin** 828-349-9000.
Call for prices, pet fee $25, microwave, fridge, stay includes continental breakfast. Computer available
for use, free WiFi.
Mail drops for guests: 81 Allman Dr, Franklin, NC 28734

⇌△🖳⊕ **Comfort Inn** 828-369-9200.
☞ Hiker Discount. Hot Breakfast, Indoor Pool. Guest Laundry. Dog Friendly rooms available. Hotel has
access to best hiker shuttle services in area.
Mail address: 313 Cunningham Rd Franklin NC 28734

✗♦ **1st Baptist Church Free Breakfast**
AT Passport location. Serves a pancake breakfast for Hikers starting the middle of March and ending the
middle of April. Picks hikers up at the motels and take them back. We serve the breakfast M-Su 7:15am
and 8am.

♦Υ🖳⊕ **Lazy Hiker Brewing Company** 828-349-2337. (www.lazyhikerbrewing.com)
AT Passport location. Spring and Summer hours, M-Thu 12pm-9pm, F-Sa 12pm-11pm, Su 12pm-6pm.
Food Truck onsite M-Th 12pm-8pm, F-Sa 12pm-9pm, Su 12pm-7pm. Computer and printer available for
use, free WiFi. Pet friendly

♦♦♨ **Outdoor 76** 828-349-7676. (www.outdoor76.com)
🖳⊕🚗☞ AT Passort location. M—Sa 10 am-7 pm, Su closed. Specialty AT hiking store with lightweight gear, food,
fuel & draft beer, right in center of town. Fuels available. Footwear experts with Pedorthic trained staff
to deal with injuries and various foot issues. 10% off total purchase for thru-hikers. Computer available
for use, free WiFi. Shipping services, in town shuttles.
No charge for Mail drops: 35 East Main Street, Franklin, NC 28734.
Rock House Lodge taproom/restaurant: Inside Outdoor 76
M-Sa 10 am-9 pm. 18 beers on tap, wine and food. Darts, indoor shuffleboard, community instruments
for hikers, along with big screen T.V and occasional live music. Weekly food specials. Free WiFi.

NoBo	Features	Description	GPS	Elev	SoBo

Three Eagles Outfitters 828-524-9061. www.threeeaglesoutfitters.net)
AT Passport location. Open year round. M–Sa 9am–6pm, Su 12am–5pm.
Full service outfitter. 10% AT thru hiker discount. Denatured alcohol and Coleman fuel by the ounce, fuel canisters. Computer available for use, free Wifi. Coffee and espresso bar and offers free beer for shoppers. Listing of shuttel proviors avaiable.
Mail drops: Three Eagles Outfitters 78 Siler Rd. Franklin, NC 28734.

Ruby City Gems and Minerals 828-524-3967. (www.rubycity.com) gems@rubycity.com
AT Passport location. M-Closed, Tu-Sa 10am-5pm, Su-Closed.

Currahee Brewing Co. 828-634-0078. (www.curraheebrew.com)
AT Passport location. Hours: M-Th 12am-9pm, F-Sa 12am-10pm, SU 2pm-7pm.

Lenzo Animal Hospital 828-369-2635 (www.lenzoanimalhospital.tripod.com) M-F 8:30 am-5 pm, Sa 8:30 am-12pm, Su sometimes open. Emergency clinic 828-665-4399.

Jim Granato 828-342-1571. Atlanta to Davenport Gap. Speaks Italian, German, and Spanish. Please call a week in advance if wanting to get shuttled into the mountains for availability. Based in Franklin.

Zen Shuttles 828-332-0228. Slackpacking/section hiking shuttles, long and short distance from GA to VA. Will also shuttle from Atlanta to the Smokies. Call for availability. Based in Franklin.

Chuck Allen 828-371-6460. Call after 1pm. Shuttles from Springer to Fontana. Based in Franklin.

Beverly Carini 850-572-7352. Not available Su 9-noon. Shuttles from Amicalola to Davenport Gap. Based in Franklin.

Franklin (north side)

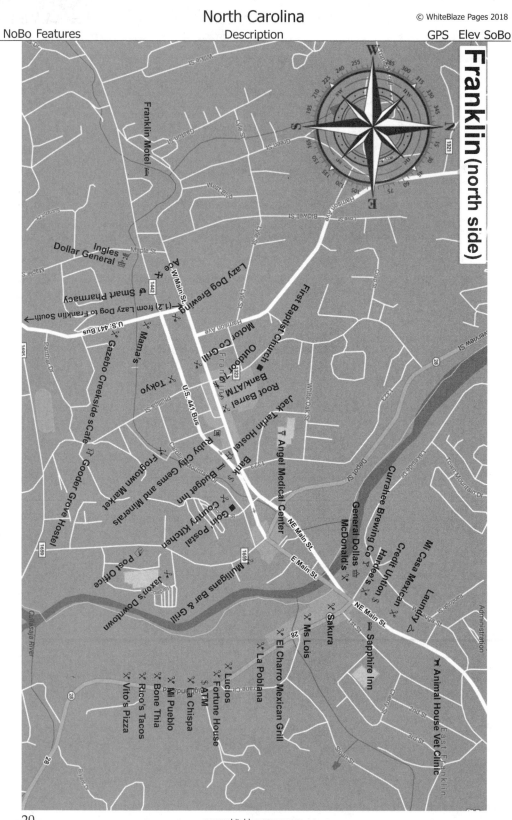

Franklin Motel

Ingles
Dollar General

Maple St.

Smart Pharmacy

(1.2) from Lazy Dog to Franklin South →

U.S. 441 Bus

Mama's

Tokyo

Gazebo Creekside sCafe

Gooder Grove Hostel

Panther Dr.

Ace

N. W Main St.

Lazy Dog Brewing

First Baptist Church

Harrison Ave.

Motor Co Grill

Outdoor 76

Bank/ATM

Root Barrel

Jack Tarlin Hostel

Angel Medical Center

U.S. 441 Bus

Ruby City Gems and Minerals

Bank

Budget Inn

Country Kitchen

Goin' Postal

Post Office

Frogtown Market

Jaxon's Downtown

Mulligans Bar & Grill

NE Main St.

E Main St.

McDonald's

General Dollar
Hardee's

Currahee Brewing Co

Credit Union

Mi Casa Mexican

Laundry

Sapphire Inn

NE Main St.

Sakura

Ms Lois

28

El Charro Mexican Grill

La Poblana

Lucios

Fortune House

ATM

La Chispa

Mi Pueblo

Bone Thia

Rico's Tacos

Vito's Pizza

Animal House Vet Clinic

East E Franklin

Administration

Cullasaja River

Franklin (south side)

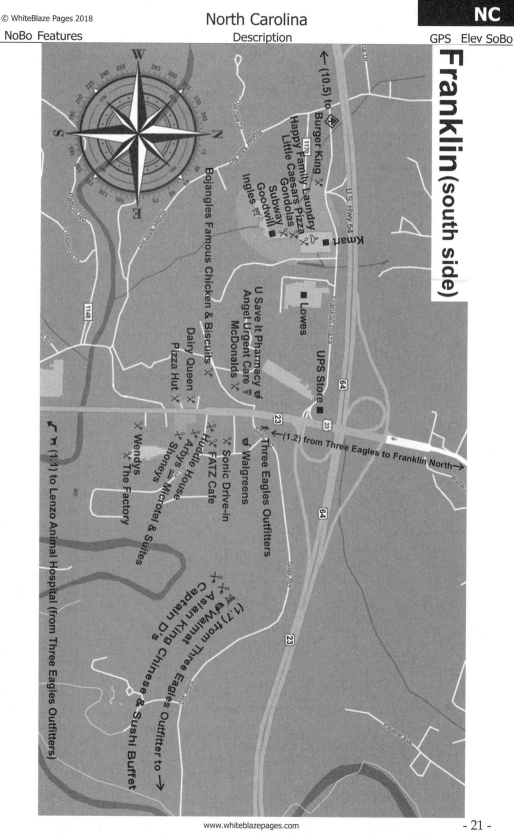

← (10.5) to Burger King

Happy Family Laundry
Little Caesars Pizza
Gondolas
Subway
Goodwill
Ingles

Kmart

Bojangles Famous Chicken & Biscuits

U Save It Pharmacy
Angel Urgent Care
McDonalds

Dairy Queen
Pizza Hut

Lowes

UPS Store

Wendys
The Factory

Sonic Drive-in
Huddle House
Arbys
Shoneys
Microtel & Suites

Walgreens

Three Eagles Outfitters

FATZ Cafe

← (1.2) from Three Eagles to Franklin North →

(1.1) from Three Eagles Outfitter to →

Asian King
Captain D's
Chinese & Sushi Buffet

Walmart

↙ ⚲ (1.1) to Lenzo Animal Hospital (from Three Eagles Outfitters)

U.S. Hwy 64

Franklin Plaza

NoBo	Features	Description	GPS	Elev	SoBo
109.5	♦	Cross east fork of Moore Creek, stone steps.		3676	2081.4
109.7	♦⌒	Cross east fork of Moore Creek, bridge.		3803	2081.2
110.1	♦⋀	Cross west fork of Moore Creek. Campsite to west.		3970	2080.8
110.3	♦	Swinging Lick Gap, water		4100	2080.6
111.2	📷	Panther Gap, view		4480	2079.7
112.9	♦Y⋀ ⊏(8)☾☂	Northern end of blue blaze of Siler Bald Loop(0.5E) **Siler Bald Shelter**, water (spring) is located 300 feet south of shelter on loop trail, tenting, privy, bear cable, south end of loop trail to shelter. 19.6◄10.9◄7.5◄►7.3►12.1►17.9	N 35 08.648, W 83 34.350	4600	2078.0
113.4	♦Y⋀ ⊏(8) ⌣☾☂	Southern end of blue blaze of Siler Bald Loop Trail (0.6E) to **Siler Bald Shelter**.	N 35 08.648, W 83 34.350	4178	2077.5
115.1	⋀🏕	**NC. 1310**, Wayah Gap, picnic area	N 35 09.240, W 83 34.842	4180	2075.8
116.4	Y	Wilson Lick Ranger Station is located to the west.		4650	2074.5
116.9	♦⋀P(4-5)	Cross **USFS 69**, water (piped spring) is located a few yards to the east		4900	2074.0
117.4	♦Y⋀⌣	Wine Spring, Bartram Trail is yellow blazed, tents sites and water (pipe spring) is located a few yards to the east.		5290	2073.5
117.6	⋀	Woods road intersects.		5008	2073.3
119.0	⋀	Cross woods road.		5158	2071.9
119.2	🚻⋀P	USFS Road termination, restrooms and parking to the east.		5302	2071.7
119.3	📷🍴○ P(20)	**Wayah Bald**, stone observation tower. Has a parking lot and a paved footpath.	Tower N 35 10.816, W 83 33.643 Parking N 35 10.723, W 83 33.739	5342	2071.6
119.5	⋀	Cross dirt road.		5178	2071.4
119.6	♦	Spring to the west of Trail.		5035	2071.3
119.7	♦⋀Y	Yellow blazed Bartram Trail comes in from the east and joins the AT for (2.4). Reliable stream 200 yards east on the Bartram Trail. Not an ATC approved camping spot		5200	2071.2

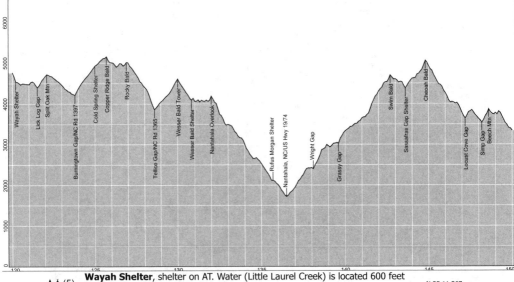

120.2	♦⋀(5) ⊏(8)⌣☾	**Wayah Shelter**, shelter on AT. Water (Little Laurel Creek) is located 600 feet west of AT on blue blazed trail, tent sites, privy. 18.2◄14.8◄7.3◄►4.8►10.6►15.5	N 35 11.367, W 83 33.864	4480	2070.7
121.5	♦⋀	Licklog Gap, logging road, water is locater (0.5) west		4440	2069.4
123.8	⋀P(7)	Cross **NC. 1397**, Burningtown Gap, large clearing with apple trees.	N 35 13.338, W 83 33.732	4236	2067.1
125.0	♦⋀⊏(6) ⌣☾☂	**Cold Spring Shelter**, water located 5 yards in front of the shelter, privy, tent sites located (0.1) north on AT, bear cables. 19.6◄12.1◄4.8◄►5.8►10.7►18.6	N 35 13.854, W 83 33.594	4920	2065.9
125.1	⋀⌣	Cold Spring Shelter tent sites. Water, privy and bear cables are located near the shelter.		4958	2065.8
125.7	📷	Vista to east near Copper Ridge Bald.		5080	2065.2

NoBo	Features	Description	GPS	Elev	SoBo
126.9	Y▲🎫	Trail to Rocky Bald summit (0.2) east to view.		5030	2064.0
127.2	🌢	Good spring		4900	2063.7
128.6	▲P(10) ★★★★★	Cross N~~~ ~o Gap	N 35 16.092, W 83 34.339	3850	2062.3

🏠🛏◈⊛ (4.3W~ ~ntain Lodge 828-321-2340. Out of hours (after 7pm) 828-321-9949
⛺🏚✕🍴 AT ~
🛵🚗P▣ P~ ~ker Wiggy.
~ 1st June
~GHTLY RATES INCLUDE BREAKFAST. Bunks $35 per person (bedding provided), bedding
~ivate room with 2 twin beds $75. Private room with king bed, private bathroom $85. Three
~ning meal available $12.50. Laundry $5.00. Cash payments only under $50. Short term
~ available. Free wiFi. Shuttle pickup and return to or from: Wayah Gap (115.1) $5PP per trip,
~gtown Gap (123.8) $5PP per trip, Telico Gap (128.6) $5PP per trip. Slackpacking options Rock
~ to Fontana w/reservations. Parking for section hikers $4 day (no charge if booking a two night
~ay)/shuttles to start point available. Cash payment only if stay is under $50. There is a $3 surcharge
for use of Credit Cards if stay is over $50.
Mail drops for guests only: 63 Britannia Drive, Topton. NC 28781

	Y🎫🗼	Wesser Bald summit. Observation tower is located east 40 yards on side trail. Formerly a fire tower, the structure atop Wesser Bald is now an observation deck offering panoramic views. The Great Smoky Mountains and Fontana Lake dominate the view to the north.	N 35 16.623, W 83 34.641	4627	2060.9
~0.7	🌢	Water (spring) on blue blazed trail 125 feet to the east.		4100	2060.2
130.8	Y▲ ⊏(8) ⌄☾🛜	(0.1W) **Wesser Bald Shelter**, water (spring) located (0.1) south on AT then 75 yards on a blue blazed trail, tenting, privy, bear cables. Blue blazed Wesser Bald Trail (2.0) east to Wesser Creek Road. 17.9◀10.6◀5.8◀▶4.9▶12.8▶21.9	N 35 16.941, W 83 34.932	4115	2060.1
132.4	🎫	Vista to the west.		4162	2058.5
132.6	🎫	Jump-up, rocky outcrop with outstanding views, not the same as the other jump-up within the next 10 miles north.		4000	2058.3
135.7	🌢Y▲ ⊏(6)⌄☾	200 feet east to **A. Rufus Morgan Shelter**, water (stream) located west of shelter AT, tenting, privy. 15.5◀10.7◀4.9◀▶7.9▶17.0▶23.1	N 35 19.451, W 83 35.412	2300	2055.2
136.5	▲P(10) ★★★★★	Cross **US 19/74**, Nantahala Gorge, Nantahala Outdoor Center. **See map of NOC**	N 35 19.872, W 83 35.532	1723	2054.4

🏠🛏◈⛟ **Nantahala Outdoor Center** 828-785-5082. (www.noc.com)
⛺🍴✕🍴 AT Passport location.
🛢🚶🚗▣ Walk in's with and without out reservation must check in at General Store between 10am and 7pm. Credit Cards accepted.
Motel rooms: $79.99 and up, free WiFi.
Base Camp Bunkhouse 828-785-5082, reservatons are recommended, $39.99 for 2 people, $79.99 for 4 people, $109.99 for 6 people, $139.99 for 8 people, all include shower, common area and community kitchen, free WiFi.
River's End Restaurant Serves breakfast, lunch and dinner. Opens mid-March. M-Thu 8am-7pm. No breakfast in the fall. F-Sa 8am-8pm, Sun 8am-7pm. Free WiFi.
NOC Outfitters: Open daily. Lots of gear, trail food, fuel by the ounce, free WiFi. They will do gear shakedowns if you would like them to, just ask. You can print Smoky Mountain permits from here. Ask about shuttles.
Mail drops: dated and marked "Hold for AT Hiker", 13077 Hwy 19W, Bryson City, NC 28713.

🏚 **Wesser General Store** Open Mar thru Oct
🚗 **Jude Julius** 828-736-0086. Based in Bryson City, NC. Shuttle ranges from Hiawassee, GA to Newfoun d Gap, NC.

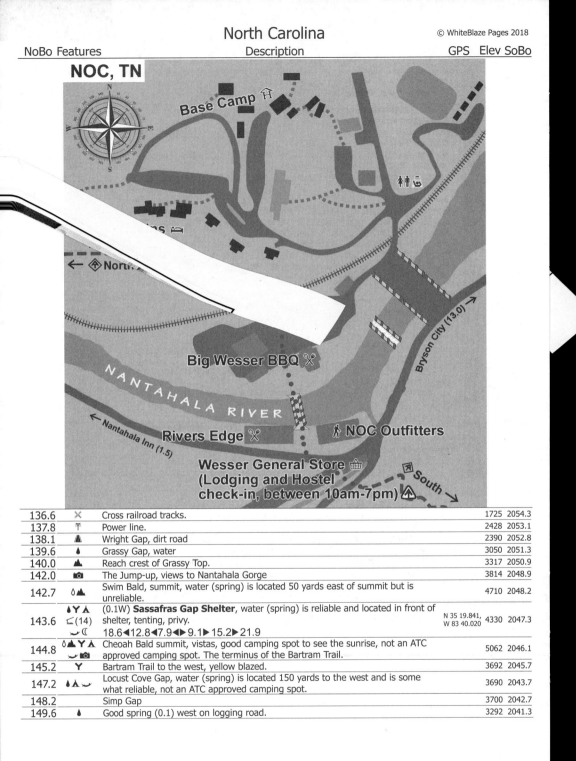

136.6	✕	Cross railroad tracks.		1725 2054.3
137.8	⊤	Power line.		2428 2053.1
138.1	▲	Wright Gap, dirt road		2390 2052.8
139.6	◊	Grassy Gap, water		3050 2051.3
140.0	▲	Reach crest of Grassy Top.		3317 2050.9
142.0	📷	The Jump-up, views to Nantahala Gorge		3814 2048.9
142.7	◊▲	Swim Bald, summit, water (spring) is located 50 yards east of summit but is unreliable.		4710 2048.2
143.6	◊Y⋏ ⊏(14) ⌣☾	**(0.1W) Sassafras Gap Shelter**, water (spring) is reliable and located in front of shelter, tenting, privy. 18.6◀12.8◀7.9◀▶9.1▶15.2▶21.9	N 35 19.841, W 83 40.020	4330 2047.3
144.8	◊▲Y⋏ ⌣📷	Cheoah Bald summit, vistas, good camping spot to see the sunrise, not an ATC approved camping spot. The terminus of the Bartram Trail.		5062 2046.1
145.2	Y	Bartram Trail to the west, yellow blazed.		3692 2045.7
147.2	◊⋏⌣	Locust Cove Gap, water (spring) is located 150 yards to the west and is some what reliable, not an ATC approved camping spot.		3690 2043.7
148.2		Simp Gap		3700 2042.7
149.6	◊	Good spring (0.1) west on logging road.		3292 2041.3

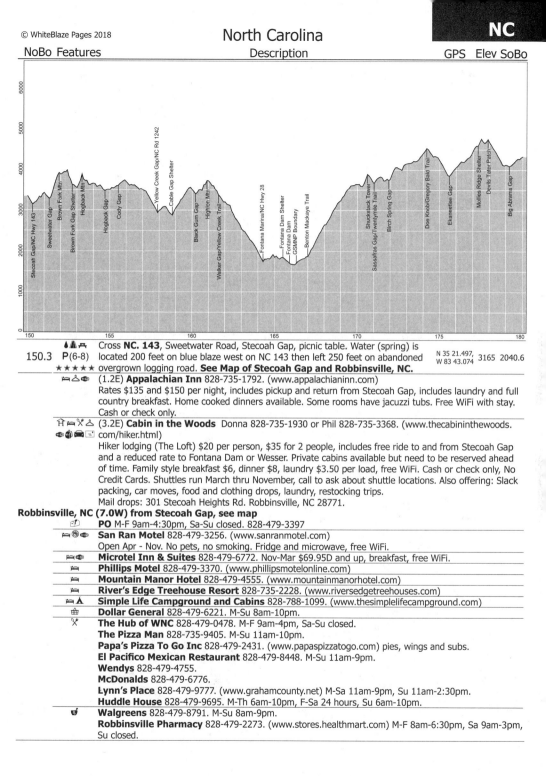

150.3 **♠▲☐ P(6-8)** Cross **NC. 143**, Sweetwater Road, Stecoah Gap, picnic table. Water (spring) is located 200 feet on blue blaze west on NC 143 then left 250 feet on abandoned ★★★★★ overgrown logging road. **See Map of Stecoah Gap and Robbinsville, NC.**   N 35 21.497, W 83 43.074   3165 2040.6

☐△⌂ **(1.2E) Appalachian Inn** 828-735-1792. (www.appalachianinn.com)
Rates $135 and $150 per night, includes pickup and return from Stecoah Gap, includes laundry and full country breakfast. Home cooked dinners available. Some rooms have jacuzzi tubs. Free WiFi with stay. Cash or check only.

⌂☐✕△ **(3.2E) Cabin in the Woods** Donna 828-735-1930 or Phil 828-735-3368. (www.thecabininthewoods.
☐⌂☐☐ com/hiker.html)
Hiker lodging (The Loft) $20 per person, $35 for 2 people, includes free ride to and from Stecoah Gap and a reduced rate to Fontana Dam or Wesser. Private cabins available but need to be reserved ahead of time. Family style breakfast $6, dinner $8, laundry $3.50 per load, free WiFi. Cash or check only, No Credit Cards. Shuttles run March thru November, call to ask about shuttle locations. Also offering: Slack packing, car moves, food and clothing drops, laundry, restocking trips.
Mail drops: 301 Stecoah Heights Rd. Robbinsville, NC 28771.

Robbinsville, NC (7.0W) from Stecoah Gap, see map
☐ **PO** M-F 9am-4:30pm, Sa-Su closed. 828-479-3397
☐☐⌂ **San Ran Motel** 828-479-3256. (www.sanranmotel.com)
Open Apr - Nov. No pets, no smoking. Fridge and microwave, free WiFi.
☐⌂ **Microtel Inn & Suites** 828-479-6772. Nov-Mar $69.95D and up, breakfast, free WiFi.
☐ **Phillips Motel** 828-479-3370. (www.phillipsmotelonline.com)
☐ **Mountain Manor Hotel** 828-479-4555. (www.mountainmanorhotel.com)
☐ **River's Edge Treehouse Resort** 828-735-2228. (www.riversedgetreehouses.com)
☐▲ **Simple Life Campground and Cabins** 828-788-1099. (www.thesimplelifecampground.com)
☐ **Dollar General** 828-479-6221. M-Su 8am-10pm.
✕ **The Hub of WNC** 828-479-0478. M-F 9am-4pm, Sa-Su closed.
The Pizza Man 828-735-9405. M-Su 11am-10pm.
Papa's Pizza To Go Inc 828-479-2431. (www.papaspizzatogo.com) pies, wings and subs.
El Pacifico Mexican Restaurant 828-479-8448. M-Su 11am-9pm.
Wendys 828-479-4755.
McDonalds 828-479-6776.
Lynn's Place 828-479-9777. (www.grahamcounty.net) M-Sa 11am-9pm, Su 11am-2:30pm.
Huddle House 828-479-9695. M-Th 6am-10pm, F-Sa 24 hours, Su 6am-10pm.
☐ **Walgreens** 828-479-8791. M-Su 8am-9pm.
Robbinsville Pharmacy 828-479-2273. (www.stores.healthmart.com) M-F 8am-6:30pm, Sa 9am-3pm, Su closed.

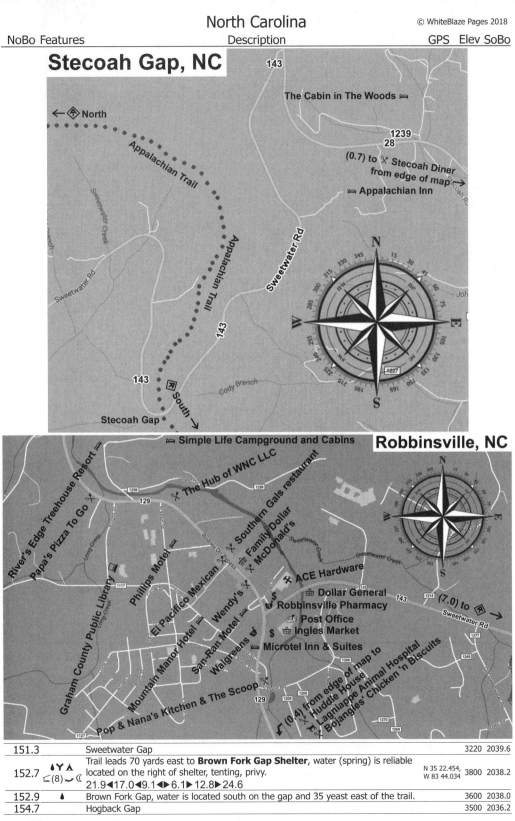

Stecoah Gap, NC

The Cabin in The Woods

← North

Appalachian Trail

Appalachian Trail

143

143

Stecoah Gap

1239
28

(0.7) to ✗ Stecoah Diner
from edge of map →

Appalachian Inn

Sweetwater Rd

Robbinsville, NC

Simple Life Campground and Cabins

River's Edge Treehouse Resort

Papa's Pizza To Go

The Hub of WNC LLC

Southern Gals restaurant

Graham County Public Library

Phillips Motel

El Pacifico Mexican

Mountain Manor Hotel

San-Ran Motel

Pop & Nana's Kitchen & The Scoop

Wendy's

Walgreens

Family Dollar

McDonald's

ACE Hardware

Dollar General

Robbinsville Pharmacy

Post Office

Ingles Market

Microtel Inn & Suites

(0.4) from edge of map to
Huddle House
Lagniappe Animal Hospital
Bojangles' Chicken 'n Biscuits

(7.0) to →
Sweetwater Rd

143

151.3	Sweetwater Gap	3220 2039.6
152.7	Trail leads 70 yards east to **Brown Fork Gap Shelter**, water (spring) is reliable located on the right of shelter, tenting, privy. 21.9◄17.0◄9.1◄►6.1►12.8►24.6	N 35 22.454, W 83 44.034 3800 2038.2
152.9	Brown Fork Gap, water is located south on the gap and 35 yeast east of the trail.	3600 2038.0
154.7	Hogback Gap	3500 2036.2

NoBo	Features	Description	GPS	Elev	SoBo
155.5	◊ ▲ ⌣	Cody Gap, water (spring) is known to go dry during dry weather.		3600	2035.4
156.3		Cross knob.		4000	2034.6
157.5	◊	Cross stream above Yellow Creek Gap.		3374	2033.4
157.9	▲P(3) ★★★★★	Cross **NC. 1242**, Yellow Creek Mountain Road, Yellow Creek Gap. **See map**.	N 35 24.630, W 83 45.942	2980	2033.0
	⇔▲⛺⊕	(1.5W) **Creekside Paradise Bed and Breakfast** 828-346-1076. Cynthia and Jeff.			
	🍴�car🖨	Room rates, $60 per person, $45PP if 2 per room. Camping $10. Stays include pickup and return from Yellow Creek Gap, laundry, hot tub, and free slackpack. Breakfast and resupply trip to Robbinsville included with room rental, $10 for campers. Dinner $15 per person. Free WiFi. Pickup and return from Stecoah Gap and Fontana $5, NOC $15. Pets welcome. Mail drops: 259 Upper Cove Rd, Robbinsville, NC, 28771.			

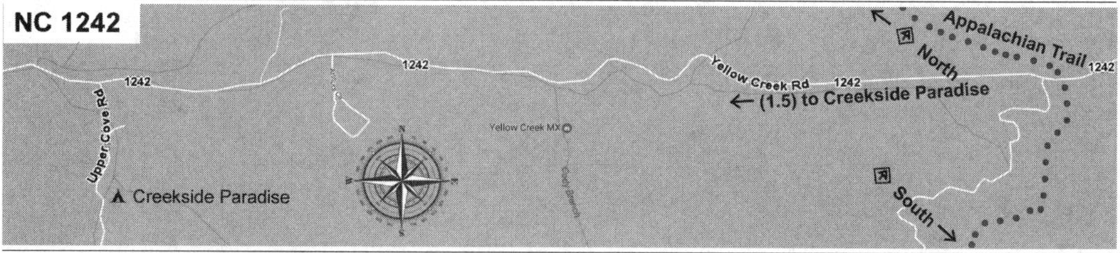

NC 1242

Creekside Paradise · ← (1.5) to Creekside Paradise · Appalachian Trail · North · South · Yellow Creek Rd · Upper Cove Rd · Yellow Creek MX · 1242

NoBo	Features	Description	GPS	Elev	SoBo
158.8	◊▲⌂(6) ⌣☾🔥	**Cable Gap Shelter**, water (spring) located in front of shelter, tenting privy. 23.1◄15.2◄6.1◄►6.7►18.5►21.6	N 35 24.913, W 83 46.416	2880	2032.1
160.2		Black Gum Gap		3490	2030.7
161.6	Y	Walker Gap.		3450	2029.3
161.9	◊	Cross small stream		3629	2029.0
162.0	◊▲⌣	Campsite is not an ATC approved camping spot, water		3200	2028.9
164.3	Y▲ ★★★★★	Cross **NC. 28**, Benton Mackaye Trail **Fontana Dam Village (2.0W)** Hostel, **The Hiker Inn (6.0E) See Notes at mile 166.3.**	N 35 26.484, W 83 47.808	1810	2026.6
164.5	▲P(10) ★★★★★	Cross **SR 1245** at parking lot. **See map of Fontana area.**	N 35 26.496, W 83 47.743	1802	2026.4
	🚹🚻	Fontana 28 AT Crossing. Bathrooms, free phone, vending machines.			
	🚗	**Fontana Shuttle** 828-498-2211. Shuttles for $3 per person each way between AT Crossing, Visitor Center and Fontana Village. 8:30-6 daily Feb 15 thru May 15. Call for rides outside these dates.			

Fontana Village, NC (2W from NC 28) **See map.**

📧	**PO** M-F: 11:45am-3:45pm. 828-498-2315	
⇔Ⓡ	**Fontana Lodge** 800-849-2258, 828-498-2211.	
⊕🖥☎🖨	No pets. Offers thru hiker rate $79 for up to 4 people. Cabins $100 and up. Computer available for use with printer in lobby, free WiFi, ATM. Mail drops: free for guests, $5 for non-guest. Fontana Village Resort, ATTN: Front Desk, 300 Woods Rd., Fontana Dam, NC 28733.	
🛒🖥♨	**General Store Grocery** Mar 10-Thanksgiving. Open M-Th 9am-7pm, F-Sa 9am-9pm, Su 9am-7pm. Offers freeze dried food, canister fuel, coleman and alcohol by the ounce.	
🍴✗♨	**Fontana Pit Stop** M-Thu 8am-7pm, F-Saturday 8am-8pm, Su 8am-7pm. Pizza, hot dogs and other light food, soda and coffee. Stocks some hiker food and fuel when the General Store is closed.	
✗	**Mountview Restaurant** 828-498-2115, **Wildwood Grill**, Apr-Sept.	
⌂	**Laundromat** Open year round, 7 days a week, detergent available in General Store.	
🚗🍴	**Steve Claxton "Mustard Seed"** (2016 thru hiker) 828-736-7501, 828-479-9608. steve@steveclaxton.com (www.steveclaxton.com) Shuttle range from Hiawasee to Hot Springs and some area airports. Also offers slackpacking.	

Fontana Dam, NC

NoBo		Description	GPS	Elev	SoBo
165.5	♦Y⚠ ⊑(24) ⌐ ♦♦♦	(0.1E) on paved sidewalk to **Fontana Dam Shelter "Fontana Hilton"**, water, tenting, shower, restroom. 21.9◀12.8◀6.7◀▶ 11.8 ▶ 4.9▶ 17.8	N 35 26.912, W 83 47.638	1775	2025.4
165.8	Y	Fontana Dam bypass trail to the west.		1773	2025.1
165.9	♦⚠⚠ P(10) ★★★★★	Fontana Dam Visitor Center, water. Southern end of dam.	N 35 27.113, W 83 48.137	1700	2025.0
166.3	O⚠P ★★★★★	Cross **Fontana Dam**, Little Tennessee River. Southern boundary of **Great Smoky Mountains National Park. North bounders must have a backcountry permit before entering Great Smoky Mountains National Park. Dogs are not permitted inside the Great Smoky Mountains National Park.**		1740	2024.6
	①◈ ♦♦♦⚏	**Fontana Dam Visitor Center** 828-498-2234. AT Pasport loaction. Open daily April 2 - Sept 30: 9am-7 pm; October 9 am-6 pm. Soda machine outside. Restrooms, showers, free WiFi.			
	⇌⚠🚗	(6.3E) **The Hike Inn** 828-479-3677. (www.thehikeinn.com) Open year round. Only services hikers. Only takes reservations. Thru hiker $75 for one per room, $100 for two per room. Section hikers $50 per room for 1 or 2 hikers. Potential thru-hikers should contact them pre-hike. No Credit Cards Accepted, cash or personal check only. No walk-ins. Laundry available. Shuttles can be arranged, call or email to make arrangements. Mail Drops: for guests only. 3204 Fontana Road. Fontana Dam, NC. 28733.			
166.4	O⚠P ★★★★★	Cross **Fontana Dam**, Little Tennessee River. Southern boundary of **Great Smoky Mountains National Park. North bounders must have a backcountry permit before entering Great Smoky Mountains National Park. Dogs are not permitted inside the Great Smoky Mountains National Park.**		1740	2023.4
	🐕⊡	**Loving Care Kennels** 865-453-2028 (www.LovingCareKennels.com) Will pickup your dog at Fontana Dam and return him/her to Davenport Gap. $375 for one dog, $500 for two. Will deliver maildrops upon pickup and return. Call at least 2 days in advance if you are heading north bound. 3779 Tinker Hollow Rd, Pigeon Forge, TN 37863.			
	🐕	**Standing Bear Farm** 423-487-0014. Listed under Green Corner Road in Davenport Gap at the north end of the Smoky Mountinas.			
	🐕	**Barks and Recreation** 865-325-8245 (www.barksandrecgatlinburg.com) Does not offer rides, but you can drop off and pickups. Located at 2159 East Pkwy Gatlinburg, TN. M-Sa 8am-8pm, Su 10am-6pm.			

© WhiteBlaze Pages 2018

North Carolina/Tennessee

NC/TN

NoBo Features

Description

GPS Elev SoBo

Great Smoky Mountains National Park, Backcountry Permit Fees

As of February, 2013, a backcountry permit must be obtained for overnight stays before entering the Great Smoky Mountains National Park. Backcountry permits can be obtained up to 30 days in advance. Hikers who meet the definition of an Appalachian Trail thru-hiker (those who begin and end their hike at least 50 miles outside the park and only travel on the A.T. in the park) are eligible for a thru-hiker permit of $20.00 per permit. The cost of the permit is non-refundable. A Thru-Hiker Permit is valid for up to 38 days from the date you obtain it. Thru-Hikers have 8 days to get through the Smokies. A break to rest or resupply in a nearby town does not negate one's standing as a thru-hiker. Thru-Hikers may tent in the immediate area around shelters only if the shelter is full. Thru-hikers are required to stay in shelters when there is space available. Thru-Hikers must always give up bunk space in shelters to those with shelter reservations. Permits are available at (https://smokiespermits.nps.gov/).

You may also obtain a permit in person at the park's Backcountry Office (at the Sugarlands Visitor Center near Gatlinburg, TN) or over the phone; with permits issued by fax, mail or email. Hikers staying overnight in the backcountry are required to have a printed copy of the permit.

No dogs or other pets are allowed on any park trails. No dogs or other pets may be carried into the backcountry. See mile 166.4 for kennel providers.

NoBo	Features	Description	GPS	Elev	SoBo
166.5	Y	Fontana Dam bypass trail to the west.		1725	2024.4
167.1	Y ▲ P(7)	**Lakeview Drive West**, Benton MacKaye Trail and Lakeshore Trail and Benton MacKaye Trail lead east. Roadside parking.	N 35 26.485, W 83 47.729	1800	2023.8
169.2	◊	Unreliable water source a few yards east at bend in trail.		3621	2021.7
170.6	⌁	Old road leads (0.1) east to Shuckstack Fire Tower. Coordinates are for fire tower.	N 35 29.128, W 83 48.909	3800	2020.3
171.0	Y	Sassafras Gap. Intersection of Lost Cove Trail east and Twentymile Trail to west.	N 35 33.757, W 83 50.748	3648	2019.9
171.9	◊▲🛏🐾	Birch Spring Gap, Tent pads are located 100 yards to west down slope, **camping not permitted along AT**, spring, bear cables.		3680	2019.0
174.0	Y▲	Doe Knob summit, intersects with Gregory Bald Trail to the west.		4520	2016.9
174.5		Mud Gap.		4331	2016.4
175.6	◊	Ekaneetlee Gap, spring 300 feet west		3842	2015.3
177.3	◊⌐(12)🐾	**Mollies Ridge Shelter**, water (spring) located 200 yards to the right of the shelter, bear cables. 24.6◄18.5◄11.8◄►3.1► 6.0►12.1	N 35 32.753, W 83 47.618	4570	2013.6
177.8		Devil's Tater Patch		4775	2013.1

178.9		Little Abrams Gap		4120	2012.0
179.2		Big Abrams Gap.		4121	2011.7
180.4	◊Y⌐(14)🐾	**Russell Field Shelter**, water (spring) located 150 yards down the Russell Field Trail toward Cades Cove, bear cables. 21.6◄14.9◄3.1◄►2.9► 9.0►14.7	N 35 33.704, W 83 45.996	4360	2010.5

NoBo	Features	Description	GPS	Elev	SoBo
180.7		MacCampbell Gap.		4329	2010.2
183.3	♦Y ⊏(12) ⟨⟨☎	(0.15) east down Eagle Creek Trail to **Spence Field Shelter**, water (spring) 150 yards down the Eagle Creek Trail, privy, bear cables. Bote Mountain Trail to the west. 17.8◄6.0◄2.9◄▶6.1▶11.8▶3.5	N 35 33.708, W 83 43.962	4915	2007.6
183.7	Y	Jenkins Ridge Trail leads east.		4936	2007.2
184.4	📷	Rocky Top, views of Fontana Lake.		5440	2006.5
185.0	▲📷	Thunderhead summit, east peak, views of Fontana Lake and southwest.		5527	2005.9
186.1	♦	Beechnut Gap, water (spring) is located 75 yards west		4920	2004.8
186.7		Mineral Gap		5030	2004.2
187.1	📷	Eastern shoulder of Brier Knob, vista		5210	2003.8
188.4		Sugar Tree Gap, sugar maple trees.		4435	2002.5
189.4	♦⊏(12)☎	**Derrick Knob Shelter**, water (spring), bear cables. 12.1◄9.0◄6.1◄▶5.7▶7.4▶13.0	N 35 33.991, W 83 38.514	4880	2001.5
189.7	♦Y P(15-20)	Sams Gap, water (spring) is located 300 feet west, junction with Greenbrier Ridge Trail to the west (4.2) to Tremont Road and parking.		4995	2001.2
190.0	♦Y	Miry Ridge Trail, water (spring) is located 600 feet west on Miry Ridge Trail.			2000.9
192.1	♦	Buckeye Gap		4817	1998.8
195.1	♦⊏(12)☎	**Silers Bald Shelter**, water (spring) located to the right on a trail 75 yards, bear cables. 14.7◄11.8◄5.7◄▶1.7▶7.3▶15.3	N 35 33.857, W 83 34.099	5460	1995.8
195.3	📷	Silers Bald, partially wooded summit, view		5607	1995.6
195.5	Y	Welch Ridge Trail to east.		5432	1995.4
196.8	♦⊏(12) ⟨⟨☎	**Double Spring Gap Shelter**, water that is reliable is located on the North Carolina side, 15 yards from the crest. A second source is on the Tennessee side, 35 yards from the crest. Privy, bear cables. Gap is named for two springs that are unreliable in late summer. 13.5◄7.4◄1.7◄▶5.6▶13.6▶21.0	N 35 33.915, W 83 32.558	5505	1994.1
199.1	📷	Mt. Buckley, vista		6582	1991.8
199.6	♦Y ◈📷 ⑃O ♦♦▲ P(20)	**Clingmans Dome** AT Passport location, in visitors center. Highest point on the AT. Observation tower provides 360-degree views. Trail east (0.5) to Clingman's parking area with restroom.	N 35 33.775, W 83 29.900	6643	1991.3
200.1	▲	Mt. Love, summit		6446	1990.8
202.4	♦Y ⊏(12) ⟨⟨☎	Sugarland Mountain Trail leads (0.5W) **Mt. Collins Shelter**, water (spring) located 200 yards beyond shelter on Sugarland Mountain Trail, privy, bear cables. 13.0◄7.3◄5.6◄▶8.0▶15.4▶20.6	N 35 35.645, W 83 28.263	5900	1988.5
202.6	Y▲ P(4-5)	Side trail leads east 35 yards to **Clingmans Dome Access Road** and Fork Ridge Trail.	N 35 36.418, W 83 28.175	5269	1988.3
205.6	Y▲ P(8-10)	Indian Gap, intersection of Road Prong Trail. Parking 19 yards east off **Clingmans Dome Access Road**.	N 35 36.572, W 83 26.793	5286	1985.3
207.3	♦▲♦♦⊕ 📷P(20) ⌐ ★★★★★	Cross **U.S. 441**, Newfound Gap. Rockefeller Memorial. Restrooms. The only road crossing along the Trail in the Smokies.	N 35 36.665, W 83 25.519	5045	1983.6

Gatlinburg, TN (15.0W) see map of Gatlinburg.

⊡	**PO** M-F 9am-5pm, Sa 9am-11am. 865-436-3229.	
🛏⊕🖵	**Microtel Gatlinburg** 865-436-0107. $69.99 to 89.99, includes continental breakfast. Pets fee $10. Free WiFi. Mail drops for guests and advance reservations: 211 Historic Nature Trail, Gatlinburg, TN 37738.	
🛏⊕🛏🖵	**Motel 6** 865-436-7813. Reaonable rates, call for pricing. Pets under 25 lbs are free, There is a pet fee of over 25 lbs. Microwave, fridge, outdoor pool, free WiFi. Accepts Credit Cards. Mail drops for guests: 309 Ownby St, Gatlinburg, TN 37738.	
🛏⊕	**Days Inn & Suites** 865-436-5811. Call for pricing, free WiFi.	
🚶🛏🖵	**NOC Great Outpost** 865-277-8209. (noc.com/retail-locations/noc-gatlinburg) M-Th 10am-6pm, F-Sa 10am-8pm, Su 10m-6pm. Coleman and alcohol by the ounce. Free showers and pack storage. Mail drops: 1138 Parkway, Gatlinburg, TN 37738.	
🚶	**The Day Hiker** 865-430-0970. (www.thedayhiker.com)	
🚗	**Highlands Shuttle Service** (Ron McGaha) 423-625-0739 (home), 865-322-2752 (cell). (high-landsshuttleservice.com) Shuttle area is from Wesser, North Carolina (NOC), to Damascus Virginia. Shuttles anywhere in the Great Smoky Mountains National Park and the McGhee/Tyson Airport in Knoxville, Tennessee.	
🚗	**A Walk in the Woods** 865-436-8283. (www.awalkinthewoods.com) M-Su 9am-5pm, except holidays. Resupply and shuttling hikers. Shuttles range from Springer Mtn, GA to Damascus, VA. Ask about thru hiker rates.	

NoBo	Features	Description	GPS Elev SoBo

🛒 **Old Dad's General Store & Deli** 865-430-1644. (www.olddadsgeneralstore.com) Deli, Grill, Grocery. Also serves hot foods. M-Su 7am-11pm.

🍴 Other restaurants intown include.

Bennett's BBQ, (bennetts-bbq.com) AYCE Breakfast bar include 50 items. AYCE Soup and Salad bar for lunch.

Smoky Mountain Brewery (www.smoky-mtn-brewery.com)

Park Grill Steakhouse (www.parkgrillgatlinburg.com)

Pizza Hut, TGI Friday's, Five Guys, Shoney's, Loco Burro fresh mex cantina

Cherokee, NC. (18.0E) (all major services)

💊 **Walgreens** M-Su 8 am-10 pm; **Pharmacy** M-F 11am-7pm, Sa-Su closed.

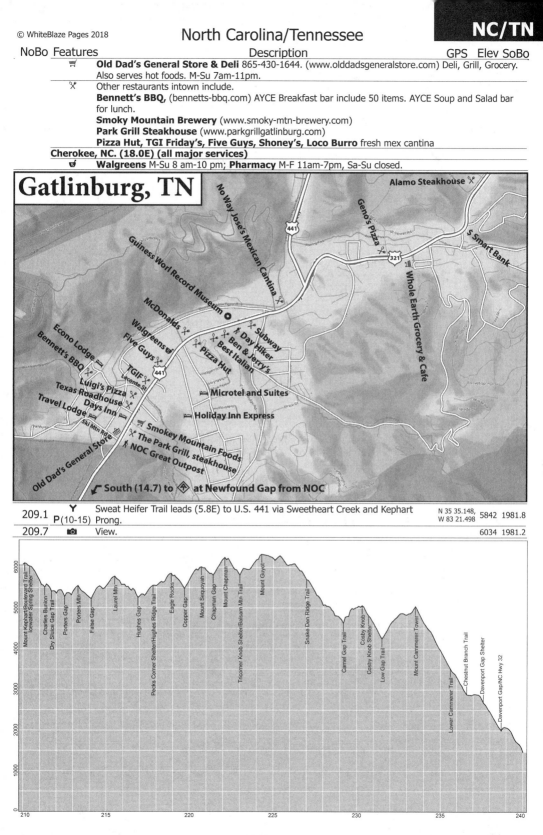

Gatlinburg, TN

| 209.1 | Y P(10-15) | Sweat Heifer Trail leads (5.8E) to U.S. 441 via Sweetheart Creek and Kephart Prong. | N 35 35.148, W 83 21.498 | 5842 | 1981.8 |
| 209.7 | 📷 | View. | | 6034 | 1981.2 |

NoBo	Features	Description	GPS	Elev	SoBo
210.1	Y 📷	Boulevard Trail leads (5.5W) to Mt. LeConte.		5695	1980.8
210.4	♦Y ⊏(12) ⟪🔥	East 75 feet to **Icewater Spring Shelter**, water (spring) located 50 yards north of AT, privy, bear cables. 15.3◀13.6◀8.0◀▶7.4▶12.6▶20.3	N 35 37.789, W 83 23.179	5920	1980.5
211.0	♦	Spring on the west.		5884	1979.9
211.3	Y 📷 ⊙	**Charlies Bunion** (0.1) on loop trail west around Fodder Stack. From here to Porters Gap there are some spectacular views.	N 35 38.246, E 83 22.604	5500	1979.6
211.7		Dry Sluice Gap.		5314	1979.2
211.8	Y	Dry Sluice Gap Trail leads (8.7) east to Smokemont Campground.		5443	1979.1
212.7		Porters Gap, the Sawteeth. From here to Charlies Bunion there are some spectacular views.		5577	1978.2
213.4		False Gap.		5500	1977.5
214.6	▲	Cross Woolly Top Lead.		5880	1976.4
215.8	📷	Bradley's View, views east into deep-cut gorge of Bradley Fork.		5200	1975.1
217.6	📷	Cross Hughes Ridge.		5571	1973.3
217.8	♦Y ⊏(12) ⟪🔥	Hughes Ridge Trail leads east, continue (0.4E) **Peck's Corner Shelter**, water (spring) located 50 yards in front of shelter, privy, bear cables. From the shelter Hughes Ridge Trail leads to Smokemont Campground. 21.0◀15.4◀7.4◀▶5.2▶12.9▶19.6	N 35 39.049, W 83 18.511	5280	1973.1
218.7	📷	Good view of slopes and gorges.		5884	1972.2
220.2	▲	Mt. Sequoyah, summit		6069	1970.7
221.9		Reach high point on Mt. Chapman.		6417	1969.0
223.0	♦Y ⊏(12) ⟪🔥	Trail leads 100 yards east to **Tri-Corner Knob Shelter**, water (spring) located 10 yards in front of shelter, privy, bear cables. 20.6◀12.6◀5.2◀▶7.7▶14.4▶25.3	N 35 41.630, W 83 15.399	5920	1967.9
223.3	Y	Balsam Mountain Trail leads (10.1) along ridge of Balsam Mountains to Pin Oak Gap at Balsam Mountain Road, closed in winter.		5970	1967.6
224.4	♦Y	Cross Guyot Spur, AT skirts around Mt Guyot		6360	1966.5
225.0	♦	Guyot Spring, located on AT		6150	1965.9
225.7	📷	Good view.		6271	1965.2
227.0	Y	Snake Den Ridge Trail leads (5.3) west to Crosby Campground		5600	1963.9
230.3		Ridgecrest on west side of ridge near Cosby Knob.		5150	1960.6
230.7	♦Y ⊏(12) ⟪🔥	Trail leads 150 feet east to **Cosby Knob Shelter**, water (spring) is located 35 yards downhill in front of shelter, privy, bear cables. 20.3◀12.9◀7.7◀▶6.7▶17.6▶25.9	N 35 43.697, W 83 10.924	4700	1960.2
231.4	Y ⅄	Low Gap Trail leads (2.5) west to Crosby Campground.		4240	1959.5
233.5	Y 🗼	Side trail leads (0.6) west to Mt. Cammerer fire tower. Historic stone and timber structure rebuilt in 1994 that provides panoramic views from its platform. Not your run of the mill fire lookout, it's an octagonal rock tower.		5000	1957.4
233.9	♦	Water (spring) is located on AT west side.		4300	1957.0
234.1	📷	Large rock provides good views east.		4387	1956.8
235.4	♦Y	Water (spring) is located 80 feet to the east		3700	1955.5
235.6	Y	Lower Mt. Cammerer Trail leads west (7.8) public road at NPS Cosby Campground.		3469	1955.3
236.6	Y P(10)	Chestnut Branch Trail, leads (2.0) east to parking at Big Creek Ranger Station and to the north end of BMT	N 35 45.592, W 83 06.333	2900	1954.3
237.6	♦Y ⊏(12)	Trail leads 200 yards west to **Davenport Gap Shelter**, water (spring) located to left of shelter. 19.6◀14.4◀6.7◀▶10.9▶19.2▶24.0	N 35 46.153, W 83 07.422	2600	1953.3
238.7	▲P(5-6)	**Cross TN. 32, Davenport Gap, Cove Creek Road.** (Old NC. 284), eastern boundary, Great Smoky Mountain National Park. Parking is not recommend here, location has a reputation of vandalism with car thefts. **See Notes about Great Smoky Mountains National Park, Backcountry Permit Fees at NOBO mile 166.4.**	N 35 46.466, W 83 06.729	1975	1952.2
	🏪🛒	(1.2E) **Big Creek Country Store** 828-476-4492 Open Daily 10 AM – 6 PM. Hours may vary." Winter hours are Mondays, and Thursday through Sunday 10:00 til 5 PM Close mid December until spring.			
239.1	▲	Cross woods road.		1799	1951.8
239.4	⟙	Power line.		1822	1951.5
240.0	♦⅄⌄	State Line Branch, water at the base of a fine series of cascades. Not an ATC approved camping spot.		1600	1950.9
240.2	▲P(1-2)	Junction with Tobes Creek Road, Waterville Road, Pigeon River. Parking at intersection.	N 35 47.104, W 83 06.771	1400	1950.7

© WhiteBlaze Pages 2018

North Carolina/Tennessee

NC/TN

NoBo Features

Description

GPS Elev SoBo

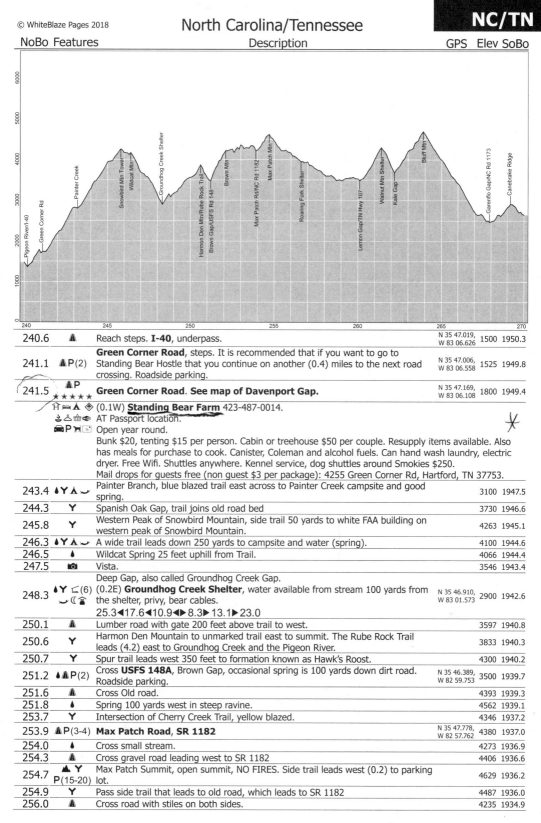

			GPS	Elev	SoBo
240.6	⛺	Reach steps. **I-40**, underpass.	N 35 47.019, W 83 06.626	1500	1950.3
241.1	⛺P(2)	**Green Corner Road**, steps. It is recommended that if you want to go to Standing Bear Hostle that you continue on another (0.4) miles to the next road crossing. Roadside parking.	N 35 47.006, W 83 06.558	1525	1949.8
241.5 ★★★★★	⛺P	**Green Corner Road**. See map of Davenport Gap.	N 35 47.169, W 83 06.108	1800	1949.4
	⛺⛺🛖🛏🛆◈ ♨️⛺🏚🚿 🚗P🐾🖥	(0.1W) **Standing Bear Farm** 423-487-0014. AT Passport location. Open year round. Bunk $20, tenting $15 per person. Cabin or treehouse $50 per couple. Resupply items available. Also has meals for purchase to cook. Canister, Coleman and alcohol fuels. Can hand wash laundry, electric dryer. Free Wifi. Shuttles anywhere. Kennel service, dog shuttles around Smokies $250. Mail drops for guests free (non guest $3 per package): 4255 Green Corner Rd, Hartford, TN 37753.			
243.4	⛺Y⛆⌣	Painter Branch, blue blazed trail east across to Painter Creek campsite and good spring.		3100	1947.5
244.3	Y	Spanish Oak Gap, trail joins old road bed		3730	1946.6
245.8	Y	Western Peak of Snowbird Mountain, side trail 50 yards to white FAA building on western peak of Snowbird Mountain.		4263	1945.1
246.3	⛺Y⛆⌣	A wide trail leads down 250 yards to campsite and water (spring).		4100	1944.6
246.5	⛆	Wildcat Spring 25 feet uphill from Trail.		4066	1944.4
247.5	📷	Vista.		3546	1943.4
248.3	⛆Y⛺(6) ⌣☾🐻	Deep Gap, also called Groundhog Creek Gap. (0.2E) **Groundhog Creek Shelter**, water available from stream 100 yards from the shelter, privy, bear cables. 25.3◀17.6◀10.9◀▶8.3▶13.1▶23.0	N 35 46.910, W 83 01.573	2900	1942.6
250.1	⛺	Lumber road with gate 200 feet above trail to west.		3597	1940.8
250.6	Y	Harmon Den Mountain to unmarked trail east to summit. The Rube Rock Trail leads (4.2) east to Groundhog Creek and the Pigeon River.		3833	1940.3
250.7	Y	Spur trail leads west 350 feet to formation known as Hawk's Roost.		4300	1940.2
251.2	⛆⛺P(2)	Cross **USFS 148A**, Brown Gap, occasional spring is 100 yards down dirt road. Roadside parking.	N 35 46.389, W 82 59.753	3500	1939.7
251.6	⛺	Cross Old road.		4393	1939.3
251.8	⛆	Spring 100 yards west in steep ravine.		4562	1939.1
253.7	Y	Intersection of Cherry Creek Trail, yellow blazed.		4346	1937.2
253.9	⛺P(3-4)	**Max Patch Road, SR 1182**	N 35 47.778, W 82 57.762	4380	1937.0
254.0	⛆	Cross small stream.		4273	1936.9
254.3	⛺	Cross gravel road leading west to SR 1182		4406	1936.6
254.7	⛰Y P(15-20)	Max Patch Summit, open summit, NO FIRES. Side trail leads west (0.2) to parking lot.		4629	1936.2
254.9	Y	Pass side trail that leads to old road, which leads to SR 1182		4487	1936.0
256.0	⛺	Cross road with stiles on both sides.		4235	1934.9

NoBo	Features	Description	GPS	Elev	SoBo
256.1	♦	Cross stream.		4237	1934.8
256.6	♦ Υ ⅄ (8) ⊏ (10) ◡ ⊄ 🕿	50 yards east to **Roaring Fork Shelter**, water located 800 feet north and south on the AT from the shelter, tent pads, privy, bear cables. 25.9◀19.2◀8.3◀▶4.8▶14.7▶28.9	N 35 49.340, W 82 56.316	3950	1934.3
256.7	♦	Cross stream.		4080	1934.2
256.9	⌒	Cross footbridge.		4020	1934.0
257.5	🝔	Nice cascades below the trail to the east.		3861	1933.4
257.6	♦⌒	Cross creek on footbridge.		3863	1933.3
258.4	⚠	Cross old woods road.		3612	1932.5
259.9	♦⅄	Cross stream with nice camping spot nearby.		3488	1931.0
260.1	⚠ P(4-6)	Cross **SR 1182**, TN. 107, Lemon Gap. Small clearing with three way road junction.	N 35 49.522, W 82 56.250	3550	1930.8
260.8	♦	Cross two branches of stream 150 feet apart.		3937	1930.1
261.4	◊ ⅄ ⊏ (5) ◡ ⊄ 🕿	**Walnut Mountain Shelter**, water is located down a blue blazed trail to the left of Rattlesnake Trail and is difficult to locate, tenting, privy, bear cables. Walnut Mountain Trail to west 24.0◀13.1◀4.8◀▶9.9▶24.1▶32.7	N 35 50.187, W 82 56.202	4260	1929.5
262.9	📷	Catpen Gap, views.		4146	1928.0
263.1	♦	Cross brooks.		4251	1927.8
263.8	▲	Bluff Mountain, large boulders on summit.		4686	1927.1
264.6	♦	Spring west on blue blazed trail 50 yards.		4036	1926.3
265.4	♦	Big Rock Spring, water (spring) is located 50 yards east at base of log steps.		3730	1925.5
265.7	⚠	Cross old road.		3466	1925.2
266.1	⚠	Cross woods road.		3366	1924.8
266.5	♦	Cross brook.		3081	1924.4
266.6	♦	Cross brook with cascades below trail.		3022	1924.3
267.1	⚠	Cross old road that is now grassed over.		2679	1923.8
267.4	Υ 📷	Blue blaze leads (0.1) east to vista.		2649	1923.5
267.7	⚠	Cross old road.		2499	1923.2
267.9	Υ ⚠ P(6-8)	**Garenflo Gap Road**, Garenflo Gap. Shut-In Trail yellow blazed trail leads (2.0) west to Upper Shut-in Road/SR 1183.	N 35 51.204, W 82 52.554	2500	1923.0

NoBo	Features	Description	GPS	Elev	SoBo
271.3	♦ Υ ⅄ ⊏ (5) ◡ ⊄ 🕿	Gragg Gap. (0.2E) **Deer Park Mountain Shelter**, water (spring) is located on the trail about half way to the shelter, tenting, privy, bear cables. Gravestones west of trail. 23.0◀14.7◀9.9◀▶14.2▶22.8▶30.1	N 35 52.550, W 82 51.684	2330	1919.6
274.0	📷	View of Spring Creek at switchback.		1593	1916.9
274.1	⚠	Cross Serpentine Street near parking area.		1404	1916.8
274.5	○ ⚠ P(15-20) ★★★★★	**U.S. 25/70, N.C. 209, Hot Springs, NC**. See Map of Hot Springs. Notice the AT logos in the sidewalks **South bounders must have a backcountry permit before entering Great Smoky Mountains National Park.**	N 35 53.370, W 82 49.938	1326	1916.4

North Carolina/Tennessee

NoBo Features	Description	GPS Elev SoBo

PO M-F 9am-11:30am & 1pm-4pm, Sa 9am-10:30am 828-622-3242.

Elmers Sunnybank Inn 828-622-7206. (www.sunnybankretreatassociation.org)
AT Passport location.
Open year round. No Pets. No Smoking. Located across from Dollar General. Traditional thru-hikers $25 per person for private room, includes linens, towel and shower. Breakfast for guests only $6 dinner $12; gourmet organic vegetarian meals. Inn offers an extensive library and a well-equipped music room. Work exchange possible. Does not take Credit Cards.
Mail drops for guests: PO Box 233, Hot Springs, NC 28743. FEDX drops: 26 Walnut St. , Hot Springs, NC 28743.

Hostel at Laughing Heart Lodge
828-206-8487. (www.laughingheartlodge.com)
AT Passport location.
Open year round. Pets welcome. $20 bunks, $25 per person for semi private, $35 per person for single private, $45 double occupancy in a private room. Pets fee $5, few pet rooms. All rooms include morning coffee, shower, towel, movies, use of hiker kitchen. Lodge rooms $100 and up, includes continental breakfast, must call to reserve at 828-622-0165. Tenting with shower $10 per person $15 for 2 (in one tent). Quiet time at night from 10 pm to 7 am. Free WiFi. Laundry $5 includes soap. Shower only $5. Karoake and outdoor movie theater with 10 foot screen. Massage available, please call Glenda at 603-204-7893
Mail drops for guests: 289 NW US Hwy 25/70, Hot Springs, NC 28743.

Iron Horse Station 866-402-9377. (www.theironhorsestation.com)
Restaurant, tavern and coffee shop. Serves lunch and dinner, offers few vegetarian options, free WiFi.

Little Bird Cabins
828-206-1487. natalie@littlebirdcabinrentals.com (www.littlebirdcabinrentals.com)
Open year round.
Located 500 feet east from the southern AT trail head in town. Cabin sleeps 7, includes kitchenette. 10% Hiker's Discount. Use code WHITEBLAZE at checkout (online) or mention this guidebook's discount when booking by phone. Pet fee $15. Free Wifi. Credit Cards accepted

Mountain Magnolia Inn 800-914-9306. (www.mountainmagnoliainn.com)
Discount hiker rates $75S, $100D, includes big country breakfast, free WiFi. Dinner Th-M, is open to everyone.
Mail drops for guests: 204 Lawson St, Hot Springs, NC 28743.

Creekside Court 828-215-1261. Call or text for availability 828-206-5473. (www.lodginghotspringsnc.com)
$79 and up, ask for hiker discount, pets allowed, pet fee $25. Free WiFi.

Hot Springs Resort & Spa 828-622-7676. (www.nchotsprings.com)
Tenting $24 up to 4 people. Camping cabins $50 and up. Pets $10. Mineral water spa $20 per person before 6pm; 3-person rate $38 before 6pm, $43 after 6pm. Camp store carries snacks and supplies. Take Out Grill inside the campstore. Free WiFi. Also offers massage therapy. Accepts Credit Cards.

Spring Creek Tavern 828-622-0187. (www.thespringcreektavern.com)
AT Passport location.
M-Th 11am-10pm, F-Sa 11:30am-11pm, Su 11am-10pm. special AT burger. Limited amount of rooms to rent, call for availability and pricing. Fre WiFi.

Alpine Court Motel 423-721-0450 Tax-included prices; $57S, $67D, $10 EAP. No Credit Cards.

Smoky Mountain Diner 828-622-7571
AT Passport location.
M-W 6am-8pm, Th-Sa 6:30-8pm, Su 6:30am-2pm.

ArtiSun Gallery and Marketplace 828-622-3573
AT Passport location.
M-Th 9am-4pm, F 9am-6pm, Sa 9am-7pm, Su 9am-5pm. Local art, local Ice-Cream, Espresso, coffee, tea, wine, baked goods. Free WiFi.
Mail drops: FedEx/UPS 16 S. Andrews Ave, Hot Springs, NC 28743.

Visitor Center 828-622-9932 Free WiFi, signal still accessible outside after closed.

Hiker's Ridge Ministries Resource Center
828-691-0503 godswayeen@gmail.com (www.hikersridge.com)
AT Passport location.
Open M-Sa 9am-3pm, Mar 21 - May. Place to relax, coffee, drinks, snacks, restroom. Computer available for use, free WiFi.

Bluff Mountain Outfitters 828-622-7162. (www.bluffmountain.com)
AT Passport location.
M-Thu 9am-5pm, F-Sa 9am-6pm, Su 9am-5pm. Full service outfitter, fuel by the ounce. Long term resupply. Computer available for use, ask about WiFi. ATM. Shuttles; Springer to Roanoke and area airports and bus stations. Hikers can print GSMNP permits here.
Mail drops: (USPS) PO Box 114 Hot Springs, NC 28743 or (FedEx/UPS) 152 Bridge St.

Hot Springs Library 828-622-6584. M-F 10 am-6 pm, Sa 10 am-2 pm, Su closed.

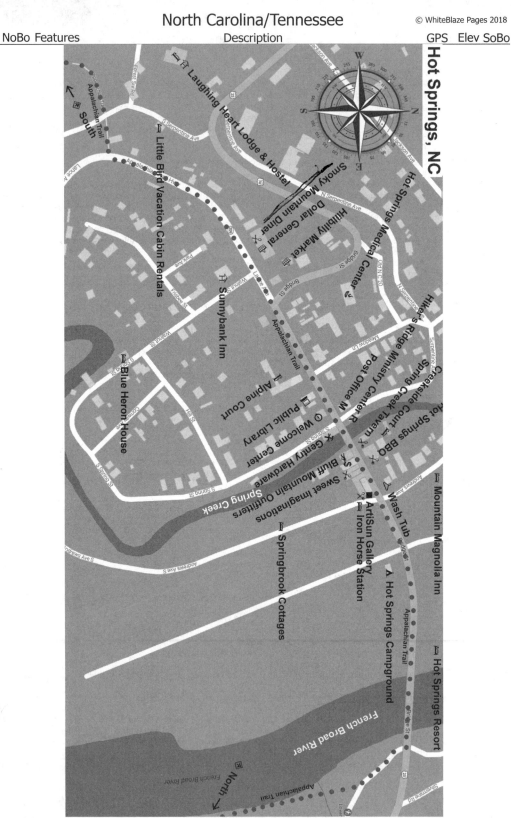

Hot Springs, NC

NoBo	Features	Description	GPS	Elev	SoBo
275.9	Y📷	Lovers Leap Rock, Pump Gap Trail leads to the west		1820	1915.0
276.2	📷	Viewpoint overlooking the French Broad River 600 feet below.		1980	1914.7
277.8	Y	Pump Gap, another blue blaze trail crosses here		2130	1913.1
279.4	♦⋏	Reach saddle then turn right downhill to pond and campsite, not an ATC approved camping spot.		2490	1911.5
280.4	⋏P	Cross **U.S. 25 & 70** overpass, Tanyard Gap. Trail follow fire road 70 feet.	N 35 54.622, W 82 47.467	2278	1910.5
281.8	♦	Cross foot log below good spring.		3097	1909.1
282.2	⋏	Trail is on road for about 50 feet.		3283	1908.7
282.3	Y	Roundtop Ridge Trail, yellow blazed leads (8.2) west back to Hot Springs.		3257	1908.6
282.7	♦Y⋏📷	Rich Mountain. Side trail (0.1) west to Fire Tower and views, water (piped spring) is located north on AT. Campsite is located (0.1) west on side trail.		3600	1908.2
282.8	♦⋏	Head of ravine with camp site and spring to the west.		3030	1908.1
283.3	♦	Spring west on trail.		3321	1907.6
283.6	⋏	Cross road, **USFA 3514** leads east.		3019	1907.3
283.8	⋏	Junction with **USFS 467**, Hurricane Gap. Trail follows fire road 70 feet.		2900	1907.1
285.5	♦⋏⊑(5) ☾☂	**Spring Mountain Shelter**, water is located 75 yards down a blue blazed trail on the east side of the AT, tenting, privy, bear cables. 28.9◀24.1◀14.2◀▶8.6▶15.9▶22.6	N 35 57.089, W 82 47.412	3300	1905.4
287.0	♦Y	Water (spring) 10 feet west on trail in ravine.		3190	1903.9
289.1	⋏	Cross logging road.		2466	1901.8
289.2	♦⋏P	Cross **NC. 208, TN. 70**, Allen Gap, Paint Creek, water to the west 350 yards	N 35 59.216, W 82 47.232	2234	1901.7
290.2	⋏	Cross old dirt road.		2494	1900.7
290.8	⋏ ★★★★★	Log Cabin Drive. Private home in view to 100 yards east, please do not trespass. **See map of Log Cabin Rd.**		2560	1900.1

⌂⍭⋏ (0.7W) **Hemlock Hollow Inn** 423-787-1736 (www.hemlockhollowinn.com) Owners Russ and Dianna
◈✕🛏🖂 Rosa.
P🚗🖂 AT Passport location.
Open year-round. West on Log Cabin Dr. to paved Viking Mountain Rd. Bunkroom $25PP with linens, $20 without. Cabin for couples with linens $60. All rooms heated. Tent site $12 per person. Pets fee $5. All stays include shower. Non guest shower and towel for $5. Camp store stocked with long term resupply, some gear, cold drinks, foods, fruit, stove fuels. Cafe (not re-opened yet). Parking free for guests, fee for non-guests. Credit cards accepted. Mail drops free if you stay, $5 without staying. Mail drops (ETA mandatory): 645 Chandler Circle, Greeneville, TN 37743.

Log Cabin Rd NC

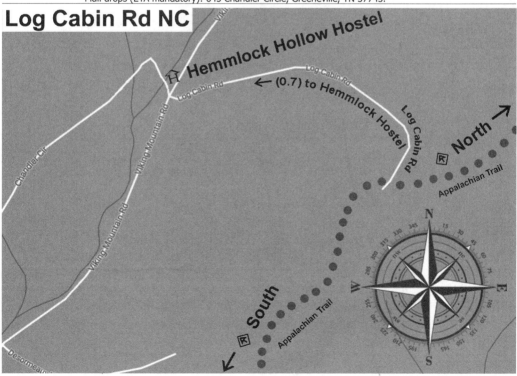

© WhiteBlaze Pages 2018

NoBo	Features	Description	GPS	Elev	SoBo
294.1	♦🅐⛺(5) 🥾《🐻	**Little Laurel Shelter**, water (boxed spring) is located 100 yards down blue blazed trail behind shelter to west, tent sites are south of shelter, privy, bear cables. 32.7◄22.8◄8.6◄▶7.3▶14.0▶22.8	N 36 00.899, W 82 44.154	3300	1896.8
295.9	⅄🔦📷🔺	Camp Creek Bald Trail leads (0.2) west to Camp Creek Bald Lookout Tower, catwalk is often locked. Trail least (6.2) east to Shelton Laurel Road.		4750	1895.0
297.6	♦⅄	Water (spring), creek, blue blaze trails on both sides of the AT		4390	1893.3
297.7	⅄📷	White Rock Cliffs are located 50 feet east with views.		4450	1893.2
297.8	⅄	Wide side trail to west.		4494	1893.1
297.9	⅄📷	Blackstack Cliffs are located 200 feet west with views.		4420	1893.0
298.1	⅄	Trail to west is a bad weather route.		4434	1892.8
298.9	♦📷	Big Firescald Knob		4360	1892.0
299.1	⅄	Pass blue blaze trail.		4410	1891.8
299.7	⅄	Trail to west is a bad weather route.		4211	1891.2

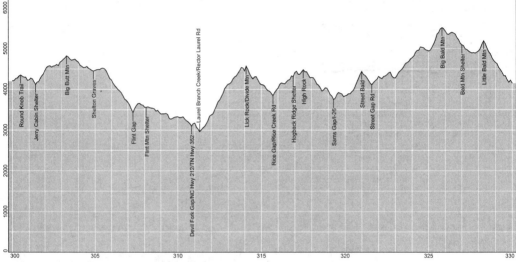

NoBo	Features	Description	GPS	Elev	SoBo
300.3	⅄	Round Knob Trail leads (3.0) to picnic area and Round Knob Spring and into Round Knob Campground Road.		4260	1890.6
301.2	⅄	USFS Fork Ridge Trail leads (2.0) east to parking area at Big Creek Road.		4272	1889.7
301.4	♦🅐⛺(6) 《🐻	**Jerry Cabin Shelter**, water is located 100 yards down a blue blazed trail behind the shelter, tenting, privy, bear cables. 30.1◄15.9◄7.3◄▶6.7▶15.5▶25.6	N 36 03.392, W 82 39.431	4150	1889.5
303.0	🔺	Cross dirt road.		4477	1887.9
303.3	⅄🅐	Big Butt, summit to west, short bypass trail. Trail turns abruptly here.		4750	1887.6
304.4	♦	Water (spring) is seasonal and known to go dry.		4480	1886.5
304.9	○	**Shelton Graves,** William and David Shelton, uncle and nephew. When returning to a family gathering during the war, they were ambushed near here and killed by Confederate troops.		4490	1886.0
306.0	🔺	Cross old logging road on Snake Den Ridge crest.		4577	1884.9
306.5	◊	Seasonal water.		4067	1884.4
307.3	🔺	Flint Gap, cross old logging road.		3616	1883.6
308.1	♦⛺(8) 🥾《	**Flint Mountain Shelter**, water (spring) located 100 feet north of shelter on the AT, there are two streams between the shelter and the spring, privy. 22.6◄14.0◄6.7◄▶8.8▶18.9▶29.5	N 36 02.087, W 82 35.814	3570	1882.8
309.0	♦🅐	Campsite, water		3400	1881.9
310.8	🔺P ★★★★★	Cross **NC. 212**, Devil Fork Gap, hostel and resupply (2.5E) **See map of NC 212.**	N 36 00.631, W 82 36.506	3100	1880.1
	🏠🅐🏛 🛒⛺🚗	(2.5E) **Laurel Trading Post** 828-656-2016 Open year round. M-Su days 7am-7pm. Bunkroom $25, tenting $10, includes shower, laundry $5, full kitchen. Shower and towel without stay $5. Lots of resupply items. Free shuttle to store and return to trail. Credit cards accepted.			

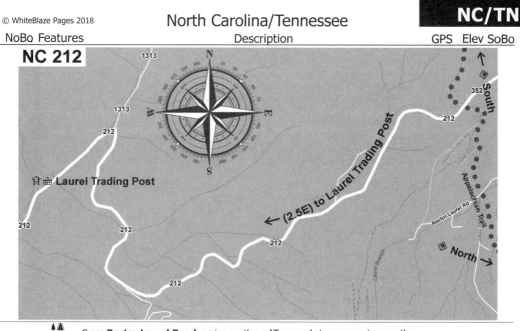

NC 212

Laurel Trading Post

← (2.5E) to Laurel Trading Post

311.3 ★★★★★	♦▲	Cross **Rector Laurel Road**, spring north on AT, several stream crossings on the AT north of road		2960 1879.6

⌂⊏▲⛺ **Hiker Paradise** 423-735-4437
Located (0.7) west on Rector Laurel from the AT. Bunkroom $20PP, tenting $5PP. Shuttles and slack-packing for a fee. Rides to Erwin $20, Hot Springs $30, ask about all other destinations. Laundry $5 for small loads. Full service resupply. Mail drops: 778 Rector Laurel Rd. Flag Pond, TN. 37657

311.6	♦	Small cemetery, water (stream).		3060 1879.3
311.9	♦	Cross stream and woods road.		3258 1879.0
312.2	♦�	Cross stream at waterfall.		3589 1878.7
312.6		Sugarloaf Gap. Sugarloaf Knob to the east.		4000 1878.3
313.0	♦	Pass spring and big rocks.		4203 1877.9
314.0		Pass apples trees from remnants of farm.		4477 1876.9
314.1	▲	Frozen Knob/Lick Rock, summit.		4579 1876.8
314.7	♦Y▲	Big Flat is located east of rock formation, water, campsite to east		4160 1876.2
315.7	▲	Rice Gap, dirt road		3800 1875.2
316.9	♦Y⊏(6) ↩((☂	(0.1E) **Hogback Ridge Shelter**, water (spring) (0.3) on a side trail near the shelter, privy, bear cables. 22.8◀15.5◀8.8◀▶ 10.1▶20.7▶31.2	N 35 57.837, W 82 35.232	4255 1874.0
317.5	Y🄿	High Rock, blue blazed trail leads 150 feet to the west for view		4460 1873.4
319.3 ★★★★★	⚊▲P	Cross Flag Pond Road, US. 23, I-26, Sams Gap.	N 35 57.149, W 82 33.655	3800 1871.6

⌂🛏▲ (2.8W) **Natures Inn Hostel** 828-216-1611 (www.naturesinnhostel.com)
↩(4)◈✕ AT Passport location.
⛺♨⚰⚆ Pets allowed but they must be leashed when on property
♨🍴🚗P Two bunkhouses,($20PP) both have electricity, twin mattress, bed linens $5, heaters available for rent
☒ $5, covered outdoor space between the two buildings. Cabins $40 per nite, 2 People, $20 EAP up to a total of 4, electricity, queen and twin bed with mattress, bed linens $5, heaters are available for rent $5, fire ring (firewood for sale), picnic table, charcoal grill (charcoal for sale). Bath house; bath towels, soap and shampoo included with stay. Private rooms available in house, 2 queen beds $40 each, 1 king beds $50. Tenting, $15 per tent, includes shower. 4 hammock spots (in ground poles), $12 per hammock, includes shower. WiFi. Laundry facilities on site, $6 per load, includes laundry powder. Showers; with out stay $5, if shuttle to and from trail head needed, add $5. Small resupply store for Hiker food stuffs and we offer pizza, soft drinks, hamburgers, hot dogs, etc. Shuttle: to and from trail head at Sams Gap, free with stay. To and from Devil's Fork trail head, $15. Slackpacking: available, negotiated pricing dependent upon, where, when, etc. Parking: No charge with stay, $3 per day with out stay. We accept CC and cash. Reservations recommended. All reservations must provide CC to reserve or pay in advance. Full refund if cancelled 7 days prior to reservation, 50% refund if cancelled during 6 days up to check in date.
Mail Drops: 4871 Old Asheville Highway, Flag Pond, TN 37657
✕ (2.8E) **Little Laurel Cafe** 828-689-2307. M-Th 6am-2pm, F 6am-7:30pm, Sa 7am-2pm, Su closed.

NoBo	Features	Description	GPS	Elev	SoBo
	✗⌂☎	(3.5E) **Wolf Creek Market** 828-689-5943. Open M-F 6am-10pm, Sa 8am-9pm, Su closed. **Hunts Bros. Pizza**, M-Sa 6am-10pm, Su 8am-9pm. **Convenience Store**, M-Sa 6am-10 pm, Su 8am-9 pm.			
320.0	♦	Water, two springs about 660 feet apart.		4000	1870.9
320.7		Pass around the east edge of an old abandoned talc mine, woods road to the west.		4357	1870.2
321.6	⚑P	Cross Street Gap, gravel road.	N 35 58.133, W 82 32.429	4100	1869.3
321.7	⟙	Power line.		4219	1869.2
322.8	♦Y	Blue blaze trail to east leads 20 yards to spring.		4342	1868.1
323.0	♦⚑	Low Gap, water (piped spring) is located by campsite that are located downhill and to the west		4300	1867.9
323.6	♦	Pass spring.		4533	1867.3
324.5		Reach crest of ridge extending northwest.		4908	1866.4
325.0	♦	Blue blaze trail leads west 100 yards down slope to spring.		4850	1865.9
325.1	Y	Junction of blue blaze bypass trail east.		4959	1865.8
325.3	♦	Cross small streams in the area.		4965	1865.6
325.5		Slipper Spur, southern end of grassy bald.		5461	1865.4
325.8	⚑⚑	Big Bald, open summit.		5516	1865.1
326.1	♦Y⚑⚑	Big Stamp is a treeless saddle at the base of Big Bald, bypass trail to east. Water is located near campsite that is (0.3) west. Blue blaze bypass trail and road from Wolf Laurel ski resort.		5300	1864.8
327.0	♦Y⚑ ⊏(10) ⌣《☎	(0.1W) **Bald Mountain Shelter**, water (spring) is located on the side trail to the shelter, tenting, privy, bear cables. 25.6◄18.9◄10.1◄► 10.6►21.1►33.9	N 36 00.011, W 82 28.692	5100	1863.9
327.2	♦	Spring beside trail. Stream crosses path.		4993	1863.7
327.4	♦Y⚑	Blue blazed side trail leading west to a good campsite and continuing down (0.2) to Tumbling Creek and a reliable spring. This campsite is a good place to tent if the shelter is crowded.		4890	1863.5
328.4	⚑	Little Bald, wooded summit		5185	1862.5

330.4	♦⚑⌣	Whistling Gap, a trail leads 0.1 to west and small clearing, water, campsite.		3650	1860.5
330.7	Y	Blue blaze trail leads (0.1) east to High Rocks.		4100	1860.2
332.1	♦	Cross several small streams in the area.		3715	1858.8
332.2	♦⚑	Stone steps. Stream and campsite to east.		3490	1858.7
332.7	♦⚑P	Cross **U.S. 19W**, Spivey Gap, stream south of gap. Parking (0.5W)	N 36 01.914, W 82 25.212	3200	1858.2
332.8	⚑	Cross woods road.		3307	1858.1
333.1	♦⌒	Cross Oglesby Branch on plank bridge.		3806	1857.8
333.3	♦⌒	Cross Oglesby Branch on plank bridge.		3800	1857.6
334.0	♦	Cross stream.		3809	1856.9
334.2	⚑	Intersection of old logging road and gravel **USFS 278**.		3752	1856.7
334.5		Reach small gap on crest.		3749	1856.4

NoBo	Features	Description	GPS	Elev	SoBo
335.0		Devils Creek Gap		3400	1855.9
337.4	♦	Spring to west in hemlock grove, water for No Business Knob Shelter		3300	1853.5
337.6	▲ ⊑(6) ⏝	**No Business Knob Shelter**, water is located (0.2) south of the shelter on the AT, tenting. 29.5◄20.7◄10.6◄► 10.5►23.3►32.4	N 36 04.006, W 82 26.016	3180	1853.3
340.0	Y	Temple Hill Gap, Side trails east and west from here.		2850	1850.9
340.7	▲	Access road to former fire tower.		2930	1850.2
342.1	📷	View of railroad and Unaka Springs below.		2671	1848.8
343.9	▲ ⌒ P ★★★★★	Cross **River Road**, Chestoa Bridge, Nolichucky River **Erwin, TN. (3.8W) (all major services). See maps of Erwin.**	N 36 06.312, W 82 26.794	1700	1847.0

    ⛺🛏▲ ◈ **Uncle Johnny's Nolichucky Hostel and Outfitters** 423-735-0548. (www.unclejohnnys.net)
    🛉♨△🛒 AT Passport location.
    🖥🍴🍴🍺 Open year round. $20 per person per bunk. Private cabins range from $30-$95, includes fridge, micro-
    🚲♿🏧P wave, and linens. Camping $10 per person. Included with stay are showers, shampoo, conditioner, and
    🚗🖥 soap. Work for Stay possible, just ask. Coleman and alcohol by the ounce. Laundry $5. Full resupply.
    Computer available for use, free Wifi. Outfitters store carries water filtration systems and filters, head-
    lamps and lots more hiker gear. Bike, kayak and raft rentals. Shower without stay $5, includes soap and
    towel. Pay phone available. Accepts Mastercard, Visa. Parking fees for non-guests - $3.00 per vehicle
    per day. Free town shuttles for guests, shuttle runs for breakfast, lunch and dinner. Longer shuttles for a
    fee. Parking available for guest. $2/day.
    Mail drops: 151 River Rd, Erwin, TN 37650.

    📫 **PO** M-F 8:30-4:45, Sa 10-12, 423-743-9422

    🛏 ◈♿△ **(0.9W) Cantarroso Farm & Apiary** 423-833-7514 or 423-360-1697. cantarrosofarm@gmail.com
    🍴🍴🚗P (www.cantarrosofarm.com)
    🖥 AT Passport location.
    Located (0.9W) from Chestoa/Nolichucky River Bridge.
    Open year-round. No pets. CLEAN & QUIET setting with personal service. Free beverage and candy bar
    at pick up. Two cabins: $30PP (2-7) or $45/$65 private, Cabins offer free wifi, heat/AC, coffee/tea, full
    size beds, linens, shower, toiletries, towel, refrigerator, microwave, toaster oven, cooking gear, grill and
    fire pit. Stay includes pickup & return to Chestoa trail head, access to river and fishing gear Additional
    charge for laundry, town shuttles, bikes. Offer slack packing options.
    Mail drops: 777 Bailey Lane, Erwin TN 37650.

    🛏♿△🖥 **Mountain Inn & Suites** 423-743-4100. (www.erwinmountaininn.com)
    🍴🖥 No pets. Hiker rate $79.99 single, $10 each additional person up to four people, includes breakfast
    buffet. Coin laundry, Computer in lobby for guest. Free WiFi. Hot tub & swimming pool open (Memorial
    Day to Labor Day).
    Mail drops for registered guests only: 2002 Temple Hill Rd, Erwin TN 37650.

    🛏🍴🖥 **Best Southern** 423-743-6438. $50 and up. Pet fee $10, free WiFi.
    Mail drops for guests only: 1315 Jackson Love Hwy, Erwin, TN 37650.

    🛏♿△🖥 **Super 8** 423-743-0200.
    🍴🖥 No pets. $49.99 single, $59.99 double for two persons, $10 each additional person, max 4, includes
    breakfast. Microwaves, fridge, laundry, computer in lobby for guests, WiFi.
    Mail drops for guests only: 1101 N Buffalo St, Erwin TN 37650.

    🛒 **Price Less Foods** M-Su 7am-9pm.
    ✗ **Pizza Plus**, 423-743-7121. M-Su 11am-11pm. (AYCE 11am-2pm)
    🚐 **Shuttles by Tom** 423-330-7416, 910-409-2509. hikershuttles@gmail.com (www.hikershuttles.com)
    Owners Tom "10-K" Bradford and Marie "J-Walker" Bradford. Licensed and insured, permitted to shuttle
    in Pisgah and Cherokee National Forests. Based out of Erwin, TN. Shuttles to all area trail heads, bus
    stations, airports, outfitters, etc. Shuttle ranges from Springer to Harpers Ferry.
    ■ **Baker's Shoe Repair** 423-743-5421. Full service repair shop for shoes, leather, backpacks, etc. M
    10am-5pm, Tu-Thurs 10am-3:30 pm. F 10am-5pm. Sa-Su closed. Sat--sometimes open but do not
    advertise any hours. Located across the street from the courthouse.
    🚗P **Shuttles by Tom** 423-330-7416, 910-409-2509 (www.hikershuttles.com) Shuttles from Springer to
    Harpers Ferry, all trail heads, bus stations, airports, outfitters and more. Free parking.

| 344.1 | ✗ | Cross CSX railroad track. | | 1714 | 1846.8 |
| 344.9 | 📷 | Nolichucky River Gorge view | | 1707 | 1846.0 |

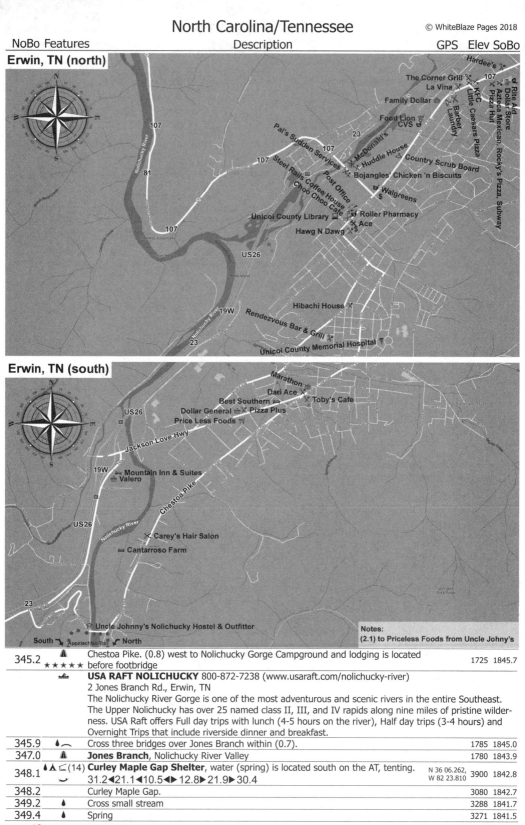

Erwin, TN (north)

Erwin, TN (south)

Notes:
(2.1) to Priceless Foods from Uncle Johny's

345.2	▲ ★★★★★	Chestoa Pike. (0.8) west to Nolichucky Gorge Campground and lodging is located before footbridge		1725	1845.7
	⛵	**USA RAFT NOLICHUCKY** 800-872-7238 (www.usaraft.com/nolichucky-river) 2 Jones Branch Rd., Erwin, TN The Nolichucky River Gorge is one of the most adventurous and scenic rivers in the entire Southeast. The Upper Nolichucky has over 25 named class II, III, and IV rapids along nine miles of pristine wilderness. USA Raft offers Full day trips with lunch (4-5 hours on the river), Half day trips (3-4 hours) and Overnight Trips that include riverside dinner and breakfast.			
345.9	♦⌒	Cross three bridges over Jones Branch within (0.7).		1785	1845.0
347.0	▲	**Jones Branch**, Nolichucky River Valley		1780	1843.9
348.1	♦▲⛺(14)⌣	**Curley Maple Gap Shelter**, water (spring) is located south on the AT, tenting. 31.2◄21.1◄10.5◄► 12.8►21.9►30.4	N 36 06.262, W 82 23.810	3900	1842.8
348.2		Curley Maple Gap.		3080	1842.7
349.2	♦	Cross small stream		3288	1841.7
349.4	♦	Spring		3271	1841.5

NoBo	Features	Description	GPS	Elev	SoBo
350.7		Cross through a gap.		3432	1840.2
352.2	⛺P ★★★★★	Cross **TN. 395, NC. 197**, Indian Grave Gap, water is located (0.1) east on outside of curve in road. **Erwin, TN (7.0W) See NOBO mile 343.9.**	N 36 06.646, W 82 21.665	3360	1838.7
	⛺	(3.3W) **Rock Creek Recreation Area** (USFS) 423-638-4109 Tent site $12, Open mid-May to mid-Nov.			
352.9	⊤	Power line.		3749	1838.0
353.3	⛺	Cross **USFS 230**, Beauty Spot Gap Road, gravel road		3980	1837.6
354.5		Beauty Spot, summit.		4437	1836.4
355.0	♦⛺P	**USFS 230**, Beauty Spot Gap (northern end), water (spring) is located across from gated road. Parking is located to the west.		4120	1835.9
355.2	▲	Cross summit.		4358	1835.7
356.0	♦⋏	Deep Gap, field		4100	1834.9
356.6	⛺	USFS 230, Unaka Mountain Road is a few feet to the east.		4660	1834.3
357.6		Unaka Mountain, large stand of red spruce atop its summit.		5180	1833.3
359.8	♦	Low Gap, water (stream) is located (0.1) west		3900	1831.1
360.7	⌒	Cross bog bridge.		3902	1830.2

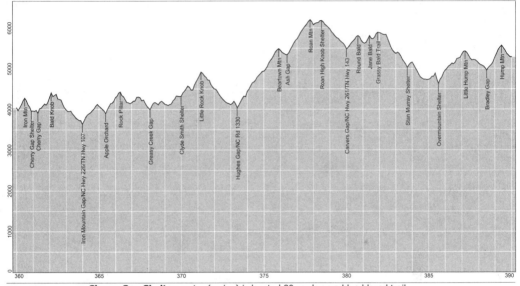

360.9	♦⊏(6)↘	**Cherry Gap Shelter**, water (spring) is located 80 yards on a blue blazed trail from the shelter. 33.9◀23.3◀12.8◀▶9.1▶17.6▶22.8	N 36 07.754, W 82 15.852	3900	1830.0
361.3		Cherry Gap.		4016	1829.6
361.6		Reach several gaps within the next mile heading north.		3833	1829.3
363.4	⛺	Trail intersects with road several time in this area.		3807	1827.5
364.0	⛺P ★★★★★	Cross **TN 107, NC 226**, Iron Mountain Gap **Unicoi, TN.**	N 36 08.589, W 82 13.998	3723	1826.9
	✗	(4.0E) **Mountain Grill** 828-688-9061. M-Sa 11am-8pm, Su closed. Cash only.			
364.5	Y📷	Trail west provides good views across Stone Mountain.		3942	1826.4
364.8	📷	Open field to the west provide good view of Unaka Mountain.		4096	1826.1
365.2	♦⋏	Campsite at north edge of orchard and blue blaze down to water		3950	1825.7
365.4		Weedy Gap		3913	1825.5
366.3		Pass a large rock formation.		4426	1824.6
366.8		Pass through Gap		4390	1824.1
367.4		High point near summit of knob.		4332	1823.5
368.1	Y ★★★★★	Greasy Creek Gap, blue blaze trail leads west 300 yards to good campsite and water (spring) , campsite is located at the at gap. Old road bed to Greasy Creek Road To the east a trail leads (0.6) **Greasy Creek Hostel. See map of Greasy Creek Gap, NC.**		4034	1822.8

NoBo	Features	Description	GPS	Elev	SoBo

⌂ Å ◈ (0.6E) **Greasy Creek Friendly** 828-688-9948. greasycreekfriendly@gmail.com (www.greasycreek-
✕ ♨ ♿ friendly.com)
△ ⊕ 🚐 AT Passport location.
🖥P ☐ Open year round, except during Trail Days. Call ahead during Dec-Feb, self serve during the Sabbath (sundown Friday to sundown Saturday).
Directions; from Greasy Creek Gap; take old woods road Trail east, follow flags on branches and painted arrows downhill. You should be going downhill all the way. Hostel is first house to your right with gravel path, follow gravel path past bunk house to main house back door to check in. Pets okay outside, we have a shed where guest can stay with their pets we call it the Pup Shed. Bunk house $10 per person (8 bunks available) Indoor beds $15 per person (3 single beds available). Tenting $7.50 per person, stay includes shower. Shower without stay $3. Limited kitchen privileges. Free WiFi. Resupply options include multi-day resupply including snacks, meals, alcohol and coleman by the ounce. Free long distance calls within US. Shuttles available from Hot Springs to Damascus. Call ahead to schedule shuttles. Parking $2 per night. Credit cards accepted.
Mail drops: 1827 Greasy Creek Rd, Bakersville, NC 28705.

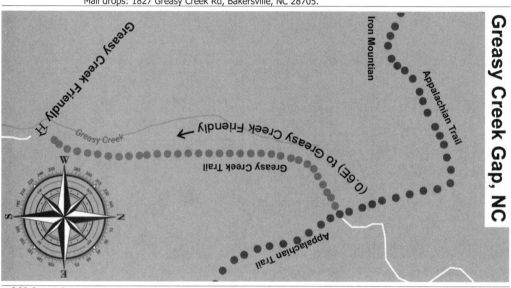

368.9	♦Å	Campsite, water (spring) is located (0.1) west		4110	1822.0
369.7		Reach shallow Gap.		4335	1821.2
370.0	♦Y Å ⌐(10)↵	(0.1W) **Clyde Smith Shelter**, water is located 100 yards behind the shelter on a blue blazed trail, tent sites. 32.4◄21.9◄9.1◄►8.5►13.7►15.6	N 36 08.906, W 82 09.678	4400	1820.9
370.4	♦	Reach gap, spring (0.1) west in a hollow.		4460	1820.5
371.1	📷	Pass many overlooks with good views		4646	1819.8
371.2	📷	Little Rock Knob, high point near summit.		4918	1819.7
372.6		Series of rock steps.		4224	1818.3
372.8		Pass through Gap.		4120	1818.1
373.4	Å～♦P	**Hughes Gap Road**, Hughes Gap	N 36 08.208, W 82 08.460	4040	1817.5
373.8	Y	Blue blaze trail leads 65 yards west to small pipe spring.		4524	1817.1
375.9	▲	Summit of Beartown Mountain.		5481	1815.0
376.4	♦Å～	Ash Gap, campsite at gap, water (spring) is located (0.1) east.		5350	1814.5
377.7		Trail gets steep with many switchbacks		6151	1813.2
377.8	♦Y⚶🗑 ⇐♦P	Trail to Roan High Bluff leads (0.1) east to parking, picnic area. Open Memorial Day thru the first of October.	N 36 06.238, W 82 07.990	6200	1813.1
378.0	▲	Southern end of **old Hack Line Road** in small open gap. Pass old chimney.		6085	1812.9
378.5	◊YÅ ⌐(15)↵	(0.1E) **Roan High Knob Shelter**, piped spring, tenting. This is the highest shelter on AT. 30.4◄17.6◄8.5◄►5.2►7.1►25.1	N 36 06.298, W 82 07.362	6285	1812.4
379.6	▲	Old Hack Line Road.		5574	1811.3
379.7	⌒	Cross several board bridges.		5756	1811.2
380.0	♦▲⚶👤 ⊂P	Cross **TN. 143, NC. 261**, Carvers Gap, water (spring), restroom, picnic area.	N 36 06.372, W 82 06.631	5512	1810.9
380.2		Southern end of wooded path.		5742	1810.7
380.4		Northern end of wooded path.		5836	1810.5

NoBo	Features	Description	GPS	Elev	SoBo
380.7		Trail skirts the side of Round Bald summit on gravel trail.		5801	1810.2
381.0		Engine Gap		5620	1809.9
381.3	📷	Passes a rock formation with several locations for good views between Jane Bald and Round Bald.		5708	1809.6
381.4	📷	Summit of Jane Bald.		5785	1809.5
381.9	Y📷	Side trail to Grassy Ridge and views, AT to west		5770	1809.0
382.0	💧	Spring east of trail.		5770	1808.9
383.7	💧⊏(6)⌣	Low Gap. **Stan Murray Shelter**, water (spring) is located east on a blue blazed trail opposite the shelter. 22.8◀13.7◀5.2◀▶1.9▶19.9▶29.5	N 36 06.736, W 82 03.954	5050	1807.2
384.1	Y	Crest of Elk Hollow Ridge, view a short distance on trail.		5180	1806.8
384.8		Buckeye Gap.		4730	1806.1
385.6	💧Y⋀ ⊏(20) ⌣(📷	Yellow Mountain Gap. (0.25E) **Overmountain Shelter**, water is located on way to the shelter, tenting, privy. 15.6◀7.1◀1.9◀▶18.0▶27.6▶35.8▶	N 36 07.411, W 82 03.260	4682	1805.3
386.8	💧	Saddle in open field. Spring is about 100 yards east.		5272	1804.1
387.2	⋀📷	Little Hump Mountain, grassy summit with outstanding views.		5459	1803.7
387.4	Y	Reach small gap, be careful of side trails.		5196	1803.5
388.5	💧⋀	Bradley Gap, grassy, water (spring) is located 100 yards east		4950	1802.4
389.4	📷	Hump Mountain, Stan Murray plaque		5587	1801.5

NoBo	Features	Description	GPS	Elev	SoBo
391.6	💧⋀⌣	Doll Flats a grassy area. A blue blaze trail leads west to water. North Carolina–Tennessee State Line		4600	1799.3
392.2	📷	Crest of rocky spur, overlook 50 feet east with views of Elk River Valley pastures.		4400	1798.7
392.3		Cliff with overhanging rock over trail.		4153	1798.6
393.8	⊤	Power line.		3420	1797.1
394.2	⋀	Campsite and water west of trail in Wilder Mine Hollow, water is located 100 yards north on AT		3200	1796.7
394.6	⛰	Northern end of old road in Wilder Mine Hollow.		3008	1796.3
394.8	⋀P ★★★★★	Cross **U.S. 19E** **Elk Park, NC. (2.5E)**.	N 36 10.647, W 82 00.707	2895	1796.1

🛏🏠⋀ (0.3W) **Mountain Harbour B&B and Hiker Hostel** 866-772-9494. welcome@mountainharbour.net
◈✗ (www.mountainharbour.net)
🍴♨⛺🚮 AT Passport location.
🍴🚗P🖵 Open year round.

Food Truck open during NOBO Season. Hostel located over barn, $25 per person, king bed $55. Treehouse $75, Tenting with shower $10. Stay includes linens, shower, towel, full kitchen, wood burning stove, video library. Non guest shower with towel $5. Coin operated laundry, Breakfast $12 when available. B&B rooms $125-$165 includes breakfast, A/C, refrigerator, cable TV, WiFi. General Store on site with hiker supplies, full resupply. Shuttles can be arranged for slackpacking. Parking $10 per day or $2 per day with shuttle.
Mail drops of non-guests $5. Mail drops for guests, 9151 Hwy 19E, Roan Mountain, TN 37687.

NoBo Features	Description	GPS Elev SoBo

⌂ ◈ 🛒 ✗ (0.5E) **The Station at 19E** 575-694-0734.
🍴🚗P▣ (www.thestationat19e.com)
AT Passport location.
Open year round.
$30pp (flat rate), private rooms available, Includes bunk, shower, laundry, fresh linens. Craft beer and food available on site. Full outfitter/resupply, shuttles and slack pack options. Secure parking $10/day or $2/day with shuttle.
Mail drops to 9367 HWY 19E Roan Mountain, TN 37687. Mail drop free with stay $5 non-stay .

⌂ 🛒 ✗ ☎ (6.0W) **Doe River Hiker Rest** 575-694-0734.
🍴🚗P▣ Open year round.
Free shuttle with stay. $30pp (flat rate), includes private room, shower, laundry, and fresh linens. Shuttles to town. Slack pack available. Fast wifi. Send Mail drops to The Station at 19E hostel and they will be forwarded here.

⌂ ⊛ ⊛ ⛺ (9.8E) **Harmony Hostel** 828-898-6200 (www.harmony-hostel.com)
☎🚗P No Pets, No smoking, No alcohol. Not the typical hiker hostel.
$50.00pp + tax, clean and spacious with semi-private sleeping areas, includes linen, shower. Communal kitchen equipped with refrigerator, microwave, large bake/broil toaster oven, crock-pot, toaster and dishwasher. Laundry $6. Free breakfast includes toast and jam, oatmeal, fruit, tea/coffee & boiled eggs (limit 2) on request. Free shuttle from Hwy 19E at 3p & 6p for hostel guests, additional shuttle services available for a fee. Section hiker parking.
Mail drops: 444 S. Beech Mountain Parkway Banner Elk, NC 28604.

Roan Mountain, TN 37687 (3.5W)

⌖ **PO** M-F 8am-12pm & 1pm-4pm, Sa 7:30am-9:30am 423-772-3014.

🛏 ◈ ⛺ ☎ (4.8W) **Roan Mountain B&B** 423-772-3207. campbell79@comcast.net (www.roanmtbb.com)
🍴🚗P▣ AT Passport location.
Open year round. Pets considered, no alcohol, no smoking inside. Hiker rate $75 single, $95 double includes full hot breakfast. Free pickup and return at Hwy 19E and 5pm town shuttle. Do it yourself laundry $5. Some resupply items on site. Free WiFi. Free 5pm shuttle into town for restaurants and restock for guests. Shuttles and slackpacking Sam's Gap to Watauga Lake. Parking for section hikers. Credit Cards accepted.
Mail drops; must have both the PO and physical address both on the mailing label. P.O. Box 227, 132 W. B. Mitchell Rd. Roan Mountain, Tennessee 37687

✗ ☎ **Happy's Cafe** 423-772-3400 Mon-Su 7am-3pm. Ask for ride availability after eating if going back to 19E trail head.

✗ ◈ ☎ **Bob's Dairyland** 423-772-3641. (www.bobsdairyland.com) M-Su 6am-9pm.

✗ ☎ **Smoky Mountain Bakers** 423-957-1202. M closed, Tu-Sa 8 am-8 pm, Su closed. Wood fired pizza.

✗ ☎ **Frank & Marty's Pizza** 423-772-3083. M closed, Tu-Sa 4 am-9 pm, Su closed.

🛒🛒 **Redi Mart** 423-772-3032. M-Sa 8am-10pm, Sun 10am-8pm.

🛒 **Cloudland Market** 423-772-3201. M-Sa 8am-7pm.

Roan Mountain, TN

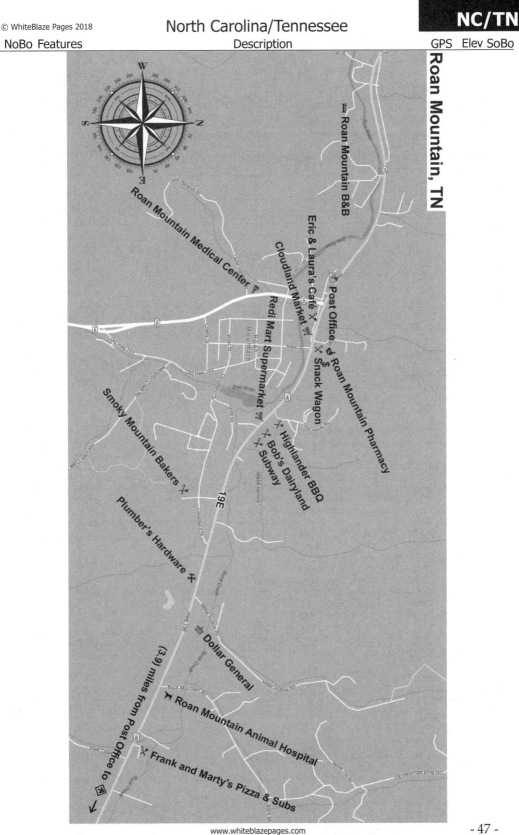

Roan Mountain B&B

Eric & Laura's Café

Cloudland Market

Roan Mountain Medical Center

Post Office

Roan Mountain Pharmacy

Redi Mart Supermarket

Snack Wagon

Highlander BBQ

Bob's Dairyland

Subway

Smoky Mountain Bakers

19E

Plumber's Hardware

Dollar General

(3.9) miles from Post Office to

Roan Mountain Animal Hospital

Frank and Marty's Pizza & Subs

NoBo	Features	Description	GPS	Elev	SoBo
394.9		High point on ridge.		2911	1796.0
395.0	♦⛺P	Cross **Bear Branch Road**, water (streams) are located north of road	N 36 10.764, W 82 00.768	2900	1795.9
395.9		Lower end of Bishop Hollow.		3344	1795.0
396.3		High end of Bishop Hollow.		3623	1794.6
397.3	📷	Reach summit and stile. Many views in this area.		3820	1793.6
397.7		Circle around Isaacs Cemetery.		3602	1793.2
398.1	♦⛺	Cross **Buck Mountain Road**, water (spigot) is located (0.1) east at church.		3340	1792.8
398.3	♦	Cross small stream.		3461	1792.6
398.4	♦⛺	Cross **Campbell Hollow Road**, water (streams) are located south of road.		3330	1792.5
398.7	⌒	Cross small bridge.		4335	1792.2
399.1	♦	Pass by spring.		3422	1791.8
400.2	Y⛏	Side trail (0.1) east to Jones Falls.		3148	1790.7
401.2	♦⚠	Campsite, water		3590	1789.7
402.4	♦	Cross creek.		2925	1788.5
403.0	⌒	Cross small log bridge.		2935	1787.9
403.4	♦⚠⛏	Cross small stream below waterfall, blue blaze west to campsite.		3130	1787.5
403.6	♦Y⚠ ⌐(17)↷	**Mountaineer Falls Shelter**, water is located 200 feet on blue blaze in front of shelter, tenting. 25.1◄19.9◄18.0◄►9.6►17.8►26.4	N 36 12.212, W 81 59.141	3470	1787.3
404.4	♦⚠	Blue blaze trail east leads to campsite, water		3260	1786.5
404.9	♦	Cross small stream.		3531	1786.0
405.0	⛺	Cross worn Forest Service Road.		3572	1785.9
405.2	⛺P	Cross **Walnut Mountain Road**	N 36 13.327, W 82 00.258	3550	1785.7
406.4	♦⛺P	Stream, **Howard Harrison Road**		3400	1784.5
406.9	Y📷	Viewpoint, memorial bench.		3350	1784.0
407.4	Y⌒ ★★★★★	Upper Laurel Fork, footbridge, side trail (0.3) west to **Vango/Abby Memorial Hostel.**		3290	1783.5

Y🏠⬧⛏⚠ Blue blazed side trail (0.3W) to hostel originates at the hand railed footbridge.
⚓🏠⛏⛏ (0.3W) **Vango/Abby Memorial Hostel**
⚓⛏ 423-772-3450. vangoabby@gmail.com.
AT Passport location.
CLOSED from mid Nov thru mid Feb UNLESS called first.
Call for availability off season Nov-Feb. Overnights must sign registration form. Bunk rooms with heat $10, without heat $5 night, includes shower. Private room and deck, queen bed with linens, heat, $20 single/$30 double. Pets okay if picked up after. No toilet, but privy, shovels ,TP, hand sanitizer provided. Shower without stay is $2, if also using provided towel $3. Piano, guitar and fiddle available for use if you play. Cash or paypal only. Offers slackpacking from 19E, ask about rates. Short term resupply available daily 4-8: beverages, pizza, Ben & Jerry's ice cream and stove fuels. Hike in and out only, no parking or drive ins. WiFi is on satellite; need to ration hours; 8-10 pm, 2-8 am daily; $3 per hour otherwise. Mail drops are free if sent in advance. Otherwise it is $15 round trip to the PO in Roan Mountain. PO Box 185, Roan Mountain, TN 37687.

408.4	⛺	Cross **USFS 293**		3442	1782.5
409.2	♦	Cross stream.		3410	1781.7
410.1	♦⚠	Cross small stream, campsite.		3378	1780.8
412.5		Cross high point on White Rocks Mountain.		4121	1778.4
413.2	♦⚠⌐(6) ↷	**Moreland Gap Shelter**, water is located (0.2) down the hollow across from the shelter and steep, tenting. 29.5◄27.6◄9.6◄►8.2►16.8►24.0	N 36 13.207, W 82 05.310	3815	1777.7
414.4	⛺	Cross **Tower Road**, White Rocks Mountain		4206	1776.5
415.3	♦⚠	Campsite on southern end of field, blue blaze trail leads to water.		3700	1775.6
415.6	Y⛺	Cross forest road. Lacy Trapp Trail.		3810	1775.3
415.7	⟘	Power line.		3825	1775.2
416.3	📷	Vista with views to the west.		4102	1774.6
417.8	Y⛏	Trail to Coon Den Falls is located to the east (0.8)		2660	1773.1
417.9	📷	Cliffs with views.		3450	1773.0
418.3	📷	Cliffs with views.		3442	1772.6
419.3	♦⛺	Follow farm road by pond and field.		2606	1771.6
419.5	♦⛺P ★★★★★	Cross **USFS 50**, Dennis Cove.	N 36 15.854, W 82 07.389	2550	1771.4

🏠⚠⬧Ⓢ (0.3W) **Kincora Hiking Hostel** 423-725-4409.
⛺⛏🏠⛏ AT Passport location.
No dogs. Bunks $5 a night recommended donation, 3 night limit. Cooking facilities, laundry. Coleman and alcohol by the ounce.
Mail drops free for guests, non-guest $5. 1278 Dennis Cove Rd, Hampton, TN 37658.

NoBo	Features	Description	GPS	Elev	SoBo
	🏠 ⛺ ◈ 🚐 ⛺ 💻 🚗 🖥	**(0.4E) Black Bear Resort** 423-725-5988 (www.blackbearresorttn.com) AT Passport location. Open Mar 1 - Oct 31. Pet friendly. Hostel bunks $20, upper bunkhouse $25 per person, tenting $15 per person. Cabins available $50-$65 up to 4 people per cabin, $20 EAP with a max of 6 people. Laundry $5. Computer available for use. Camp store with long-term resupply items, snacks, sodas, pizza, beer, ice cream and food that can be bought and cooked on-site with microwave and stove. Fuel by the ounce and canister fuel. Credit Cards accepted. Shuttles available. Parking free for guest who stay one night, $3 per day for non guests. Mail drops free for guests, non-guest $5. 1511 Dennis Cove Rd, Hampton, TN 37658.			
419.6	⛺ ⌣	Pass two small bridges and a campsite that is near the area used for the old railroad.		2499	1771.3

NoBo		Description	GPS	Elev	SoBo
420.3	♦⌒	Cross Koonford Bridge over Laurel Falls.		2118	1770.6
420.4	Y	Unmarked trail junction to Potato Top		2450	1770.5
420.6	Y	High water bypass to Laurel Fork Shelter, reconnects again at Laurel Fork Shelter		2200	1770.3
420.7	♦⛟	Laurel Fork Falls, Laurel Fork Gorge. **Do not swim near or close to the falls. Hikers have been pulled in and drowned here.**		2120	1770.2
420.9		Skirt edge of cliff on walkway. If the walkway is flooded or icy, use high water bypass trail.		2211	1770.0
421.4	♦Y⊏(8)	Blue blaze trail 300 feet to **Laurel Fork Shelter**, water (stream) is located 50 yards behind the shelter. Also high water bypass trail. 35.8◀17.8◀8.2◀▶ 8.6▶ 15.8▶22.6		2450	1769.5
421.7	♦⌒	Waycaster Spring, there are a few footbridges that go over Laurel Fork in this area	N 36 16.714, W 82 08.184	1900	1769.2
421.8	♦⌒	Cross stream on footbridge.		2082	1769.1
422.0	♦⌒	Cross stream on footbridge.		2137	1768.9
422.2	♦Y	Water, blue blaze side trail to leads west (0.8) to US. 321, Hampton TN is west on 321. **See Notes Below 428.1.**		1900	1768.7
424.6		Pond Flats (south end).		2682	1766.3
424.7	♦	Spring located in rocky bottom of drainage.		3304	1766.2
425.0	♦⛺⌣	Pond Flats (north end), water (spring) is located (0.1) north on AT, campsite		3780	1765.9
427.6	Y⛺	Campsite to the east		2200	1763.3
428.0	Y⛺	Trail and **Shook Brach Road** intersect with gravel road to the east.		2023	1762.9
428.1	♦⊞🚻⛲⛺P ★★★★★	Cross **US. 321**, Shook Branch Picnic Area. **See map of Hampton.**	N 36 18.112, W 82 07.735	1990	1762.8

Boots Off Hostel & Campground 239-218-3904.
AT Passport location.
Call ahead if you have dogs. 142 Shook Branch Rd, Hampton, TN 37658. Campsites, Tent or Hammock Camping, $10 per night per person. Bunkhouse, $20 per person. Cabin bunks, $20 per person, up to four people. Call for private space options. Includes continental breakfast, town shuttle, WifI. $5 Laundry. Showers free for guest, non guest $5. Bonfire pit, short term resupply, kayaks, canoes, stand up paddleboards for rent. (Watauga Lake is a 5 minutes walk). Section hiker parking. Ask about shuttle service from Damascus to Erwin.
Mail drops: Free for guest, $5 for non guests. 142 Shook Branch Rd. Hampton, TN 37658.

(0.8E) **Dividing Ridge Campground** 424-957-0821
Open until July. Donation based. Hot shopwers, charging stations, wash tub and local shuttles. Call for pickup.

Hampton, TN 37658 (2.6W). See map.

Brown's Grocery & Braemar Castle Hostel 423-725-2411, 423-725-2262.
AT Passport location.
Open year round. Operated by Sutton Brown; check-in at grocery to stay at the hostel or for shuttles. Pets okay. WiFi at hostel only. **Store:** Open M-Sa 8am-6pm, Su closed. Store accepts Credit Cards; hostel is cash only.

Hampton Trails Bicycle Shop 423-725-5000. (www.hamptontrails.com)
Offers shuttles and has few supplies in shop. M, T, Th, F 11am-6pm, Sat 10pm-3pm, closed Wed & Sun.

Hampton, TN

NoBo		Description	GPS	Elev	SoBo
428.3		Paved road to Shook Branch Recreation Area.		1970	1762.6
428.4		Footbridge across stream.		1964	1762.5
428.8		Go through gate in old road.		2046	1762.1
429.6		Griffith Branch		2100	1761.3
430.0	(6)	50 yards west to **Watauga Lake Shelter**, water is located south of shelter on AT. This shelter and area has been known for bear activity. **Closed for 2017 and may be permanently closed.** 26.4◄16.8◄8.6◄►7.2►14.0►21.6	N 36 18.833, W 82 07.770	2130	1760.9
431.0		**Lookout Road**, Watauga Dam, AT travels along this road for (0.4) miles, keep an eye out for the blazes		1915	1759.9
432.0		Reach summit, views of Watauga Lake.		2480	1758.9
432.5	P	**Wilbur Dam Road**	N 36 19.728, W 82 06.690	2250	1758.4
434.9		Cross summit		3420	1756.0
435.1		Cross summit		3400	1755.8
435.5		Water (spring)		3360	1755.4
436.5		Large rock formation to the east.		3482	1754.4

NoBo	Features	Description	GPS	Elev	SoBo
437.2	⌐(6)📷	**Vandeventer Shelter**, water is located is (0.3) down a steep, blue blazed trail south of the shelter (0.1) south of shelter. Views from shelter. 24.0◄15.8◄7.2◄►6.8►14.4►22.7	N 36 22.026, W 82 03.525	3620	1753.7
438.2	📷	Lookout to the east.		3632	1752.7
439.2	📷	Lookout to the east.		3947	1751.7
440.7	Y	Side trail leading west to private property.		3993	1750.2
441.0	♦⅄	Water (spring) is located about 40 yards east beyond bog. There are good tent sites 175 yards north.		3900	1749.9
442.4		Turkeypen Gap		3840	1748.5
443.0	▲	Reach high point of Iron Mountain.		4190	1747.9
443.3	⊤	Power line. Views of fields around Doeville, TN.		4138	1747.6
443.8	♦Y	Water (spring) is also water for Iron Mountain Shelter, a more reliable spring is located 100 yards compass-south on blue blaze trail.		4000	1747.1
444.0	⅄⌐(6)↵	**Iron Mountain Shelter**, water (spring) 500 yards south on AT, tenting. 22.6◄14.0◄6.8◄►7.6►15.9►35.6	N 36 26.132, W 81 59.460	4125	1746.9
445.3	●	Nick Grindstaff Monument, person was a hermit living here before the trail came through.		4090	1745.6
445.4	♦Y	Water (spring) on blue blazed trail west 100 yards to spring.		4090	1745.5
445.8		Cross over high point.		4113	1745.1
446.8		Reach top of ridge.		3750	1744.1
447.8	♦	Water (stream), two streams 100 yards apart.		3500	1743.1
448.0	⌢	Cross several bog bridges.		3625	1742.9
448.1	▲	Cross USFS logging road.		3620	1742.8
448.6	▲P ★★★★★	Cross **TN 91**.	N 36 28.882, W 81 57.622	3450	1742.3

⊨⅄△☎ (2.6E) **Switchback Creek Campground** 407-484-3388. (www.switchbackcreek.com)
Open Apr 1 - Oct 31.
Location; (1.8) miles east to Sluder Rd, turn right for (0.2) miles, then right on Wallace Rd. (0.6) miles to 570 Wallace Rd, Shady Valley, TN 37688. Cabin for two $40, campsite $12, cash only. Pets allowed for camping only. Free WiFi. Showers, laundry, call for ride at TN. 91 or Low Gap.

Shady Valley, TN (3.5E) See NOBO mile 455.1

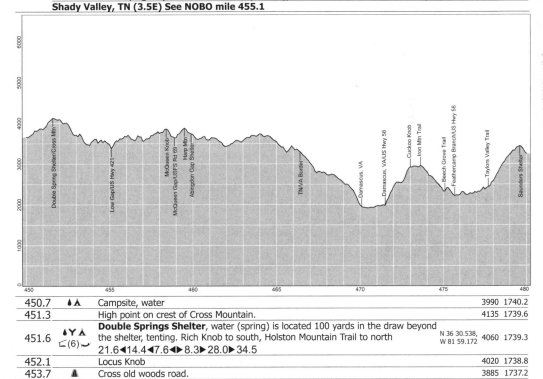

450.7	♦⅄	Campsite, water		3990	1740.2
451.3		High point on crest of Cross Mountain.		4135	1739.6
451.6	♦Y⅄ ⌐(6)↵	**Double Springs Shelter**, water (spring) is located 100 yards in the draw beyond the shelter, tenting. Rich Knob to south, Holston Mountain Trail to north 21.6◄14.4◄7.6◄►8.3►28.0►34.5	N 36 30.538, W 81 59.172	4060	1739.3
452.1		Locus Knob		4020	1738.8
453.7	▲	Cross old woods road.		3885	1737.2
453.8	📷	Views in the open field.		3712	1737.1

NoBo	Features	Description	GPS	Elev	SoBo
455.0	⋏	Pass campsite on ridge crest.		3495	1735.9
455.1	⏚⊞⚑P ★★★★★	Cross **U.S. 421**, Low Gap, picnic table, spring.	N 36 32.331, W 81 56.893	3384	1735.8

Shady Valley, TN.(2.7E)

	⌂	**PO** M–F 8am-12pm, Sa 8am-10am, 423-739-2073.			
	🏪✕⚖	**Shady Valley Country Store & Deli** 423-739-2325. (www.shadyvalleycountrystore.com) Open in the Spring until Thanksgiving: M-F 7 am-8 pm, Sa 8 am-8 pm, Su 9 am-6 pm. Deli serves burgers and sandwiches. Coleman fuel.			
	✕	**Raceway Restaurant** 423-739-2499. M-Tu 7am-8pm, W 7am-2pm, Th-Sa 7am-8pm, Su 8am-2pm.			

NoBo	Features	Description	GPS	Elev	SoBo
456.1		Cross a summit.		3643	1734.8
457.0	◊	Double Spring Gap, water is known to be unreliable at times		3650	1733.9
457.4		Gap, evidence of old farmstead.		3642	1733.5
458.4		McQueens Knob, little remains of old fire tower.		3900	1732.5
458.5		Old unused shelter, emergency use only shelter		3816	1732.4
458.8	⚑P	**USFS 69**, McQueens Gap	N 36 34.443, W 81 55.927	3680	1732.1
459.9	Y⋏⊏(5) ⏝	**Abingdon Gap Shelter**, water (spring) is located spring (0.2) east on a steep, blue blazed side trail, downhill behind the shelter, tenting. Maple Spring Gap. 22.7◀15.9◀8.3◀▶ 19.7▶ 26.2▶ 38.6	N 36 34.861, W 81 54.132	3785	1731.0
465.3	Y	Junction of Backbone Rock Trail		3466	1725.6
466.4	State Line	Tennessee–Virginia State Line, Mt. Rogers NRA sign		3302	1724.5
468.0	◆	Spring on blue blaze trail (0.1) east at and abandon homestead.		2600	1722.9
469.2	Y	Wooded path intersects with old woods road.			1721.7
470.1	⚑P(25) ★★★★★	Junction with **U.S. 58**. **Damascus, VA**. 24236. **See map of Damascus**.	N 36 38.160, W 81 47.376	1928	1720.8

	⌂	**PO** M-F 8:30-1 & 2-4:30, Sa 9-11, 276-475-3411			
	🛒🛍	**Food City** (0.5W on US 58) 276-475-3653, M-Sa 6am-12am, Su 8am-12pm. Pharmcy, M-F 9am-7pm, Sa 9a,-3pm, Su closed.			
	🏠🛏⋏ ◈⛺	**The Broken Fiddle Hostel** 275-608-6220 AT Passport location. Pets OK outside. Located on the AT. 4 single beds in shared space, $25PP. Two private rooms, $45/2. Tent or hammock $10PP. Laundry $5. Stay includes continental breakfast. Shower with out stay $3. Credit cards accepted with but includes a processing fee.			
	🛏🏠◈ ⛺📶	**Hikers Inn** 276-475-3788. hikersinn@gmail.com (www.hikersinndamascus.com) AT Passport location. Closed in winter. $25 bunks, hostel private room $50. Rooms in house and Airstream $75 or $65/night for multi-night stays. Guest laundry $5. A/C everywhere. Smoking outside, dogs allowed in hostel and airstream, free WiFi, cash/check/credit/debit.			
	🏠⋏◈ ◈🅿⚖	**The Place** 276-492-3983. AT Passport location. No Pets, , alcohol or smoking anywhere on the premises. Methodist Church run bunkrooms, tenting, pavilion, showers with towel and soap. Suggested donation $7. Seasonal caretaker, please help to keep the bunkroom clean. Two night max unless sick/injured. Check-in from 1-10pm. Open early Mar until mid-Nov (depending on weather). No vehicle-assisted hikers (except during Trail Days).			
	🏠⋏◈ ⛺📶�car📧	**Crazy Larry's** 276-475-7130. AT Passport location. Hostel $40+tax, tenting $20+tax, stay includes laundry, breakfast and morning coffee. Hostel has A/C and heat. Free WiFi. Nightly rental that sleeps 12 or more, WiFi , satellite TV , 3 bathrooms laundry room fully stocked kitchen HVAC, $300 plus. Can call ahead for reservations. Shuttles 276-206-1245 or 276-274-0907. Mail drops: 209 Douglas Drive, Damascus, VA 24236.			
	🏠⋏◈ ⚖📶�car📧	**Woodchuck Hostel** 406-407-1272. (woodchuckhostel.com) AT Passport location. Open year-round. No drugs or Alcohol. Bed with linens $25. One private cabin $45S $55D. Teepee $20. Tent or hammock $12. Hot breakfast with stay ($2 extra for tenter or hammocker). Laundry $5 with stay, $8 without stay. Shower without stay $5. Kitchen privileges, common area, large yard, pavilion with gas grill. Dogs welcome. Alcohol by the ounce, cold drinks and snacks available. Free WiFi. Free shuttles to Food City, other shuttles by arrangement. Credit cards and Debit cards accepted for a $2 fee. Physical address is: 533 Docie St, Damascus Va. 24236. Mail drops sent to: PO Box 752, Damascus VA, 24236.			
	🛏◈🅿⛺ 📧	**Montgomery Homestead Inn** 276-492-6283. (www.montgomeryhomestead.com) AT Passport location. No smoking, no alcohol, no pets. Rooms $75 and up, includes laundry. Open Mar-Oct, cash or check only. Mail for guest only: (USPS) PO Box 12, (FedEx/UPS) 103 E. Laurel Ave, Damascus, VA 24236.			

Virginia

NoBo Features	Description	GPS Elev SoBo

Dancing Bear B&B 423-571-1830. (www.dancingbearrentals.com)
No smoking, no pets. $70-$150. Breakfast for $5PP, free WiFi. Credit cards accepted.
Mail for guest only: PO Box 252, 203 E Laurel Ave, Damascus, VA 24236.

Lazy Fox B&B 276-475-5838.
Open year round.
No pets, no smoking. $75/up includes tax and breakfast. Check or cash only.
Mail for guests only: PO Box 757, 133 Imboden St, Damascus, VA 24236.

Mountain Laurel Inn 276-475-8822.
(www.mountainlaurelinn.com)
$85-$145, includes breakfast. Discounts for extended stay. Optional dinners, Laundry for registered
guests, saltwater pool, free wifi. Located across from food city and dollor store.

Virginia Creeper Lodge 276-492-1143. (www.virginiacreeperlodge.com)
$125 and up.

Appalachian Folk School 423-341-1843. (www.warrendoyle.com)
Open Mar-April and mid-Sept-Nov.
Nonprofit run by Warren Doyle offers work for stay weeknights (M-Th) only (2-3 hrs/night) for all hikers
who have a spiritual or poetic connection to the white blazes. Kitchen privileges, shower, free WiFi,
laundry and rides to and from the AT between Route 321 (Hampton) and VA 603 (Fox Creek).

Mt. Rogers Outfitters 276-475-5416 (www.mtrogersoutfitters.com)
AT Passport location.
No Dogs, No alcohol.
Private rooms $21. Full service outfitter, fuel by the ounce. Parking $5 per day. Shuttles to many area in
TN and VA. Shower with towel $3.
Mail drops: PO Box 546, 110 W Laurel Ave, Damascus, VA 24236.

Adventure Damascus 888-595-2453 or 276-475-6262 (www.adventuredamascus.com)
AT Passport location.
Open year round, 7 days a week. Catering to thru hikers with backpacking gear. Offers hiker foods,
alcohol and coleman by the ounce, other fuels, bike rentals. Showers $3. Shuttles to area trail heads by
arrangement
USPS and UPS Mail drops: PO Box 1113, 128 W. Laurel Ave. Damascus, VA 24236.

Sundog Outfitter 276-475-6252. (www.sundogoutfitter.com)
AT Passport location.
Open year round, 7 days a week. Backpacking gear and clothing, repairs, hiker food, coleman and
alcohol by the ounce, other fuels. Shuttles to area trail heads by arrangement,
Mail drops: PO Box 1113 or 331 Douglas Dr, Damascus, VA 24236.

Damascus Library 276-475-3820
M 9am-5pm, Tu 11am-7pm, W 9am-5pm, Th 11am-7pm, F 9am-5pm, Sa 9am-1pm, Sun closed.
Computers available for use, one hour internet limit. Free WiFi. Charging stations are set up for hikers to
charge their phones, IPads, tablets, etc.

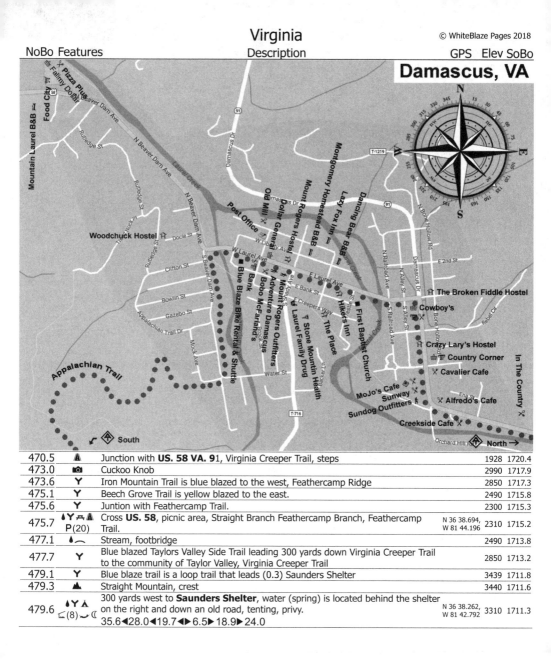

Damascus, VA

NoBo		Features / Description	GPS	Elev	SoBo
470.5	▲	Junction with **US. 58 VA. 9**1, Virginia Creeper Trail, steps		1928	1720.4
473.0	📷	Cuckoo Knob		2990	1717.9
473.6	Y	Iron Mountain Trail is blue blazed to the west, Feathercamp Ridge		2850	1717.3
475.1	Y	Beech Grove Trail is yellow blazed to the east.		2490	1715.8
475.6	Y	Juntion with Feathercamp Trail.		2300	1715.3
475.7	♦ Y ⊟ ▲ P(20)	Cross **US. 58**, picnic area, Straight Branch Feathercamp Branch, Feathercamp Trail.	N 36 38.694, W 81 44.196	2310	1715.2
477.1	♦ ⌒	Stream, footbridge		2490	1713.8
477.7	Y	Blue blazed Taylors Valley Side Trail leading 300 yards down Virginia Creeper Trail to the community of Taylor Valley, Virginia Creeper Trail		2850	1713.2
479.1	Y	Blue blaze trail is a loop trail that leads (0.3) Saunders Shelter		3439	1711.8
479.3	▲	Straight Mountain, crest		3440	1711.6
479.6	♦ Y ⋀ ⊏(8) ⌣ ☾	300 yards west to **Saunders Shelter**, water (spring) is located behind the shelter on the right and down an old road, tenting, privy. 35.6◀28.0◀19.7◀▶6.5▶18.9▶24.0	N 36 38.262, W 81 42.792	3310	1711.3

NoBo	Features	Description	GPS	Elev	SoBo
481.9	Y	Bear Tree Gap Trail, (3.0) west to Bear Tree Recreation Area		3050	1709.0
482.1	♦ ⋏	Campsite with man made pond.		3020	1708.8
483.7	⋒	Cross **VA. 728**, Creek Junction Station, old railroad bed		2720	1707.2
484.3	Y⋒P	Virginia Creeper Trail, Whitetop Laurel Creek	N 36 38.964, W 81 40.344	2690	1706.6
484.9	⋒	Cross **VA. 859**, Grassy Ridge Road		2900	1706.0
485.1	♦	Streams		3040	1705.8
487.7		Lost Mountain		3400	1703.2
486.1	♦⋏⊑(8) ⌣ℂ	**Lost Mountain Shelter**, water is located on a trail to the left of the shelter, tenting, privy. 34.5◄26.2◄6.5◄► 12.4► 17.5► 23.5	N 36 38.644, W 81 39.378	3360	1704.8
487.2	♦🚻⋒P	Cross **US. 58**. Summit Cut, VA.	N 36 38.393, W 81 39.921	3160	1703.7
487.3	♦⋏	Campsites located near water (stream)		3300	1703.6
488.5	♦⋒P(5)	Cross **VA. 601**, Beech Mountain Road	N 36 38.237, W 81 38.422	3600	1702.4
491.0	📷	Buzzard Rock on the south slope of Whitetop Mountain		5080	1699.9
491.8	♦	Water (spring) on east side of trail, pipes		5100	1699.1
491.9	♦⋏🚻⋒ P(15)	Cross **USFS 89**, Whitetop Mountain Road to summit, parking 100 feet to the east.	N 36 37.908, W 81 36.076	5150	1699.0
493.7	♦	Small creek at log steps.		4763	1697.2
494.3	ℂ🚻📷⋒ P(12)	Cross **VA. 600**, Elk Garden, Whitetop, VA.	N 36 38.781, W 81 34.979	4463	1696.6
494.8		Boundary Lewis Fork Wilderness, fence		4640	1696.1
495.7	Y⋏	Campsites are uphill to the east on blue blaze trail		4850	1695.2
496.3	♦	Deep Gap, **No camping permitted here**, water is located (0.2) east		4900	1694.6
496.4	Y	Virginia Highlands Horse Trail, Mt. Rogers Trail, (4.0) west to USFS Grindstone campground, tenting		5200	1694.5
497.4	📷	Brier Ridge Saddle, views in meadows		5125	1693.5
498.3	Y	Spur Trail to summit of Mt. Rogers (0.5W)		5490	1692.6
498.5	♦⊑(16) ℂ📷	**Thomas Knob Shelter**, water is located in an enclosed area in a pasture behind the shelter and please lock the gate after getting water as this will keep the feral ponies in the area from polluting the water, privy, views. **No camping or open fires permitted around the shelter.** 38.6◄18.9◄12.4◄► 5.1► 11.1► 16.0	N 36 39.396, W 81 32.114	5400	1692.4
499.5	Y⋏	Rhododendron Gap, Pine Mountain Trail is a blue blaze trail to the west. Many large, established campsites between Thomas Knob and Rhododendron Gap		5440	1691.4
500.0	Y	Wilburn Ridge Trail is a blue blazed trail to the east.		5440	1690.9
500.1	O	**Fatman Squeeze**, a narrow rock passage in the rocks.		5300	1690.8
500.7	Y	Wilburn Ridge Trail is a blue blazed trail to the east.		4900	1690.2
501.5	⋒P	**Park service road** descending (0.5) west to Grayson Highlands State Park with parking at to Massie Gap	N 36 38.009, W 81 30.312	4800	1689.4
502.2	YP	Blue blaze AT Spur Trail leads (0.8) east to backpackers parking lot.	N 36 38.009, W 81 30.312	4882	1688.7

NoBo	Features	Description	GPS	Elev	SoBo
502.7	♦	Cross Quebec Branch		4629	1688.2
503.6	♦⊏(8)☾	Grayson Highlands State Park. **Wise Shelter**, water (spring) is located south of the shelter on a trail east of the AT, **no tenting around the shelter**; tent sites are located in the Mt. Rogers NRA, across Wilson Creek (0.3) north. Privy. 24.0◄17.5◄5.1◄►6.0►10.9►20.1	N 36 39.242, W 81 29.906	4460	1687.3
503.7	♦⌒	Big Wilson Creek, footbridge		4300	1687.2
503.9	Y	Wilson Creek Trail		4300	1687.0
504.0	Y	Junction with Scales Trail, open to horses and hikers.		4650	1686.9
505.0	♦	Water (spring)		4610	1685.9
506.2	📷	Stone Mountain		4820	1684.7
506.6	☾❂P(8)	**The Scales**, livestock corral, a grassy fenced in area used by campers and horse riders.	N 36 40.194, W 81 29.245	4620	1684.3
507.3	♦	Cross small stream.		4797	1683.6
508.0	Y	Pine Mountain Trail is a blue blazed trail to the west,		4960	1682.9
509.6	♦☾⊏(6)⌣	**Old Orchard Shelter**, water is located 100 yards west on blue blazed trail to right of shelter, privy. 23.5◄11.1◄6.0◄►4.9►14.1►23.9	N 36 40.993, W 81 30.672	4050	1681.3
509.7	Y	Upper Old Orchard Trail		4020	1681.2

510.4	Y	Old Orchard Trail.		3750	1680.5
511.3	♦⚑☾⚑P(10)	Cross VA. 603, Fox Creek Horse camp, (2.5) west leads to USFS Grindstone campground. 100 yards east to parking and port-a-potty.	N 36 41.796, W 81 30.381	3480	1679.6
511.4	♦⌒	Cross Fox Creek on long footbridge.		3450	1679.5
513.3		Ridge crest on Hurricane Mountain on the Tennessee New River Divide.		4360	1677.6
513.6	Y	Iron Mountain Trail, Chestnut Flats		4240	1677.3
514.5	♦Y⚑⊏(8)⌣☾	Side trail across from stream leads 160 yards west to **Hurricane Mountain Shelter**, water (creek), tenting, privy. 16.0◄10.9◄4.9◄►9.2►19.0►26.0	N 36 42.921, W 81 30.570	3850	1676.4
515.1	Y	Hurricane Creek Trail, old logging road		3300	1675.8
515.9	♦	Water (stream)		3000	1675.0
516.2	⊤	Power line.		3013	1674.7
517.6	Y ★★★★★	Dickey Gap Trail, USFS Hurricane campground (0.5W) **USFS Hurricane Creek Campground.**		3090	1673.3
	♦⚑⌣ 🚿🛠⛱	**USFS Hurricane Creek Campground** 276-783-5196 Tent site $16, shower $2. Open mid Apr-Oct. Restroom and shower. N 36 43 21, W 81 29 26			
518.3	Y	Comers Creek Falls Trail		3120	1672.6
518.4	♦⌒⚓	Comers Creek, footbridge, waterfalls		3100	1672.5
519.6	⚑P ★★★★★	Cross **VA. 650**, Dickey Gap. 100 yards to VA. 16 **Troutdale, VA.(2.6E). See map of Troutdale.**	N 36 43.218, W 81 27.677	3300	1671.3

⌂ ⋀ ◈ ♨ **(2.6E) Troutdale Church Hostel** 276-677-4092.
AT Passport location.
Open Mar 15 thru Nov 15.
62 Sapphire Lane, Troutdale. Donations are appreciated. Bunkhouse with microwave, tenting, shower available. Pets stay outside, no alcohol. Hikers welcome to services in hiker attire. Pastor Ken Riggins.
No mail drops to here.

⇌ ◈ ⛍ ⊷ **(3.2E) Sufi Lodge** 276-677-0195 (www.sufilodge.org)
$35PP for hiker room. Those staying in the Hiker Rooms are offered a boxed breakfast that may include a homemade cheesy egg biscuit, fruit and other treats easily consumed on the trail. This provides hikers and others with the option to take their breakfast to go and eat it later or enjoy it in their comfy bed. Free WiFi. Shuttles for guests to and from, Dickey Gap (VA 650), Sugar Grove Highway (VA 16). Call ahead to have the shuttle waiting at the trailhead for you but drivers will typically not wait more than fifteen minutes unless receiving a call telling them you will be late. Notify us about 3 miles away from Dickey Gap. Hikers have reported cell phone service in this area.
Mail drops free for guests, non guests $10: Please include your full legal name on the package along with a date you will be arriving. Packages may be returned to sender one week after the date of arrival indicated. Proper legal ID required to pickup package. 67 High Country Lane, Troutdale, Virginia 24378 Attn: Mail Drop Service.

⛪ ◈ ✕ ⚓ **(6.2E) Fox Creek General Store**
AT Passport location.
276-579-6033. M-F 7 am-7 pm, Sa 7 am-6 pm, Su closed.
Located 4 miles south on route 16. Resupply food, short order grill, burgers, pizza, and deli items. Fuel, denatured alcohol and canister fuel.

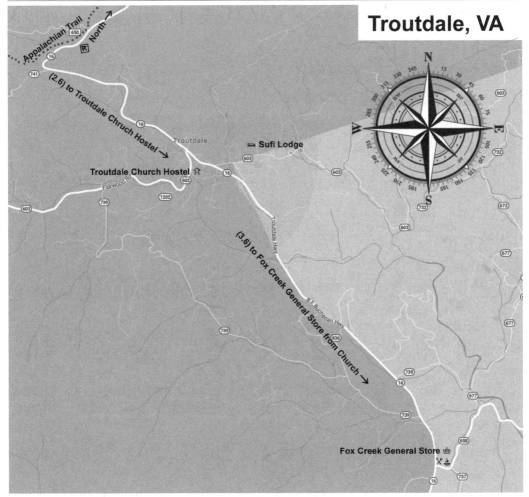

Troutdale, VA

NoBo	Features	Description	GPS	Elev	SoBo
520.4	Y	Virginia Highlands Horse Trail		3450	1670.5
521.1	Y人	Bobby's Trail leads (2.0) east to Raccoon Branch campground.		3570	1669.8
521.6	📷	High Point 200 yards on blue blazed trail.		4040	1669.3
523.7	♦Y人 ⌐(8) ⌣(⛺	**(1.0E) Trimpi Shelter**, water (spring), tent sites in front of shelter, tenting, privy. 20.1◄14.1◄9.2◄►9.8►16.8►36.1	N 36 44.955, W 81 28.824	2900	1667.2
524.9	🛆(4)	Cross **VA. 672**, Slabtown Road, gravel		2700	1666.0
525.6	Y	Blue blaze Slabtown Trail to the east.		2645	1665.3
525.8	🛆⌒P(4)	Cross **VA. 670, Teas Road**, South Fork Holston River, bridge	N 36 45.789, W 81 29.588	2450	1665.1
527.3	人⌣	Campsite located in the pines in small hollow west.		2933	1663.6
527.4	♦	Stream, unreliable.		2674	1663.5
529.6	🛆P(3)	Cross **VA. 601, Pugh Mountain Road**, gravel. A parking pull-off.	N 36 47.202, W 81 28.299	3250	1661.3
531.2	⊤	Power line.		3316	1659.7
532.1	♦⌒	Cross creek on bridge.		3052	1658.8
532.8	🛆	Junction of two roads.		3227	1658.1
533.5	♦⌐(16) (⛺	**Partnership Shelter**, water from faucet, bathroom, warm shower, no tenting around shelter, **No tenting permitted here.** Can call for pizza delivery at Visitor Center. 23.9◄19.0◄9.8◄►7.0►26.3►35.7	N 36 48.564, W 81 25.356	3360	1657.4
533.7	♦♦♦🛆P ★★★★★	Cross **VA. 16**, Mount Rogers NRA Headquarters. Parking is not recommend here, location has a history of vandalism with car thefts.	N 36 48.695, W 81 25.279	3220	1657.2
	⊕◈🅱P	**Mount Rogers National Recreation Area HQ** 276-783-5196. AT Passport location. Permit required for overnight parking (or park outside of gate).			

Sugar Grove, VA 24375 (3.2E)

     📪   **PO** M-F 8:30-12:30 & 1:30-3:30, Sa 8:15-10:30, 276-677-3200

Marion, VA 24354 (6.0W). See map of Marion.

     📪   **PO** M-F 9am-5pm, Sa 9:30am-12pm, 276-783-5051.

🛏🛆⌨🖥 **Travel Inn** 276-783-5112 (www.travelinnmarion.com)
    $43 and up. Include microwave, fridge, free coffee in the morning. Free WiFi.
    Mail drops for guests: 1419 N Main St, Marion VA 24354.

🛏◈⌨🖥 **Econo Lodge** 276-783-6031.
    AT Passport location.
    Special Hiker Rate: $54 - $64. Pet fee. Includes Free Hot Breakfast, microwave, fridge, free WiFi.
    Mail drops: 1420 N. Main St, Marion, VA 24354.

🛏⌨ **America's Best Value Inn** 276-378-0481. Continental breakfast, coffee, microware, fridge, pool. Free WiFi.

✗🖥⌨🖥 **Kohi Cafe** 276-613-7385. (www.mkt.com/store/kohi-cafe)
    M-F 8am-4pm, Sa 10am-2pm, Su closed. Coffee, breakfast , lunch, and deli. Computer with printer, free WiFi.
    Mail drops: 201 E Main St Suite 102, Marion, VA 24354

📷 **Park Place Drive-In Park Place Drive-In** 276-781-2222. More than welcome to walk in. Offers mini golf, arcade, and ice cream shop.

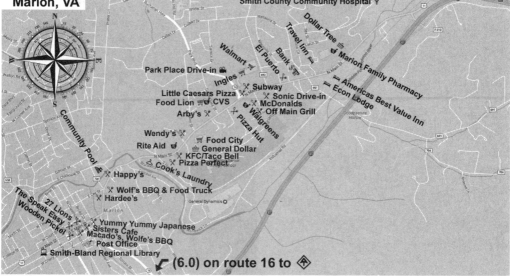

Marion, VA

NoBo	Features	Description	GPS	Elev	SoBo
534.4	▲	Cross **VA. 622/Nick's Creek Road**		3270	1656.5
534.9		Brushy Mountain		3600	1656.0
537.3	▲	Locust Mountain, wooded knoll.		3900	1653.6
537.7	♦▲▲ P(15)	Cross **USFS 86, Glade Mountain Road**, Water (spring). Private road, permission required, may not be passable for vehicles.	N 36 50.089, W 81 22.232	3650	1653.2
539.0	▲	Glade Mountain		4093	1651.9

Elevation profile labels (left to right): Chatfield Shelter; Settlers Museum/VA Rd 615; Kegley Ln/VA Rd 729; Middle Holston River; Atkins, VA/I-81/US Hwy 11; Dry Run Creek; Davis Cemetery/VA Rd 617; Davis Path Campsite; Little Brushy Mtn; Reed Creek/Crawfish Trail; Big Walker Mtn/Tilson Gap; Rich Valley Rd/VA Rd 610; North Holston River/VA Rd 742; Olystery Pavilion/VA Hwy 42; Brushy Mtn; Knot Maul Shelter; Knot Maul Creek; Lynn Camp Creek; Lynn Camp Mtn; Lick Creek; Lick Creek Rd/VA Rd 625; Chestnut Ridge; Chestnut Knob Shelter

NoBo	Features	Description	GPS	Elev	SoBo
540.5	♦⊏(6)☾	**Chatfield Shelter**, water (creek) is located in front of shelter, privy. 26.0◄16.8◄7.0◄► 19.3► 28.7► 39.4	N 36 50.995, W 81 21.798	3150	1650.4
540.8	▲	Cross **USFS 644**, stile.		3100	1650.1
542.0	Y	Trail intersects with old farm road. Farm road is part of Settlers Museum.		2731	1648.9
542.3	○◈▲ P(15)	Cross **VA. 615, Rocky Hollow Road**. (0.1E) **Settlers Museum, Lindamood Schoolhouse** 276-686-4401. (www.settlersmuseum.com) Parking available at farm. (Apr 1-Nov 15) AT Passport location.	N 36 52.248, W 81 21.462	2600	1648.6
542.8	▲(3)	Cross **VA. 729**, Kegley Lane, gravel	N 36 52.507, W 81 21.589	2540	1648.1
543.1	Y▲	Junction with Kegley Trail, old road		2540	1647.8
543.9	📷	Good view at top of meadow of Brushy Mountain and Great Valley.		2560	1647.0
544.2	⌒✕	Cross Middle Fork of Holston River, railroad tracks		2420	1646.7
545.1	▲P(30) ★★★★★	Cross **U.S. 11, I–81, VA. 683. Atkins, VA.**	N 36 53.171, W 81 22.408	2420	1645.8
	🏤	(3.0W) **PO** M-F 8:30am-12pm & 12:30am-3:15pm, Sa 9am-10:45am, 276-783-5551.			
	🛏⛺☕🚗 P✉	**Relax Inn** 276-783-5811. $50S $55D, $5EAP (max 4), pets $10. Call for shuttle availability. Lanudrt, free WiFi for guests. Parking $3 per day. Mail drops free for guests, $5 for non guests. Government issued ID require to pick up mail drops and for room registration. Relax Inn, 7253 Lee Hwy, Rural Retreat, VA 24368.			
	✕◈P✉	**The Barn Restaurant** 276-686-6222. AT Passport location. M-Sa 7am-8pm, Su 7am-3pm. Sunday buffet from 11am-2pm. Parking for section hikers $5 per day, $25 a week. Mail drops: 7412 Lee Highway, Rural Retreat, VA 24368.			
	🏪☎	**Shell Convenience Store** M-Su 24 hours, ATM inside.			
	■	**Rambunny and Aqua** 276-783-3754 Shuttles and referrals for other help.			
	🚗	**Skip Skip** 276-783-3604 by appointment only. Will know of accesses to trail from the 2016 fire damage, water levels and weather. Covers From Damascus to Pearisburg.			
	🛏🖥☕✉	(3.7W) **Comfort Inn** 276-783-2144 $79 and up. Sometimes there is a discount book coupon at Exxon or ask for hiker rate.			
545.3	▲⌒	**VA 683**, pass under **I-81** over pass.		2431	1645.6
545.7	⌒	Cross puncheon and bridge over Dry Run.		2433	1645.2
546.0	○	**Davis Fancy** historical marker. Path to east leads 100 yards to Davis cemetery.		2451	1644.9

NoBo	Features	Description	GPS	Elev	SoBo
546.1	▲P(3)	Cross **VA. 617**, Davis Valley Road	N 36 53.842, W 81 22.152	2580	1644.8
546.8	♦Y	Water, year round spring is located 300 yards east, blue blaze		2610	1644.1
547.9	⋏ ☾	Davis Path campsite, no water		2840	1643.0
549.6	▲	South Ridgecrest of Little Brushy Mountain, limited views.		3300	1641.3
551.8	♦⋏	Reed Creek in Crawfish Valley on east side of trail. Good campsites.		2600	1639.1
551.9	Y	Intersection with Crawfish Trail (Channel Rock), marked with orange diamonds.		2622	1639.0
553.7	▲	Tilson Gap, Big Walker Mountain, wooded crest.		3500	1637.2
555.2	▲P ★★★★★	Cross **VA. 610**, Old Rich Valley Road.		2700	1635.7

⌂⋏ ◈⌂ (0.8W) **Quarter Way Inn** 276-522-4603. tina@quarterwayinn.com (www.quarterwayinn.com)
🏠🍴P AT Passport location.
No dogs. Open April 1 – June 30. Renovated 1910 farmhouse in idyllic setting, run by 2009 thru-hiker Tina (Chunky) and husband, Brett.
$30pp for indoor bunkroom with comfy mattress, pillow, shower, towel, laundry, loaner clothes, & morning coffee. $45S $75D private room; $18pp tenting, includes same. Gourmet breakfast available for $12 when 3 or more request it – includes honey and apple butter from our bees and trees. Resupply (canister, gas, and alcohol fuel; Mountain House; pasta sides; snacks; oatmeal; etc.), pizza, pop & ice cream. Guests can enjoy extensive VHS collection, free phone calls, a cuddly cat, and hammock chairs hanging from a majestic Sycamore tree. Slackpacking from Marion/Partnership shelter and Atkins often available – call in advance. Parking $3/day. Credit cards accepted. ID required. NOBOs turn left, SOBOs turn right at VA 610.

556.7	♦〰▲	**VA. 742**, Shady Grove Road, North Fork of Holston River, bridge		2460	1634.2
557.1	♦	Blue blaze trail 25 yards downhill to reliable spring.		2550	1633.8
557.7	▲P(10) ★★★★★	Cross **VA. 42**. O'Lystery Pavilion **(private, do not use)**. See map of VA 42.	N 36 58.998, W 81 24.384	2650	1633.2

⌂ (2.5W) **Appalachian Dreamer Hiker Hostel** 276-682-4061 (www.appalachiandreamerhikerhostel.
◈◈⚲⌂ com)
🏠⊕🍴🚗 AT Passport location.
P🖥 Open April thru October.
No pets or animals of any kind allowed.
May accept guest at other times with advanced reservations call for availability. $20.00 donation requested for stay, cash only (last ATM heading North is at Shell Station in Atkins or if heading South, the trail crossing of HWY 52 at Bland VA. Space for 8 hikers, 2 full baths for hikers, large screened in porch, full kitchen for hikers where meals are served and hikers can prepare meals. Laundry facilities, WiFi, land line phone, towels, bath cloths and pillow case furnished. Photo I.D. required, max. 2 night stay must sign hold harmless hiker agreement and accept rules which we have in place. Visit web site for rules and more info. We are Christians and promote Christian Values. Complimentary meals, short term resupply, fuel, (shuttle service when availably for slack packing). No cell service from trail crossing of Hwy 42 or Va. 610. Call for pickup from top of Walker Mt. if heading north or from Chestnut Ridge if heading south. Will pick up from either Hwy 42 or Va. 610. Photo I.D. required, max. 2 night stay must sign hold harmless hiker agreement and accept rules which we have in place. Visit web site for rules and more info. We are Christians and promote Christian Values. Complimentary meals, short term resupply, (shuttle service when availably for slack packing). Ask about parking. **Located:** at, 502 Dotson Ridge Rd. Ceres, VA. 24318. It is located west of where trail crosses VA 42 and also west of where trail crosses Old Rich Valley Rd.
Mail drops: 502 Dotson Ridge Rd. Ceres, VA. 24318.

VA 42

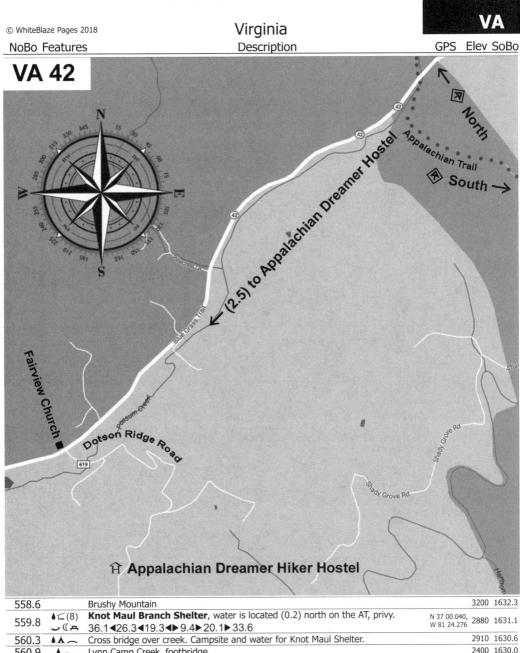

Fairview Church

Dotson Ridge Road

619

possum Creek

Blue Grass Trail

Pine Creek Trail

(2.5) to Appalachian Dreamer Hostel

42

42

42

Appalachian Trail

North

South →

Shady Grove Rd

Shady Grove Rd

⌂ **Appalachian Dreamer Hiker Hostel**

558.6		Brushy Mountain		3200 1632.3
559.8	♦⌐(8) ⌣((⚲	**Knot Maul Branch Shelter**, water is located (0.2) north on the AT, privy. 36.1◀26.3◀19.3◀▶9.4▶20.1▶33.6	N 37 00.040, W 81 24.276	2880 1631.1
560.3	♦▲⌐	Cross bridge over creek. Campsite and water for Knot Maul Shelter.		2910 1630.6
560.9	♦⌐	Lynn Camp Creek, footbridge		2400 1630.0
562.0		Lynn Camp Mountain		3000 1628.9
563.2	♦⌐▲⌣	Lick Creek, footbridge. Good campsites in the area.		2300 1627.7
564.4	♦	Cross creek.		2311 1626.5
564.6	▲P(4)	Cross **USFS 222, VA. 625**, gravel	N 37 01.372, W 81 25.559	2300 1626.3
567.4	♦	Spring-fed pond, water for Chestnut Knob Shelter		3800 1623.5
568.5		Chestnut Ridge		3700 1622.4
569.2	⌐(8)((⚲	**Chestnut Knob Shelter**, no water at shelter but is sometimes found (0.2) south on the AT and then 50 yards east on an old Jeep road, privy. 35.7◀28.7◀9.4◀▶10.7▶24.2▶33.9 Burkes Garden Overlook	N 37 03.468, W 81 23.969	4409 1621.7

NoBo	Features	Description	GPS	Elev	SoBo
570.6	♦⚑P(5)	Walker Gap, water for Chestnut Knob Shelter is located on blue blaze trail along dirt road 130 yards to spring.	N 37 03.288, W 81 22.672	3520	1620.3
557.7	♦	Water (spring) is located (0.2) east		3570	1633.2
575.3	📷	Cliffs on west side of trail.		3948	1615.6
575.4	⚑P(6)	Cross **VA. 623, Burkes Garden Road**, Garden Mountain	N 37 04.623, W 81 18.424	3880	1615.5
576.4	Y♦⚑(2)	Blue blaze trail leads (0.4) west to Davis Farm campsite with seasonal spring in fenced area 165 yards further down the trail.		3850	1614.5
579.0	♦	Water (stream), unreliable		3700	1611.9
579.9	♦Y⚑ ⊑(6) ⌇⚑	80 yards west to **Jenkins Shelter**, water (stream) is located 100 yards north on blue blazed trail, tenting, privy. 39.4◄20.1◄10.7◄► 13.5►23.2►37.7	N 37 05.603, W 81 14.868	2470	1611.0
580.0	♦	Hunter Camp Creek		2388	1610.9
581.2		Brushy Mountain		3080	1609.7
584.3	♦⌇⚑⌇ ⚑P(20)	Cross **VA. 615, Suiter Road**, Laurel Creek on footbridge, **treat water**. Two parking options.	N 37 06.177, W 81 12.133 N 37 06.605, W 81 12.360	2450	1606.6
586.3	Y	Trail junction with Trail Boss Trail.		3095	1604.6
589.2	⚓	Pass under telephone line.		2737	1601.7
590.7	Y⚑P(3) ★★★★★	Trail intersects with **USFS 282**.	N 37 08.308, W 81 08.141	3086	1600.2
590.9	⚓	Power line.		3028	1600.0
591.2	⚑ P(10) ★★★★★	Intersects with **U.S. 52**.		2920	1599.7

Bland, VA (2.5E). See map of Bland.

✉	**PO** M-F 8:30am-11:30am & 12pm-4pm, Sa 9am-11am, 276-688-3751.
🛏🍴💲	**Big Walker Motel** 276-688-3331 $64.33(1-2), $69(3-4), pets okay. Fridge and microwave. Mail drops for guests only: (UPS) 70 Skyview Lane, Bland VA 24315, (USPS) PO Box 155, Bland VA 24315.
✗	**Subway, Dairy Queen**
🛒	**Grants Supermarket** 276-688-0314 (www.shopatgrants.com) M-Sa8am-8pm, Su 10am-7pm.
🏪✗🍴☎	**Citgo, Bland Square Grill** 276-688-3851. Open year round, M-Su 6:30am-7pm. Groceries, Canister fuel and Heet, Grill serves Breakfast, lunch and dinner, payphone, ATM.
🏪	**Dollar General** Open M-Su 8am-10pm.
⚕	**Bland Family Clinic** 276-688-0500. M 10am-6pm, Tu 11am-7pm, W closed, Th 9am-5pm, F 10am-2pm, Sa-Su closed. Call ahead because they sometimes close early.
💻🖥	**Bland County Library** 276-688-3737. M 10am-4:30pm, 10am-7:30pm, W 10am-4:30pm, Th 10am-7:30pm, F-Sa 10am-7:30pm, Su closed. Located at 697 Main Street. Computers available for use, free WiFi.
🚗	**Bubba's Shuttles** 276-730-5869. barnes.james43@yahoo.com Shuttles from Damascus to Pearisburg and Roanoke Airport.

Bastian, VA 24314 (3.0W)					

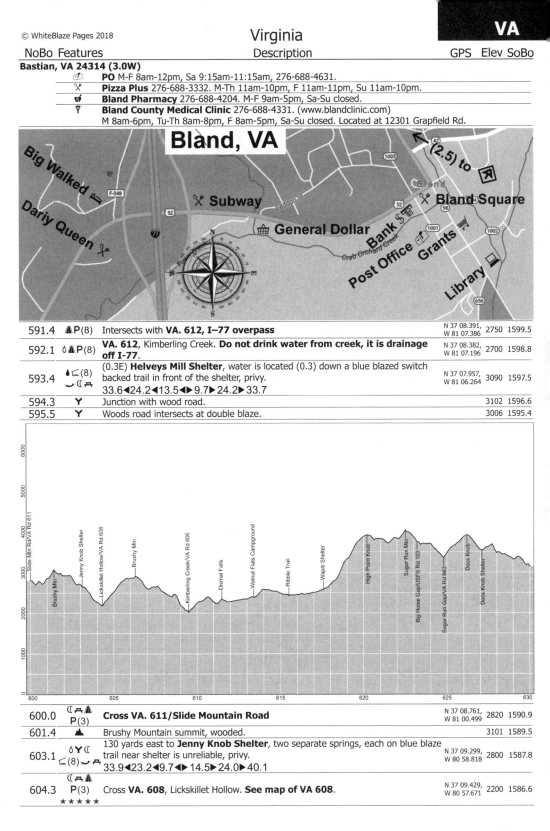

	📪	**PO** M-F 8am-12pm, Sa 9:15am-11:15am, 276-688-4631.			
	✕	**Pizza Plus** 276-688-3332. M-Th 11am-10pm, F 11am-11pm, Su 11am-10pm.			
	⚕	**Bland Pharmacy** 276-688-4204. M-F 9am-5pm, Sa-Su closed.			
	⚕	**Bland County Medical Clinic** 276-688-4331. (www.blandclinic.com) M 8am-6pm, Tu-Th 8am-8pm, F 8am-5pm, Sa-Su closed. Located at 12301 Grapfield Rd.			

591.4	⛰P(8)	Intersects with **VA. 612, I–77 overpass**	N 37 08.391, W 81 07.386	2750	1599.5
592.1	⬦⛰P(8)	**VA. 612**, Kimberling Creek. **Do not drink water from creek, it is drainage off I-77.**	N 37 08.382, W 81 07.196	2700	1598.8
593.4	⬦⌐(8) ⌣((🚻	(0.3E) **Helveys Mill Shelter**, water is located (0.3) down a blue blazed switch backed trail in front of the shelter, privy. 33.6◄24.2◄13.5◄► 9.7►24.2►33.7	N 37 07.957, W 81 06.264	3090	1597.5
594.3	Y	Junction with wood road.		3102	1596.6
595.5	Y	Woods road intersects at double blaze.		3006	1595.4

600.0	((🚻⛰ P(3)	**Cross VA. 611/Slide Mountain Road**	N 37 08.761, W 81 00.499	2820	1590.9
601.4	⛰	Brushy Mountain summit, wooded.		3101	1589.5
603.1	⬦Y((⌐(8)⌣🚻	130 yards east to **Jenny Knob Shelter**, two separate springs, each on blue blaze trail near shelter is unreliable, privy. 33.9◄23.2◄9.7◄► 14.5►24.0►40.1	N 37 09.299, W 80 58.818	2800	1587.8
604.3	((🚻⛰ P(3) ★★★★★	Cross **VA. 608**, Lickskillet Hollow. **See map of VA 608.**	N 37 09.429, W 80 57.671	2200	1586.6

命 ⊛ 🛢 🖳   (0.8E) **Lickskillet Hostel** 276-779-5447.

Open 01 March. Donations accepted, laundry, TV with dvd collection, pool table, slackpacking available. Limited kitchen, fridge, microwave, hotplate. Pets OK.
Mail drops for guest only: 35 Price Ridge Rd Bland, VA 24315

VA 608

604.5	◊	Stream, unreliable.		2733	1586.4
605.5	⊤	Power line.		2739	1585.4
607.7	▲	Brushy Mountain, crest.		2800	1583.2
609.5	◊〜Å	Kimberling Creek, suspension bridge		2090	1581.4
609.6	▲P(4) ★★★★★	Cross **VA. 606**	N 37 10.542, W 80 54.498	2040	1581.3
	Å⌂✕ ◈ 🛢🛆🚗 🖳	(0.5W) **Trent's Grocery** 276-928-1349. AT Passport location. Open year round. M-Sa 7am-8pm, Sun 9am-8pm. Deli with pizza, hamburgers, hot dogs and more. Camping $6, shower $3, laundry $3. Coleman and alcohol by the ounce and canister fuel. Soda machines outside. Accepts Credit Cards. Shuttles. Mail drops: 900 Wilderness Rd, Bland, VA 24315.			
	🚗	**Larry Richardson** 540-921-4724. Shuttle range Bland to Pearisburg.			
611.5	◊Y♨	Dismal Creek Falls Trail, waterfalls located (0.3) west, camping on side trail		2320	1579.4
612.6	〜	Cross bridge over deep gully.		2387	1578.3
613.4	Y〜Å	Side trail leads (0.4) west to Walnut Flats campground.		2400	1577.5
615.4	▲P(4)	Cross **Lion's Den Road**, gated forest service road.	N 37 12.774, W 80 51.389	2519	1575.5
615.5	YÅ	Ribble Trail south junction, trail leads (0.5) west to USFS White Cedar Horse campground		2400	1575.4
615.8	◊〜	Water (stream), bridge.		2500	1575.1
616.8	▲	Intersects with woods road.		2493	1574.1
617.6	◊Y⊑(6) 〜⟨⟨	100 yards east to **Wapiti Shelter**, water (Dismal Creek) just south of the turn off to the shelter, privy. 37.7◀24.2◀14.5◀▶9.5▶25.6▶38.2	N 37 13.436, W 80 49.446	2600	1573.3
617.7	Y	Unmarked trail leads (0.1) to Wapiti Shelter		2662	1573.2

NoBo	Features	Description	GPS	Elev	SoBo
618.2	⬧	Upper branch of Dismal Creek.		2656	1572.7
619.0	Y	Intersects with woods road.		3417	1571.9
620.2	▲ 🗻	Sugar Run Mountain, rocky outcropping		3800	1570.7
623.1	⬧Y	Junction with blue blazed Ribble Trail north junction		3800	1567.8
623.2	⚑P(4)	Cross **USFS 103**, Big Horse Gap	N 37 14.521, W 80 51.835	3752	1567.7
624.4	⚑	Cross **Nobusiness Creek Road**.		3711	1566.5
624.8	⚑P(6) ★★★★★	Cross **VA. 663, Sugar Run Gap Road**, Sugar Run Gap. **See map of VA 663/** **Sugar Run Gap Rd.**	N 37 15.353, W 80 51.328	3450	1566.1

🛏🏠⛺◈ (0.5E) **Woods Hole Hostel & Mountain B&B**
🍴🏪♿△ 540-921-3444. woodsholehostel@gmail.com (www.woodsholehostel.com)
🖥🚗🚌✉ AT Passport location.
Opened in 1986 by Roy & Tillie Wood. Granddaughter, Neville, continues the legacy with husband Michael. Organic farming, gardening, pottery, yoga (free), & massage therapy.
Directions: Turn East at Sugar Run Gap/Dirt Road. Take a left at fork on gravel road to Hostel. Bunkhouse $20/person: Wood Stove, mattresses, electricity, and hot shower. Camping $12/person. Open Seasonal. Pet friendly. Indoor rooms: $30/person shared/$60private (thru-hiker rate). Guests often invited to share local organic communal meals. Dinner $14, breakfast $8. Computer access, laundry, smoothies, cheese, home roast coffee, baked goods . Coleman and alcohol by the ounce, fuel canisters. Shuttles and Slack Pack for fee. Credit or cash (discount).
Please call or email to inquire about available services.
Mail drops for guests only/or $5 fee: Woods Hole Hostel, 3696 Sugar Run Rd, Pearisburg, VA 24134.

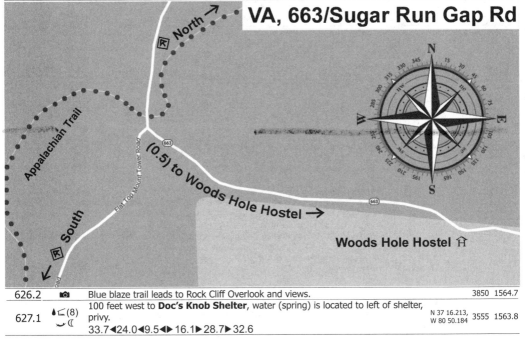

VA, 663/Sugar Run Gap Rd

| 626.2 | 🗻 | Blue blaze trail leads to Rock Cliff Overlook and views. | | 3850 | 1564.7 |
| 627.1 | ⬧⌂(8) ☕☽ | 100 feet west to **Doc's Knob Shelter**, water (spring) is located to left of shelter, privy. 33.7◀24.0◀9.5◀▶16.1▶28.7▶32.6 | N 37 16.213, W 80 50.184 | 3555 | 1563.8 |

NoBo	Features	Description	GPS	Elev	SoBo
630.7	⍽	Power line.		3225	1560.2
632.8	📷	Near the summit of Pearis Mountain, pass rock ledges with panoramic views.		3770	1558.1
633.0	♦⚑	Campsite, water (spring)		3750	1557.9
633.5	Y📷	Blue blaze to Angels Rest on north end of Pearis Mountain, vista		3555	1557.4
634.5	⍽	Power line.		3438	1556.4
634.9	♦	Water (spring)		2300	1556.0
635.5	⚠	Cross **VA. 634**, Cross Ave.		2200	1555.4
635.9	⚠	Intersects with **Lane Street to US. 460**		1650	1555.0

Pearisburg, VA (0.9E) (all major services). See map of Pearisburg.

⌂   **PO** M-F 9am-4:30pm, Sa 10am-12pm, 540-921-1100.

⌂🛏⚑⤳ **Angels Rest Hiker's Haven** 540-787-4076, Cell: 540-922-2178. Your host Doc Peppa. (www.angelsre-
◈⚐🐾🚐 sthikershaven.com)
💻   AT Passport location.
$12-$45 pp a night. Tenting, Hammocking, Bunks and Private Rooms available. Laundry $4, Day Passes
$7 (includes laundry, shower, and use of the many amenities until 6pm, then upgrade to a stay if you
can't tear yourself away). Courtesy shuttle to and from local trail head.
Local Shuttles $2-$4. Slack Packing Packages Available. Chiropractic and Acupuncture Services Available
by appt. Well behaved canines $5 for entire stay. Some limited WiFi available.
Mail drops: 204 Douglas Ln. Pearisburg, VA 24134.

⌂🛏◈ **Holiday Motor Lodge** 540-921-1552.
⚐🐾🍴💻 AT Passport location.
Open year round.
Lodging; Limited economy rooms $40, no reservations (first come first serve). Standard rooms $50,
$10 for each addition person after 2, $10 pet fee, microwave, fridge, TV.
Bunkroom; open May 15 thru Aug 30, weather permitting.
$20 per bed, limited spave, no reservations (first come first serve), pets free, shower, microwave, fridge,
TV, coin laundry. Pet friendly. Coffee in office. Pool. Free WiFi. ATM.
Mail drops: 401 N Main St, Pearisburg, VA 24134.

🛏◈⚐ **Plaza Motel** 540-921-2591 $44S $55D includes tax, no pets, accepts credit cards. Laundry, computer
💻🍴💻 available to use, free WiFi.
Mail drops: 415 N. Main St, Pearisburg, VA 24134.

⌂🛏◈⚑🐾 **Holy Family Hostel** Pat Muldoon 540-626-3337.
Open Mar-Nov. No Pets, drugs or alcohol allowed. Volunteer caretaker on hand please don't call for a
ride, no pickup. Donations are requested, suggested $10PP, 2 night max. Hot shower, bath room, elec-
tric stove, micro-wave, fridge, pots ,pans & dishes. Clean Towels provided. Bed mats, tables & benches,
library, tents allowed on grounds. Wood Stove for heating. Keep hostel clean and neat. Coed sleeping
area.

🛒   **Food Lion** M-Su 7am-11pm. **Walmart** M-Su 24 hours. **Grant's** M-Su 8am-9pm.

🏪◈🚐 **Pearis Mercantile** 540-921-2260. M-Sa 10am-5:30pm. Has a small selection of hiker food, small gear
items, fuel.

⚐   **EZ Way Laundry** M-Sa 6am-9pm, Su 6am-8pm.

🍴   **Dairy Queen, Pizza Hut, Wendys, La Barranca Mex. Grill, Lucky Star Chinese** (AYCE).

Virginia

NoBo Features	Description	GPS Elev SoBo

The Hardware Store 540-921-1456. (www.harveystreethardwareandelectronics.com) M-F 9am-5pm, Sa 9am-4pm, Su closed. Canister fuel, alcohol by the ounce, tent repair kits.

Pearisburg Library 540-921-2556. M 12pm-8pm, T 12pm-5pm, W 9am-5pm, TH 9am-8pm, F 9am-5pm, Sa 9am-1pm, Su closed.

Community Health Center 540-921-3502. M-F 8am-4:30pm, Sa-Su closed. Located at 219 South Buchanan Street Quick, low cost healthcare, hikers welcome.

Don Raines 540-921-7433 ratface20724@aol.com Anytime, anywhere. Slackpacking available.

Tom Hoffman 540-921-1184. gopullman@aol.com. Mid-range shuttles centered in Pearisburg area.

Narrows, VA (3.6W on VA 100)

PO MF 9:30am-1:15pm & 2pm-4: 15pm, Sa 9am-11am , 540-726-3272.

MacArthur Inn 540-726-7510. (www.macarthur-inn.com)

AT Passport location.

Hiker room $45 includes two doubles with hall bath. Price goes up with different accommodations. Free long distance phone, cable TV, WiFi and use of guest kitchen. Shower without stay $8. On site restaurant serves breakfast is served Fri.-Sun. 7-11 a.m.; dinner is served Thurs. 5-8 p.m. with Old Time Mountain Music Jam. AT gear shop with dried foods, socks, small gear items, bike rentals and brewery. Located in center of town with all major services, restaurants, laundry all within close walking distance. All within close walking distance. Call for ride from Pearisburg area trail heads, ride $5 round trip. Longer shuttles and slack-packing can be arranged.
Mail drops; 117 MacArthur Lane, Narrows, VA 24124.

Camp Success Camping (www.townofnarrows.org) Primitive camping- tents or hammokcs only. $5 tenting per night, no showers. Checkin at Town Office 540-726-3020 M-F 9 am-5 pm. Discount of $20 for 5 days (1 tent). They do have an outhouse and a slop-sink. Call ahead for after-hours arrivals or print permit form . 37°20'4.83"N 80°48'42.68"W

Grants Supermarket 540-726-2303 M–Sa 8am–8pm, Sun 9am–8pm.

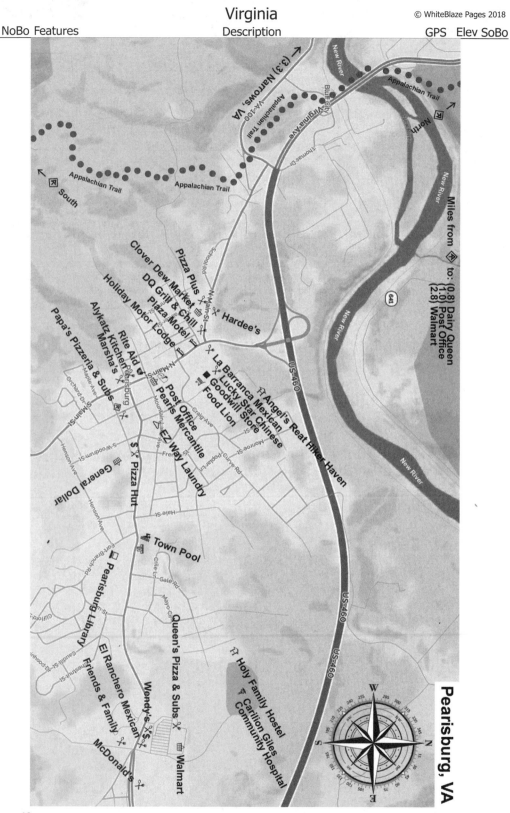

Pearisburg, VA

Current corrections to 2018 WhiteBlaze Pages

Page 33 - Add, Davenport Gap, TN map left out of book. See image below.

Page 50 - Closed, mile 430.0. Watuaga Lake Shlter is being removed.
Keep in mind the next three shelters mileage (north/soouth) reference points prior to and after this point will not be accurate, in the descriptions.

Page 52 - UPDATE "The Place" new phone number is 276-206-0440.

Page 59 - NEW OWNERSHIP - "The Barn Restaurant". Mon-closed, Tu-Sa 6am-8pm, Su 11am-3pm.

Page 66 - REMOVE. Remove the entire mileage line 635.9. This was overlooked and hould have been removed.

Page 71 - Changed, mile 668.0 should be 700.9.

Page 112 - Change, mile 1135.0 should be 1147.4.

Page 112 - Change, mile 1147.2 should be 1147.5.

Page 117 - Rock 'n Sole Hostel is now CLOSED.

Page 141 - Change, mile 1423.1 the second mention of this mileage, should delete the while line (Intersects with NY. 301 (north side).

Page 141 - Change, mile 1423.2 should change (south side) to (north side).

Page 146 - Closed, Backcoutry Outfitter closed December 2018.

Page 185 - Change, second mention of mile 1853.5 should be1854.7.

Page 157 - Closed, Lee, MA. Price Chooper Supermarket is now Closed.

Insert Davenport Gap map into page 33.

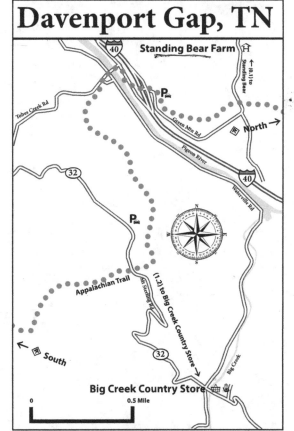

Current corrections to 2018 WhiteBlaze Pages

Insert Rutland, VT maps into page 171.

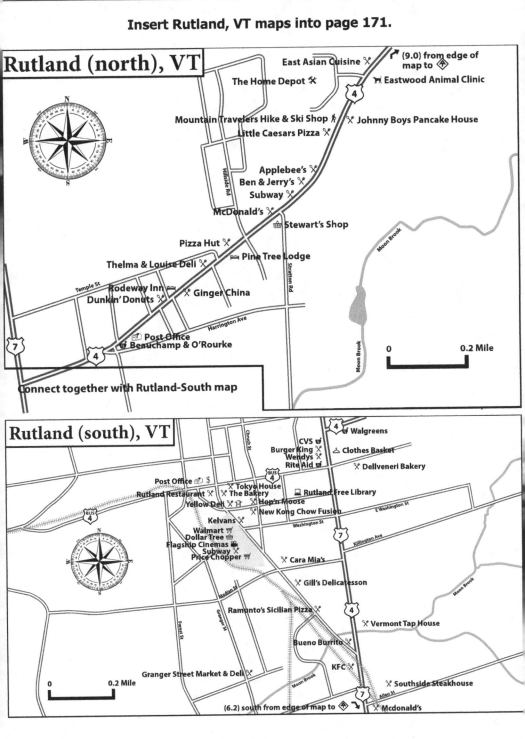

Rutland (north), VT

East Asian Cuisine ✗

(9.0) from edge of map to 🏠

The Home Depot ✗

🐾 Eastwood Animal Clinic

Mountain Travelers Hike & Ski Shop 🏃

✗ Johnny Boys Pancake House

Little Caesars Pizza ✗

Applebee's ✗
Ben & Jerry's ✗
Subway ✗

McDonald's ✗

🏛 Stewart's Shop

Pizza Hut ✗

🛏 Pine Tree Lodge

Thelma & Louise Deli ✗

Temple St

Rodeway Inn 🛏
Dunkin' Donuts ✗

✗ Ginger China

Hillside Rd

Stratton Rd

Moon Brook

Harrington Ave

📮 Post Office
♿ Beauchamp & O'Rourke

Moon Brook

0   0.2 Mile

Connect together with Rutland-South map

Rutland (south), VT

4 🅿 Walgreens

Church St

CVS 🅿
Burger King ✗
Wendys ✗
Rite Aid 🅿

⚕ Clothes Basket

✗ Delivneri Bakery

Post Office 📮 $
Rutland Restaurant ✗
Yellow Deli ✗

✗ Tokyo House
✗ The Bakery

🖥 Rutland Free Library

Hop'n Moose
New Kong Chow Fusion

E Washington St

Kelvans ✗

Washington St

Walmart 🛒
Dollar Tree 🛒
Flagship Cinemas 🎬
Subway 🛒
Price Chopper 🛒

7

Killington Ave

✗ Cara Mia's

Moon Brook

Madison St

✗ Gill's Delicatesson

Granger St

Forest St

Ramunto's Sicilian Pizza ✗

4

✗ Vermont Tap House

Bueno Burrito ✗

KFC ✗

Granger Street Market & Deli ✗

0   0.2 Mile

Moon Brook

✗ Southside Steakhouse

7 Allen St

(6.2) south from edge of map to 🏠

✗ Mcdonald's

Insert Rutland, VT maps into page 171.

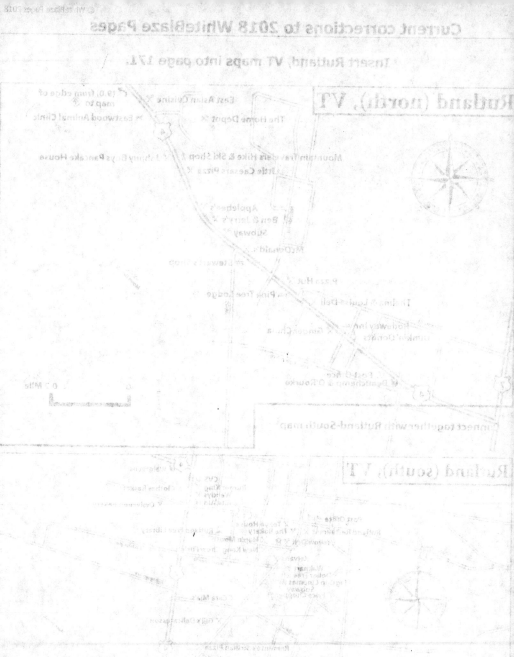

Rutland (north), VT

Rutland (south), VT

NoBo	Features	Description	GPS	Elev	SoBo
636.5	Y⚑P(8)	Intersects with **Narrows Road, VA. 100**, Side trail leads (0.2) west to parking.	N 37 20.064, W 80 45.372	1617	1554.4
636.9	⌒⚑	Intersects with **U.S. 460**, Cross Senator Shumate Bridge (east shore) over New River.		1600	1554.0
640.3		Hemlock Ridge		2470	1550.6
640.8	⚑P(4)	Intersects with **VA. 641, Clendennin Road**	N 37 21.880, W 80 44.983	2220	1550.1
640.9	⚑	**Pocahontas Road**, re-enter woods		2230	1550.0
641.9	⬥	Stream		2230	1549.0
643.0	⬥⚑	Water (springs)		3200	1547.9
643.2	⬥Y⊏(8)☾	(0.3E) **Rice Field Shelter**, water is located on a steep downhill trail (0.3) behind and to the left of the shelter that is not always reliable, privy. 40.1◀25.6◀16.1◀▶12.6▶16.5▶25.3	N 37 22.487, W 80 45.516	3400	1547.7
644.8	⬥⚑	Campsite, water (spring)		3450	1546.1
648.3	⬥⚑	**Symms Gap Meadow**. A mountain meadow with views into West Virginia. This is a small pond downhill from the AT with spots for camping nearby.		2480	1542.6
649.3	Y	Blue blazed Groundhog Trail		3400	1541.6
650.9		Dickerson Gap		3300	1540.0
653.1	▲▲	Peters Mountain Ridgecrest		3860	1537.8
653.3	Y	Yellow blazed Allegheny Trail Junction west		3740	1537.6
655.8	⬥⊏(6)⌣☾🍴	**Pine Swamp Branch Shelter**, water (stream) is located 75 yards down a blue blazed trail on the west of the side trail to the shelter, privy. 38.2◀28.7◀12.6◀▶3.9▶12.7▶18.5	N 37 25.325, W 80 36.528	2530	1535.1
656.1	⚑P(6)	Blue blazed trail leads east to **VA. 635**, Stony Creek Valley, USFS parking area (1.0E)	N 37 25.119, W 80 36.276	2370	1534.8
656.2	⬥	Cross Pine Swamp Branch.			1534.7
656.6	⬥	Cross Stony Creek tributary.			1534.3
657.2	⬥⌒⚑ ★★★★★	Cross Dismal Branch on bridge.		2480	1533.7
		~~Captain's~~ AT Passport location. 30 yards east of trail, use zip line to cross the creek. 4464 Big Stony Creek Rd. Camping, this is not a hostel; do not enter the house. You may camp even when no one is home. Dogs bark but they are friendly and are contained by an invisible electric fence. If it rains, you may stay on back porch. **No mail drop accepted here.**			
657.3	⚑	Intersects with old road.			1533.6
658.2	⚑P(15)	Cross **VA. 635** (paved), Stony Creek	N 37 24.860, W 80 35.000	2450	1532.7
658.3	⚑	Cross woods road.			1532.6
659.3	⚑	Cross **VA 734**, gravel fire road.			1531.6
659.5	⬥	Blue blazed side trail leads 125 yards east to water (spring)		3490	1531.4
659.7	⬥⊏(6)⌣☾🍴	**Bailey Gap Shelter**, water is located (0.2) south on the AT and then east down a blue blazed trail, privy. 32.6◀16.5◀3.9◀▶8.8▶14.6▶21.0	N 37 24.052, W 80 34.632	3525	1531.2

NoBo	Features	Description	GPS	Elev	SoBo
662.3		Rock ledge west of trail.			1528.6
663.4	▲P(14)	Cross **VA. 613** (gravel), Mountain Lake Road, Salt Sulphur Turnpike	N 37 24.719, W 80 31.360	3950	1527.5
663.6	Y▣	Wind Rock is located 100 feet west on side trail, vista		4121	1527.3
664.5	▲Y	Cross old woods road, Side trail Potts Mountain Trail is 100 feet north on trail.			1526.4
664.8	♦▲	Campsite, water (spring) located north of open area.		4000	1526.1
665.3	Y	Junction of old trail leading 150 yards west to Potts Mountain Trail.			1525.6
666.0		West side of Pine Peak.		4054	1524.9
666.5	Y	Junction with connector trail that leads to War Spur Trail to the east.			1524.4
666.8	♦	Water on east side of trail, rock field on west side.			1524.1
667.0	◊	Seasonal spring west on trail.			1523.9
668.5	♦⊏(6) ⌣⟨⛺	**War Spur Shelter**, water (stream) is located 80 yards north of the shelter on the AT, privy. 25.3◀12.7◀8.8◀▶5.8▶12.2▶18.2	N 37 23.852, W 80 28.440	2340	1522.4
669.3	♦▲P(6)	Cross **USFS 156**, Johns Creek Valley	N 37 23.280, W 80 28.135	2102	1521.6
670.3	◊	Water (stream), seasonal		2700	1520.6
671.3	▲P(3)	Cross **VA. 601**, gravel road, Rocky Gap		3250	1519.6
671.8	Y	Intersection with Johns Creel Mountain Trail east side.		3757	1519.1
672.9	Y	Unmarked trail west.		3779	1518.0
673.1	Y	Blue blaze trail leads 100 yards east to White Rock.		3809	1517.8
673.4		Kelly Knob.		3735	1517.5
674.3	♦Y⊏(6) ⟨⛺	Blue blaze trail 100 feet to **Laurel Creek Shelter**, water is located to the west on the AT and 45 yards south of the shelter trail junction, privy. 31.1◀14.6◀5.8◀▶6.4▶12.4▶22.5	N 37 21.535, W 80 25.272	2720	1516.6
675.3	♦	Water (spring), seasonal		2400	1515.6
676.7	▲ ★★★★★	Cross **VA. 42**, Sinking Creek Valley		2200	1514.2

Newport, VA 24128 (8E) No much located here.

	⊠	**PO** M-F 8:15am-11:30am & 12:30pm-3:15pm, Sa 9am-11pm, 540-544-7415.			
	⛒	**Super Val-U** 540-544-7702. M-Th 6am-10pm, F-Sa 6am-10:30pm, Su 6am-10pm.			
677.2	▣	Top of hill with views.		2354	1513.7
677.6	♦▲P (5)	Cross **VA. 630**, Sinking Creek	N 37 21.093, W 80 22.752	2100	1513.3
677.7	♦⌐	Cross stream over footbridge.		2183	1513.2
678.1	●	**Keffer Oak**, this is the largest oak tree on the AT in the south		2240	1512.8
678.4	⟙	Power line.		3232	1512.5
679.1	▲	Sinking Creek Mountain (south)		3200	1511.8
680.7	♦Y⊏(6) ⟨⛺	(0.4E) **Sarver Hollow Shelter**, water (spring) is located on a blue blazed trail near the shelter, privy. 21.0◀12.2◀6.4◀▶6.0▶16.1▶29.7	N 37 21.286, W 80 20.245	3000	1510.2
683.1	▣	Walk along rock ledge with views east.		3364	1507.8
684.3	▲▣	Sinking Creek Mountain (north)		3490	1506.6
686.0	♦▲	Cross Cabin Branch		2490	1504.9
686.7	♦▲⊏(6) ⌣⟨⛺	**Niday Shelter**, water is located 75 yards down a blue blazed trail west of the AT, tenting, privy. 18.2◀12.4◀6.0◀▶10.1▶23.7▶24.7	N 37 23.249, W 80 15.864	1800	1504.2
687.3	♦	Cross small stream.		1689	1503.6
688.0	▲P(10)	Cross **VA. 621**, Craig Creek Valley	N 37 22.755, W 80 15.004	1560	1502.9
688.1	⟙	Power line.		1539	1502.8
688.3	♦	High bridge over Craig Creek.		1571	1502.6

			GPS	Elev	SoBo
691.2	Y▲ P(10)	Intersection with grassy wood road at top of Brushy Mountain. Follow grassy wood road to Audie Murphy Monument Parking (0.1E)	N 37 21.462, W 80 14.250	3100	1499.7
691.8	Y○	At intersection of woods road a Blue blaze trail leads 50 yards to **Audie Murphy Monument,** Murphy was most decorated American soldier of World War II. After the war, he starred in many Hollywood war movies and westerns. He died in a 1971 plane crash near this site. Monument on blue blazed trail to west.	N 37 21.871, W 80 13.544	3100	1499.1
692.6	Y	Intersects old road at ridge crest of Brushy Mountain.		1810	1498.3
693.9	📷	Pass vista as trail turns west.		1809	1497.0
694.0	📷	Brushy Mountain, vista on east side of trail.		2600	1496.9
695.6	♦▲P(5)	Cross **VA. 620**, Trout Creek, Miller Cove Road	N 37 23.393, W 80 11.780	1525	1495.3
696.0	⊤	Power line.		1738	1494.9
696.8	♦Y▲ ⌣(6) ⌣《🍴	(0.3E) **Pickle Branch Shelter**, water (stream) is located below the shelter, tenting along trail to shelter, privy. 22.5◄16.1◄10.1◄►13.6►14.6►17.0	N 37 23.286, W 80 11.466	1845	1494.1
699.4	📷	Pass Hemlock Point, a rocky outcrop with views 100 feet west.		2134	1491.5
688.0	▲	Cove Mountain Summit.		3005	1502.9
701.0	▲📷○	Crest of Cove Mountain, **Dragons Tooth**. Coordinates are to Dragons Tooth.	N 37 21.654, W 80 10.407	3020	1489.9
702.0	Y	Lost Spectacles Gap, Blue blazed trail to the west.		2550	1488.9
702.1	📷	Pass Devils Seat to east.		2346	1488.8
702.2	📷	Viewpoint Rock on the west side of trail.		2376	1488.7
702.5	📷	Rawies Rest, ridge narrows to knife-edge.		2350	1488.4
703.1	Y	Blue blazed Scout Trail with access to North Mountain Trail.		2102	1487.8
703.5	Y▲P(3) ★★★★★	Cross **VA. 624**, Newport Road, North Mountain Trail. Parking at Dragons Tooth Trail head on VA 311. **See map of Catawba, VA.**	N 37 22.778, W 80 09.355	1810	1487.4
	🏠◈ ⛺🖥🍴🚗 🖦	(0.3E) **Four Pines Hostel** Owner Joe Mitchell, cell: 540-309-8615. AT Passport location. Open year round. Hostel is a 3 bay garage with shower. Please leave a donation. Laundry $3 wash and $3 to dry. Pet friendly. Computer available, free Wifi. Shuttles to and from The Homeplace Restaurant (Th-Su) and to Catawba Grocery. Longer shuttles for a fee. Mail drops: 6164 Newport Rd. Catawba VA 24070.			
	🛒🍴	(0.4W) **Catawba Grocery** 540-384-8050. (0.3) west to VA 311 and then left (0.1) mile to store. Open M-Su 6am-10pm. Grill serves breakfast, pizza, burgers, ice cream.			

Catawba, VA

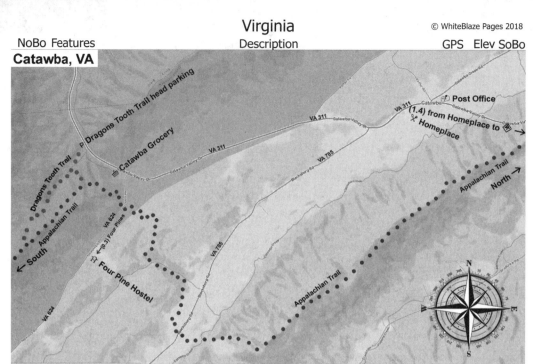

NoBo	Features	Description	GPS	Elev	SoBo
704.2	🅰	Intersects woods road.		1867	1486.7
704.4	🌢︎〜	Cross stream on bridge.		1833	1486.5
705.1	🅰	**Cross VA. 785, Blacksburg Road**		1790	1485.8
705.2	🌢︎〜	Bridge over Catawba Creek.		1762	1485.7
705.4	◊〜	Cross stream on bridge, unreliable.		1761	1485.5
709.1	Y📷	Side trail east to rock outcrops and views.		2121	1481.8
709.4	🅰P(20) ★★★★★	Cross **VA. 311, Catawba Valley Drive** **Catawba, VA. (1.0W) See map for Catawba, VA.**	N 37 22.811, W 80 05.371	1990	1481.5
	📪	(1.0W) **PO** M-F 9am-12pm & 1pm-4pm, Sa 8:30am-10:30am, 540-384-6011.			
	✗	(1.4W) **Homeplace Restaurant** 540-384-7252 Th-F 4pm-8pm, Sa 3pm-8pm, Su 11am-6pm. Closed mid Dec thru mid-Jan and two weeks over the 4th of July. AYCE family style meals including drink, $15 (two meats) $16 (three meats) $9 kids, all means include drink and tax.			
710.4	◊🅰⊏(6) ((🔥	**Johns Spring Shelter**, water (spring) in front of shelter is unreliable, privy, tenting. 29.7◄23.7◄13.6◄► 1.0► 3.4► 9.4	N 37 23.119, W 80 04.446	1980	1480.5
711.3	Y	Intersects old road.		2306	1479.6
711.4	◊Y🅰 ⊏(6) 〜((🔥	Blue blaze trail leads to **Catawba Mountain Shelter**, water (piped spring) is located 50 yards south on the AT, tenting to the north, privy. 24.7◄14.6◄1.0◄►2.4► 8.4► 22.8	N 37 23.292, W 80 03.444	2580	1479.5
711.5	🅰	Primitive campsite at turn in trail.		2261	1479.4
711.8	🅰	Dirt fire road.		2347	1479.1
712.3	🕇	Power line.		2448	1478.6
712.7	📷	Rock outcrop on west side of trail with views.		3192	1478.2
712.8	Y	Intersects old woods road.		2698	1478.1
713.0	Y📷	Side trail west leads to cliffs.		3171	1477.9
713.1	📷	Side trails lead to **McAfee Knob**, NO CAMPING. Coordinates are to McAfee Knob.	N 37 23.549, W 80 02.175	3199	1477.8
713.7	🌢🅰〜🔥	Pig Farm campsite, picnic tables. Blue blaze trail a few yards south on AT leads (0.1) east to large spring.		3000	1477.2
713.8	🌢Y🅰 ⊏(6) 〜((🔥	100 feet east to **Campbell Shelter**, water (spring) is located on a blue blazed trail to the left and behind the shelter and follow the trail through meadow, tenting, privy. 17.0► 3.4► 2.4◄► 6.0► 20.4► 26.6	N 37 23.447, W 80 01.770	2580	1477.1
715.2	🅰	Intersects old road.		2372	1475.7
716.9	Y	Brickey's Gap and a blue blazed trail.		2250	1474.0
718.7	📷	Tinker Cliffs, 1/2 mile cliff walk		3000	1472.2
719.2	Y	Scorched Earth Gap, Yellow blazed west to Andy Layne Trail.		2600	1471.7

NoBo	Features	Description	GPS	Elev	SoBo
719.8	◊♈⚠ ⌂(6)☽⚲	50 yards east to **Lamberts Meadow Shelter**, water is located 50 yards down the trail in front of the shelter, tenting, privy. 9.4◀8.4◀6.0◀▶14.4▶20.6▶27.9	N 37 26.074, W 79 59.268	2080	1471.1
719.9	◊⌒	Cross bridge over stream.		2077	1471.0

720.1	◊⚠⌇	Lamberts Meadow campsite, Sawmill Run, 100 yards north is a blue blazed trail.		2000	1470.8
723.5		Angels Gap		1800	1467.4
724.5	⟙	Power line.		2125	1466.4
725.2	📷	Hay Rock, Tinker Ridge. A climb to the top of Hay Rock provides some good views.		1900	1465.7
726.5	📷	Pass rock outcrop on east side of trail with view.		1951	1464.4
728.0	⟙	Power line.		1207	1462.9
728.4	⟙	Power line.		1167	1462.5
728.7	◊⌒	Cross Tinker Creek, Trail crosses gated concrete bridge.		1165	1462.2
729.2	⚠P(25) ★★★★★	Cross **U.S. 220**	N 37 23.461, W 79 54.380	1350	1461.7

	⌂	(0.7W) from AT on Hwy 11 to PO M-F 9am-12pm & 1pm-5pm, Sa 9am-11am, 540-992-1472.
	⚠⊛♰⚲ ⚐⊞	**Troutville Park and Fire Station**. Free camping at town park, no pets. Free laundry and showers at fire station.
	⇌⟐⚐ 🖥	**Howard Johnson Express** 540-992-1234. AT Passport location. ⊞⟘⊠ $49.95 hiker rate, continental breakfast microwave, fridge. Coin laundry. Pets $10. Game room and pool. Computer available, free WiFi. ATM in lobby. Mail drops for guest: 437 Roanoke Road, Daleville, VA 24083.
	⇌⊛⚐🖥 ⊞	**Super 8** 540-992-3000. No pets. $67.95 and up, includes continental breakfast, microwave, fridge. Laundry. Outdoor pool. Computer available for use, free WiFi. Accepts Credit Cards.
	⇌🖥⊞	**Comfort Inn** 540-992-5600. No smoking. Hiker rate $59.51 double bed, $10 each additional person up to four people, pets $25. Includes continental breakfast. Microwave, fridge, computer available, free WiFi. There is a $150 fine if caught smoking in the room. Outdoor pool is open Memorial Day thru Labor day. Credit card is required even if you pay in cash.
	⇌🖥⊞	**Quality Inn** 540-992-5335. $72 and up, king or 2 doubles (hikers rate). $25.00 pet fee nonrefundable. Includes free Full Hot Breakfast. Seasonal Pool Microwaves/refrigerators/coffee makers in each room, computer available for use, free WiFi. Free WiFi/HD TV/Fitness Center.
	⇌⊛⚐🖥 ⊞	**Holiday Inn Express** 540-966-4444 No pets. $109-129, includes continental breakfast. Coin laundry. Computer available for use, free WiFi. Mail drops for guests: 3200 Lee Hwy, Troutville, VA 24175.
	⇌⊞⊠	**Red Roof Inn** 540-992-5055. Hiker special Su-Th $49.99, $10 extra F-Sa, continental breakfast, coffee in lobby, microwave, fridge, coin laundry, free WiFi, pets stay for free. Mail drops: 3231 Lee Highway South Troutville, VA 24175
	⇌⚐⊞	**Motel 6** 540-992-6700. $59.99 and up $6EAP, microwave, fridge, pets stay for free.

🍴⚜ **Three Li'l Pigs Barbeque** 540-966-0165. (www.threelilpigsbbq.com)
AT Passport location.
Open year-round, extended summer hours. M-W 7 am-9 pm, Th 7 am-9:30 pm, F-Sa 7 am-10:30 pm, Su 7 am-9 pm.
Hiker friendly, "hand-chopped BBQ, ribs, wings, fresh-ground burgers and a good selection of beer, much of it locally-brewed." In addition, during peak season (mid-April-June), we offer free Banana Pudding to thru-hikers with a meal purchase.

🛒🍴 **Kroger Grocery Store and Pharmacy** 540-992-4920. M-Su 24 hours, pharmacy M-F 8am-9pm, Sa 9am-6pm, Su 12pm-6pm.

🚶⚜ **Outdoor Trails** 540-992-5850 (www.outdoortrails.com)
⛽☕🚗✉ AT Passport location.
Full service outfitter. May 1 -Jul 1, Open M-F 9 am-8 pm, Sat 9 am-6 pm. All other dates open M-F 10 am-8 pm, Sat 10 am-6 pm. White gas and denatured alcohol by the ounce, free WiFi, shuttle service. Mail drops, please address Outdoor Trails, Hold for AT Hiker, Your Realname: Botetourt Commons, 28 Kingston Dr, Daleville, VA 24083.

🚗 **Homer Witcher** 540-266-4849. Shuttles from Daleville to Front Royal or south to Damascus. Based in Daleville.

Daleville, VA 24083
📬 (1.1W) from AT on route 220 to **PO** M-F 8am-5pm, Sa 8am-12pm, 540-992-4422.

Daleville, VA   Troutville, VA

730.1	⌒	Cross bridge.		1346	1460.8
730.3	▲P	**U.S. 779, I-81 underpass**	N 37 24.282, W 79 53.772	1400	1460.6
730.5	⌒	Cross low bridge.		1378	1460.4
730.7	▲✕P(6)	Cross **U.S. 11**, Norfolk Southern Railway.	N 37 24.270, W 79 53.370	1300	1460.2
	★★★★★	**Troutville, VA. See note NOBO mile 729.2**			

NoBo	Features	Description	GPS	Elev	SoBo
731.2	⚠	Cross **VA. 652, Mountain Pass Road**		1450	1459.7
731.5	Y	Intersects old farm lane.		1484	1459.4
734.2	♦Y⚠ ⊑(6) ⌣((⛺	(0.1E) **Fullhardt Knob Shelter**, water is from cistern behind shelter. This is the last shelter on the AT that has a cistern. Tenting, privy. 22.8◄20.4◄14.4◄►6.2►13.5►20.0	N 37 23.908, W 79 51.234	2676	1456.7
735.1	⚠P(2)	Intersects Fullhardt Knob fire road.	N 37 24.204, W 79 50.381	2213	1455.8
737.0	⚠P(2)	Cross **USFS 191**, Salt Pond Road	N 37 25.014, W 79 49.146	2260	1453.9
737.8	♦	Cross Curry Creek		1680	1453.1
738.5	♦	Cross Wilson Creek		1690	1452.4
740.4	♦Y⚠ ⊑(6) ⌣((⛺	150 feet west to **Wilson Creek Shelter**, water (stream) is located 200 yards in front of the shelter, tenting, privy. 26.6◄20.6◄6.2◄►7.3►13.8►20.8►	N 37 25.156, W 79 47.142	1830	1450.5
740.8	◊	Unreliable spring		2050	1450.1
741.7	📷	Cross spur with views		1975	1449.2
742.5	📷	Narrow side trail with views.		1675	1448.4
742.8	Y⚠P	Trail east to USFS 186; **BRP MP 97.7** Old Fincastle Road, Black Horse Gap	N 37 25.497, W 79 45.436	2402	1448.1
743.6	⚠📷 P(12)	Cross **BRP MP 97.0** at Taylors Mountain Overlook	N 37 25.884, W 79 44.999	2350	1447.3
744.5	Y	Blue blazed Spec Mines Trail leads south to milepost 96.		2451	1446.4
744.7		Montvale Overlook; BRP MP 95.9		2400	1446.2
745.3	⚠📷🚻 P(20)	Cross Harveys Knob Overlook; **BRP MP 95.3**	N 37 26.714, W 79 43.597	2550	1445.6
746.9	Y	Blue blazed Hammond Hollow Trail west.		2335	1444.0
747.7	♦Y⊑(6)(	(0.2W) **Bobblets Gap Shelter**, water (spring) is located to the left of the shelter but frequently goes dry but look farther downstream if dry, privy. 27.9◄13.5◄7.3◄►6.5►13.5►18.4	N 37 28.032, W 79 42.084	1920	1443.2
748.4	⚠P	Cross Peaks of Otter Overlook; **BRP MP 92.5**	N 37 28.464, W 79 41.525	2350	1442.5
749.1	P(15)	Mills Gap Overlook; **BRP MP 91.8**, parking west.	N 37 28.773, W 79 40.931	2450	1441.8

| 750.8 | ⚠P(6) ★★★★★ | Intersects with **VA. 43** for (0.1), Bearwallow Gap; **BRP MP 90.9**. | N 37 28.976, W 79 40.133 | 2228 | 1440.1 |

🛏⚠✗🍴 (5.5E) **Peaks of Otter Lodge & Restaurant** 540-586-1081 (www.peaksofotter.com).
(0.1) east on to the Blue Ridge Parkway overpass, then follow BRP to the left (5.0).
Motel rooms $126 weekdays, $169 weekends, higher in fall. Restaurant is open for breakfast, lunch and dinner. Sunday buffet brunch 11:30 am-3:30 pm. Limited supplies in camp store. Off season operation Dec-Mar reduced to Th-Su and lower lodging pricing. Camping is managed separately, 540-586-7321, Open end of Apr - end of Oct, $16-19.

Buchanan, VA (downtown) (5.0W) see NOBO mile 756.3

📬 **PO** M & Th 9am-7pm; Tu, W, F 9am-5pm; Sa 9am-1pm, 540-254-2538.

✗⛟ **Rasones Fountain & Grille** 540-254-1800, Pharmacy 540-254-2904. located at 19771 Main St.

✗	**Burger King**, M-Sa 6am-12am, Su 7am-12am.	
💻	**Library** 540-254-2538. M 9am-7pm, T-W 9am-5pm, Th 9am-7pm, F 9am-5pm, Sa 9am-1pm, Su closed.	

Buchanan, VA

(5.0) on VA 43 to

Brink of the James Bistro

Roanoke Bagel
Ransone's Drug Store

Exxon
Burger King
The Swingin Bridge Case
Post Office

DJ Produce

Family Dollar

Good Time Cafe

James River

🏪 **Dollar General**
🏪 **Happy Food Mart**

752.4	▲	Cove Mountain summit.	2707	1438.5
752.8	Y	Little Cove Mountain Trail	2600	1438.1
754.2	Y ▲ ⊏(6) ☾	East to **Cove Mountain Shelter**, water (stream) is located on a steep unmarked trail to left of the shelter leads (0.5) downhill, tenting, privy.	N 37 30.703, W 79 39.066	
		20.0◀13.8◀6.5◀▶7.0▶11.9▶17.2	1925	1436.7
754.3	📷	Pass rocky outlook to west.	1735	1436.6
755.9	Y	Buchanan Trail	1790	1435.0
756.7	◊	Intermittent stream.	1339	1434.2
757.4	◐▲▲▲ P(15) ★★★★★	Intersects with **VA. 614** and crosses **Jennings Creek Road** on bridge, Jennings Creek. **See map of VA. 614.**	N 37 31.755, W 79 37.368 955	1433.5

🛏▲⟡🏪 (1.2E) **Middle Creek Campground** 540-254-2550. (www.middlecreekcampground.com)
✗🛁⚲🍴 AT Passport location.
📷 If walking off AT go east on 614 for (0.2), and then left 1 mile on 618.
Thru hiker rates, Camping/hammocking $15 per person, includes showers and pool or $5.00 for just shower and pool use. Cabins begin at $60, A/C rec room with couches, outlets, movies. Night registration is available. Grill serves burgers, fries, milkshakes, nachos, wings, and more. Resupply, pouch meats, instant food, spices, oatmeal, tuna, denatured alcohol, fuel. Laundry. Free WiFi. Call for free shuttle to and from trail head, phone signal strongest near parking area.
Mail drops for guest only: 1164 Middle Creek Rd, Buchanan, VA 24066.

Buchanan, VA (west side) (4.6W on VA 614) see NOBO mile 750.8
🛏✗🍴 **Wattstull Inn** 540-254-1551. (wattstullinn.com)
Hiker rates starting at $60, pets $15, includes continental breakfast, fridge, free WiFi, outdoor pool. Free ride to and from trail head with stay.
Foot of the Mountain Café, on site restaurant.
✗ **Mountain View Restaurant** 540-254-1333. M 7am-8pm, Tu-W closed, Th-Su7 am-8pm. Serves breakfast, lunch and dinner.

VA 614

NoBo	Features	Description	GPS	Elev	SoBo
759.0	▲	Fork Mountain		2042	1431.9
759.6	⋎P	Blue blazed side trail leads (0.8) east to VA. 714 terminus.	N 37 31.806, W 79 35.381	1656	1431.3
760.1	♦	Cross creek on two large rocks		1350	1430.8
760.9	♦	Cross Hamps Branch.		1256	1430.0
761.2	♦⋎⊏(16) ⌣⟜	Steps up to **Bryant Ridge Shelter**, water (stream) is located 25 yards in front of the shelter and also crossed on the trail to the shelter, privy. Blue blazed trail (0.1N) of shelter leads (0.5E) to VA 714. 20.8◀13.5◀7.0◀▶4.9▶10.2▶22.6	N 37 31.802, W 79 35.136	1330	1429.7
761.3	♦⋎⩑P	Cross stream junction, campsite and blue blaze trail that leads (0.5) east to VA. 714 terminus.	N 37 31.806, W 79 35.381	1467	1429.6
761.5	⋎	Intersects old road.		1543	1429.4
762.6	▲	Cryant Ridge crest.		2246	1428.3
765.5	▲	Floyd Mountain crest, wooded.		3560	1425.4
766.1	♦⋎⩑ ⊏(6) ⌣⟜⌂	(0.1E) **Cornelius Creek Shelter**, water is located on trail to shelter, tenting, privy. 18.4◀11.9◀4.9◀▶5.3▶17.7▶21.6	N 37 29.635, W 79 32.832	3145	1424.8
767.0	⋎	Side trail leading west 200 feet to Black Rock.		3450	1423.9
767.3	♦	Cross stream.		3373	1423.6
767.6	⋎	Intersects with Cornelius Creek Trail Recreation Trail west.		3246	1423.3
768.7	⋎	Intersects with Apple Orchard Falls Trail (1.1W) to 200 foot waterfall		3250	1422.2
768.8	⩑P	Cross **USFS 812, Parkers Gap Road; BRP MP 78.4**	N 37 30.642, W 79 31.355	3410	1422.1
770.2	▲	Top of Apple Orchard Mountain, radar dome		4206	1420.7
770.5	⊙	The Guillotine, a large rock boulder suspended over the trail in a narrow rock cleft.		4090	1420.4
771.1	⩑P(2)	Cross Upper **BRP crossing MP 76.3**	N 37 31.315, W 79 30.237	3900	1419.8
771.2	▲	Cross woods road.		3883	1419.7
771.4	♦⩑⊏(6) ⌣⟜⌂⌃	**Thunder Hill Shelter**, water is a walled in spring south on AT and unreliable during dry seasons, privy, tent sites north of shelter. Bear box. 17.2◀10.2◀5.3◀▶12.4▶16.3▶25.1	N 37 31.643, W 79 30.252	3960	1419.5
772.3	⋎	Hunter Creek Trail east (2.0) to USFS 45.		3607	1418.6
772.4	▲	Cross Lower **BRP crossing MP 74.9**		3650	1418.5
772.7	⋎	Thunder Ridge loop trail leads east.		3518	1418.2
773.0	📷♦⩑P	Unmarked trail leads east 85 feet to Thunder Hill Overlook; **BRP MP 74.7**	N 37 32.321, W 79 29.511	3525	1417.9
773.9	⋎📷	Path west leads to view of Arnold Valley and Devils Marblehead.		3672	1417.0
774.0	▲	Thunder Hill summit, wooded		3666	1416.9
774.7	♦⩑	Harrison Ground Spring, tenting.		3200	1416.2
775.0	📷	Ridgecrest with views.		3113	1415.9
775.2	◊	Intermittent spring.		2932	1415.7
775.7	▲	Intersects old road to east.		2640	1415.2
776.1	⩑P(6)	Cross **Pettties Gap Road/SR 781**, Petties Gap; **BRP MP 71.0**	N 37 33.565, W 79 27.520	2369	1414.8
777.3	▲	Highcock Knob summit.		3054	1413.6
778.3	♦⩑	Marble Spring, campsite in sag.		2290	1412.6
778.6	📷	Pass area with open view.		2567	1412.3
778.8	⋎	Sulphur Spring Trail to east (south crossing)		2400	1412.1

NoBo		Features / Description	GPS	Elev	SoBo
780.6	Y	Gunter Ridge Trail to west, Hickory Stand		2650	1410.3
781.1	Y	Sulphur Spring Trail to east (north crossing)		2588	1409.8
781.5	📷	View of James River Gorge.		2322	1409.4
781.9	♦	Big Cove Branch		1890	1409.0
783.8	♦YΛ ⌐(6) ⌣ℂ⇞	**Matts Creek Shelter**, water (Matts Creek) in front of the shelter, tent spaces nearby, privy. Several small swimming holes are nearby. Matts Creek Trail (2.5E) to US 501 22.6◄17.7◄12.4◄► 3.9►12.7►22.2	N 37 35.967, W 79 24.810 835		1407.1
783.9	Y	Matts Creek Trail to east.		816	1407.0
784.6	♦Λ	Campsite, water		700	1406.3
785.8	⌒o	Cross **James River Foot Bridge**, James River. This bridge is the longest foot bridge on the AT.	N 37 35.738, E 79 23.455	678	1405.1
786.0	⛰P(25) ★★★★★	Cross **U.S. 501/VA. 130**. See map of Glasgow, VA.	N 37 35.818, E 79 23.477	680	1404.9
	🚐	**Ken Wallace** 434-609-2704 Shuttles from Buchanan to Waynesboro areas.			

Glasgow, VA 24555 (5.9W)

	📪	**PO** M-F 8am-11:30am & 12:30pm-4:30pm, Sa 8:30am-10:30pm, 540-258-2852.
	🏛	**Town Hall** 540-258-2246 Maintains shelter and Knick Field restrooms.
	🏠◈⛾ 🖥🍴🚐📠	**Stanimal's 328 Hostel & Shuttle Service Glasgow** 540-480-8325. AdamStanley06@gmail.com (www.stanimals328.com) AT Passport location. Guests enjoy complimentary pickup and drop off from 501 James River trailhead, WiFi, complimentary laundry services, shower, clean linens and bunks with mattresses. Property is ultra clean and features 55" flat screen with Netflix. Pizza, drinks & ice cream plus snacks avail. for purchase at reasonable prices. Caretaker provides breakfast for $6 and dinner for $10. Full house available to hikers plus kitchen privileges. $30/night plus private room options available for additional fee. Paid shuttles available. for guests and non-guests at lowest rates. No cell service at 501 trailhead. Guests can call ahead from ridge to arrange for pickup at 501. Owned and operated by Adam Stanley "STANIMAL" AT '04 PCT '10 Mail drops free for guest, $5 for non guests: 1131 Rockbridge Road, Glasgow, VA 24555.
	🛒⛾	**Glasgow Grocery Express** 540-258-1818. M-Sa 6am-11:30pm, Su 8am-1130pm. Large selection of Grocery's and hiker foods. Hardware section, beer, dairy, frozen, ice cream. Coleman and alcohol by the ounce, heat in bottles, Isobutane fuel in two size cans. Hiker Friendly Store.
	🐾	**Natural Bridge Animal Hospital** 540-291-1444. Located at 466 Buck Hill Rd, Natural Bridge Station Va 24579 M-F 8am-6pm, Sa 8am-12pm Sunday and all Major holidays Closed.
	⛾	**Lew's Laundromat**, M-Su 24 hours.
	🖥	**Library** 540-258-2509. M 10am-6pm, Tu-W 10am-5:30pm, Th 10am-7pm, F-Sa 10am-2pm.
	🚐	**Gary Serra** 757-681-2254. Pickups at Glasgow and Buena Vista trail heads. Shuttles along the AT, to Roanoke, Lynchburg and Charlottesville airports, and to Amtrak station. Will also do long distance shuttles. Sells fuel canisters.
	🚐	**Stanimal's Shuttle Service** 540-480-8325 covers all of Virginia.

Big Island, VA 24526 (5.6E)

NoBo Features		Description	GPS	Elev	SoBo

	PO M-F 8:15am-12pm & 1pm-4pm, Sa 8am-10am. 434-299-5072.		
	H&H Food Market 434-299-5153. M-Su 6am-9pm, 7 days a week, serves breakfast, lunch, and dinner 6:30am-8pm. Mail drops: 11619 Lee Jackson Hwy, Big Island, VA 24526.		
	Big Island Family Medical Center 434-299-5951 M-Tu 8:30am-5pm, W closed, Th-F 8:30am-5pm, Sa-Su closed.		

Glasgow, VA

786.1	Lower Rocky Row Run Bridge	740	1404.8
786.2	Upper Rocky Row Run Bridge.	663	1404.7
786.3	Intersects woods road.	674	1404.6
786.6	Power lines.	669	1404.3
786.8	Johns Creek, swimming hole below in Rocky Row Run.	684	1404.1
787.0	Rocky Row Run with cascades and swimming holes, campsites along creek	760	1403.9
787.1	P(6) Cross **VA. 812, USFS 36**	N 37 36.294, W 79 23.301 825	1403.8
787.7	400 feet east to **Johns Hollow Shelter**, water (springs) are located to left and right of shelter, tenting, privy.	N 37 36.780, W 79 23.526	
	(6) 21.6◄16.3◄3.9◄►8.8►18.3►23.9	1020	1403.2
788.1	Cross woods road.	1323	1402.8
788.2	Cross logging road.	1344	1402.7
788.4	Old road intersects.	1545	1402.5
788.8	Cross old road.	2045	1402.1
789.7	Rocky Row Trail to west	2400	1401.2
789.8	Fullers Rocks, Little Rocky Row, several view points.	2486	1401.1
790.3	Unmarked trail to west 40 feet to large flat rock with view.	2800	1400.6
790.8	Big Rocky Row summit.	2974	1400.1
790.9	Cliff east of the trail offers good views.	2952	1400.0
792.3	Saddle Gap, Saddle Gap Trail	2600	1398.6
793.4	Saltlog Gap (south)	2573	1397.5
794.1	Cross pipeline in small clearing.	2775	1396.8
794.7	Old Trail intersects.	2803	1396.2

NoBo	Features	Description	GPS	Elev	SoBo
794.9	📷⊙	Bluff Mountain, **Ottie Cline Powell Memorial.** On 9 November 1891 at a school located 7 miles down the mountain from here, a teacher sent the kids out to collect kindling. Ottie Cline Powell who was going to turn five later that month, wondered off to help collect kindling but did not return. A search was organized later to find little Ottie with no luck. In April 1892 hunter's crossing over Bluff Mountain found Ottie's body. It has become somewhat of a little tradition for hikers that pass by this monument to leave a small toy or something at the monument.	N 37 39.597, W 79 20.785	3391	1396.0
795.4	▲	Intersects old road.		2933	1395.5
795.8	▲	Cross old road.		2770	1395.1
796.0	▲▲	Punchbowl Mountain summit, wooded.		2850	1394.9
796.5	♦Y▲ ⊏(6)⌣⊄	(0.2W) **Punchbowl Shelter**, water (spring) is located by a tree next to the pond drainage in front and to the left of the shelter, tenting, privy. 25.1◀12.7◀8.8◀▶9.5▶15.1▶25.3	N 37 40.665, W 79 20.328	2500	1394.4
796.9	♦▲ P(8)📷	Cross Punchbowl Mountain crossing; **BRP MP 51.7**, water north of road	N 37 40.428, W 79 20.082	2170	1394.0
797.0	♦	Trail to the east leads 150 feet to a reliable pipe spring.		2147	1393.9
797.2	▲P	Cross **VA. 607, Robinson Gap Road**	N 37 40.566, W 79 19.920	2100	1393.7
799.1	▲▲	Rice Mountain summit, wooded.		2169	1391.8
799.8	♦	Spring west sided of trail.		1602	1391.1
800.2	▲	**USFS 311A**, dirt road.		1235	1390.7
801.0	▲P(5)	**USFS 39/Reservoir Road**, possible camping (0.2) south on road.	N 37 40.257, W 79 16.988	990	1389.9
801.1	⌒	Pedlar River Bridge		970	1389.8
803.6	♦	Cross Swapping Camp Creek.		1088	1387.3
804.0	▲P	Cross USFS 38, Swapping camp Road	N 37 41.134, W 79 16.281	1000	1386.9
804.6	▲	Cross old logging road.		1409	1386.3
805.0	♦⌣♨☇	Cross footbridge over Brown Mountain Creek. Swimming hole and waterfalls upstream.		1249	1385.9
805.1	♦☇	Swimming hole on east side of trail.		1178	1385.8
806.0	♦▲⊏(6) ⊄⌂	**Brown Mountain Creek Shelter**, water (spring) us located in front of and uphill from, the shelter, tenting across the creek, privy. 22.2◀18.3◀9.5◀▶5.6▶15.8▶22.4	N 37 42.614, W 79 16.092	1395	1384.9
806.2	♦Y	Old walled spring 15 yards east of tail.		1484	1384.7
806.9	♦	Cross branch of Brown Mountain Creek.		1684	1384.0
807.7	▲	Intersects old road.		2049	1383.2
807.8	▲人⌐ P(15) ★★★★★	Cross **U.S. 60, Lexington Turnpike**, Long Mountain Wayside, picnic table.	N 37 43.412, W 79 15.029	2060	1383.1
	🚐P	**Three Springs Shuttles** 434-922-7069 Shuttles year-round. Range Daleville-Waynesboro VA. Parking available for section hikers. **See notes under NOBO mile 813.0.**			

Buena Vista, VA 24416 (9.3W) See map of Buena Vista, VA.

	🏤	**PO** M-F 8:30am-4:30pm, 540-261-8959.			
	人🛁☇	**Glen Maury Park Campground** 540-261-7321. (www.glenmaurypark.com) Open Apr-Oct. Located at south end of town across river. AT hiker special $5 tent site. Free shower, even without stay. South end of town across river. Yearly Maury River Fiddlers Convention and Beach Music Festival takes place in mid-June.			
	🛏🍴🚗	**Buena Vista Motel** 540-261-2138. (http://buenavistamotel.us) $45 and up, microwave, fridge, free local calls. Free WiFi. Shuttle to and from trail for a fee.			
	🛏🛁🍴	**Budget Inn** 540-261-2156. (www.budgetinnbv.net) $59.95 and up, microwave, fridge, pets $10 and must use smoking room.			
	🏪🍴	**Amish Cupboard** 540-264-0215 (www.theamishcupboard.com) M-F 10am-7pm, Deli open till 6 pm, Sa 10 am-5:30 pm, Su closed. Deli, Ice Cream, jerky, and dried foods.			
	🏪🍴	**Lewis Grocery** 540-261-6826. M-F 10am-9pm, Sa-Su 11am-8:30pm, short order grill.			
	🛒	**Food Lion** 540-261-7672, M-Su 7am- 10pm.			
	🚌	**Maury Express** 800-964-5707, 540-343-1721. M-F 8am-6pm, Sa 10am-4pm, Su closed. Area bus makes hourly loops though Buena Vista and connects with a Lexington loop bus. Fee (small).			
	🚗	**Ken Hawkins** 540-817-9640. Shuttle range from Punchbowl Overlook (BRP 51.7) to Reeds Gap.			
	🐕	**Edgewater Animal Hospital** 540-261-4114 (www.edgewateranimalhospitalpc.com) M-F 8am-6pm, Sa 8am-1 pm.			
	ⓘ ♿P	**Regional Visitor Center** 540-261-8004 Allows multi day parking.	N 37 44.645, W 79 20.332		

Lexington, VA. (15.0W of Buena Vista)

Buena Vista, VA

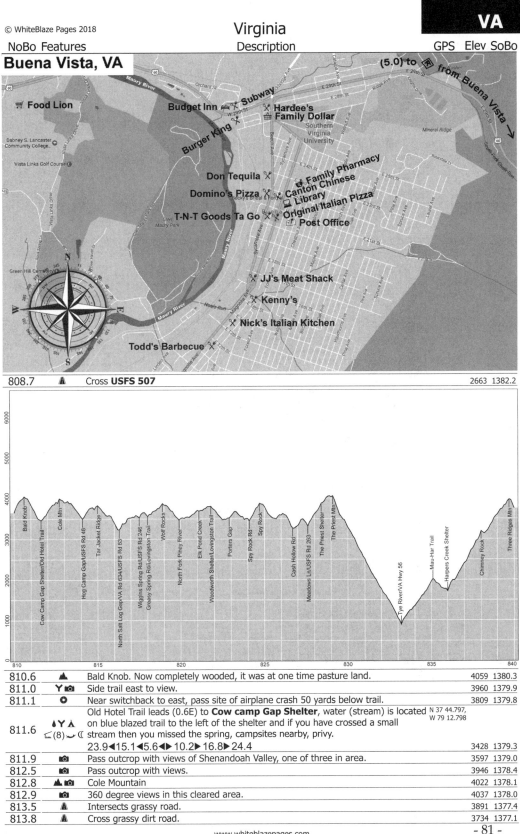

🍴 Food Lion

Budget Inn ⭐🍴 Subway

Burger King 🍴

🍴 Hardee's
🏛 Family Dollar

Southern
Virginia
University

Dabney S. Lancaster
Community College

Vista Links Golf Course ⛳

Mineral Ridge

Don Tequila 🍴

Domino's Pizza 🍴   Family Pharmacy 💊
Canton Chinese 🍴

T-N-T Goods Ta Go 🍴🍴   📖 Library
Original Italian Pizza

📮 Post Office

Green Hill Cemetery

🍴 JJ's Meat Shack

🍴 Kenny's

🍴 Nick's Italian Kitchen

Todd's Barbecue 🍴

| 808.7 | ⛺ | Cross **USFS 507** | | 2663 | 1382.2 |

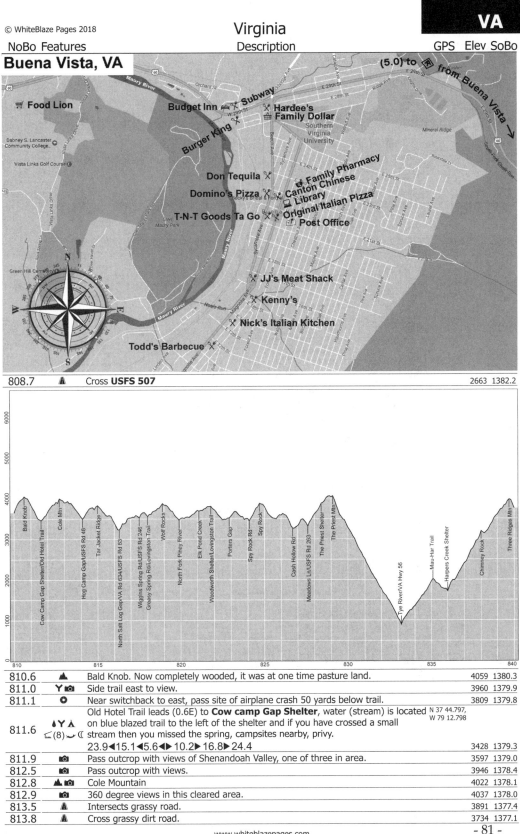

810.6	▲	Bald Knob. Now completely wooded, it was at one time pasture land.		4059	1380.3
811.0	Y📷	Side trail east to view.		3960	1379.9
811.1	⊙	Near switchback to east, pass site of airplane crash 50 yards below trail.		3809	1379.8
811.6	♦Y⚡ ⌐(8)⌣☾	Old Hotel Trail leads (0.6E) to **Cow camp Gap Shelter**, water (stream) is located on blue blazed trail to the left of the shelter and if you have crossed a small stream then you missed the spring, campsites nearby, privy.	N 37 44.797, W 79 12.798		
		23.9◄15.1◄5.6◄► 10.2►16.8►24.4		3428	1379.3
811.9	📷	Pass outcrop with views of Shenandoah Valley, one of three in area.		3597	1379.0
812.5	📷	Pass outcrop with views.		3946	1378.4
812.8	▲📷	Cole Mountain		4022	1378.1
812.9	📷	360 degree views in this cleared area.		4037	1378.0
813.5	⛺	Intersects grassy road.		3891	1377.4
813.8	⛺	Cross grassy dirt road.		3734	1377.1

NoBo	Features	Description	GPS	Elev	SoBo
814.1	♦⚑⌇⚑P ★★★★★	Cross **USFS 48, Wiggins Spring Road**, Hog Camp Gap. Grassy meadow with lots of campsites. Water (spring) is located (0.3) north on road.	N 37 45.582, W 79 11.713	3485	1376.8
	🚗P	**Three Springs Shuttles** 434-922-7069 Shuttles year-round. Range Daleville-Waynesboro VA. Parking available for section hikers.			
814.7	📷	Tar Jacket Ridge		3840	1376.2
816.3	⚑P(6)	Cross **USFS 63, VA. 634**, Salt Log Gap (north)	N 37 46.797, W 79 10.918	3290	1374.6
817.5	⚑	Cross **USFS 246**		3500	1373.4
818.0	Y⚑	**Greasy Spring Road**, just north is blue blazed Lovingston Spring Trail.		3600	1372.9
818.2	♦	Unmarked spring 20 yards east.		4919	1372.7
819.0	Y📷	Wolf Rocks 50 yards to the west.		3785	1371.9
819.9	♦⚑	Cross two branches of the North Fork of Piney River.		3500	1371.0
821.1	♦⚑	Cross Elk Pond Branch.		3750	1369.8
821.8	♦Y⚑ ⊑(6) ⌇《🚿	120 yards east to **Seeley–Woodworth Shelter**, water (pipe spring) is located (0.1) beyond shelter downhill to right, campsites nearby, privy. 25.3◄15.8◄10.2◄►6.6►14.2►20.4	N 37 49.136, W 79 09.306	3770	1369.1
822.9	♦⚑	Porters Field, spring 100 feet down old road to the west. Camping both east and west of trail.		3650	1368.0
824.1	⚑⚑⌇ P(15) ★★★★★	Cross **Spy Rock Road, formerly Fish Hatchery Rd**, gravel. Parking (1.0W).	N 37 50.514, W 79 07.869	3454	1366.8
		Montebello, VA. (2.0W) Location from AT; (1.0W) West downhill gravel road (Spy Rock Rd.) to parking area, (0.2E) from the parking lot (Fish Hatchery Rd.), (0.4W) at intersection of Crabtree Falls Hwy (VA 56), from here it is (0.4) miles.			
	✉	**PO** M-F 10am-2pm, Sa 10am-1pm, 540-377-9218.			
	⚑🏪⛺	**Montebello Camping & General Store** 540-377-2650. (www.montebellova.com) Store open year-round. Apr thru Oct 8am-6pm, summer months 8am-8pm, Dec thru March 9am-5pm. Campground open Apr 1 - Oct 31. Thru-hiker rate on tentsite $14 EAP, 7 Laundry. Sometimes they have fuel by the ounce.			
	🚗	**Earl Arnold** 540-377-2119. When available, shuttles from James River to Rockfish Gap.			
824.6	📷	Spy Rock with 360 degree views from the top, wonderful camping area and has great views. Water needs to be carried in.		3680	1366.3
825.7	📷	Cash Hollow Rock		3550	1365.2
826.7	⚑	Cross **Cash Hollow Road**, dirt		3280	1364.2
827.5	♦⚑	Cross **VA. 826, Crabtree Farm Road**, Crabtree Falls Trail, water is located (0.5) west		3350	1363.4
828.4	♦⊑(6) ⌇《	(0.1E) **The Priest Shelter**, water (spring) is located left of the shelter, privy. 22.4◄16.8◄6.6◄►7.6►13.8►29.6	N 37 49.065, W 79 04.236	3840	1362.5
828.8	Y📷	Path west 150 feet to boulders with 180 degree view.		4088	1362.1
828.9	📷	The Priest summit, wooded. There are 36 switchbacks.		4063	1362.0
831.9	♦	Cripple Creek		1800	1359.0
833.2	⌐⚑ P(20)	Cross **VA. 56, Crabtree Falls Highway**, River suspension bridge.	N 37 50.307, W 79 01.395	997	1357.7
833.3	♦⚑	Tye River		950	1357.6
834.8	⚑	Cross old logging road.		1323	1356.1
835.1	Y	Mau-Har Trail		2090	1355.8
836.0	♦⚑⊑(6) ⌇《🚿	Cross the creek west to **Harpers Creek Shelter**, water (Harpers Creek) in front of shelter, tent sites, privy. 24.4◄14.2◄7.6◄►6.2►22.0►34.7	N 37 51.385, W 79 00.072	1800	1354.9
837.6	📷	Flat-rock overlook to the east with view.		3188	1353.3
838.0	📷	Chimney Rocks, a faint unblazed trail ascends steeply for 25 yards, then passes around the left side of the summit to the Chimney Rock overlook.		3190	1352.9
839.3	Y📷	Blue blazed trail to rocky outcrop with views.		3514	1351.6
833.2		Three Ridges summit, wooded.		3970	1357.7

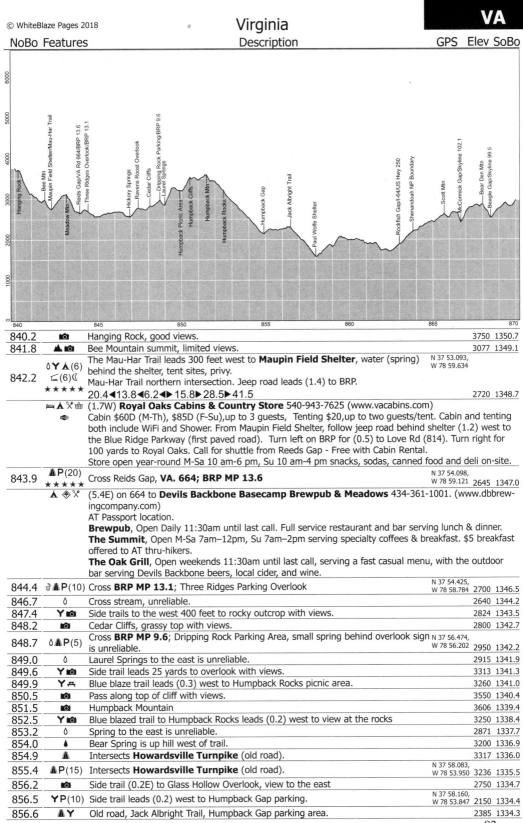

NoBo	Features	Description	GPS	Elev	SoBo
840.2	📷	Hanging Rock, good views.		3750	1350.7
841.8	▲📷	Bee Mountain summit, limited views.		3077	1349.1
842.2	◊ Υ ⋏(6) ⌐(6)☾ ★★★★★	The Mau-Har Trail leads 300 feet west to **Maupin Field Shelter**, water (spring) behind the shelter, tent sites, privy. Mau-Har Trail northern intersection. Jeep road leads (1.4) to BRP. 20.4◄13.8◄6.2◄▶ 15.8▶28.5▶41.5	N 37 53.093, W 78 59.634	2720	1348.7
	🛏⋏✕⛪ 🍺	**(1.7W) Royal Oaks Cabins & Country Store** 540-943-7625 (www.vacabins.com) Cabin $60D (M-Th), $85D (F-Su),up to 3 guests, Tenting $20,up to two guests/tent. Cabin and tenting both include WiFi and Shower. From Maupin Field Shelter, follow jeep road behind shelter (1.2) west to the Blue Ridge Parkway (first paved road). Turn left on BRP for (0.5) to Love Rd (814). Turn right for 100 yards to Royal Oaks. Call for shuttle from Reeds Gap - Free with Cabin Rental. Store open year-round M-Sa 10 am-6 pm, Su 10 am-4 pm snacks, sodas, canned food and deli on-site.			
843.9	▲P(20) ★★★★★	Cross Reids Gap, **VA. 664; BRP MP 13.6**	N 37 54.098, W 78 59.121	2645	1347.0
	⋏ ◈✕	(5.4E) on 664 to **Devils Backbone Basecamp Brewpub & Meadows** 434-361-1001. (www.dbbrewingcompany.com) AT Passport location. **Brewpub**, Open Daily 11:30am until last call. Full service restaurant and bar serving lunch & dinner. **The Summit**, Open M-Sa 7am–12pm, Su 7am–2pm serving specialty coffees & breakfast. $5 breakfast offered to AT thru-hikers. **The Oak Grill**, Open weekends 11:30am until last call, serving a fast casual menu, with the outdoor bar serving Devils Backbone beers, local cider, and wine.			
844.4	⯑▲P(10)	Cross **BRP MP 13.1**; Three Ridges Parking Overlook	N 37 54.425, W 78 58.784	2700	1346.5
846.7	◊	Cross stream, unreliable.		2640	1344.2
847.4	Υ📷	Side trails to the west 400 feet to rocky outcrop with views.		2824	1343.5
848.2	📷	Cedar Cliffs, grassy top with views.		2800	1342.7
848.7	◊▲P(5)	Cross **BRP MP 9.6**; Dripping Rock Parking Area, small spring behind overlook sign is unreliable.	N 37 56.474, W 78 56.202	2950	1342.2
849.0	◊	Laurel Springs to the east is unreliable.		2915	1341.9
849.6	Υ📷	Side trail leads 25 yards to overlook with views.		3313	1341.3
849.9	Υ🛏	Blue blaze trail leads (0.3) west to Humpback Rocks picnic area.		3260	1341.0
850.5	📷	Pass along top of cliff with views.		3550	1340.4
851.5	📷	Humpback Mountain		3606	1339.4
852.5	Υ📷	Blue blazed trail to Humpback Rocks leads (0.2) west to view at the rocks		3250	1338.4
853.2	◊	Spring to the east is unreliable.		2871	1337.7
854.0	◊	Bear Spring is up hill west of trail.		3200	1336.9
854.9	▲	Intersects **Howardsville Turnpike** (old road).		3317	1336.0
855.4	▲P(15)	Intersects **Howardsville Turnpike** (old road).	N 37 58.083, W 78 53.950	3236	1335.5
856.2	📷	Side trail (0.2E) to Glass Hollow Overlook, view to the east		2750	1334.7
856.5	ΥP(10)	Side trail leads (0.2) west to Humpback Gap parking.	N 37 58.160, W 78 53.847	2150	1334.4
856.6	▲Υ	Old road, Jack Albright Trail, Humpback Gap parking area.		2385	1334.3

NoBo	Features	Description	GPS	Elev	SoBo
857.4	Y📷	Pass cleared overlook with views.		3296	1333.5
858.0	▲⌐(10) ⏜((☂♨♨	**Paul C. Wolfe Shelter**, water (Mill Creek) is located 50 yards in front of shelter, privy. Waterfall with pool 100 yards. Bear pole. Swimming hole with small water-falls just downstream.	N 37 59.138, W 78 53.034		
		29.6◀22.0◀15.8◀▶ 12.7▶25.7▶38.9		1700	1332.9
859.7	⊙	Pass remnants of Mayo cabin that dates back to the 1900's, chimney and hearth remain.		2085	1331.2
861.2	▲	Cross stream.		1992	1329.7
863.0	▲P(15) ⊨♦♨♟ ★★★★★	Cross **U.S. 250, I-64**, Rockfish Gap.	N 38 01.866, W 78 51.541	1902	1327.9

⊨ ♦ ♟♟⊨▲P	**Rockfish Gap Tourist Information Center** 540-943-5187. AT Passport location. Open most days 9-5. Info on town services. Maintains a listing of local trail angels. If the center is closed, the listing is dis-played in the window. Some lodging facilities offer free pickup and return from here. Long-term parking is permitted here but not encouraged; it's a "park at your own risk" situation. It is recommended to park for free in Waynesboro at the police-monitored lot near Kroger's (fill out a waiver at the police depart-ment). Hikers that leave their car in town can then catch a ride to the AT with one of the trail angels.
⊨▲⚐⊨ 📠	(0.5W on 250) **Colony House Motel** 540-942-4156. $42-70, microwave and fridge. Ask about tenting. Pets $10. Laundry. Free WiFi. Mail drops for guest: 494 Three Notched Mountain Hwy, Waynesboro, VA 22980.

Waynesboro, VA 22980 (3.7W) on route 250 (all major services) See Map of Waynesboro, VA.

⊡	**PO** M-F 9am-5pm, Sa pickup (only) 8am-12pm, 540-942-7320.
▲⚐⊨	**YMCA** 540 943-YMCA(9622). Free camping and showers. Use of YMCA facilities for $10. Free WiFi. Check-in at front desk, need photo ID.
⌂ ♦⚐ 🖥 ⊨🍴🚗⊡	**Stanimal's 328 Hostel Waynesboro** 540-290-4002 AdamStanley06@gmail.com (www.stanimals328.com) AT Passport location. $30 hiker only hostel includes pickup and return to trail, mattress with clean linens, shower with towel, soap, loaner clothes, laundry. Private rooms available plus full kitchen privileges. Private area including sunroom and finished basement, laptop, WiFi and DVDs. Fridge, freezer and microwave. Snacks, drinks, and ice cream for sale. Discounted slackpacking for multi-night guests. Large property located downtown near grocery, restaurants, and fastfood. Please respect noise level. Hikers are required to call ahead and speak with owner prior to staying. Owned by Adam Stanley AT '04, PCT '10. Mail drops free for guest, $5 for non guests: 1333 West Main Street, Waynesboro, VA 22980.
⌂ ♦⊛🖥⊨	**Grace Hiker Hostel** - Supervised Lutheran Church Hostel AT Passport location. Open May 16-June 19, closed Su nights, 2-night limit. 20 hiker maximum. Please do not call the church office. No pets, smoking, drugs, alcohol, firearms or foul language. Donations gratefully accepted. Check-in 5 pm-8pm, check-out 9 am; hikers staying over may leave packs. Cots in air-conditioned Fellowship Hall, showers, internet, big-screen TV and DVD, hiker lounge with kitchenette, snacks and breakfast foods. Laundry. Free WiFi. Congregation cooks free dinner Thursday nights followed by option-al vespers service.
⊨⊛⊨⊡	**Tree Streets Inn** 540-949-4484. (www.treestreetsinn.com) No pets. $80 and ip, includes breakfast, microwave, fridge, free WiFi, pool, snacks. Free pickup and return from Rockfish Gap with stay. Mail drops for pre-registered guests only: 421 Walnut Avenue, Waynesboro, VA 22980.
⊨⊛⊨⊡	**Belle Hearth B&B** 540-943-1910. (www.bellehearth.com) No pets, no smoking, no alcohol. $85S +tax, $99D +tax, higher on weekends, includes breakfast, pool, pickup and return. 10 day cancel-lation policy. Mail drops guest only: 320 S. Wayne Ave, Waynesboro, VA 22980
⊨🖥⊨	**Quality Inn** 540-942-1171. Hiker rates $62S $67 up to 4 plus tax, pets $10. Includes continental breakfast, microwave, fridge, outdoor pool. Computer available for use, free WiFi.
✗	**Heritage on Main** 540-946-6166. (www.heritageonmainstreet.com) M-Th 11am-12am, F-Sa11 am 1am, Su 11am-12am. Hiker friendly sports bar, beer, burgers, salads.
✗	**Weasie's Kitchen** 540-943-0500. M-F 5:30 am-8 pm, Sa 5:30 am- 2 pm, Su 7 am-2 pm.
✗ ♦	**Ming Garden** 540-942-8800. (www.minggardenwbo.com) AT Passport location. M-F 10 am- 10pm, Sa-Su 10 am- 11 pm. **All you can eat meals**.

NoBo	Features	Description	GPS	Elev	SoBo
	🚶 ◈	**Rockfish Gap Outfitters** 540-943-1461. AT Passport location. Full service outfitter, Coleman an alcohol by the ounce, other fuels, shuttle info. Freeze dried foods. Located between town and trail.			
	🚐	**Stanimal's Shuttle Service** 540-290-4002 covers all of Virginia.			
	🚐	**DuBose Egleston** "Yellow Truck" 540-487-6388 shuttles Roanoke to Harpers Ferry.			
	✕	**Ace Hardware** 540-949-8229. M-F 7:30am-6pm, Sa 8am-5pm, Su closed. Coleman by the ounce.			
863.1	🅐P	Cross **I-64 overpass**, Rockfish Gap	N 38 01.866, W 78 51.541	1902	1327.8
863.3	🅐P	**Skyline Drive MP 105.2**	N 38 01.912, W 78 51.502	1902	1327.6

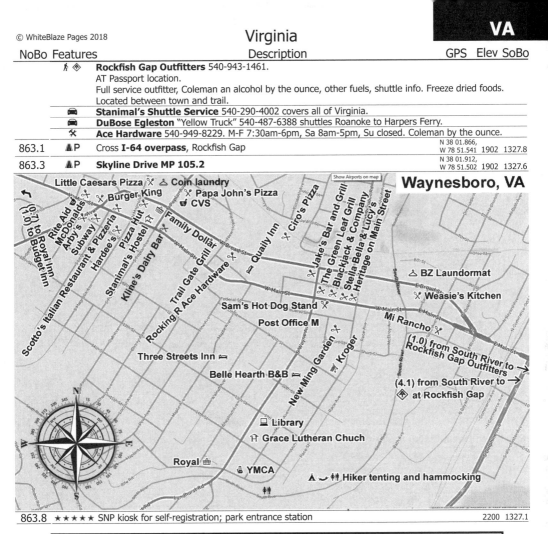

Waynesboro, VA

| 863.8 | ★★★★★ | SNP kiosk for self-registration; park entrance station | | 2200 | 1327.1 |

Backcountry Permits are required for overnight hikes within the park. There is no charge for the permit, There is a fine for not having a permit. Permits are available from self registration sites at the north and south entrances of the AT in the Shenandoah National Park, from any park visitor center, or by mail. Shenandoah National Park 540-999-3500 (www.nps.gov/shen) Emergency line: 800-732-0911

Concrete 4"x4" signposts are used to mark intersections thoughout the SNP. Information is stamped into an aluminum band around the top of the post.

Groups are limited to 10 people. Campfires are only permitted at preconstructed fire rings at the huts. Pets must be leashed.
Campgrounds information. 877-444-6777. (www.recreation.gov). Campsites allow for 2 tents and up to 6 people. All have All have coin operated laundry and showers except Mathews Arm. Most close November-May.

	🚕	**Yellow Cab of the Shenandoah** 540-692-9200 serves all of SNP (24/7). Pet friendly, accepts Credit cards.			
866.7	🅐P(20)	Cross **Skyline Drive MP 102.1**; McCormick Gap.	N 38 03.581, W 78 49.056	3450	1324.2
868.0	📷 ⓞ	Bear Den Mountain. **Old tractor seats**, The tractor seats were put here because the family that owned this property used to have picnics and cookouts and bonfires, particularly to watch the fireworks on July fourth. Vista	N 38 04.016, W 78 47.923	2885	1322.9
868.5	🅐P(12)	Cross **Skyline Drive MP 99.5**; Beagle Gap	N 38 04.387, W 78 47.601	2550	1322.4

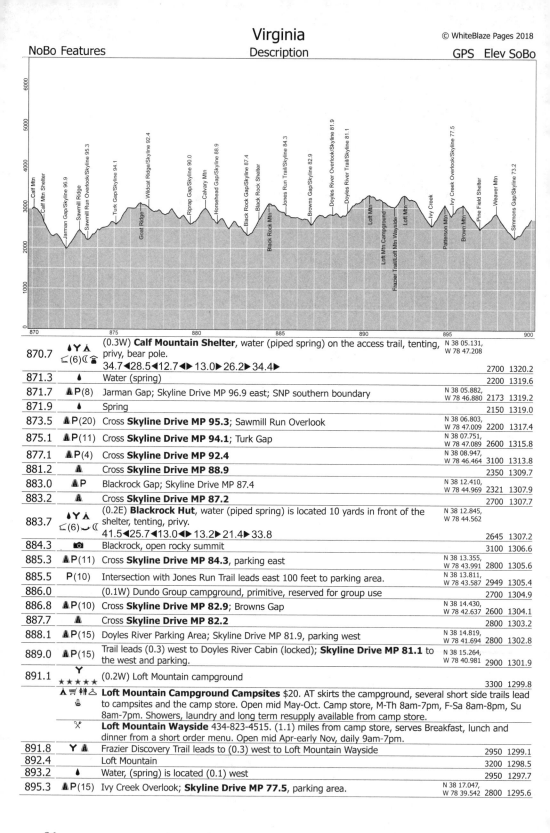

NoBo	Features	Description	GPS	Elev	SoBo
870.7	▲Y⅄ ⊏(6)☾☏	(0.3W) **Calf Mountain Shelter**, water (piped spring) on the access trail, tenting, privy, bear pole. 34.7◄28.5◄12.7◄►13.0►26.2►34.4►	N 38 05.131, W 78 47.208	2700	1320.2
871.3	▲	Water (spring)		2200	1319.6
871.7	▲P(8)	Jarman Gap; Skyline Drive MP 96.9 east; SNP southern boundary	N 38 05.882, W 78 46.880	2173	1319.2
871.9	▲	Spring		2150	1319.0
873.5	▲P(20)	Cross **Skyline Drive MP 95.3**; Sawmill Run Overlook	N 38 06.803, W 78 47.009	2200	1317.4
875.1	▲P(11)	Cross **Skyline Drive MP 94.1**; Turk Gap	N 38 07.751, W 78 47.089	2600	1315.8
877.1	▲P(4)	Cross **Skyline Drive MP 92.4**	N 38 08.947, W 78 46.464	3100	1313.8
881.2	▲	Cross **Skyline Drive MP 88.9**		2350	1309.7
883.0	▲P	Blackrock Gap; Skyline Drive MP 87.4	N 38 12.410, W 78 44.969	2321	1307.9
883.2	▲	Cross **Skyline Drive MP 87.2**		2700	1307.7
883.7	▲Y⅄ ⊏(6)⌣☾	(0.2E) **Blackrock Hut**, water (piped spring) is located 10 yards in front of the shelter, tenting, privy. 41.5◄25.7◄13.0◄►13.2►21.4►33.8	N 38 12.845, W 78 44.562	2645	1307.2
884.3	📷	Blackrock, open rocky summit		3100	1306.6
885.3	▲P(11)	Cross **Skyline Drive MP 84.3**, parking east	N 38 13.355, W 78 43.991	2800	1305.6
885.5	P(10)	Intersection with Jones Run Trail leads east 100 feet to parking area.	N 38 13.811, W 78 43.587	2949	1305.4
886.0		(0.1W) Dundo Group campground, primitive, reserved for group use		2700	1304.9
886.8	▲P(10)	Cross **Skyline Drive MP 82.9**; Browns Gap	N 38 14.430, W 78 42.637	2600	1304.1
887.7	▲	Cross **Skyline Drive MP 82.2**		2800	1303.2
888.1	▲P(15)	Doyles River Parking Area; Skyline Drive MP 81.9, parking west	N 38 14.819, W 78 41.694	2800	1302.8
889.0	▲P(15)	Trail leads (0.3) west to Doyles River Cabin (locked); **Skyline Drive MP 81.1** to the west and parking.	N 38 15.264, W 78 40.981	2900	1301.9
891.1	Y ★★★★★	(0.2W) Loft Mountain campground		3300	1299.8
	▲🛒🕍⚠ 🛖	**Loft Mountain Campground Campsites** $20. AT skirts the campground, several short side trails lead to campsites and the camp store. Open mid May-Oct. Camp store, M-Th 8am-7pm, F-Sa 8am-8pm, Su 8am-7pm. Showers, laundry and long term resupply available from camp store.			
	✗	**Loft Mountain Wayside** 434-823-4515. (1.1) miles from camp store, serves Breakfast, lunch and dinner from a short order menu. Open mid Apr-early Nov, daily 9am-7pm.			
891.8	Y▲	Frazier Discovery Trail leads to (0.3) west to Loft Mountain Wayside		2950	1299.1
892.4		Loft Mountain		3200	1298.7
893.2	▲	Water, (spring) is located (0.1) west		2950	1297.7
895.3	▲P(15)	Ivy Creek Overlook; **Skyline Drive MP 77.5**, parking area.	N 38 17.047, W 78 39.542	2800	1295.6

NoBo	Features	Description	GPS	Elev	SoBo
896.9	◊ Y ▲ ⌂(6) ⌒~ ((☂	(0.1E) **Pinefield Hut**, water (spring) is located behind the shelter 50 yards and it is known to fail during dry seasons, tenting located past the privy, privy. Bear box. 38.9◄26.2◄13.2◄▶8.2▶20.6▶32.1	N 38 17.433, W 78 38.760	2430	1294.0
897.1	▲P(5)	Cross **Skyline Drive MP 75.2**; Pinefield Gap, parking 50 yards west.	N 38 17.468, W 78 38.515	2590	1293.8
899.0	▲P(7)	Cross **Skyline Drive MP 73.2**; Simmons Gap, Simmons Gap ranger station on paved road (0.2E) from where AT crosses Skyline. Water available at pump outside buildings.	N 38 18.105, W 78 37.361	2250	1291.9

Elevation profile with labeled features: Flat Top Mtn, Powell Gap/Skyline 69.9, Smith Roach Gap/Skyline 68.6, High Top Shelter, High Top Mtn, High Top Gap/Skyline 66.7, Swift Run Gap/US Hwy 33/Skyline 65.5, Saddleback Mtn, South River Trail, Baldface Mtn, Pocosin Cabin, Lewis Mtn Campground, Bearfence Mtn Shelter, Bearfence Mtn, Bootens Gap/Skyline 55.1, Hazeltop, Milam Gap/Skyline 52.8, Lewis Spring, Big Meadows Campground, David Spring, Fishers Gap/Skyline 49.3, Rock Spring Shelter, Salamander Trail

NoBo	Features	Description	GPS	Elev	SoBo
902.3	▲P(4)	Cross **Skyline Drive MP 69.9**; Powell Gap. Parking 80 yards east.	N 38 19.273, W 78 35.475	2294	1288.6
902.7	◙	Little Roundtop Mountain		2700	1288.2
903.9	▲P(8)	Cross **Skyline Drive MP 68.6**; Smith Roach Gap	N 38 19.716, W 78 34.500	2600	1287.0
905.1	◊ Y ▲(8) ⌂(6)~((	(0.1W) **Hightop Hut**, water (piped spring) is located (0.1) from the shelter on a side trail, tenting, privy. 34.4◄21.4◄8.2◄▶12.4▶23.9▶34.8	N 38 19.982, W 78 33.516	3175	1285.8
905.6	◊	Water (box spring)		3450	1285.3
905.7	▲(7)	Hightop Mountain, south on A.T. there are three tent sites, side trail to top of High Top has room for four more tents.		3587	1285.2
907.2	▲P(6)	Cross **Skyline Drive MP 66.7**, parking west	N 38 20.688, W 78 33.191	2650	1283.7
908.5	◊ Y ▲ ★★★★★	Cross **Skyline Drive MP 65.5 over U.S. 33** on overpass; Swift Run Gap; Spotswood Trail.		2367	1282.4
	⛺△⊜▤	(2.9W) **Country View Motel** 540-298-0025 (www.countryviewlodging.com) Room with 1 queen bed $75.11 including tax for single bed, two queen beds $91.20 including tax for double beds. All rooms have microwave and fridge. No charge for laundry, but you must have detergent which they sell. Free WiFi. Mail drops for guests only: 19974 Spotswood Trail, Elkton, VA 22827.			
	▲ ✗ ⊜	(3.2W) **Swift Run Campround** 540-298-8086. (www.shenandoahvalleyweb.com/swiftrun) Open year-round. $20 campsite, shower, pool, and snack bar, game room, seasonal pool, Wifi signal is weak at the campgound but good at the store up form the campground.			
	🛒	**Bear Grocery & Deli** 540-298-9826. M-F 5am-8pm, Sa 6am–8pm, Su 8am-7pm.			
Elkton, VA 22827 (6.5W)					
	✉	**PO** M-F 8:30am-4:30pm, Sa 9am-11am, 540-298-7772.			
	🛒	**Food Lion** M-Su 7am-11pm.			
	✗	**Pizza Hut** 540-298-9439. M-F 11am-10pm, F-Sa 11am-11pm, Su 11am-10pm.			
	💊	**Rite Aid** M-Sa 8am-8pm, Sun 10am-8pm. **Pharmacy**; M-F 8am-8pm, Sa 9am-6pm, Sun 10am-6pm.			
911.5	◊ Y ♔⛺ ((P	(0.1) west to South River Parking Area, Picnic Grounds. Falls Trail to east, parking west	N 38 22.902, W 78 31.152	3200	1279.4
914.8	◊P	Pocosin Cabin (locked), parking (0.15) west on Skyline Drive	N 38 24.816, W 78 29.382	3150	1276.1
915.1	◊	Water (spring)		3100	1275.8
916.8	▲P(20) ★★★★★	(0.1W) **Lewis Mountain campground and Cabins, Skyline Drive MP 57.6**, parking west	N 38 26.232, W 78 28.740	3500	1274.1

		▭ ⌂ ⋏ ⛪ **Lewis Mountain Campground & Cabins** 540-999-2255. Reservations 877-247-9261.			
		⚑ ⌂ Open mid May-Oct. Campsites $20, small bunkhouse, cabin rates seasonal. Camp store open same dates, M-Th 9am-6pm, F-Sa 9am-7pm, Su 9am-6pm.			
917.5	◊ Y ⋏ (7) ⌐(6) ⤳ ☾ ☎	(0.1E) **Bearfence Mountain Hut**, water (piped spring) is located in front of the shelter, tent sites, privy. 33.8◄20.6◄12.4◄► 11.5►22.4►26.8	N 38 26.645, W 78 28.242	3110	1273.4
919.1	⋏(5) ⤳	Campsite		3400	1271.8
920.1	⛺P(6)	Cross Conway River Fire Road; **Skyline Drive MP 55.1**, parking is 50 feet west; Bootens Gap		3243	1270.8
921.0		Hazeltop		3812	1269.9
922.9	⛺ (25)	Cross **Skyline Drive MP 52.8**; Milam Gap	N 38 29.994, W 78 26.744	3300	1268.0
923.8	◊	Water (spring)		3380	1267.1
924.6	◊⛺P	Lewis Spring; Big Meadows Wayside; Harry F. Byrd Sr. Visitor Center is located (0.2) east.	N 38 31.016, W 78 26.520	3390	1266.3
925.5	Y ★★★★★	(0.1E) Big Meadows Lodge, Big Meadows campground		3500	1265.4
	✕ ⛽ ◈	**Big Meadows Wayside** Open late-March through Nov. M-Su 8am-8pm, daily. Resupply foods, breakfast, lunch, dinner from a short order menu, fuel by the ounce at gas station. Open Mar 24-Nov 13.			
	▭✕ ☏	**Big Meadows Lodge** 877-847-1919. Open 11 May- 06 Nov. Lodge rooms, cabins and suites, reservations required. Some pet-friendly rooms. Breakfast 7:30am-10am, lunch 12pm-2pm, dinner 5:30pm-9p.m. ATM.			
926.1	◊	David Spring		3490	1264.8
927.1	⛺	Fishers Gap; Skyline Drive MP 49.3		3050	1263.8
929.0	◊ Y ⋏(9) ⌐(8)⤳☾	(0.2W) **Rock Spring Hut and (locked) Cabin**, water is located down a steep trail in front of the hut and flows from beneath a rock, tent sites, privy. 32.1◄23.9◄11.5◄► 10.9►15.3►28.4	N 38 33.211, W 78 24.492	3465	1261.9
929.3	Y ⛺ ⛺	Trail to Hawksbill Mountain (0.9E), Byrd's Nest #2 Picnic Shelter		3600	1261.6

930.3	⛺P(15)	Hawksbill Gap; Skyline Drive MP 45.6	N 38 33.701, W 78 22.983	3361	1260.6
930.7	Y	Trail to Crescent Rock Overlook; Skyline Drive MP 44.4		3450	1260.2
932.8	⛺P(5)	Cross **Skyland Service Road (south)**; horse stables	N 38 35.202, W 78 23.004	3550	1258.1
933.6	⛺P(20) ★★★★★	Cross **Skyland Service Road (north)**, best access to Skyland leads (0.2) west	N 38 35.569, W 78 22.560	3790	1257.3
	▭✕☏♦	**Skyland Resort and Restaurant** 540-999-2212. Open Mar 30-Dec. Rates seasonal, reservations required. Snack foods and sodas sold at gift shop and vending machines. Dining breakfast 7:30am-10:30am, lunch 12pm-2:30pm, dinner 5:30 pm-9:00pm.			
934.0	Y ⛺	Trail to Stony Man Mountain summit.		3837	1256.9
935.6	◊Y📷⛺P	Hughes River Gap; Trail to Stony Man Mountain Overlook (0.2W), Skyline Drive MP 38.6. parking east.	N 38 36.617, W 78 21.829	3097	1255.3
937.8	◊⛺⛺P(15)	Pinnacles Picnic Ground; Skyline Drive MP 36.7	N 38 37.505, W 78 20.466	3390	1253.1

NoBo	Features	Description	GPS	Elev	SoBo
937.9	Y	Trail to Jewell Hollow Overlook; **Skyline Drive MP 36.4**		3350	1253.0
938.9	📷	The Pinnacle		3730	1252.0
939.9	♦Y⋏ ⌐(8)☾	**Byrds Nest #3 Hut**, water (spring) is located (0.3) east and down the fire road, tenting, privy.	N 38 38.066, W 78 19.423		
		34.8◄22.4◄10.9◄►4.4►17.5►28.0		3290	1251.0
940.6	♦	Water (Meadow Spring) is located (0.3) west		3100	1250.3
941.2	📷	Mary's Rock, vista		3514	1249.7
943.1	⚠P(30) ★★★★★	Cross **U.S. 211**; Thornton Gap, Panorama **Skyline Drive MP 31.5**. Two parking options.	N 38 39.594, W 78 19.198 N 38 39.637, W 78 19.317	2307	1247.8

🛏✕🍴 **(4.5W on US 211) Brookside Cabins & Restaurant** 540-743-5698 (www.brooksidecabins.com) $85-$200 cabins open year-round, range in size (2-6 persons). Restaurant AYCE M- Th closed, F 10 am-8 pm, Sa 9 am- 8pm, Su 9 am-5 pm. Closed Dec-Mar. Free WiFi.

🛏⋏✕🏠 **(5.3W) Yogi Bear's Jellystone Park** 540-743-4002. (www.campluray.com)
△ Open late Mar to late Nov. Has some pet friendly sites. Cabins $66-$552.Tent sites $37-75, 2-night min. All stays include free water slide, paddle boat, mini golf. Snack Shop: Open Memorial to Labor Day, serves hamburgers, hot dogs, pizza. Camp store, coin laundry, pool. Showers for guests only.

🛏△🖥🍴 **(6.9W) Days Inn** 540-743-4521. (www.daysinn-luray.com)
Rates: $79.00 - $140.00, $10 extra person, $10.00 for extra bed, pets under 50lbs $15.00. Includes continental breakfast. Microwave, fridge, laundry, seasonal outdoor pool, computer available for use, free Wi-Fi.

Luray, VA 22835 (9.0W) (all major services) See map of Luray, VA.
📫   **PO** M-F 8:30am-4:30pm, 540-743-2100.
🏠⋏◈△ **Open Arms at the Edge of Town** 540-244-5652, call or text for availability and to schedule a pickup.
🖥🍴P🖨 (www.OpenArmsLuray.com)
AT Passport location.
Open year round. Located within a mile of town. Beds $30, camping $15PP with shower and kitchen privileges. Breakfast, soda and snacks for sale on-site. Laundry $5 per load. Computer for guests. Free WiFi. Complimentary pick-up & drop-off at trail head and for resupply (Rt. 211/ Thornton Gap) for guests. Shuttles for a fee from DC airports, Harper's Ferry, SNP, and south to Waynesboro. $1.50/ mile from pick-up to drop-off with $15 minimum
Mail for guests: 1260 E. Main St., Luray, VA 22835

🛏🍴🖥 **Budget Inn** 540-743-5176. (www.hotelluray.com)
🖨 $69.95-$129.95, $10EAP, pets $10. 10% off if you mention that you saw 10% on there web site. Microwave, fridge. Fre WiFi.
Mail drops (non-guests $10): 320 W. Main St, Luray, VA 22835.

🛏🍴 **Cardinal Inn** 540-743-5010. (www.cardinalinn.com)
Hiker rate: winter $55, summer $75. Microwave, fridge. Free local calls. Free WiFi.

🛏✕🖥🍴 **Best Western** 540-743-6511
No smoking. $80 and up, pet fee $20. Microwave, fridge. Outdoor pool. Computer avail be for use, free WiFi.
Restaurant onsite.

🥾♿🍴🖨 **Appalachian Outdoors Adventures** 540-743-7400 (www.aoaluray.com/)
M-Th 10 am-6 pm, F-Sa 10 am-8 pm, Su 1 pm-5 pm.
Full-service outfitter. Coleman and alcohol by the ounce, canisters, Dr. Bonner's by the ounce, freeze dried foods. Free WiFi. Have a brochure with information, places to stay, eat, trail angles, and shuttles.
Mail drops: 2 West Main St, Luray, VA 22835.

Luray, VA (north east)

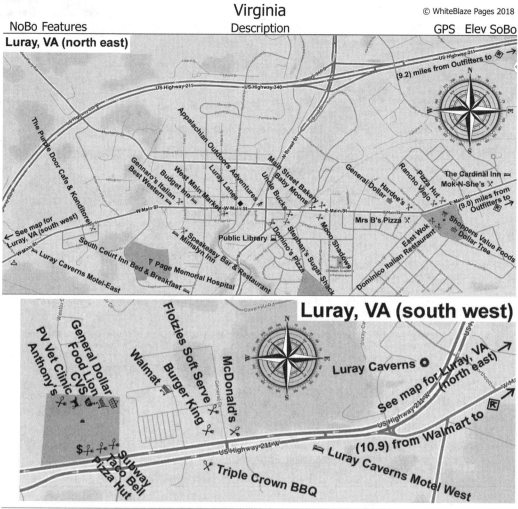

Luray, VA (south west)

NoBo		Description	GPS	Elev	SoBo
944.3	♦Y⋏ ⌐(8)☾☂	(0.2E) **Pass Mountain Hut**, water (piped spring) is located 15 yards behind shelter, privy, tenting, bear box and pole. 26.8◄15.3◄4.4◄►13.1►23.6►31.7	N 38 40.600, W 78 19.137	2690	1246.6
945.1	⋏	Pass Mountain, wooded summit.		3052	1245.8
946.2	⋔	Cross **Skyline Drive MP 28.6**		2490	1244.7
946.5	⌧⋏ P(25)	Side trail leads (0.1) east to Skyline Drive MP 28.5; Beahms Gap.	N 38 41.949, W 78 19.235	2490	1244.4
946.6	⋏(2)	Tenting, west side of trail. Space for 2 tents, maybe 3. 350 feet south of spring on AT.	N 38 41.795, W 78 19.299	2495	1244.3
946.7	♦	Formal piped Spring on the west side of trail, 150 feet off trail.	N 38 41.828, W 78 19.340	2457	1244.2
947.5	♦⌂	Neighbor Mtn, Trail to **Byrds Nest #4 Picnic Shelter** (0.6) east, water is located (0.5) east.	N 38 42.199, W 78 19.924	2600	1243.4
950.1	⋏(2)	Tenting, east side of trail. Space for 2 tents.	N 38 43.906, W 78 19.288	2484	1240.8
950.4	⋏(2)	Tenting, west side of trail. Space for 2 tents, maybe 3. 350 feet south of spring on AT.	N 38 44.170, W 78 19.211	2773	1240.5
951.2	♦	Small stream crossing, possibly from spring.	N 38 44.541, W 78 19.057	2600	1239.7
951.5	♦	Formal piped SNP spring on the east side of trail, 50 feet off trail.	N 38 44.571, W 78 18.832	2341	1239.4
951.7	⌂P	Elkwallow Gap picnic area.	N 38 44.288, W 78 18.566	2396	1239.2
952.0	✕⋔⌸⋏ P(30)	Cross **Skyline Drive MP 23.9**; Elkwallow Gap, (0.1E) to Elkwallow Wayside and parking on Skyline Drive.	N 38 44.288, W 78 18.566	2480	1238.9
952.5	♦	(0.1E) Range View Cabin (locked)		2950	1238.4
953.2	⌧⋏P(8)	Rattlesnake Point Overlook Skyline Drive MP 21.9, parking (0.1) east.	N 38 45.095, W 78 17.331	3100	1237.7

NoBo	Features	Description	GPS	Elev	SoBo
953.8	Y A	Tuscarora Trail (southern terminus) to (0.7W) Matthews Arm campground. The Tuscarora Trail recoonects back to the AT in PA at Blue Mountain.		3400	1237.1
954.2	▲P(15)	Cross **Skyline Drive MP 21.1**, parking west.	N 38 45.681, W 78 16.913	3350	1236.7
954.4		Hogback Third Peak		3400	1236.5
954.5	📷 A P(15)	Skyline Drive MP 20.8	N 38 45.772, W 78 16.789	3350	1236.4
954.7		Hogback Second Peak		3475	1236.2
954.9	♦A(4)	Water (spring) is located (0.2) east at N38° 45.543' W78° 16.365'. 100 yards down the trail to the spring are a few tent sites on the left. There is room for 4 tents, coordinates N38° 45.664' W78° 16.328'		3250	1236.0
955.0		Hogback First Peak		3390	1235.9
955.7	Y A P(10)	Little Hogback Overlook; Skyline Drive MP 19.7, side trail leads 50 feet east to parking.	N 38 45.531, W 78 15.764	3000	1235.2
955.8	📷	Little Hogback Mountain, views 30 feet west.		3050	1235.1
956.3	A	Cross **Skyline Drive MP 18.9**		2850	1234.6
957.4	♦Y A ⌐(8)☾☎	Bluff Trail leads (0.2E) to **Gravel Springs Hut**, water (boxed spring) is located on side trail near the shelter, tent sites on a blue blazed trail, privy. A bear pole at the shelter and another up towards the tent sit, also a box. 28.4◄17.5◄13.1◄►10.5►18.6►24.1	N 38 45.834, W 78 14.018	2480	1233.5
957.6	▲P(8)	Cross **Skyline Drive MP 17.7**; Gravel Springs Gap, parking.	N 38 46.074, W 78 14.014	2666	1233.3
958.7		South Marshall Mountain		3212	1232.2
959.2	▲P(12)	Cross **Skyline Drive MP 15.9**, parking west.	N 38 46.514, W 78 12.652	3050	1231.7
959.9		North Marshall Mountain		3368	1231.0

NoBo	Features	Description	GPS	Elev	SoBo
960.8	♦	Hogwallow Spring	N38° 47.042' W78° 11.629	2950	1230.1
961.4	▲P	Cross **Skyline Drive MP 14.2**; Hogwallow Gap, parking west.	N 38 47.388, W 78 11.322	2739	1229.5
963.1	▲P(14)	Side trail leads east parking at Skyline Drive MP 12.3; Jenkins Gap.	N 38 48.395, W 78 10.842	2400	1227.8
964.0	♦	Compton Springs	N38° 48.966' W78° 10.632	2700	1226.9
964.4	📷	Compton Peak, blue blaze trail (0.2) east to Columnar Jointing Geologic Feature- and, west to views.		2909	1226.5
965.2	▲P(14)	Cross **Skyline Drive MP 10.4**; Compton Gap	N 38 49.418, W 78 10.231	2550	1225.7
965.5	♦	Water (Indian Run Spring) is located (0.2) west		2350	1225.4
967.0	Y ★★★★★	Compton Gap Horse Trail, Trail to Chester Gap. **See Map of Terrapin Station Hostel.**		2350	1223.9

⌂ ◈ ◉⛺ (0.5E) **Terrapin Station Hostel** 540-539-0509. Owned by Mike Evans
◔🍴🛏✉ AT Passport location.

Open Apr 30-July 1, 2018.

No dogs. At concrete post in SNP the AT turns left. North bounders go straight and follow Compton Gap Trail (0.5) to paved road. On paved road the Hostel is first home on left. Enter in back through marked gate. Hikers only, picture ID required, bunk only $25, shower with soap and shampoo $3, laundry $3. One night hiker special $30 includes bunk, shower, laundry, pizza and soda. Two night hiker special $50 also includes slackpack and 2nd night but not 2nd dinner. Free WiFi, charging stations, TV, library, music, room to chill. All visits include free town shuttle. Other shuttles for a fee. Reservations recommended.

Mail drops for guests only: 304 Chester Gap Rd, Chester Gap, VA 22623.

🚗 **Mobile Mike's** 540-539-0509 shuttles and more (Mike Evans)

Terrapin Station Hostel

Terrapin Station Hostel ⌂

← ⚑ **North**

Appalachian Trail

Compton Gap Trail

Appalachian Trail

⚑ **South**

				GPS	Elev	SoBo
967.2	📷○	Possums Rest Overlook with 180 degree views, SNP kiosk for self-registration, SNP northern boundary			2300	1223.7
967.9	◔🏕⛲(6) 🛏☾	Path west to **Tom Floyd Wayside**, water is located (0.2) on a blue blazed trail to the right of the shelter and is not reliable, tent sties, privy, bear pole. 28.0◀23.6◀10.5◀▶8.1▶13.6▶18.1		N 38 51.023, W 78 09.834	1900	1223.0
968.0	◔🏕	Blue blaze trail leads west (0.2) to Ginger Spring and tent site. Built for shelter overflow.			1956	1222.9
968.2	Y	Blue blaze trail leads west (0.3) VA. 601.			1762	1222.7
968.6	⼲	Power line.			1480	1222.3
968.7	Y🚶 P(10) ★★★★★	Side trail leads (0.3) west to Northern Virginia 4-H Swimming Pool.			1350	1222.2
	✕🚶⛴⛽ P	**Northern VA 4H Center (0.4W)** 540-635-7171 (www.nova4h.com/appalachian-trail) Swimming pool open Memorial Day thru Labor Day, shower $1, concession stand. Free parking up to 30 days, register on-line or check in at office. Donations graciously accepted.				
969.3	◊	Cross stream, not reliable. **Do not use water from stream because of houses upstream.**			1280	1221.6
969.4	⚠	Cross **VA. 602**			1150	1221.5
970.8	⚠P(10) ★★★★★	Cross **U.S. 522**.		N 38 52.679, W 78 09.033	950	1220.1

Front Royal, VA. (4.0W) (all major services) See map of Front Royal, VA.

PO M-F 8:30am-5pm, Sa 8:30am-1pm, 540-635-8482.

Visitors Center 540-635-5788. (www.discoverfrontroyal.com)
AT Passport location.
Open 7 days a week 9am-5pm, except Thanksgiving, Christmas, and New Years. Hiker goody bags, hiker box, pack storage. Cold drinks for sale. Sells stamps. Trolley runs form trail head to the town of Front Royal Mid-May thru July, call for details. Fifty cents to ride the trolley.

A new base camp is being established on Main Street that will include shower and laundry facilities. It is expected to be open early spring. Ask for details.

Mountain Home "Cabbin" 540-692-6198. MountainHomeAT@gmail.com.
Lisa & Scott Jenkins, 3471 Remount Rd (US 522).
AT Passport location.
Open year round, call/email ahead recommended, drop-ins are OK.
Located; 120 steps east of AT, where it bends north from Route 522. Look for long stone wall on left and red brick "Cabbin" on the hill. Sleeps 6-8. $30PP includes bed, fresh linens, shower, breakfast, WiFi, some cell, hiker clothes, hiker box, boot dryers, town shuttle for meals and resupply. $5 laundry onsite. Max 1 dog per night for $5; outdoor kennel available for short day use. Pizza, ice cream, snacks & fuel for sale on site. All are welcome to lemonade, cookies, water from faucet on southwest corner of Cabbin. Parking $3 per day for non-guests. Some shuttling. Historic home (tours optional and as available). Mail drops: 3471 Remount Rd., Front Royal, VA. 22630.

Quality Inn 540-635-3161.
Call for rate, $10EAP (up to 4) includes hot continental breakfast. Pets $15. Guests laundry, microwave, fridge, flat screen TV and HBO, free WiFi. Outdoor pool. When you check in let them know if you need a ride back to the AT in the morning(free). Thai restaurant onsite
Mail drops of guests: 10 Commerce Avenue, Front Royal, VA 22630.

Parkside Inn 540-631-1153. (www.parksideinnfrontroyal.com)
Clean, hiker friendly: $50-75, microwave, fridge, laundry, free WiFi.Trail pickup and drop off when available.

Super 8 540-636-4888.
$62.60 ands up, 10% hiker discount. Pets $10. Microwave, fridge, computer available for use, free WiFi.

Scottish Inn 540-636-6168.
$50/up. Pets $10. Microwave, fridge, free WiFi.

Budget Inn 540-635-2196. (www.budgetinnfrontroyal.com)
$49.95 and up, Pet fee. Microwave, fridge, free WiFi.

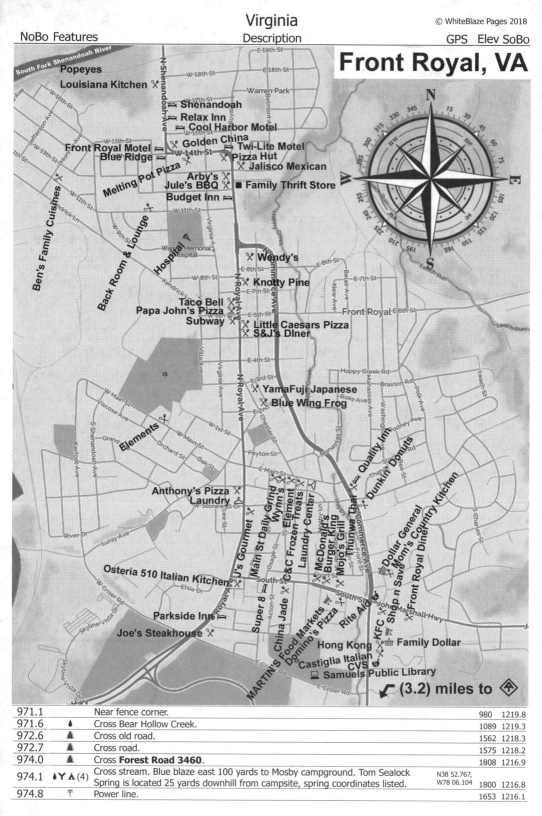

Front Royal, VA

971.1		Near fence corner.		980	1219.8
971.6	⬧	Cross Bear Hollow Creek.		1089	1219.3
972.6	⚠	Cross old road.		1562	1218.3
972.7	⚠	Cross road.		1575	1218.2
974.0	⚠	Cross **Forest Road 3460**.		1808	1216.9
974.1	⬧Y⛺(4)	Cross stream. Blue blaze east 100 yards to Mosby campground. Tom Sealock Spring is located 25 yards downhill from campsite, spring coordinates listed.	N38 52.767, W78 06.104	1800	1216.8
974.8	ⵣ	Power line.		1653	1216.1

Virginia

NoBo	Features	Description	GPS	Elev	SoBo
976.0	♦Y⚥♿⚑ ⊏(7)↭ ⟨⟨🍴☂♿🚻	50 yards west to **Jim and Molly Denton Shelter**, water (spring) is located on the AT, lots of tent places, privy, solar shower, bear pole, picnic table and pavilion, horseshoe pit. 31.7◀18.6◀8.1◀▶5.5▶10.0▶18.4	N 38 53.405, W 78 04.998	1310	1214.9
976.1	▲	Old road intersects west.		1342	1214.8
976.8	Y	Intersection with another trail.		1164	1214.1
976.9	♦	Small stream.		1088	1214.0
977.1	▲P ★★★★★	Cross **VA. 638**	N 38 54.557, W 78 03.200	1150	1213.8
Linden, VA. (0.9W)					
	⌂	**PO** M-F 8-am12pm & 1pm-5pm, Sa 8am-12pm, 540-636-9936, packages only held for 15 days.			
	✕🚗	**Apple House Restaurant** 540-636-6329. (www.theapplehouse.net) Open M 7am-5pm, Tu-Su 7am-8 pm. Hiker specials, supplies and rides sometimes available.			
	🛒	**Monterey Convenience Store**			
978.9	✕	Cross railroad tracks.		867	1212.0
979.0	▲P(4) ★★★★★	Junction of **VA. 55 and VA, 725**, Manassas Gap	N 38 54.557, W 78 03.198	800	1211.9
Linden, VA .(1.2W) See notes at NoBo mile 977.1					
980.0	Y	Blue blaze trail leads east to overgrown view.		1339	1210.9
981.5	♦Y▲ ⊏(6) ↭⟨⟨🍴	70 yards east to **Manassas Gap Shelter**, water (spring) is located near the shelter on a side trail, tenting, privy, bear pole. Blue-blazed trail south of shelter leads (0.9W) to VA 638. 24.1◀13.6◀5.5◀▶4.5▶12.9▶19.8	N 38 55.844, W 78 01.962	1655	1209.4
982.7	♦	Stream, unreliable.		1789	1208.2
983.4	YP(10)	Trico Tower Trail (aka Trillium Trail) leads (0.3) west to Trico Road just short of Trillium parking area on VA. 638.		1900	1207.5
986.0	♦Y▲ ⊏(4)⊏(9) ↭⟨⟨🍴	(0.2E) **Dick's Dome Shelter** and **Whiskey Hollow Shelter**, water TREAT WATER (Whiskey Hollow Creek) is located in front of the shelter, tenting, hammocking, privy, bear pole. 18.1◀10.0◀4.5◀▶8.4▶15.3▶26.3	N 38 58.195, W 77 59.820	1230	1204.9
986.1	▲P(8)	Cross dirt road.	N 38 59.127, W 77 59.985	1546	1204.8
987.0	♦▲	Water (spring)		1578	1203.9
987.1	YP(10)	Side trail (0.1) west AT parking area for 10 cars on Signal Knob.	N 38 59.127, W 77 59.983	1799	1203.8
987.7	YP(10)	Pass path to the west side leading (0.1) to Orchard parking area for 10 cars.	N 38 59.509, W 77 59.693	1821	1203.2
988.2	♦Y▲ P(6)📞 🚻🏕	Blue blaze trail leads (1.3) to Sky Meadows campground or (1.7) to Sky Meadows State Park Side and parking.		1780	1202.7
988.3		Cross gas pipeline.		1761	1202.6
989.6	▲	Cross old roadbed.		1372	1201.3
989.7	Y	Old Trail, purple blazed.		1380	1201.2

Elevation profile with labeled landmarks: Ashby GapUS Hwy 17/50, Myron Glaser Cabin, Duke Hollow, Rod Hollow Shelter, Rod Hollow, Fishers Hill, Morgan Mill Stream, Piney Ridge, Ashby Hollow, Morgan Mill Rd/VA Rd 605, Reservoir Hollow, Buzzard Hill, Wiley Hollow, Tomblin Hill, Sam Moore Shelter, Taylor Hill, Spout Run Creek, Bears Den Rocks, Snickers Gap/VA Hwy 7, Pigeon Hollow, Round Hill, Raven Rocks Hollow, VA/WV Border, Raven Rocks, Rocky Branch Creek, Sunny Ridge, Wilson Gap, Blackburn Trail Center, Potts Springs, Buzzard Rocks, David Lesser Shelter, Keys Gap/WV Hwy 9

NoBo	Features	Description	GPS	Elev	SoBo
990.8		Cross U.S. 50, US. 17, Ashby Gap		900	1200.1
991.0	Y P(6)	Blue blaze trail leads 85 yards east to PATC trail head parking lot.	N 39 0.992, W 77 57.721	1084	1199.9
992.3	♦	Cross creek		1095	1198.6
992.6	Y	Blue blaze leads to Myron Glaser Cabin, reserved for PATC members only.		1100	1198.3
992.8	♦	Cross creek		1022	1198.1
993.1	Y	Blue blaze leads (0.2) to Myron Glaser Cabin, reserved for PATC members only.		1015	1197.8
994.4	◊Y▲ ⊏(7) ﹀ℂ⇌	(0.1W) **Rod Hollow Shelter**, water (spring) is located in the streams just south of the shelter, tenting, privy. 18.4◄12.9◄8.4◄►6.9►17.9►21.1	N 39 02.869, W 77 56.664	840	1196.5
994.7	Y	Fishers Hill Loop Trail to west.		800	1196.2
994.8	⌒	30 foot boardwalk.		826	1196.1
996.1	♦	Cross creek.		1189	1194.8
996.7	📷	Piney Ridge knoll, view.		1342	1194.2
997.6	♦⌒	Cross footbridge over Morgans Mill Stream.		772	1193.3
998.1	▲P(6)	Cross **VA. 605, Morgans Mill Road**	N 39 04.326, W 77 54.725	1140	1192.8
998.9	♦	Cross creek.		1096	1192.0
999.3	♦	Old foundation, spring located 50 yards south		1016	1191.6
999.9	Y📷	Trail west leads to summit of Buzzard Hill with nice views.		1183	1191.0
1000.5	♦	Cross creek.		775	1190.4
1000.7	▲	Cross old road.		1028	1190.2
1000.9		Top of Tomblin Hill		1169	1190.0
1001.3	♦▲(2) ⊏(6) ﹀ℂ⇌🐻	Cross branch of Spout Run. Blue blaze 35 yards south leads east to unreliable Sawmill Spring and to continue of 90 yards to **Sam Moore Shelter**, water (Sawmill Spring) is located in front of shelter or spring to left of shelter, tenting, privy. Bear pole. 19.8◄15.3◄6.9◄►11.0►14.2►29.8	N 39 05.438, W 77 53.196	990	1189.6
1001.4	▲	Cross old road.		932	1189.5
1002.5		Cross Spout Run		741	1188.4
1003.7	♦⌒	Cross creek on footbridge.		864	1187.2
1004.3	♦Y📷⛺ ★★★★★	Bears Den Rocks with good views, (0.2E) Bears Den Hostel, tap water available.	Bears Den Hostel N 39 06.666, W 77 51.255	1350	1186.6
	⛺▲◈⛲ ⏚♨💻⛾ 🍴P▦	(0.2E) **Bears Den Hostel** 540-554-8708. (www.bearsdencenter.org) AT Passport location. Stone lodge, ATC owned and PATC operated. Bunk $20PP, tenting $12PP includes full house privileges. Hiker Special: Bunk, laundry, pizza, soda and pint of Ben & Jerry's ice cream $30PP. All stays include shower and self serve pancake breakfast. Laundry, computer available for use, free WiFi. Hiker room with TV, shower, Internet and sodas, accessible all day by entering a mileage code at the hostel door. Upper lodge, kitchen, camp store and office open 5 am-9 pm daily. Check-out 9am. Slackpacking and shuttles may be available during summer months. Parking $3 per day. Credit Cards accepted. Mail drops, picked up during office hours: Bears Den Hostel, 18393 Blue Ridge Mountain Rd, Bluemont, VA 20135			
1004.7	Y P(10)	Blue blaze trail to parking lot. Same parking as Snikers Gap.	N 39 06.934, W 77 50.919	1139	1186.2
1004.9	▲P(10) ★★★★★	Cross **VA. 7, VA. 679**, Snickers Gap. Caution against parking on the shoulders of VA 679 if the VA 679 parking lot is full - vehicles parked on either shoulder will be towed. Alternate parking is available nearby at the intersection of VA 7 and VA 601, where a rather large parking lot is located. If your car is towed, contact the Clarke County Communications Center at 540-955-1234.	N 39 06.934, W 77 50.919	1000	1186.0

Bluemont, VA 20135

	⌖	(1.7E) **PO** M-F 10am-1pm & 2pm-5pm, Sa 8:30am-12pm, 540-554-4537.			
	✗	(0.3W) **Horseshoe Curve Restaurant** 540-554-8291 M Closed, Tu-W 5pm-9pm, Th-Su 12 pm-9pm.			
	✗⊛☎	(0.9W) **Pine Grove Restaurant** 540-554-8126. M-Sa 7am-8pm, Su 7am-2pm. Welcomes hikers, serves breakfast, lunch and dinner, breakfast served all day. Free WiFi, ATM			
1005.7	♦	Pigeon Hollow, stream.		850	1185.2
1007.1	♦	Water (spring)		1083	1183.8
1007.4	📷 State Line	Virginia–West Virginia State Line. View to the west.		1140	1183.5
1007.5	📷	Crescent Rock		1252	1183.4
1008.1	♦▲Y	Old road leading west 70 yards to Sand Spring (seasonal), 20 yards further to a dependable spring and Ridge to River Trail..		1150	1182.8
1008.2	⊤	Power line. Devils Racecourse, boulder field.		1200	1182.7

NoBo		Features / Description	GPS	Elev	SoBo
1011.1		Wilson Gap		1380	1179.8
1012.0	Y A	Side trail leads (0.2) east **Blackburn AT Center** see **notes below** (0.1) east to campground.		1651	1178.9
1012.3	◗Y A ⌐(8)☾ P(6) ★★★★★	Side trail leads (0.2) east to **Blackburn Trail Center**, water, tenting, privy. 26.3◀17.9◀11.0◀▶3.2▶18.8▶22.9	N 39 11.262, W 77 47.868	1650	1178.6
	Y ⌂ A ◈▤◗⌂	(0.2E) **Blackburn Trail Center** 540-338-9028. AT Passport location. Open year round. The Center offers a hiker cabin with four double bunks with a picnic pavilion; six tent sites and a tent platform are located below the hiker cabin. Water is available from an outside spigot and a solar shower is located on the lower lawn. On porch of main building are logbook, donation box, pay phone, and electrical outlets. (0.1E) **Group campground** with tent sites, picnic tables, and a privy is located on the north blue blaze trail. The Trail Center is owned and operated by the Potomac Appalachian Trail Club and is used to house trail crews, hold meetings, training seminars and retreats. A caretaker lives on site.			
1012.4	◉	Path west to outcrop with views.		1666	1178.5
1014.4	A	Clearing with campsites.		1527	1176.5
1014.9	Y	Blue blazed trail west (0.1) to Buzzard Rocks, left branch in trail has limited views, right branch of trail has no views.		1512	1176.0
1015.5	◗Y A ⌐(6) ⌣☾⌂	115 yards east to **David Lesser Memorial Shelter**, water (spring) is located (0.4) downhill from the shelter, tenting, privy. 21.1◀14.2◀3.2◀▶15.6▶19.7▶24.7	N 39 13.635, W 77 46.746	1430	1175.4
1016.5	▲	Cross old road.		1516	1174.4
1017.4	A	Primitive campsite.		1229	1173.5
1018.1		Cross polluted stream, **Do not drink water from stream**.		1048	1172.8
1018.5	▲P(12) ★★★★★	Cross **W.VA. 9**, Keys Gap	N 39 15.684, W 77 45.747	935	1172.4
	⇞✗- ♨☎▨	(0.3E)**Sweet Springs Country Store** 540-668-7200. Good selection of hiker foods. Fuel available. Full deli, sandwiches, hamburgers, subs and fried chicken. M-Sa 4am-11pm, Su 7am-11pm. Mail drops: 34357 Charles Town Pike, Purcellville, VA 20132.			
	🏠✗	(0.3) west at intersection) **Mini-Mart & Torlone's Pizza** 304-725-0916. M-Th 11am-9pm, F-Sa 11am-10pm, Su 12pm-8pm. Restaurant and conveyance store.			
	⌂♦✗⛺ ▨	(2.0E) **Stoney Brook Organic Farm** 703-622-7526, 571-442-2834, 540-668-9067. Offers Work for stay, meals, shower, laundry. Market hours M-Th 6 AM–8 PM, F6 am-3 pm, Sa closed, Su 9 am-8 pm. Pickup and return from Bears Den, Blackburn Trail Center, Keys Gap, Harpers Ferry. Grocery and outfitter located nearby. Mail drops for guest: 37091 Charles Town Pike Hillsboro, VA 20132			

Keys Gap

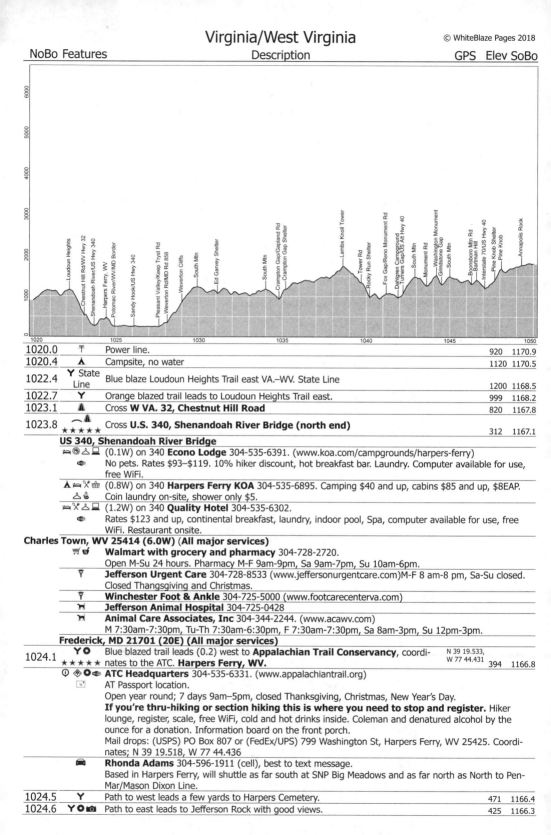

NoBo	Features	Description	GPS	Elev	SoBo
1020.0	⸙	Power line.		920	1170.9
1020.4	⋏	Campsite, no water		1120	1170.5
1022.4	Y State Line	Blue blaze Loudoun Heights Trail east VA.–WV. State Line		1200	1168.5
1022.7	Y	Orange blazed trail leads to Loudoun Heights Trail east.		999	1168.2
1023.1	⚠	Cross **W VA. 32, Chestnut Hill Road**		820	1167.8
1023.8 ★★★★★	⌒⚠	Cross **U.S. 340, Shenandoah River Bridge (north end)**		312	1167.1

US 340, Shenandoah River Bridge

🛏🅿⛺🚻 (0.1W) on 340 **Econo Lodge** 304-535-6391. (www.koa.com/campgrounds/harpers-ferry)
🐾 No pets. Rates $93–$119. 10% hiker discount, hot breakfast bar. Laundry. Computer available for use, free WiFi.

⋏🛏✕🏧 (0.8W) on 340 **Harpers Ferry KOA** 304-535-6895. Camping $40 and up, cabins $85 and up, $8EAP.
⛺ Coin laundry on-site, shower only $5.

🛏✕⛺🚻 (1.2W) on 340 **Quality Hotel** 304-535-6302.
🐾 Rates $123 and up, continental breakfast, laundry, indoor pool, Spa, computer available for use, free WiFi. Restaurant onsite.

Charles Town, WV 25414 (6.0W) (All major services)
🛒🐾 **Walmart with grocery and pharmacy** 304-728-2720.
Open M-Su 24 hours. Pharmacy M-F 9am-9pm, Sa 9am-7pm, Su 10am-6pm.
⚕ **Jefferson Urgent Care** 304-728-8533 (www.jeffersonurgentcare.com)M-F 8 am-8 pm, Sa-Su closed. Closed Thangsgiving and Christmas.
⚕ **Winchester Foot & Ankle** 304-725-5000 (www.footcarecenterva.com)
🐐 **Jefferson Animal Hospital** 304-725-0428
🐕 **Animal Care Associates, Inc** 304-344-2244. (www.acawv.com)
M 7:30am-7:30pm, Tu-Th 7:30am-6:30pm, F 7:30am-7:30pm, Sa 8am-3pm, Su 12pm-3pm.

Frederick, MD 21701 (20E) (All major services)

| 1024.1 ★★★★★ | Y◐ | Blue blazed trail leads (0.2) west to **Appalachian Trail Conservancy**, coordinates to the ATC. **Harpers Ferry, WV.** | N 39 19.533, W 77 44.431 | 394 | 1166.8 |

ⓘ◈◐🛒 **ATC Headquarters** 304-535-6331. (www.appalachiantrail.org)
🔲 AT Passport location.
Open year round; 7 days 9am–5pm, closed Thanksgiving, Christmas, New Year's Day.
If you're thru-hiking or section hiking this is where you need to stop and register. Hiker lounge, register, scale, free WiFi, cold and hot drinks inside. Coleman and denatured alcohol by the ounce for a donation. Information board on the front porch.
Mail drops: (USPS) PO Box 807 or (FedEx/UPS) 799 Washington St, Harpers Ferry, WV 25425. Coordinates; N 39 19.518, W 77 44.436

🚗 **Rhonda Adams** 304-596-1911 (cell), best to text message.
Based in Harpers Ferry, will shuttle as far south at SNP Big Meadows and as far north as North to Pen-Mar/Mason Dixon Line.

| 1024.5 | Y | Path to west leads a few yards to Harpers Cemetery. | | 471 | 1166.4 |
| 1024.6 | Y◐📷 | Path to east leads to Jefferson Rock with good views. | | 425 | 1166.3 |

NoBo	Features	Description	GPS	Elev	SoBo
1024.7 ⚐P(15) ★★★★★		**Shenandoah Street**; Harpers Ferry National Historical Park. Parking is available for up to two weeks at Harpers Ferry National Historical Park Visitor Center. You must register your vehicle with rangers at the visitors center or entrance station and pay a one-time $6.00 entrance fee. Gates are sometimes locked at night. For more information, call (304) 535-6298.	N 39 18.952, W 77 45.411	315	1166.2

Harpers Ferry, WV. See map of Harpers Ferry, WV.

PO M-F 8am-4pm, Sa 9am-12pm, 304-535-2479.

(0.5W) Teahorse Hostel 304-535-6848. (www.teahorsehostel.com)
AT Passport location.
No pets, alcohol or smoking. Open for check in 3pm-9pm. $35 per bunk plus tax includes waffle breakfast. Laundry $6. Visit their web site to reserve or check availability. For shuttles call 304-506-2890. Mail drops for guests: 1312 W. Washington St., Harpers Ferry, WV 25425.

The Town's Inn 304-932-0677. (www.thetownsinn.com)
Private room $110-$160 up to 4 persons, one pet room. Hostel $35PP. Dining available 6am-10pm daily year-round. Shop stocked for hiker resupply. Laundry $5. Shuttles $1/mile.Visa/MC accepted. No mail drops.

Laurel Lodge 304-535-2886. (www.laurellodge.com) $150-195, free WiFi. Call about mail drops.

The Outfitter at Harpers Ferry & Harpers Ferry General Store 888-535-2087. (www.theoutfitter-atharpersferry.com) Full service outfitter with good selection of shoes & trail food. Shuttle referrals. M-Su 10am–6pm, later on F-Sa. Located just steps off the AT across the street from the train station at 161 Potomac St.

Harpers Ferry National Historical Park 304-535-6029.
AT Passport location.
$10 entrance fee, parking up to 2 weeks (must register). Free shuttle bus to lower town. Gates open 9am-dusk.

HostelHiker Rideshare Shuttles 304-885-9550, 202-670-6323. info@hostelhiker.com (www.Hostel-Hiker.com)
Shuttles throughout Maryland, north to Boiling Springs, Pennsylvania, south to Swift Run Gap, Virginia, and east to Washington, D.C., and Baltimore. Airport shuttles to IAD, DCA, and BWI. Dogs allowed to ride with human hiking companion. A max of 11 people can ride together on van. Online booking is mobile friendly at (www.hostelhiker.com).

Mark "Strings" Cusic 304-433-0028. mdcusic@frontier.com. Based out of Harpers Ferry. Shuttle range Rockfish Gap to Duncannon.

Harpers Ferry, WV

Harpers Ferry (downtown)

NoBo	Features	Description	GPS	Elev	SoBo
1024.8	⌒ State Line	Cross Potomac River on Goodloe E. Bryon Memorial Footbridge, West Virginia–Maryland State Line		250	1166.1
1025.0	♦Y	C&O Canal Towpath MP 60.2 (AT west junction)		290	1165.9
1026.1	▲⌒	Cross **under US. 340 bridge**, Sandy Hook Bridge above, underpass.		290	1164.8
1027.6	Y	C&O Canal Towpath MP 58 (AT east junction) Lockhouse 38		290	1163.3
1027.7	✕▲P(8) ★★★★★	Cross Railroad tracks; Intersects with **Keep Tryst Road**.	N 39 19.785, W 77 40.928	320	1163.2

Knoxville, MD. (1.0W)

	命人⬦⛺	**Harpers Ferry Hostel** 301-834-7652. (www.hiusa.org/hostels/maryland/knoxville/harpers-ferry)
	🏠🖥🖨🚗	AT Passport location.
	P🖼	Open May 1–Nov 15 for individuals, year-round for groups. Check-in 5-10pm, check-out 10am. ID required for any stay. No drinking.

Thru-hiker rate $22.40 includes tax, shower, WiFi, linens, A/C and heat, make your own breakfast and dinner. Laundry $4. Tenting $8PP, pay extra $5 for shower, $4 for breakfast. Campers permitted inside only for shower, laundry or breakfast. Computer available for use, WiFi, soda machine and phone charging on back porch. Porta-potty, fire pits, grill on lawn. Service dogs okay inside, otherwise dogs on leash allowed only if tenting. Store with hiker snacks inside and there is often free food. Complimentary meals on Tu, Fr, & Sa. Netflix movies available. Call for trail angel help with rides. Non guest parking $5 per day.

Mail drops for guests: 19123 Sandy Hook Rd, Knoxville, MD 21758.

| | 🛏⛺⬦ | **Knights Inn** 301-660-3580 $69.99and up, fridge, microwave, continental breakfast. Hiker laundry $5. |
| | 🏠✕🍴 | **Hillside Station** 301-834-5300. Convenience store with some hot food, pizza, ATM. M-Sa 6am-9pm, Sa 7am-9pm, Su 8am-8pm. |

Brunswick, MD 21716 (2.5E from Keep Tryst Rd)

| | 📪 | **PO** M-F 8am-4:30pm, Sa 9am-12pm, 301-834-9944. |
| | ✕ | **Wing n' Pizza Shack** 301-834-5555. (www.wingnpizzashack.com) Not just pizzas, they have other foods. Delivers to Harper Ferry Hostel. M-Th 11am-9pm, F-Sa 11am-10pm, Su 12pm-9pm. |

1027.9	▲	Cross under **U.S. 340**, underpass.		400	1163.0
1028.1	▲P(24)	Intersects with **Weaverton Road**	N 39 19.992, W 77 41.002	420	1162.8
1029.0	Y📷	Weaverton Cliffs Trail. Potomac River view, Congressman Goodloe E. Bryon plaque		780	1161.9
1031.1	♦Y⅄ ⌐(12)☾	100 yards east to **Ed Garvey Shelter**, water is located in reliable spring (0.4) at the end of a steep side trail in front of the shelter, tenting, privy. 29.8◄18.8◄15.6◄►4.1►9.1►16.6	N 39 21.591, W 77 39.723	1100	1159.8
1033.1	▲	Cross Brownsville Gap, dirt road		1140	1157.8

NoBo	Features	Description	GPS	Elev	SoBo
1033.4	✪	Glenn R. Caveney Memorial Plaque		1150	1157.5
1034.8	◊▲P ★★★★★	Cross **Gapland Road, MD. 572**. Gathland State Park, Crampton Gap Monument. Frost-free spigot by restrooms.	N 39 24.341, W 77 38.386	650	1156.1
	⇌▲⌂⚐	**(0.4W) Maple Tree Campground** 301-432-5585 (www.thetreehousecamp.com) Open year round. $30 tent site for 1-3 people, $10EAP, showers. Wooded tent sites are $10/person per night and there is a 3 person minimum. Field tent sites for $8/person per night, but they are usually intended for larger groups with a 10-person minimum. Do make exceptions however for hikers when we have availability. Treehouses/Tree Cottages, Non-insulated rustic Treehouses available for $43-$72/night, and insulated Tree Cottages with mattresses and wood stoves available for $60-$74/night. Campstore has snacks, candy bars, sodas, batteries. Located: west of AT on Gapland Road, taker the right onto Townsend Road.			
1035.2	◊▲⌐(6) ⌣ℂ	**(0.25E) Crampton Gap Shelter**, water intermittent (spring) is located (0.1) south on AT, tenting, privy. 22.9◄19.7◄4.1◄►5.0►12.5►20.7►	N 39 24.752, W 77 38.256	1000	1155.7
1037.8	◊Y	Trail to Bear Spring Cabin (locked), water is located (0.5) west		1480	1153.1
1038.4	▣	White Rocks Cliff, quartzite cliff with good view		1500	1152.5
1038.6	Y▣	Lamb's Knoll, unmarked trail west leads 50 yards to antenna tower		1600	1152.3
1039.7	▲	Cross **Tower Road**		1300	1151.2
1040.2	◊Y▲ ⌐(5)⌣ℂ	**(0.2W) Rocky Run Shelter**, water (Rocky Run Spring) is located at old shelter a few hundred yards on blue blaze, tenting and hammocks sites, privy. 24.7◄9.1◄5.0◄►7.5►15.7►20.6►	N 39 27.649, W 77 37.884	970	1150.7
1040.5	▲	Intersects with old road.		967	1150.4
1040.7	⌐▣	High tension power line clearing, view.		950	1150.2
1041.2	▲P✕ ★★★★★	Cross **Reno Monument Road**, Fox Gap.	N 39 28.234, W 77 37.056	910	1149.7
	▪	(2.0E) to South Mountain Creamery 301-371-8565. (www.southmountaincreamery.com). M-Sa 10 am-6 pm, Su 12-6 pm.			
1042.0	◊Y▲♯ ⚐⇌	Dahlgren Backpacker campground west of trail.		980	1148.9
1042.2	▲P(10) ★★★★★	Cross **U.S. Alt. 40**, Turners Gap.	N 39 29.045, W 77 37.195	1000	1148.7
	✕Ϋ	**(0.1W) Old South Mountain Inn** 301-432-6155. (www.oldsouthmountaininn.com) Please shower first. Men, no sleeveless shirts.. Dining reservations preferred. Tu–F 5pm until close, Sa 4pm until close, Su 2pm until close. Brunch on Sundays 10:30am-1:30pm, except Easter and Mothers Day. Winter hours may differ.			
Boonsboro, MD (2.5W)	**See map of Boonsboro, MD.**				
	⌕	(2.5W) **PO** M-F 9am-1pm & 2pm-5pm Sa 9am-12pm, 301-432-6861.			
	✕	**Vesta Pizzeria** 301-432-6166. (www.vestapizza.com) M-Tu 11am-9pm, W-Su 11am-10pm.			
	✕	**Mountainside Deli** 301-432-6700. M-Sa 8am-7pm, Su 11am-5pm. Accepts Credit Cards.			
	⌂	**Cronise Market Place** 301-432-7377. (www.cronisemarket.com) Fruits and vegetables, limited. M-F 9am-7pm, Sa 9am-6pm, Su 12pm-6pm.			
	⊜✕	**Turn the Page Book Store Café** 301-432-4588. (www.ttpbooks.com) M-Sa 10am-6pm, Su 11am-4pm.			
	✕⌂	**Crawfords** 301-432-2903. M-F 7am-5pm, Sa 7am-3pm. Limited.			

Boonsboro, MD

✗ Boone's Restaurant and Bar
💊 Boonsboro Pharmacy

Potomac Street Creamery

💊 Weis Pharmacy

Marcy's Laundry

✂ Pete's Barber Shop
Subway

Post Office

Boonsboro Library

Dan's Restaurant & Taphouse

Washington Monument

Vesta Pizzeria & Restaurant

Cronise Market Place

Boonsboro Veterinary Hospital

Mountainside Deli

Appalachian Trail

South

Old South Mountain Inn ✗

Dahlgren Backpacker campground ⛺ 🚻

NoBo		Description	GPS	Elev	SoBo
1043.6	▲	Cross **Monument Road**		1350	1147.3
1043.8	⛺🚗▲ P(35)	Cross **Washington Monument Road**, cross road two more time after this.	N 39 29.862, W 77 37.248	1400	1147.1
1044.2	📷 ‖ ☉ ◈ ▲P(35)	Washington Monument. The first monument built dedicated to George Washington built in 1827. When open the observation deck on top of the monument offers fine views of the surrounding countryside.	N 39 29.932, W 77 37.410	1500	1146.7
1044.5	⟓	Power line.		1277	1146.4
1045.0	📷	Short path to the eat to rocks with view.		1509	1145.9
1046.3	▲P(4)	Cross **Boonsboro Mountain Road**	N 39 31.669, W 77 36.764	1300	1144.6
1046.6	⛺Y▲⛉ ★★★★★	Bartman Hill. Bartman Hill Trail leads (0.6) west to **Greenbrier State Park**, water, tenting, shower.		1380	1144.3
	⛺🚻⛉	**Greenbrier State Park** 301-791-4767 Camping first Fri of Apr to last full weekend in Oct. $5 entrance fee waived if camping or if you walk in on Bartman Trail. Prices listed as MD resident/nonresident. Tent sites with showers $26-30, higher wkends/holidays. Pets allowed at Dog Wood. Available Mem Day-Labor Day: lunch concession stand, lake swimming, row boat & paddle boat rentals.			
1047.0	▲P(2)	Cross **Boonsboro Mountain Road**.		1248	1143.9
1047.1	⛺Y⌒▲ ⛉▲P(25) ★★★★★	Cross over **US. 40, I-70 on footbridge (north end)**, Blue Blaze (1.4) west leads to **Greenbrier State Park** with water, tenting, shower. **See NoBo mile 1046.6**	N 39 32.134, W 77 36.230	1200	1143.8
1047.6	Y	Blue blazed trail west (north end) to Pine Knob Shelter, **see notes below**.		1339	1143.3
1047.7	◊▲⊏(5) ☾	(0.1W) **Pine Knob Shelter**, water (piped spring) beside shelter, tenting, privy. 16.6◀12.5◀7.5◀▶ 8.2▶13.1▶22.7	N 39 32.550, W 77 36.144	1360	1143.2
1049.3	⛺Y▲⌣ 📷	Trail (0.2) west to Annapolis Rock, water is located (0.4) west, camping is located (0.2) west.		1820	1141.6

NoBo	Features	Description	GPS	Elev	SoBo
1050.3	Y	Black Rock Cliffs 40 yards west.		1800	1140.6
1050.8	◊	Black Rock Creek.		1566	1140.1
1050.9	◊ Y Ⓐ P(6)	Pogo Memorial campsite, side trail leads (0.9) west to parking.	N 39 34.981, W 77 36.214	1500	1140.0
1051.7	▲	Junction with old road.		1762	1139.2
1053.3	📷	View to the east.		1850	1137.6
1055.7	▲ Y P ★★★★★	Cross **MD. 17, Wolfsville Road**. Blue blazed trail 400 feet to trail head parking.	N 39 37.706, W 77 33.566	1400	1135.2

Smithsburg, MD. (1.5W) See map of Smithburg, MD.

🏤	**PO** M–F 8:30am–1pm & 2pm–4:30pm, Sa 8:30am–12pm, 301-824-2828.
🏬	**Dollar General Store** 301-824-6940, M-Su 8am-10pm.
🛒	**Food Lion** 301-824-7011, M-Su 7-11.
✕	**Smithsburg Market** 301-824-2171. (www.smithsburgmarket.com) M-Sa 8am-9pm, Su 10am-9pm.
✕	**Rocky's Pizza** 301-824-2066. (www.rockyspizzasmithsburg.com) M-Sa 10am-10:30pm, Su 11am-10:30pm.
✕	**Vince's New York Pizza** 301-824-3939. (www.incespizza.net) M-Su 11am-11pm.
✕	**Dixie Diner** 301-824-5224. M closed, Tu-F 7am-8pm, Sa-Su 7am-2pm.
✕	**Subway** 301-824-3826. M-Su 24 hrs.
✕	**China 88** 301-824-7300. M-Th 11am-10pm, F-Sa 11am-10:30pm, Su 11:30am-10pm.
⚕	**Smithsburg Emergency Medical** 301-824-3314. (www.sems79.org) Like a 911 service.
🐾	**Smithsburg Veterinary Clinic** 301-416-0888
⚕	**Home Care Pharmacy** 301-824-3900
⚕	**Rite Aid** 301-824-2211, store M-F 8am-10pm, Sa 8am-9pm, Su 10am-8pm. Pharmacy M-F 9am-9pm, Sa 9am-6pm, Su 10am-6pm.
🔺	**Home Style Laundry** M-Su 5:30 am-10:30pm.
🖥	**Library** 301-824-7722. M 10am-7pm, Tu 12:30am-9pm, W-Th 10:30am-7pm, F 10:30am-6pm, Su closed.
✗	**Ace Hardware** 301-733-7940. M 7am-6pm, Tu-W 7a,-5pm, Th 7am-6pm, F 7am-5pm, Sa 7am-3pm, Su closed.

Smithsburg, MD

Dixie Diner

Post Office

Hadley Farms Bakery

Smithsburg Veterinary Clinic
Bank
General Dollar
Smithsburg Family Medical Center

← (0.4) to Rocky's New York Pizza

Debbie's Soft Service

Rite Aid
China 88
Shop n Save

(1.5) to

NoBo	Features	Description	GPS	Elev	SoBo
1055.8	♦	Side trail leads 40 yards east to spring.		1425	1135.1
1055.9	◊▲⊏(8) ⌣⊂	**Ensign Cowall Shelter**, water (boxed spring) is located south of the shelter (0.2) on the AT, tenting, privy. 20.7◄15.7◄8.2◄►4.9►14.5►16.9	N 39 37.664, W 77 33.456	1430	1135.0
1056.1	⊤	Power line.		1505	1134.8
1057.2	▲P(2)	Cross **MD. 77, Foxville Road**	N 39 38.220, W 77 32.466	1450	1133.7
1057.7	♦	Cross stream.		1272	1133.2
1058.9	♦	Spring 10 feet west.		1300	1132.0
1059.0	♦⌢▲ P(2)	Cross **Warner Gap Road**, two-board bridge across stream	N 39 39.333, W 77 32.282	1150	1131.9
1059.7	♦	Cross Little Antietam Creek.		1093	1131.2
1059.8	♦▲P(4)	Cross **MD. 491**, Raven Rock Hollow, rock-hop stream	N 39 39.870, W 77 32.139	1190	1131.1
1060.8	♦Y▲ ⊏(16) ⌣⊂🐻	(0.1W) **Raven Rock Shelter**, water (spring) is located (0.3) east of the AT on a clearly marked blue blaze trail, tenting, privy, bear cables. If you continue (0.15) past the spring (blazes painted over) you'll find the Devils Racecourse boulder field with interesting water noises beneath 20.6◄13.1◄4.9◄►9.6►12.0►13.2	N 39 40.322, W 77 31.476	1480	1130.1
1062.5	Y📷▲P	Trail to High Rock (eastern end), view. (0.1E) from either end to view and parking. Parking gated from dusk till 8am. (1.7) from parking area to Pen Mar Park via Pen Mar Road.		1809	1128.4
1062.6	Y📷▲P	Trail to High Rock (western end), view. (0.1E) from either end to view and parking. Parking gated from dusk till 8am. (1.7) from parking area to Pen Mar Park via Pen Mar Road.	N 39 41.688, W 77 31.392	1950	1128.3
1064.2	▲	Unused forest service road, east (0.15) to High Rock Road.		1472	1126.7
1064.4	▲	Unused forest service road, east (0.16) to High Rock Road.		1542	1126.5
1064.8	▲	Unused forest service road, east (0.3) to High Rock Road.		1377	1126.1
1065.5	♦📷🏕▲P ★★★★★	**Pen Mar County Park**, picnic area.	N 39 42.984, W 77 30.432	1300	1125.4

Pen Mar County Park Open first Sunday in May thru last Sunday in Oct. No camping permitted here. Vending machines, water. Restrooms locked when park closed. Bobby D's and other pizza places deliver here.

🚗   **Dennis Sewell** 301-241-3176

Waynesboro, PA 17214 (6.6W) See map of Waynseboro, PA.

     (2.1W) to Walmart, (4.5) to downtown.

📮   **PO** M-F 8:30am-1pm & 2pm-4:30pm, Sa 8:30am-11:30pm, 717-762-7050.

🛏⛺🖥 **Cobblestone Hotel** 717-765-0034 $90/up +tax, includes hot breakfast, microwave, fridge, laundry, computer available for use, free WiFi, indoor pool, outdoor grill for use, convenience Store.

✗   **Bobby D's Pizza** 717-762-0388. (www.bobbydsonline.com) M-Th: 11am-9pm, F-Sa 11am-10pm, Su 11am-9pm.

NoBo Features	Description	GPS Elev SoBo

	Burgundy Lane B&B 717-762-8112. (hwww.burgundylane.biz) AT Passport location. $90-110, includes full breakfast, free laundry and shuttle to trail head or town stop. Longer shuttles for fee. Mail drops for guests: 128 W Main St, Waynesboro, PA 17268.	
	Days Inn 717-762-9113 $59.99 and up, $5EAP, $10 pet fee. Continental breakfast, microwave, fridge, free WiFi, laundry close by.	
	Laundry Station 717-762-7203	
	Waynesboro Hospital 717-765-4000. Location 501 E Main St.	
	Waynesboro Walk-in Clinic 717-265-1154. (www.waynesborowalkin.com) M-F 8am-7pm, Sa-Su 9am-5pm.	
	Wayne Heights Animal Hospital 717-765-9636. (www.whahvet.com) M-F 8am-12pm & 2pm-6pm.	
	(2.1W) **Walmart** 540-943-4087. M-Su 24 hours; **Pharmacy** 540-943-4637 M-F 9am-9pm, Sa 9am-7pm, Su 10am-6pm.	

Cascade, MD (1.4E on Pen Mar/High Rock Rd)

	PO M-F 10am-1pm & 2pm-5pm, Sa 8am-12pm, 301-241-3403.	
	Sanders Market M 8:30am-9pm, 8:30-8pm, W-F 8:30am-9pm, Sa 8:30–8pm, Su closed.	
	Fort Ritchie Community Center 301-241-5085. (www.thefrcc.org) Showers, computer avaialble for use, free WiFi. M-Th 6am-9pm, F 6am-6pm, Sa 9am-5pm, Su 10am-4pm.	

Rouzerville, PA 17250 (1.8W) most major services.

| | **PO** M–F 8:30am–1pm & 2am–4:30pm, Sa 8:30am–11:30pm 717-762-7050. | |
| | **Cobblestone Hotel** 717-693-8262, ask for hiker discount. | |

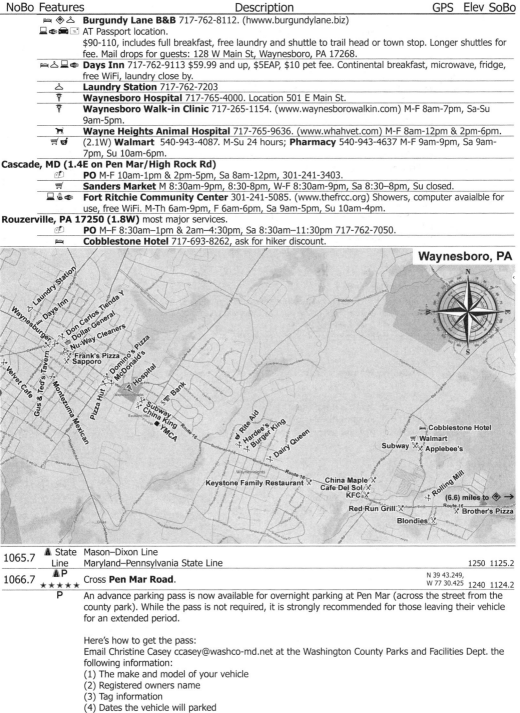

Waynesboro, PA

1065.7	▲ State Line	Mason–Dixon Line Maryland–Pennsylvania State Line		1250 1125.2
1066.7	▲ P ★★★★★	Cross **Pen Mar Road**.	N 39 43.249, W 77 30.425	1240 1124.2
	P	An advance parking pass is now available for overnight parking at Pen Mar (across the street from the county park). While the pass is not required, it is strongly recommended for those leaving their vehicle for an extended period.		

Here's how to get the pass:
Email Christine Casey ccasey@washco-md.net at the Washington County Parks and Facilities Dept. the following information:
(1) The make and model of your vehicle
(2) Registered owners name
(3) Tag information
(4) Dates the vehicle will parked

Ms. Casey will respond with a "do not tow" pass, as an attachment, that is to be printed and posted in your vehicle so local police will know that the vehicle has been registered.
The phone number to call to reach Ms. Casey is 240-313-2700 Tue-Fri. 6am - 4:30pm (reduced hours in winter and more information here.)

Rouzerville, PA.(1.5W), See Notes at mile 1065.5.

NoBo	Features	Description	GPS	Elev	SoBo
1066.4	◑⌒▲	Falls Creek Footbridge		1100	1124.5
1066.8	▲◑	Cross **Buena Vista Road**, roadside spring on the west		1290	1124.1
1068.0	▲	Cross **Old PA. 16**. Limited parking.		1350	1122.9
1068.3	▲P(5) ★★★★★	Cross **PA. 16**.	N 39 44.484, W 77 29.430	1200	1122.6
Blue Ridge Summit, PA (1.2E)					
	■	**Synergy Massage Wellness Center** 877-372-6617 (www.synergymassage.com) Massage, hiker discount. Free outdoor shower, hot tub and pool.			
	✗	**Unique Bar and Grill** 717-794-2565. (www.uniquebarandgrill.com)			
1068.5	▲P(2)	Cross **Mentzer Gap Road**, Mackie Run		1250	1122.4
1068.9	▲	Cross **Rattlesnake Run Road**		1370	1122.0
1069.1	◑	Bailey Spring, box spring 15 yards west.		1300	1121.8
1070.4	◑▲⌐(8) ⌣ℂ	**Deer Lick Shelters** (two shelters hold four hikers each), water (spring) (0.25) on a blue blazed trail to the east of the shelter, tenting, privy.	N 39 45.971, W 77 29.112		
		22.7◀14.5◀9.6◀▶2.4▶3.6▶10.2		1420	1120.5
1071.3	▲	Woods road, Rattlesnake Run Road is (0.17) east.		1408	1119.6
1072.8	◊⌒▲ ⌐(6)⌣ℂ	Old Forge Park, cross two foot bridges. **Antietam Shelter**, water is located (0.2) north on the AT at a springhouse with spigot by the ballfield in Old Forge Park, tenting, privy.	N 39 47.629, W 77 28.980		
		16.9◀12.0◀2.4◀▶1.2▶7.8▶13.4		890	1118.1
1072.9	◑♦▩⌐	Old Forge Picnic Grounds, restroom, frost free water tap-source for Antietam Shelter		900	1118.0
1073.2	▲P	Cross **Rattlesnake Run Road**.		900	1117.7
1073.8	◿▲P(20)	Cross **Old Forge Road**	N 39 48.196, W 77 28.520	1000	1117.1
1074.0	◑▲⌐(8) ⌣ℂ	30 yards west to **Tumbling Run Shelters** (two shelters hold four hikers each), water is located 100 yards to the west of the shelter, tenting, privy.	N 39 48.300, W 77 28.698		
		13.2◀3.6◀1.2◀▶6.6▶12.2▶19.6		1120	1116.9
1075.3	Y▣	Blue blaze trail east to Chimney Rocks or west to PATC Hermitage Cabin (locked)		1900	1115.6
1076.1		Pipe line.		1603	1114.8
1077.3	⟙	Power line.		1901	1113.6
1077.9	▲P(3)	Cross **Snowy Mountain Road**. Parking pull-off on the west side of the road just north of the trail crossing.	N 39 50.247, W 77 30.254	1680	1113.0
1078.2	▲	Cross dirt road.		1648	1112.7
1078.5	▲	Junction with **Swamp Road (south)**.		1560	1112.4
1078.6	▲	Junction with **Swamp Road (north)**.		1560	1112.3
1078.7	Y	Raccoon Run Trail east goes to Caledonia State Park.		1624	1112.2
1078.9	▲P(4) ★★★★★	Cross **PA. 233**.	N 39 50.982, W 77 30.529	1600	1112.0
South Mountain, PA. (1.3E)					
	⌂	**PO** M-F 12pm-4pm, Sa 8:30am-11:30am. 717-749-5833.			
	✗▲⚲	**South Mountain Tavern** 717-749-3845 Historic Bar & Grill, serves lunch and dinner. Ask about tenting M-Sa 9am-2am, Su 12pm-2am.			
Waynesboro, PA. (5.2W) see NOBO mile 1065.5.					
1079.1	▲	Gravel road.		1751	1111.8

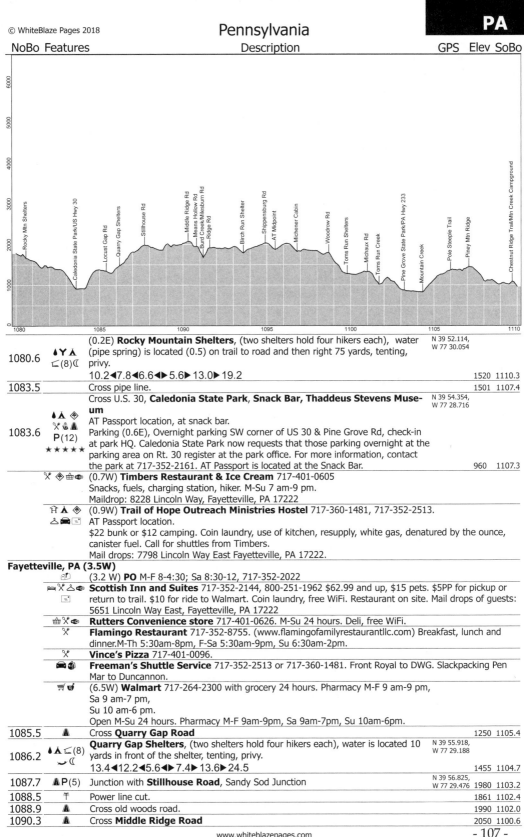

NoBo	Features	Description	GPS	Elev	SoBo
1080.6	♦ Y Å ⊏(8)ℂ	**(0.2E) Rocky Mountain Shelters**, (two shelters hold four hikers each), water (pipe spring) is located (0.5) on trail to road and then right 75 yards, tenting, privy. 10.2◄7.8◄6.6◄►5.6►13.0►19.2	N 39 52.114, W 77 30.054	1520	1110.3
1083.5		Cross pipe line.		1501	1107.4
1083.6	♦ Å ◈ ✕ 🏠 Å P(12) ★★★★★	Cross U.S. 30, **Caledonia State Park**, **Snack Bar**, **Thaddeus Stevens Museum** AT Passport location, at snack bar. Parking (0.6E), Overnight parking SW corner of US 30 & Pine Grove Rd, check-in at park HQ. Caledonia State Park now requests that those parking overnight at the parking area on Rt. 30 register at the park office. For more information, contact the park at 717-352-2161. AT Passport is located at the Snack Bar.	N 39 54.354, W 77 28.716	960	1107.3
	✕ ◈ 🏠 ⊕	**(0.7W) Timbers Restaurant & Ice Cream** 717-401-0605 Snacks, fuels, charging station, hiker. M-Su 7 am-9 pm. Maildrop: 8228 Lincoln Way, Fayetteville, PA 17222			
	⌂ Å ◈ ⛺ 🚗 ☒	**(0.9W) Trail of Hope Outreach Ministries Hostel** 717-360-1481, 717-352-2513. AT Passport location. $22 bunk or $12 camping. Coin laundry, use of kitchen, resupply, white gas, denatured by the ounce, canister fuel. Call for shuttles from Timbers. Mail drops: 7798 Lincoln Way East Fayetteville, PA 17222			
Fayetteville, PA (3.5W)					
	⊞	**(3.2 W) PO** M-F 8-4:30; Sa 8:30-12, 717-352-2022			
	⛟ ✕ ⛺ ⊕ ☒	**Scottish Inn and Suites** 717-352-2144, 800-251-1962 $62.99 and up, $15 pets. $5PP for pickup or return to trail. $10 for ride to Walmart. Coin laundry, free WiFi. Restaurant on site. Mail drops of guests: 5651 Lincoln Way East, Fayetteville, PA 17222			
	🏠 ✕ ⛺	**Rutters Convenience store** 717-401-0626. M-Su 24 hours. Deli, free WiFi.			
	✕	**Flamingo Restaurant** 717-352-8755. (www.flamingofamilyrestaurantllc.com) Breakfast, lunch and dinner.M-Th 5:30am-8pm, F-Sa 5:30am-9pm, Su 6:30am-2pm.			
	✕	**Vince's Pizza** 717-401-0096.			
	🚗 📱	**Freeman's Shuttle Service** 717-352-2513 or 717-360-1481. Front Royal to DWG. Slackpacking Pen Mar to Duncannon.			
	🛒 🛒	**(6.5W) Walmart** 717-264-2300 with grocery 24 hours. Pharmacy M-F 9 am-9 pm, Sa 9 am-7 pm, Su 10 am-6 pm. Open M-Su 24 hours. Pharmacy M-F 9am-9pm, Sa 9am-7pm, Su 10am-6pm.			
1085.5	⚑	Cross **Quarry Gap Road**		1250	1105.4
1086.2	♦ Å ⊏(8) ⌣ ℂ	**Quarry Gap Shelters**, (two shelters hold four hikers each), water is located 10 yards in front of the shelter, tenting, privy. 13.4◄12.2◄5.6◄►7.4►13.6►24.5	N 39 55.918, W 77 29.188	1455	1104.7
1087.7	⚑P(5)	Junction with **Stillhouse Road**, Sandy Sod Junction	N 39 56.825, W 77 29.476	1980	1103.2
1088.5	⟊	Power line cut.		1861	1102.4
1088.9	⚑	Cross old woods road.		1990	1102.0
1090.3	⚑	Cross **Middle Ridge Road**		2050	1100.6

NoBo	Features	Description	GPS	Elev	SoBo
1090.4	Y	Dughill Trail.		2073	1100.5
1090.8	⚑P(5)	Junction with **Ridge Road, Means Hollow Road**	N 39 58.563, W 77 27.548	1800	1100.1
1091.2	♦⚑	Cross **Milesburn Road**, (0.2) east to Milesburn Cabin (locked)		1600	1099.7
1091.6	⚑	Cross **Ridge Road**.		1909	1099.3
1092.3	Y	Cross Rocky Knob Trail.		1905	1098.6
1093.6	♦⚑⌐(8) ↶☾	**Birch Run Shelter**, water (spring) is located 30 yards in front of the shelter, tenting, privy. 19.6◄13.0◄7.4◄►6.2►17.1►25.2►	N 39 59.106, W 77 25.169	1795	1097.3
1094.9	⚑P(12)	Cross **Shippensburg Road**, Big Flat parking area	N 39 59.857, W 77 24.326	2040	1096.0
1083.6	⊙	2016 Midpoint		2000	1107.3
1096.0	⚑P(6)	Cross **old bed of Dead Woman Hollow Road. Re-route pending in this area.**	N 40 00.499, W 77 23.696	1974	1094.9
1096.8	♦	PATC Michener Cabin (locked), (0.2E) to water		1850	1094.1
1098.7	⚑P(4)	Cross **Woodrow Road**	N 40 01.765, W 77 22.088	1850	1092.2
1099.8	♦⚑⌐(4) ↶☾	**Toms Run Shelter**, water (spring) is located near old chimney, dining pavilion, numerous tent pads, privy. 19.2◄13.6◄6.2◄►10.9►19.0►37.2	N 40 02.020, W 77 21.407	1300	1091.1
1100.1	⊙	2011 Midpoint Sign		1300	1090.8
1101.0	⚑	Intersects with **Michaux Road**	N 0 02.346, W 77 20.549	1320	1089.9
1101.7	♦	Halfway Spring		1100	1089.2
1103.2	⚑P	Cross **PA. 233**		900	1087.7
1103.5	♦⊙♨⚑ P(20) ★★★★★	**Pine Grove Furnace State Park.** Pine Grove Furnace State Park requires that hikers check in with the park office before leaving a vehicle in the park and that vehicles be left for no more than one week.	N 40 01.902, W 77 18.324	850	1087.4

Pine Grove Furnace State Park

⌂ ◈ ⌂⛺▯⌨ **Ironmasters Mansion Hostel** 717-486-4108. ironmasterspinegrove@gmail.com (www.ironmasters-mansion.com)
AT Passport location.
Open Apr 1-Oct 31; sometimes closed for special events.
$25PP with breakfast; $30 also includes pizza dinner.Computer available for use, free WiFi, laundry $3.
5pm-9pm check-in, 9am check-out; closed 9am–5pm and Tuesday nights. Call or email for reservations.
Mail drops: Ironmasters Hostel, 1212 Pine Grove Rd, Gardners, PA 17324.

🏪 ◈ ✗ ☎⛽ **Pine Grove General Store** 717-486-4920.
AT Passport location.
M-Su 8am-7pm mid-May thru Labor Day; weekends only mid-Apr thru mid-May and Labor Day thru Oct. Selection of hiking food, cold drinks, canister fuel, fuel by the ounce. Short order grill. Soda machine outside. Free WiFi and phone charging.
"Home of the Half Gallon Challange".

⊙ ◈ **A.T. Museum** 717-486-8126. (www.atmuseum.org)
AT Passport location.
Hikers welcome. Artifacts and photos of past hikers, signs from Springer & Katahdin. Sells halfway patch and bandana. Open; Mar 25-April 30, Weekends only 12pm to 4pm. May 6-July 16, Every day 9am to 4pm. July 17-Aug 20, Every day 12pm to 4pm. Aug 23-Oct 29, Wed-Sun, 12pm to 4pm. (open Labor day and Columbus day)

⚑↶⛺P **Pine Grove Furnace State Park** 717-486-7174 From end of Dec to end of Mar open weekdays only; open 7 days rest of year. Campsites start at $17 weekdays, weekends are a little more, $2 off for PA residents. Dogs allowed in some sites. Check with park office before parking overnight.

1103.7	✗♨♨	Fuller Lake, beach, swimming		850	1087.2
1106.0	Y	Pole Steeple side trail		1300	1084.9
1109.3	⚑	**Lime Kiln Road**		1080	1081.6
1109.5	♦Y⚑ P(4) ★★★★★	Trail to **Mountain Creek Campground**, on Pine Grove Road, (0.7W) to tenting, long term resupply, water, shower, swimming. See below.	N 40 03.626, W 77 13.529	1050	1081.4

🏠⚑🏪⛺ ✗♨ **Mountain Creek Campground** 717-486-7681. (www.mtncreekcg.com) Open Apr-Nov, cabins $52+ tax, tentsites $27.Camp store has sodas and ice cream, laundry, short-order grill on weekends.

NoBo	Features	Description	GPS	Elev	SoBo
1110.3	▲	Side trail leads (0.1) west to spring, signed.		750	1080.6
1110.7	▲▲ ⊑(9) ☾	Tagg Run. (0.2E) **James Fry (Tagg Run) Shelter**, water is located (0.4) east of the AT on a blue blazed, tenting, privy.	N 40 03.778, W 77 12.384		
		24.5◄17.1◄10.9◄►8.1►26.3►33.6		805	1080.2
1111.3	▲✕▲	Cross **Pine Grove Road**, (0.4W) to tenting, restaurant		750	1079.6
1112.3	▲P(18) ★★★★★	Cross **PA. 34, Hunters Run Road**, parking (0.1E) **Gardners, PA.**	N 40 04.666, W 77 11.61	670	1078.6
	🏠✕☎♦	(0.2E) **Green Mountain Store & Deli** 717-486-4558 M-F 7am-8pm, Sa 8am-8pm, Su 9am-6pm.Hiker foods, prepared foods, ice cream, canister fuel, heet. Restroom.			
1113.9	▲P ★★★★★	Cross **PA. 94**.		880	1077.0
Mt. Holly Springs, PA. (2.5W)					
	✉	PO M–F 8am-1pm & 2pm-4:30pm, Sa 9am-12pm. 717-486-3468.			
	🛏✕🖥📶	**Holly Inn Lodging and Dinning** 717-486-3823. (www.hollyinn.com) $65-150, $10EAP, free WiFi, continental breakfast, free ride to and from AT with stay, $5 round trip from Pine Grove Furnace State Park. Restaurant open Su-Th 11:30am-9pm, F-Sa 11:30am-10pm.pm. Tavern open M-Th 11:30-10pm, F-Sa 11:3-12am, Sun 11:30am-11pm.			
	🏠	**Sheetz** M-Su 24 hours, **Dollar General** M-Su 8am-10pm, **Family Dollar** M-Su 8am-10pm.			
	✕	**Subway** 717-486-8655. M-Th 7am-9pm, F 7am-10pm, Sa 8am-10pm, Su 8am-9pm.			
	✕	**Sicilia Pizza** 717-486-4011. M-Th a1am-9pm, F-Sa 11am-10pm, Su 11am-9pm.			
	✇	**Holly Pharmacy** 717-486-5321			
	⊿	**Dollie's Laundromat** 717-580-0745.			
1114.1	▲P(4) ★★★★★	Cross **Sheet Iron Roof Road**, (0.4W) to tenting, restaurant, lodging, short term resupply, shower, laundry, swimming	N 40 05.581, W 77 09.873	680	1076.8
	🛏▲✕🏠 ♨⊿⚓	(0.4W)**Deer Run Campground** 717-486-8168. (www.deerruncampingresort.com) Tent with shower $10, cabin $75.			
1115.2	▲	Cross old road.		734	1075.7
1115.3	▲	Cross **old town road**.		794	1075.6
1116.7	▲▲P(4)	Cross **Whiskey Spring Road**, Whiskey Spring. Beware of parking here, vehicles have been vandalized here.	N 40 05.879, W 77 07.719	830	1074.2
1118.7	▲	Cross woods road with orange blazes, leads (1.7) to Boy Scout Camp Tuckahoe.		905	1072.2
1118.8	◊Y⊑(7) ⌣☾	580 feet east to **Alec Kennedy Shelter**, water (spring) is located on a side trail behind the shelter but is known to go dry, privy.	N 40 06.708, W 77 06.254		
		25.2◄19.0◄8.1◄►18.2►25.5►33.8		850	1072.1
1119.7	Y📷	Center Point Knob which at one time was mid point for the AT, White Rocks Trail		1060	1071.2
1121.0	⊙	Pass evidence of mining operations.		558	1069.9
1121.6	▲P	Intersects with **Leidigh Drive**. Very limited parking.	N 40 08.482, W 77 06.929	560	1069.3
1122.3	◊☾▲✕	Backpackers campsite, near railroad tracks to east. Privy after Memorial Day.		500	1068.6
1122.4	▲⊑▲▲	Intersects with **Mountain Road**, Yellow Breeches Creek, (1.5W) to shelter, tenting, shower		500	1068.5
1122.5	☾▲P	Cross **Bucher Hill Road**	N 40 08.871, W 77 07.450	500	1068.4

NoBo	Features	Description	GPS	Elev	SoBo
1122.7	♦⚠P ★★★★★	Intersects with **PA. 174**, ATC Mid-Atlantic Office, limited use parking. **Boiling Springs, PA**. Limited parking.	N 40 09.004, W 77 07.630	500	1068.2

Boiling Springs, PA. See map of Boiling Springs, PA.

✉	**PO** M-F 9am-12pm & 1pm-4:30pm, Sa 9am-12pm. 717-258-6668.	
🛏⊗⛺⊕	**Gelinas Manor** 717-258-6584 (www.gelinasmanor.com)	
▢	No pets, no packs inside. Room with shared bath $99D/up. Full breakfast at 8:30. Laundry $6 per load. Credit cards accepted.	
	Mail drops for guests only with reservation: MUST say "in care of Gelinas Manor", 219 Front Street, Boiling Springs, PA 17007.	
🛏⊗⊕	**Red Cardinal B&B** 717-245-0823. (www.redcardinalbedandbreakfast.com)	
	No pets, no smoking. $125 and up, queen bed room includes full breakfast and pickup and return from Boiling Springs, free WiFi.	
🛒	**Karn's Quality Foods** 717-258-1458. M-Su 7am–10pm.	
🏧☎	**Gettys Food Mart** 717-241-6163. ATM inside.	
🐕	**Boiling Springs Animal Hospital** 717-258-4575. (www.bsahvets2.com) M 9am-7:30pm, Tu 9a,-6pm, W 9am-7:30pm, Th-F 9am-6pm, Sa 9am-1pm.	
✗	**Anile's Ristorante & Pizzeria** 717-258-5070. M-Th 11am-10pm, F-Sa 11am-11pm, Su 11am-10pm.	
✗	**Boiling Springs Tavern** 717-258-3614. (www.boilingspringstavern.com) Serves lunch and dinner. M closed, Tu-Sa 11:30-9pm, Su closed.	
⚐	**Boiling Springs Pool** 717-258-4121.(www.bspool.com) Memorial Day-Labor Day, M-Su 11am-7pm, $2 hot shower. If you want to swim, visit ATC Regional Office for $3 off the $12 admission.	
🚶◈	**TCO Fly Shop** 610-678-1899. (www.tcoflyfishing.com)	
	AT Passport.	
	Canister fuel and some hiking items. M-F 9am-7pm, Sa 9am-5pm, Su 9am-3pm.	
🚗	**Mike's Shuttle Service** 717-497-6022	
◈⊕	**ATC Mid-Atlantic Regional Office** 717-258-5771.	
	AT Passport location.	
	M-F 8am-5pm, Sa-Su closed. Spigot on south side of building, may be off in winter. Ask staff about trail conditions and check bulletin board. Small shop with maps. Fuel by the ounce for donation. Hiker box.	

Boiling Springs, PA

NoBo	Features	Description	GPS	Elev	SoBo
1124.7	⚑P(6)	Cross **PA. 74, York Road**	N 40 10.379, W 77 07.259	580	1066.2
1125.8	⚑P(6)	Cross **Lisburn Road**	N 40 11.003, W 77 06.690	550	1065.1
1126.4	⚑P(2)	Cross **Boyer Road**		550	1064.5
1126.8	⚑P(8)	Cross **PA. 641, Trindle Road**	N 40 11.701, W 77 06.552	540	1064.1
1127.9	⚑ ★★★★★	Cross **Ridge Drive**.		460	1063.0
	🛏 ❖ ⛺💻	(0.5W) **Pheasant Field B&B** 717-258-0717. AT Passport location. (www.pheasantfield.com) $135 and up, free pickup and return to trail head with stay, big breakfast, microwave, fridge, laundry for fee, free WiFi, behaved pets ok. NOBO's call from Trindle Rd at **mile 1125.7**, or from Ridge Rd, go (0.25W) to Hickory Town Rd, turn left on road, they are located on right.			
1128.5	⚑	Cross **Old Stonehouse Road**		470	1062.4
1129.2	⚑	Cross **Appalachian Drive**		510	1061.7
1129.5	⚑	Cross over **I-76 Pennsylvania Turnpike**, overpass		495	1061.4
1130.1	✕	Cross **Norfolk Southern Railroad Tracks**		470	1060.8
1130.7	⚑ ★★★★★	Cross over **U.S. 11, pedestrian footbridge**.		490	1060.2

Carlisle, PA 17013 (0.5W)

	✕	**Middlesex Dinner** 717-241-2021, 24 hours.			
	🛏⛺💻	**Days Inn** 717-245-2242 Hiker rate $55.95, continrntal breakfast, pets $20.			
	🛏⛺💻🖨	**Super 8 Motel** 717-249-7000 $65 and up, continental breakfast, laundry, free WiFi, $10 pet fee. Mail drops for Guests: 1800 Harrisburg Pike, Carlisle, PA 17013.			
	🛏	**Red Roof Inn** 717-245-2400. Call for pricing.			
	🛏💻	**Americas Best Value Inn** 717-249-7775 $43.95 and up + tax, continental breakfast, $15 pet fee, microwave, fridge, free WiFi.			
	✕🏠🚿⛺	**Flying J Truck stop** 717-243-6659, M-Su 24hrs. Convenience store, diner, showers $12 includes towel, laundry.			

Mechanicsburg, PA 17050 (5.0E)

	💊	(3.0E) **CVS** 717-697-1645. M-Sa 8am-9pm, Su 9am-7pm; Pharmacy M-F 9am-9pm, Sa 9am-6pm, Su 9am-5pm.			
	🛒	(4.3E) **Giant Food** 717-796-6555. M-Su 24 hours			
	🛒	(4.6E) **Walmart** 717-691-3150. M-Su 24 hours.			
1131.6	⌢⚑P(5)	Cross over I-81, overpass on Bernhisel Bridge Road.		485	1059.3
1133.0	⚑🔥⌢(🚗P	Cross Conodoguinet Creek Bridge, **ATC Scott Farm Trail Work Center**, AT work center. Parking is limited; users must contact the Appalachian Trail Conservancy to determine parking availability, driving and parking on the grass are strictly prohibited. See next entry north for Sherwood Drive for alternate parking.	N 40 15.594, W 77 06.250	480	1057.9
1134.1	⚑P(6)	Intersects with **Sherwood Drive**	N 40 16.440, W 77 05.970	420	1056.8
1135.0	⚑	Cross **PA. 944**, pedestrian tunnel Donnellytown, PA.		480	1055.9
1136.0	◢Y	Spring at Wolf Trail Junction, spring is west 50 feet follow blue blaze. **NoBo's Get Water Here**.		650	1054.9
1136.9	Y	Tuscarora Trail (northern terminus), Darlington Trail		1390	1054.0
1137.0	◊Y⋏ ⊏(5) ⌣(	(0.1E) **Darlington Shelter**, water (spring) is located (0.2) on a blue blazed trail in front of the shelter but is unreliable, lots of tenting, privy. 37.2◀26.3◀18.2◀▶7.3▶15.6▶22.3	N 40 18.122, W 77 05.212	1250	1053.9
1138.1	⚑	Crest of Little Mountain.		910	1052.8
1138.9	⚑	Cross **Millers Gap Road**, paved		700	1052.0
1139.3	⚑P(6)	Cross **PA. 850, Valley Road**	N 40 19.309, W 77 04.689	650	1051.6

Elevation profile labels (left to right): Fishing Creek, Cove Mtn, Cove Mtn Shelter, Hawk Rock, Sherman Creek/Inn Rd Duncannon, PA/US Hwy 15/PA Hwy 274, Duncannon, PA/PA Hwy 849, Susquehanna River/US Hwy 22/PA Hwy 147, Peters Mtn, Clarks Ferry Shelter, Peters Mtn Rd/PA Hwy 225, Peters Mtn Shelter, Victoria Trail, Whitetail Trail, Kinter View, Shikellimy Trail, Peters Mtn, Clarks Creek/PA Hwy 325, Stony Mtn/Horseshoe Trail, Rattling Run

NoBo	Features	Description	GPS	Elev	SoBo
1140.7	♦	Cross stream.		761	1050.2
1141.8	Y 📷	Pipe line clearing with views. Unmarked trail leads west down to State Game lands parking.		1315	1049.1
1143.4	Y	Blue blaze trail leads west steeply down to service road for Duncannon Water Company.		1246	1047.5
1144.3	♦ Y ⌐(8) ⌣ ℂ	(0.2E) **Cove Mountain Shelter**, water (spring) is located 125 yards away on a steeply graded trail near the shelter, privy. 33.6◄25.5◄7.3◄►8.3►15.0►33.0	N 40 21.819, W 77 04.042	1200	1046.6
1146.2	📷	Hawk Rock, view of Duncannon		1140	1044.7
1135.0	⚠	Intersects with **Inn Road**		360	1055.9
1147.2	⌐⚠	Cross over **Sherman Creek Bridge**		360	1043.7
1147.9	⨿⚠P	Intersection with **PA. 274, U.S. 11 & 15**, underpass, (0.5W) to long term resupply		385	1043.0
1148.4	⚠ ★★★★★	Intersection of **Market and Cumberland Street**. **Duncannon, PA. See map of Duncannon, PA.**		385	1042.5

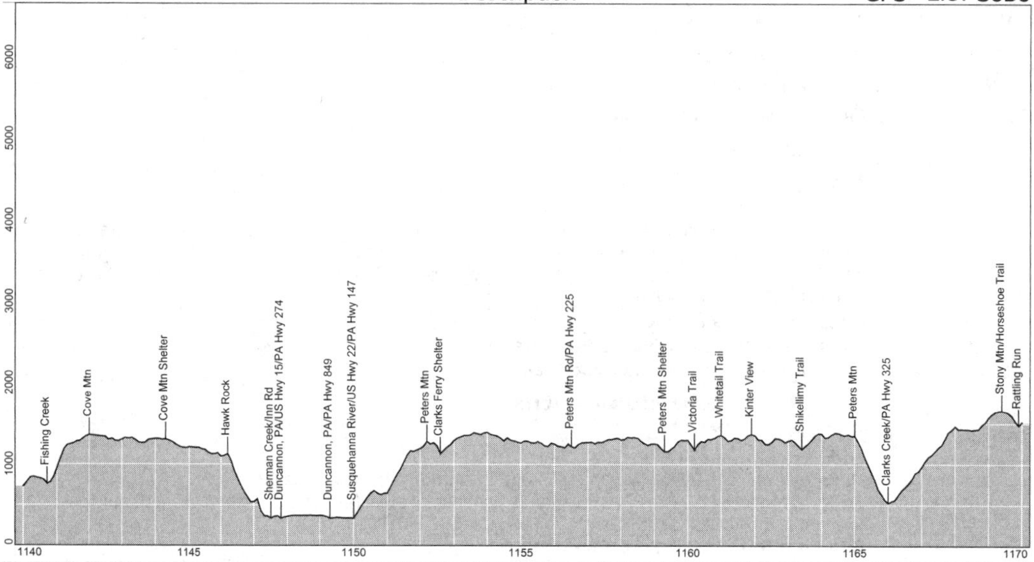

📫	**PO** ID required, M-F 8am-11am & 12pm-4:30pm, Sa 8:30am-12:30pm. 717-834-3332.	
🛏 ◈ ✗ 🖥	**Doyle Hotel** 717-834-6789. AT Passport location. $25S, $35D, $10EAP + tax, resturaunt serves lunch, dinner, homemade meals and vegan choices. Coleman, alcohol by the ounce and canister fuel. Recharging station. Pool Table. Credit cards Visa, MC, Discovery. Mail drops: Real names only as they require ID to pick up any mail drop. (USPS/UPS/FedEx) 7 North Market Street, Duncannon, PA 17020.	
🛏◈⌂	**Stardust Motel** 717-834-3191. No pets. $45S, $55D, laundry. Sometimes pickup and return rides available.	
🛏⌂⊛	**Red Carpet Inn** 717-834-3320 $55S, $60D + tax. Laundry, free WiFi. Pickup and return from Duncannon for $10.	
▲🚗	**Riverfront Campground** 717-834-5252. (www.riverfrontcampground.com) Site and shower $5PP, check-in daylight until dark. Shuttles available Take note of the railroad tracks.	
✗	**Sorrento Pizza** 717-834-5167. (www.sorrentosduncannon.com) M-Th 11am-10:30pm, F-Sa 11am-11:30pm, Su 11am-10:30pm. Bar and Lounge; every day 4pm- last call. Dinner service ends 10pm.	
✗	**Goodies Breakfast** 717-834-6300. M closed, Tu-Su 6am-11am.	
✗	**Ranch House Restaurant** 717-834-4710. (www.ranchhouseperryco.com) M-Fr 5:30am-9pm, Sa 6am-9pm, & Su 7am-9pm. Serves breakfast, lunch and dinner. Soup & Salad Bar is available everyday for lunch & dinner (11AM to 7PM). Breakfast bar on Sa-Su	
✗	**Lumberjack's Kitchen** 717-834-9099. (www.lumberjackskitchen.weebly.com) Seasonal hours, open in the summer and spring M-Th 9am-9pm, F-Sa 8am-9pm, Su 8am-8pm. In the Fall and Winter open M-Th 10am- 8pm, F-Sa 8am-9pm, Su 8am-8pm. Located near Red Carpet Inn	
🛒	**Mutzabaugh's Market** 717-834-3121. (www.mutzabaughsmarket.com) Hiker friendly, M-Su 6am-10pm. Will pickup and return to Doyle at 4pm daily.	
💊	**Rite Aid** 717-834-6303. M-F 8am-9pm, Sa 8am-7pm, Su 8am-8pm. Pharmacy M-F 9am-9pm, Sa 9am-6pm, Su 10am-6pm.	
🏧✗🚿	**Pilot Travel Plaza** 717-834-3156, M-Su 24 hours, $12 showers.	

	🐾	**Cove Mountain Animal Hospital** 717-834-5534. (www.covemountainanimalhospital.vetstreet.com) M-W 9am-8pm, Th 9am-5pm, F 9am-6pm, Sa 9am-12pm, Su closed.			
	■	**Christ Lutheran Church** 717-834-3140. (www.clcduncannon.org)Free hiker dinner Wednesdays in June & July 5pm-7pm at 115 Church St., the corner of Plum St and Church St. Sunday service 10am.			
	🚗◈	**Trail Angel Mary** 717-834-4706. AT Passport location. 2 Ann St, Duncannon, PA 17020			

Duncannon, PA

1148.5	🅰	Intersects with **High Street**.		260	1042.4
1149.4	🅰🅰	Intersects with **PA. 849, Newport Road**, Juniata River		380	1041.5
1150.2	⌒🅰P	Susquehanna River on Clarks Ferry Bridge (west end). Cross **U.S. 22 & 322, Norfolk Southern Railway**	N 40 23.756, W 77 00.510 N 40 23.774, W 77 00.465	400	1040.7
1150.3	Y	Blue blazed Susquehanna Trail, rejoins A.T. north		650	1040.6
1150.7	🅰	Old logging road.		1169	1040.2
1150.8	📷	Views of Duncannon and Susquehanna River.		1177	1040.1
1151.3	Y	Blue blazed Susquehanna Trail, rejoins A.T. south		1150	1039.6
1152.4	♦Y🅰(3)	Side trail to campsite, spring		1160	1038.5
1152.6	♦Y🅰 ⊏(8)⌣ℭ	**300 feet east to Clarks Ferry Shelter**, water (pipe spring) 0.1 beyond shelter, tenting, privy. 33.8◀15.6▶8.3◀▶6.7▶24.7▶38.1	N 40 23.536, W 76 59.630	1260	1038.3
1153.2	⟙	Power line.		1314	1037.7
1154.1		Cross pine line.		1374	1036.8
1156.5	⌒🅰 P(10)	Cross **PA. 225** on footbridge.	N 40 24.698, W 76 55.816	1250	1034.4
1156.7	📷	View.		1278	1034.2
1157.1	⟙	Power line.		1275	1033.8
1158.5	Y📷	Blue blaze east 33 yards to Table Rock View		1200	1032.4
1159.3	◊⊏(16) ⌣ℭ	**Peters Mountain Shelter**, water is located (0.3) down a steep blue blazed trail of almost 300 rock steps in front of shelter, privy. 22.3◀15.0◀6.7◀▶18.0▶31.4▶35.5	N 40 25.543, W 76 52.765	970	1031.6
1160.3	Y	Blue blazed Victoria Trail to east.		1300	1030.6
1160.9	Y	Pink blazed Whitetail Trail		1310	1030.0
1162.0	📷	Blue blazed trail to east 60 yards to Kinter View.		1320	1028.9
1163.4	Y	Blue blazed Shikellimy Trail east leads (0.9) to parking area.	N 40 26.171, W 76 49.471	1250	1027.5
1165.7	♦	Blue blaze 136 yards to spring.		700	1025.2
1166.0	♦🅰(30)	Cross **PA. 325**, Clark's Valley, Clark Creek	N 40 27.174, W 76 46.603	550	1024.9
1166.1	Y	Blue blazed Water Tank Trail to east.		570	1024.8
1166.4	♦	Spring		620	1024.5
1166.5	♦Y	Red blazed Henry Knauber Trail to east		680	1024.4
1167.0	◊	Cross stream, unreliable.		1052	1023.9

NoBo	Features	Description	GPS	Elev	SoBo
1168.2	◊	Spring, unreliable.		1453	1022.7
1168.7	◊	Spring, unreliable.		1486	1022.2
1169.2	Y	Horse-Shoe Trail (northern end). Horse-Shoe Trail leads to Valley Forge, PA, it is a total of 140 miles. See (www.hstrail.org).		1638	1021.7
1169.3	Y▲	Stony Mountain summit.		1650	1021.6
1169.9	♦	Cross Rattling Run.		1547	1021.0

Elevation profile with labeled features: Yellow Springs, Cold Spring Trail, Rausch Gap Shelter, Rausch Creek, Stony Creek, Second Mtn, Green Point Rd/PA Hwy 443, Trout Run Creek, Swatara Creek/PA Hwy 72, Swatara Gap/I-81, Blue Mtn, William Penn Shelter, Waggoners Gap/PA Hwy 645, 501 Shelter/PA Hwy 501, Round Head Knob

NoBo	Features	Description	GPS	Elev	SoBo
1172.5	Y	Yellow Springs Trail		1380	1018.4
1172.7	Y	Yellow Springs Village Site, trail register		1450	1018.2
1174.7	Y	Sand Spring Trail		1380	1016.2
1174.9	Y	Cold Spring Trail		1400	1016.0
1177.3	♦YĀ ⊏(6)↵ℂ	(0.2E) **Rausch Gap Shelter**, water (spring) next to the shelter, tenting, privy. 33.0◀24.7◀18.0◀▶ 13.4▶ 17.5▶32.6	N 40 29.918, W 76 36.010	980	1013.6
1177.8	♦⌒	Rausch Creek, stone arch bridge		920	1013.1
1177.9		Raush Gap Village, sign		920	1013.0
1178.2	♦⌒	Haystack Creek, wooden bridge		840	1012.7
1179.0		Second Mountain		1350	1011.9
1181.4	▲P(3)	Cross **Greenpoint Schoolhouse Road** then **150 feet to cross PA. 443**	N 40 29.402, W 76 33.062	570	1009.5
1182.0	▲ Ӿ⌂ ⚿▲P	Cross **PA. 443**, underpass Green Point, PA., (2.6W) to tenting, restaurant, laundry, shower.	N 40 28.946, W 76 33.012	550	1008.9
1183.4	▲P(5) ★★★★★	Cross **PA. 72**, Swatara Gap.	N 40 28.850, W 76 32.019	480	1007.5

Lickdale, PA (2.1E) See map of Lickdale, PA. Establishments are listed as Jonestown but that is because they have no post office box for Lickdale.

    ⊨⌂☐☎ **Days Inn** 717-865-4064 $85.15 and up (goes up in summer months), includes continental breakfast, pets $10. Microwave, fridge, laundry, computer available for use, free WiFi.

    ⊨⌂☐☎ **Fairfield Inn** 717-865-4234. Under construction will reopen in Feb 2017, call for pricing.

    ⊨⌂☐☎ **Comfort Inn** 717-865-8080. $127 and up, includes breakfast, microwave, fridge, laundry, computer available for use, free WiFi, pool. Pets $25

    ⊨Ā Ӿ血 **Jonestown KOA** 877-865-6411. (www.koa.com/campgrounds/jonestown) M-Su 7 days. Summer 5am-9pm. Tent site $38 and up, cabin also available. Pets on leash okay. Laundry, camp store, snack bar, free WiFi.
    ⌂☎

    血Ӿ⚿ **Love's Travel Stop with McDonalds, Chesters** 717-861-7390. $10 showers, ATM, all M-Su 24 hrs.
    ☎🕾🗑

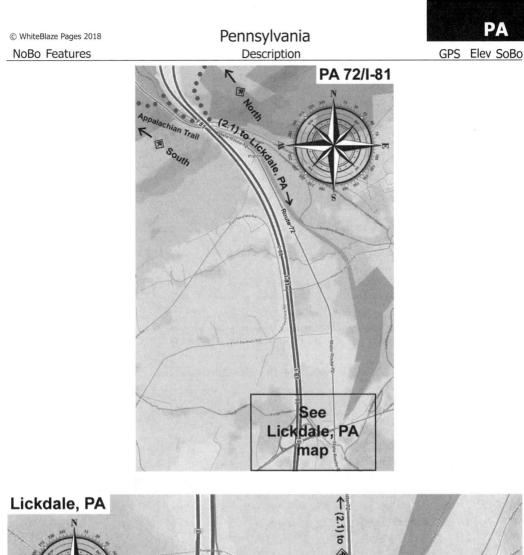

PA 72/I-81

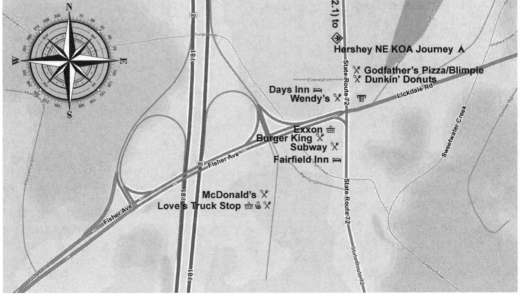

Lickdale, PA

NoBo	Features	Description	GPS	Elev	SoBo
1183.5	Y⌒	Cross Swatara Creek on Waterville Iron Bridge, Swatara Rail Trail.		460	1007.4
1183.8	⛰	Cross **I-81**, underpass		450	1007.1
1184.1	⛰	Cross woods road.		710	1006.8
1184.7		Circle of old hearth.		1187	1006.2
1188.0	📷	View of Monroe Valley to east.		1383	1002.9
1189.5		Cross pipe line.		1442	1001.4
1190.7	♦Y℃A ⊏(16)⌣	Blue Mountain Spring. Water is located 200 yards west on a blue blazed trail off the AT. (0.12E) **William Penn Shelter**, privy, tenting across AT from shelter. 38.1◄31.4◄13.4◄►4.1►19.2►33.9	N 40 29.736, W 76 24.864	1300	1000.2
1192.9	⛰P(10) ★★★★★	Cross **PA. 645**.	N 40 30.396, W 76 22.608	1250	998.0

Pine Grove, PA. (3.4W) See map of Pine Grove, PA.

      📮   **PO** M-F 8:30am-4:30pm, Sa 9am-1pm. 570-345-4955.

      ✗   **Original Italian Pizza** 570-345-5432. M closed, Tu-Th 11am-10pm, F 11am-11pm, Sa-Su 11am-10pm. Delivers to 501 shelter.

  ✗🏠⛺🚿 **Pilot Travel Center** 570-345-8800, laundry, $12 shower. M-Su 24 hours. **Subway**, **Dairy Queen** 📞

      ✗   **Pizza Town** 570-345-4041. M 11am-9pm, Tu closed, W-Th 11am-9pm, F-Sa 11am-10pm, Su closed.

      ✗   **New China** 570-345-8666. M-Th 11am-10pm, F-Sa 11am-11pm, Sun 11am-10pm.

      🛒   **Bergers Market** 570-345-3663. M-F 8am-9pm, Sa-Su 8am-6pm.

      ✗   **Original Italian Pizza, Do's Pizza, Turkey Hill Minit Market**

      ⚕   **Tri-Valley Pharmacy** 570-345-4966. (www.trivalleypharmacy.com) M-F 9am-7pm, Sa 9am-1pm, Su closed.

      ⛺   **Action Laundry**

      🚗   **Carlin's AT Shuttle Service** 570-345-0474, 570-516-3447. Shuttles anywhere in PA. Commercially insured for your safety

Pine Grove, PA

NoBo	Features	Description	GPS	Elev	SoBo
1194.7	📷	Kimmel Lookout		1330	996.2
1194.8	♦Y♠⌐ ⌣《♨⚠ P ★★★★★	Cross PA. 501 (0.1W) **501 Shelter**, water is located at faucet adjacent to house. Tenting, privy, solar shower. No smoking no alcoholic beverages allowed in shelter. Pets allowed but must be leashed. Some Pine Grove restaurants might deliver here. 35.5◄17.5◄4.1◄▶ 15.1▶29.8▶38.9▶	Shelter N 40 30.792, W 76 20.784 Parking N 40 30.753, W 76 20.678	1460	996.1

Bethel, PA (4.1E)

	📬	**PO** M-F 8am-12pm & 1:15am-4:30pm, Sa 8:30am-10:30am. 717-933-8305.			
	🏪	Several small convenience stores in the area.			
	💻	**Bethel Library** 717-933-4060. (www.berks.lib.pa.us/sbe) M-TH 10am-8pm, F 8am-6pm, Sa 10am-2pm, Su closed.			
	🐾	**Bethel Animal Hospital** 717-933-4916			
1195.3	♦Y♠	Blue blazed Pilger Ruh Spring Trail to east to spring which is a water spot dated back to colonial days. Applebee campsite to west.		1450	995.6
1196.7		Kessel Trail to the east.		1486	994.2
1197.8	📷	Unmarked trail to east leads 100 feet to unnamed lookout.		1483	993.1
1197.9	♦Y📷	Blue blaze trail to Round Head and Shower Steps with view.		1500	993.0

1200.0	▲📷	Shikellamy summit and overlook		1390	990.9
1200.4	♦⚑☂	Hertlein campsite, stream south of campsite.		1200	990.5
1200.5		Shuberts Gap		1200	990.4
1201.2		Cross pipe line.		1212	989.7
1203.8	♦	Fort Dietrich Snyder Marker, (0.2W) to spring		1440	987.1
1204.1	⚑P(6) ★★★★★	Cross **PA. 183**, Rentschler Marker. **See map of PA 183, PA.**	N 40 31.618, W 76 13.413	1440	986.8

~~(1.6W) Rock 'n Sole Hostel~~ Owners Craig and Jody Stine, 570-617-6432 text/voice, kragb@netzero. com. www.rocknsolehostel.com.
AT Passport location.
Smoke and drug free family operation that caters to those seeking a tranquil, clean, and enjoyable trail respite. A/C/heated bunkhouse, vintage camper($50 solo, $90 for couple), bunkhouse stay is $40 p/person and includes delicious home cooked dinner & breakfast, WI-FI, hot outdoor shower, sink, chemical outhouse, pickup/return to 183 trail head, and one daily resupply run to nearby Dollar General. Some options include laundry($3 p/person), package drop/mailing (free for hostel guests, $10 for non-guests), shuttles to Cabela's, Walmart, and the popular Yuengling Brewery tour. Slack packers, please contact for scheduling and shuttle costs. There are nearby farm markets, pharmacy, urgent care, bars, and central to several airports, bus, and train stops. Located midway between Duncannon and I-476 (NE Ext. of turnpike) in Schuylkill Haven, PA, 1.6 miles north of AT crossing/trail head at PA route 183.

Pine Grove, PA. (4.2W) See Notes at mile 1192.9.

PA 183

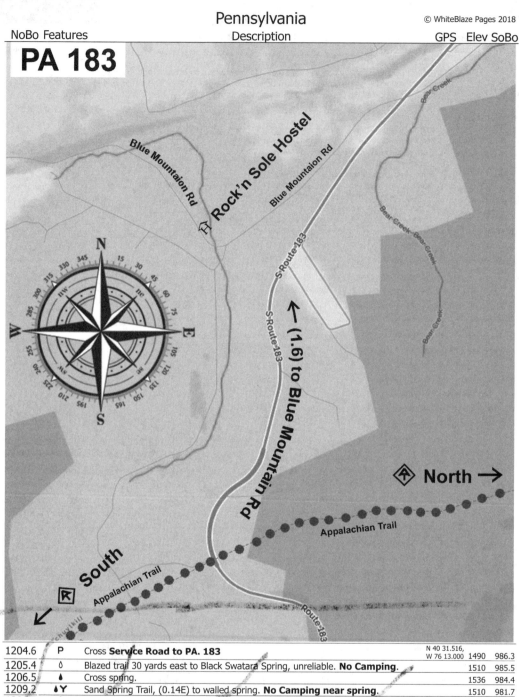

NoBo		Description	GPS	Elev	SoBo
1204.6	P	Cross **Service Road to PA. 183**	N 40 31.516, W 76 13.000	1490	986.3
1205.4	◊	Blazed trail 30 yards east to Black Swatara Spring, unreliable. **No Camping**.		1510	985.5
1206.5	◆	Cross spring.		1536	984.4
1209.2	◆Y	Sand Spring Trail, (0.14E) to walled spring. **No Camping near spring**.		1510	981.7
1209.7	▲	Cross **Game Lands Road**.		1592	981.2
1209.9	◆Y▲ ⌐(8)↶☾	Blue blaze trail leads (0.2) east to water (Yeich Spring), continue on for another (0.1) to **Eagle's Nest Shelter**, spring on trail to shelter, tenting, privy. 32.6◀19.2◀15.1◀▶ 14.7▶23.8▶31.2	N 40 32.963, W 76 09.146	1510	981.0
1211.8	▲	Cross **Shartlesville Cross–Mountain Road**		1450	979.1
1213.3	▲	Intersects with **State Game Lands Road** for about 100 yards.		1492	977.6
1214.5	◊	Unmarked Phillip's Canyon Spring trail is located east down a steep descent 135 yards in a stone enclosure, unreliable.		1500	976.4
1215.2	▲	Diagonally cross **State Game Lands Road**.		1330	975.7
1215.4	Y	Marshall's Path		1370	975.5

NoBo	Features	Description	GPS	Elev	SoBo
1216.0	Y 🖎	Auburn Lookout on trail to the east.		1400	974.9
1216.3	▲	Cross **State Game Lands Road**.		1415	974.6
1217.1		Cross pine line.		1359	973.8
1217.5		Cross pipe line.		1275	973.4
1218.3	Y ✕ ⌒	Intersection of Broad Street, Cross Schuylkill River on bridge.		420	972.6
1218.4	⌒ P	Cross Schuylkill River on bridge.	N 40 34.762, W 76 01.655	400	972.5
1218.5	▲ P(4) ★★★★★	Intersection with **Penn Street**. **Port Clinton, PA. See map of Port Clinton, PA.**	N 40 34.703, W 76 01.436	400	972.4
	🖾	**PO** M-F 12:30am-4:30pm, Sa 8am-11pm. 610-562-3787.			
	⇔ ✕ ⬧ ⌂	**Port Clinton Hotel** 610-562-3354. (www.portclintonhotel.net) AT Passport. Limited room, call for prices. $10 deposit for room key and towel. Laundry. Dining M- closed, Tu-Th 11am-9om, F-Sa 11am-10pm, Su 11am-9pm. Please shower before dine. Credit cards accepted.			
	⇔ ⌂	**Union House B&B** 610-562-3155. 610-562-4076. $65 and up. Open F-Su.			
	✕ 🖳	**3C's** 610-562-5925. Free WiFi. M-F 5am-2pm, Sa-Su 6am-2pm.			
	⛫ ⬧ ☎	**The Peanut Shop** 610-562-0610. Su-F 10am-6pm, Sa 10am-8pm, Su 10am-6pm. Sodas, candy, dried fruit, trail mixes, ATM.			
	▲ ☾	(0.2W) ojn Penn Street to **Pavilion** No alcohol or drugs. Tenting max 2 nights, no car camping. Water can be obtained from a spigot outside the Port Clinton Hotel. Permission required for more than two nights, call LaVerne Sterner 570-366-0489.			
	✕ ⬧	**Port Clinton Barber Shop** 484-336-8516. AT Passport location. Hikers are welcome to hang out. Coffee, cookies, and phone charging available. M-Sa 8am-5pm, Su closed.			

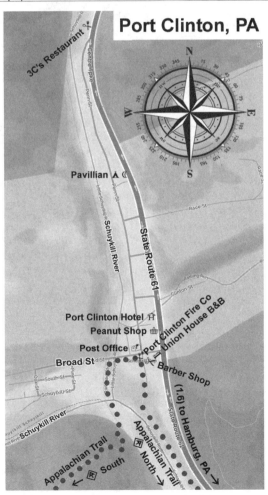

NoBo	Features	Description	GPS	Elev	SoBo
1219.2	⚑P(10) ★★★★★	Cross **PA. 61, Port Clinton Avenue** , underpass.		490	971.7

Hamburg, PA 19526 (1.6E) See map of Hamburg, PA.

	⌂	**PO** M-F 9am-5pm, Sa 9am-12pm. 610-562-7812.
	⌂✕⛺⊛	**Microtel Inn** 610-562-4234. Includes contintental breakfast.
	⌂	Mail for guest only with: 100 Industrial Drive, Hamburg, PA 19526
	🚶	**Cabela's** 610-929-7000, M-F 9am-10pm, Su 8am-10pm, Su 9am-9pm. Lots of hiking items, canister fuel. They will pickup from trail head if staff is available.
	🛒✕	**Walmart Superstore** 484-668-4001. M-Su 24 hours, with grocery and **Subway** M-Su 7am-9pm.
	✕	Many restaurants in area, **Pizza Hut, Red Robin, Logan's Steakhouse, Five Guys Burgers, Taco Bell/Long John Silver, Cracker Barrel.**
	☿	**Rite Aid** 610-562-9454, M-Su am-10pm. Pharmacy M-F 8am-9pm, Sa 8am-6pm, Su 9am-5pm.
	⌂	**Hamburg Coin Laundry** 610-562-4890
	🐕	**Hamburg Animal Hospital** 610-562-5000 (www.hamburganimalhospital.com) M-Th 9am-7pm, F 9am-5pm, Sa 9am-11am, Su closed.

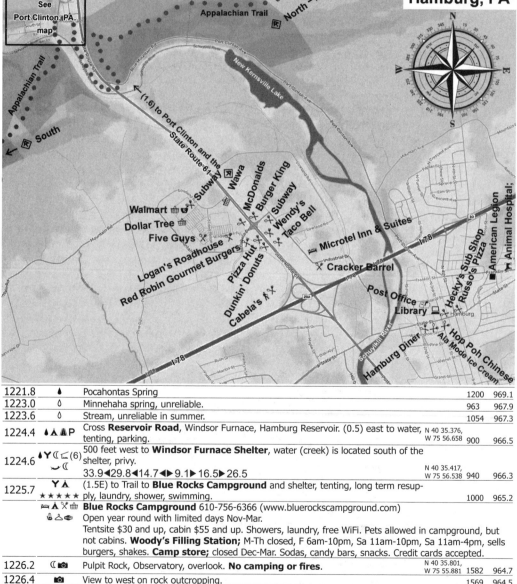

Hamburg, PA

1221.8	⬩	Pocahontas Spring		1200	969.1
1223.0	⬨	Minnehaha spring, unreliable.		963	967.9
1223.6	⬨	Stream, unreliable in summer.		1054	967.3
1224.4	⬩⛺⚑P	Cross **Reservoir Road**, Windsor Furnace, Hamburg Reservoir. (0.5) east to water, tenting, parking.	N 40 35.376, W 75 56.658	900	966.5
1224.6	⬩Y☾⛺(6) ⤵☾	500 feet west to **Windsor Furnace Shelter**, water (creek) is located south of the shelter, privy. 33.9◀29.8◀14.7◀▶9.1▶16.5▶26.5	N 40 35.417, W 75 56.538	940	966.3
1225.7	Y⛺ ★★★★★	(1.5E) to Trail to **Blue Rocks Campground** and shelter, tenting, long term resupply, laundry, shower, swimming.		1000	965.2
	⌂⛺✕⌂ ⛺⊛	**Blue Rocks Campground** 610-756-6366 (www.bluerockscampground.com) Open year round with limited days Nov-Mar. Tentsite $30 and up, cabin $55 and up. Showers, laundry, free WiFi. Pets allowed in campground, but not cabins. **Woody's Filling Station;** M-Th closed, F 6am-10pm, Sa 11am-10pm, Sa 11am-4pm, sells burgers, shakes. **Camp store;** closed Dec-Mar. Sodas, candy bars, snacks. Credit cards accepted.			
1226.2	☾📷	Pulpit Rock, Observatory, overlook. **No camping or fires**.	N 40 35.801, W 75 55.881	1582	964.7
1226.4	📷	View to west on rock outcropping.		1569	964.5

Pennsylvania

NoBo	Features	Description	GPS	Elev	SoBo
1228.0	Y A ★★★★★	Side trail leads (1.5) east to **Blue Rocks Campground** and shelter, tenting, long term resupply, laundry, shower, swimming. **See Notes at mile 1225.7.**		1150	962.9
1228.4	Y 🖾	Trail to east 80 yards leads to The Pinnacle, overlook		1615	962.5

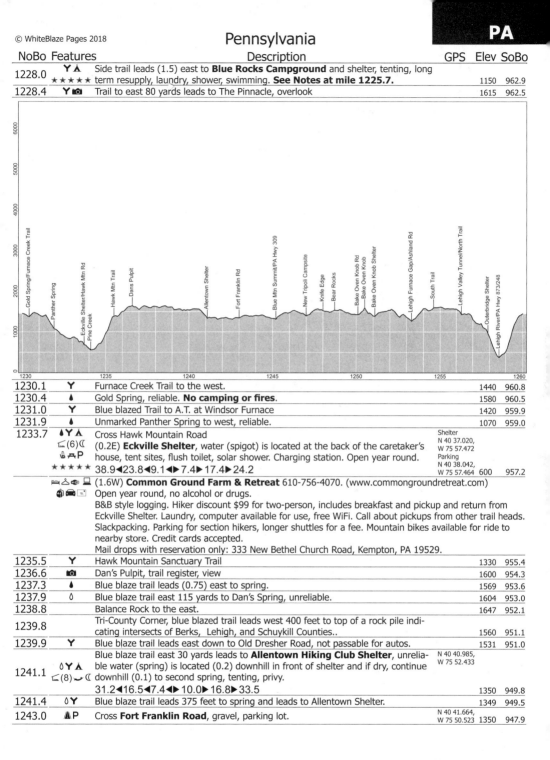

1230.1	Y	Furnace Creek Trail to the west.		1440	960.8
1230.4	◢	Gold Spring, reliable. **No camping or fires.**		1580	960.5
1231.0	Y	Blue blazed Trail to A.T. at Windsor Furnace		1420	959.9
1231.9	◢	Unmarked Panther Spring to west, reliable.		1070	959.0
1233.7	◢Y A ⊏(6)☾ ⌂🚻P ★★★★★	Cross Hawk Mountain Road (0.2E) **Eckville Shelter**, water (spigot) is located at the back of the caretaker's house, tent sites, flush toilet, solar shower. Charging station. Open year round. 38.9◄23.8◄9.1◄►7.4►17.4►24.2	Shelter N 40 37.020, W 75 57.472 Parking N 40 38.042, W 75 57.464	600	957.2
	🛏⛺🍴💻 🍴🚌📧	(1.6W) **Common Ground Farm & Retreat** 610-756-4070. (www.commongroundretreat.com) Open year round, no alcohol or drugs. B&B style logging. Hiker discount $99 for two-person, includes breakfast and pickup and return from Eckville Shelter. Laundry, computer available for use, free WiFi. Call about pickups from other trail heads. Slackpacking. Parking for section hikers, longer shuttles for a fee. Mountain bikes available for ride to nearby store. Credit cards accepted. Mail drops with reservation only: 333 New Bethel Church Road, Kempton, PA 19529.			
1235.5	Y	Hawk Mountain Sanctuary Trail		1330	955.4
1236.6	🖾	Dan's Pulpit, trail register, view		1600	954.3
1237.3	◢	Blue blaze trail leads (0.75) east to spring.		1569	953.6
1237.9	◊	Blue blaze trail east 115 yards to Dan's Spring, unreliable.		1604	953.0
1238.8		Balance Rock to the east.		1647	952.1
1239.8		Tri-County Corner, blue blazed trail leads west 400 feet to top of a rock pile indicating intersects of Berks, Lehigh, and Schuylkill Counties..		1560	951.1
1239.9	Y	Blue blaze trail leads east down to Old Dresher Road, not passable for autos.		1531	951.0
1241.1	◊Y A ⊏(8)⌣☾	Blue blaze trail east 30 yards leads to **Allentown Hiking Club Shelter**, unreliable water (spring) is located (0.2) downhill in front of shelter and if dry, continue downhill (0.1) to second spring, tenting, privy. 31.2◄16.5◄7.4◄►10.0►16.8►33.5	N 40 40.985, W 75 52.433	1350	949.8
1241.4	◊Y	Blue blaze trail leads 375 feet to spring and leads to Allentown Shelter.		1349	949.5
1243.0	⚠P	Cross **Fort Franklin Road**, gravel, parking lot.	N 40 41.664, W 75 50.523	1350	947.9

NoBo	Features	Description	GPS	Elev	SoBo
1245.2	⚠⚠⚠ P(10) ★★★★★	Cross **PA. 309**, Blue Mountain Summit. Blue blaze trail to west leads to parking area.	N 40 42.434, W 75 48.503	1360	945.7
	⚠🛏⚠⊛ ✗�car🖂	**Blue Mountain Summit B&B** 570-386-2003. (www.bluemountainsummit.com) Pending new owners in 2018. Stay tuned data may change. Open 7 days by appointment. No pets. $95–$125D, includes breakfast. Water from outside spigot at southwest corner. Please be respectful of non-hiking guests at the B&B and restaurant. Please don't loiter in front or hang clothes out to dry. Camping with permission, no fires. Ask about parking and shuttles. **Restaurant;** M-W closed, Th 12pm-9pm, F 12pm-10pm, Sa 12pm-9pm, Su 12pm-8pm. All major credit cards accepted. Mail drops for guests only (call first): 2520 W Penn Pike, Andreas, PA 18211.			
1247.0	⚠Y⚠🌲	Blue blaze trail west (0.2) leads to New Tripoli campsite, spring, power line.		1400	943.9
1248.0	📷	Knife Edge " The Cliffs", view		1525	942.9
1248.7	📷	Blue blaze west to Bear Rocks with a little difficulty but 360 degree view.		1525	942.2
1250.1	⚠P(30)	Cross State Game Lands parking lot and **Bake Oven Knob Road**, dirt road.	N 40 44.681, W 75 44.306	1450	940.8
1250.5		Bake Oven Knob		1560	940.4
1251.1	◊⚠(3) ⌐(6)🌙☾	**Bake Oven Knob Shelter**, water is located at trail in front of shelter leads downhill to multiple water sources and more reliable farther down but all sources are unreliable in dry weather, privy. Campsites are located south side below the AT. 26.5◄17.4◄10.0◄►6.8►23.5►37.2	N 40 45.247, W 75 43.644	1380	939.8
1253.5	◊⚠P	Cross **Ashfield Road** in Lehigh Furnace Gap, Ashfield, PA., radio tower, (0.7E) to spring. Parking is under the power lines.	N 40 46.170, W 75 41.656	1320	937.4
1254.6	Y	South Trail (southern jct.)		1596	936.3
1255.7	Y	South Trail (northern jct.)		1571	935.2
1256.3	Y	North Trail (southern jct.), Lehigh Valley Tunnel of PA. Turnpike is underneath A.T.		1570	934.6
1257.8	Y	North Trail		1550	933.1
1257.9	◊⌐(6)🌙	**George W. Outerbridge Shelter**, water (piped spring) is located north 150 yards on the AT north of the shelter. **The surrounding area suffers from heavy-metal contamination from the zinc plant at Palmerton.** 24.2◄16.8◄6.8◄► 16.7►30.4►61.6	N 40 46.951, W 75 37.079	1000	933.0
1258.3	🌲📷	Power lines with view.		557	932.6
1258.5	⚠ ★★★★★	Intersection with **PA. 873, Lehigh River Bridge (west end)**, Lehigh Gap		380	932.4
1258.6	⌒⚠P(8)	Intersection with **PA. 873, Lehigh River Bridge (east end)**	N 40 46.873, W 75 36.521	380	932.3
1258.8	⚠YP(3) ★★★★★	Cross **PA. 145/248.**	N 40 46.992, W 75 36.165	380	932.1

Slatington, PA. (2.0E) See map of Slatington, PA.

	🏪	**Bechtel's Pharmacy** 610-767-4121. (www.bechtelspharmacyinc.com) Open M-F 9am-8pm, Su 9am-2pm, Su closed.			
	💻	**Slatington Library** 610-767-6461. (www.slatelibrary.com) M 9am-7pm, Tu 9am-3pm, W 9am-7-m, Th closed, F 9am-5pm, Sa 8am-2pm, Su closed.			
1257.5	⌒⚠P	Intersection with **PA. 873, Lehigh River Bridge (east end)**	N 40 46.873, W 75 36.521	380	932.3
1257.7	⚠Y ★★★★★	Cross **PA. 145/248.**	N 40 46.992, W 75 36.165	380	932.1

Walnutport, PA (2.0E) See map of Walnutport, PA.

	📬	**PO** M-F 8:30am-5pm, Sa 8:30am-12pm. 610-767-2182.			
	🏪🛒	**Kmart** 610-767-1812, M-Su 8am-10pm. **Pharmacy** 610-767-2541. M-F 9am-9pm, Sa 9am-5pm, Su 10am-4pm.			
	✗	**Valley Pizza Family Restaurant** 610-767-9000. M-Th 10:30am-10pm, F-Sa 10:30am- 11pm, Su 10:30 amd-10pm. Also delivers.			
	✗	**Pizza Hut, Subway, Ritas, Burger King, Great Wall, Mamma's, Pizza**			
	🌲	**St Luke's Family Practice Center** 610-628-8922.			
	🏪	**Rite Aid** 610-767-9595. M-Su 8am-10pm, Su 9am-8pm. **Pharmacy** M-F 9am-9pm, Sa 9am-6pm, Su 9am-5pm.			
	🐾	**Blue Ridge Veterinary Clinic** 610-767-4896. (www.blueridgeveterinary.com) M-W 9am-7pm, Th 9am-6pm, F 8:30am-5:30pm, Sa 9am-12pm, Su closed. Call first.			

Palmerton, PA 18071 (1.5W) See map of Palmerton, PA.

	📬	**PO** M-F 8:30am-5pm, Sa 8:30am-12pm. 610-826-2286.			
	⌂✗⊛🛁	**Bert's Restaurant** 610-826-9921. M-T 7am-2pm, W-Th 7am-8pm, F-Sa 7am-8:30pm, Su 8am-8pm.			
	📶	WiFi in restaurant, ask about overnight stay, shower $5.			
	✗	**Palmerton Hotel Restaurant** 610-826-5454. (www.palmertonhotel.com) Dining M-Sa 11am-10pm, Su closed.			
	🛒🍴	**Country Harvest** 610-824-3663. (www.countryharvestmarkets.com) M-Su 8am-9pm.			
	✗	**Tony's Pizzeria** 610-826-6161. M-Su 11am-10:30pm. Serves lunch and dinner.			

Pennsylvania

NoBo Features	Description	GPS Elev SoBo

✗	**Joe's Place** 610-826-3730. Serves luch and dinner, deli sandwiches. M-Su 11am-8pm.	
🐾	**(3.5W) Little Gap Animal Hospital** 610-826-2793. (www.littlegapanimalhospital.com)	
△	**Towne Laundry** M-Su 5am-7pm.	
⚕	**Blue Mountain Family Medicine** 610-826-5110.	
🚗🛵	**Jason "SoulFlute"** 484-341-3356 Palmertonarea shuttles. Slackpacks Port Clinton to DWG. If you call and can not reach please send text message.	
🚗	**Brenda** 484-725-9396 Call for pricing. Shuttles ranging from local to bus terminals and airports.	

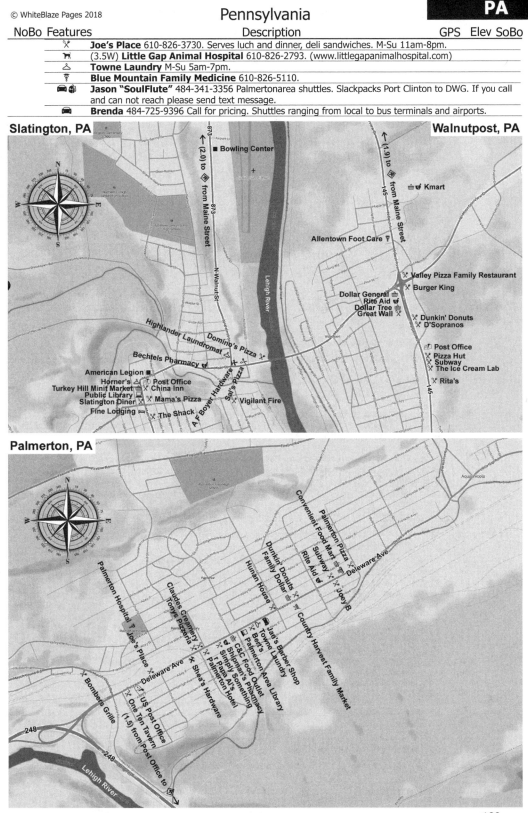

Slatington, PA

Walnutpost, PA

Palmerton, PA

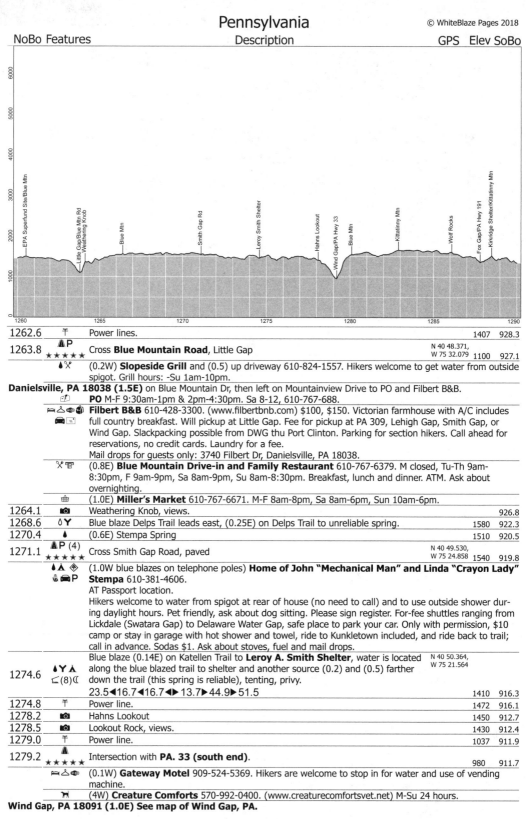

NoBo	Features	Description	GPS	Elev	SoBo
1262.6	⚡	Power lines.		1407	928.3
1263.8	⚐P ★★★★★	Cross **Blue Mountain Road**, Little Gap	N 40 48.371, W 75 32.079	1100	927.1
	▲✕	(0.2W) **Slopeside Grill** and (0.5) up driveway 610-824-1557. Hikers welcome to get water from outside spigot. Grill hours: -Su 1am-10pm.			
		Danielsville, PA 18038 (1.5E) on Blue Mountain Dr, then left on Mountainview Drive to PO and Filbert B&B.			
	✉	**PO** M-F 9:30am-1pm & 2pm-4:30pm. Sa 8-12, 610-767-688.			
	🛏⚐☎🍴 🚗✉	**Filbert B&B** 610-428-3300. (www.filbertbnb.com) $100, $150. Victorian farmhouse with A/C includes full country breakfast. Will pickup at Little Gap. Fee for pickup at PA 309, Lehigh Gap, Smith Gap, or Wind Gap. Slackpacking possible from DWG thu Port Clinton. Parking for section hikers. Call ahead for reservations, no credit cards. Laundry for a fee. Mail drops for guests only: 3740 Filbert Dr, Danielsville, PA 18038.			
	✕☎	(0.8E) **Blue Mountain Drive-in and Family Restaurant** 610-767-6379. M closed, Tu-Th 9am-8:30pm, F 9am-9pm, Sa 8am-9pm, Su 8am-8:30pm. Breakfast, lunch and dinner. ATM. Ask about overnighting.			
	🏪	(1.0E) **Miller's Market** 610-767-6671. M-F 8am-8pm, Sa 8am-6pm, Sun 10am-6pm.			
1264.1	📷	Weathering Knob, views.			926.8
1268.6	◊Y	Blue blaze Delps Trail leads east, (0.25E) on Delps Trail to unreliable spring.		1580	922.3
1270.4	◊	(0.6E) Stempa Spring		1510	920.5
1271.1	⚐P (4) ★★★★★	Cross Smith Gap Road, paved	N 40 49.530, W 75 24.858	1540	919.8
	◊▲◈ 🛏🚗P	(1.0W blue blazes on telephone poles) **Home of John "Mechanical Man" and Linda "Crayon Lady" Stempa** 610-381-4606. AT Passport location. Hikers welcome to water from spigot at rear of house (no need to call) and to use outside shower during daylight hours. Pet friendly, ask about dog sitting. Please sign register. For-fee shuttles ranging from Lickdale (Swatara Gap) to Delaware Water Gap, safe place to park your car. Only with permission, $10 camp or stay in garage with hot shower and towel, ride to Kunkletown included, and ride back to trail; call in advance. Sodas $1. Ask about stoves, fuel and mail drops.			
1274.6	◊Y▲ ⌂(8)☾	Blue blaze (0.14E) on Katellen Trail to **Leroy A. Smith Shelter**, water is located along the blue blazed trail to shelter and another source (0.2) and (0.5) farther down the trail (this spring is reliable), tenting, privy. 23.5◄16.7◄16.7◄► 13.7►44.9►51.5	N 40 50.364, W 75 21.564	1410	916.3
1274.8	⚡	Power line.		1472	916.1
1278.2	📷	Hahns Lookout		1450	912.7
1278.5	📷	Lookout Rock, views.		1430	912.4
1279.0	⚡	Power line.		1037	911.9
1279.2	▲ ★★★★★	Intersection with **PA. 33 (south end)**.		980	911.7
	🛏⚐☎	(0.1W) **Gateway Motel** 909-524-5369. Hikers are welcome to stop in for water and use of vending machine.			
	🐾	(4W) **Creature Comforts** 570-992-0400. (www.creaturecomfortsvet.net) M-Su 24 hours.			

Wind Gap, PA 18091 (1.0E) See map of Wind Gap, PA.

NoBo Features	Description	GPS Elev SoBo
PO	**PO** M–F 8:30am–5pm, Sa 8:30am–12pm, 610-863-6206.	
	Travel Inn 717-885-3101 $59.99D weekdays, $69.99D weekends. Room for 4 $69.99 weekdays, $79.99 weekends.	
	Red Carpet Inn 610-863-7782 Stay includes continental breakfast.	
	Giant Food Store M-Su 24 hours. Offers deli and salad bar.	
	K-Mart M-Sa 8am-10pm, Su 8am-9pm. **Pharmacy** M-F 8am-8pm, Sa 9am-5pm, Su closed.	
	Beer Stein 610-863-8338. (www.thebeerstein.net) M-Tu 3pm-2am, W-Su 11am-2am. Serves lunch and dinner.	
	J&R's Smokehouse 610-863-6162. Serves lunch and dinner. M-4pm-9:30pm, Tu-Th 11am-9:30pm, F-Sa 12pm-10pm, Su 9am-9pm.	
	Sal's Pizza 610-863-7565, delivers. M-W 11am-10pm, Sa 11am-11pm, Su 11am-10pm.	
	Hong Kong Chinese 610-863-9309. Lunch and dinner buffet. M-Su 11am-10:30pm.	
	CVS 610-863-5341. M-Su 8am-9m. **Pharmacy** M-F 8am-8pm, Sa 9am-6pm, Su pam-5pm.	
	Priority Care 610-654-5454. Walk- n clinic M-F 8am-8pm, Sa 10am-5pm, Su 10am-4pm.	
	Slate Belt Family Practice 610-863-3019. (www.slatebeltfamilypractice.com) M-Tu 8am-8pm, W 8am-1pm & 4pm-7pm, Th 8am-8pm, F 8am-1pm & 4pm-7pm, Sa 9am-12pm, Su closed.	
	WGM Taxi 570-223-9289	

Wind Gap, PA

NoBo	Features	Description	GPS	Elev	SoBo
1279.3	⚔ P	Intersection with **PA. 33 (north end)**.	N 40 51.642, W 75 17.561	1571	911.6
1281.3	⚔	Cross Private road to Blue Mountain Water Company.		1571	909.6
1285.6	♦ Y	Wolf Rocks Bypass Trail (south end), signed spring		1550	905.3
1286.1	📷	Wolf Rocks		1620	904.8
1286.3	Y ⌇	Wolf Rocks Bypass Trail (north end). Power line.		1510	904.6
1287.7	⚔ P(6)	Cross **PA. 191**, Fox Gap, small parking lot.	N 40 56.125, W 75 11.819	1400	903.2
1288.1	Y	Orange blazed The Great Wall Trail descends (0.8) down the mountain.		1419	902.8
1288.3	♦ Y ⌂(8) ⌇ ☾ 📷	Blue blazed trail (south end) to **Kirkridge Shelter**, water is located on outside tap to rear of shelter before the Kirkridge Retreat facility parking lot, privy. Views. 37.2◄30.4◄13.7◄► 31.2►37.8►43.6►	N 40 56.205, W 75 11.186	1500	902.6
1288.4	Y	Blue blazed trail (North end) to Kirkridge Shelter, **see notes above**.		1495	902.5
1288.5	📷	Nelson's Overlook, good views.		1527	902.4
1289.1	📷	Lunch Rock located 50 feet east, view.		1482	901.8

NoBo	Features	Description	GPS	Elev	SoBo
1290.0	⌇	Power line.		1349	900.9
1290.2	⚔	Cross Totts Gap, gravel road		1300	900.7
1292.2	⛰	Mt. Minsi, summit		1461	898.7
1292.5	📷	Panoramic view of Delaware Water Gap.		1339	898.4
1293.2	Y 📷	Side trail east to Lookout Rock, view of Delaware River and Delaware Water Gap.		800	897.7
1293.4	♦	Cross Eureka Creek.		733	897.5
1294.0	📷	Council Rock, view		600	896.9
1294.3	♦	Pass Lake Lenape. A blue blaze side trail east reconnects to the AT at (0.8) and (15.0).		492	896.6
1294.5	P	Pass hiker parking lot.	N 40 58.789, W 75 08.524	510	896.4
1294.6	⚔	Intersection of **Lake Road and Mountain Road**.		457	896.3
1294.7	⚔ ★★★★★	Intersection with **PA. 611 and Delaware Ave**. **See map of Delaware Water Gap, PA.**		400	896.2

	📫	**PO** M-F 8:30am-12pm, & 1pm-4:45pm, Sa 8:30am-11:30pm. 570-476-0304.
	⌂ ◈ ⛭	**Church of the Mountain Hiker Center** 862-268-1120, 570-476-0345, 570-992-3934. (www.churchofthemountain.org) AT Passport location. Bunkroom, showers, overflow tenting, rides to Stroudsburg when available. Donations encouraged. 2 night maximum. No laundry. There is a phone listing posted of people who can help posted in the hostel. Cars may not be parked on the property at any time. Mail drops are not accepted but the post office is next door.
	🛏 ◈ ⛺ ⊜	**Pocono Inn** 570-476-0000. (www.poconoinnwg.com) No pets. $75 and up, higher on weekends. Coin laundry, free WiFi.
	🛏 ◈ ✕	**Deer Head Inn** 570-424-2000. (www.deerheadinn.com) No pets. $120 and up. Restaurant and lounge.
	✕ 🏪	**Village Farmer & Bakery** 570-476-9440. (www.villagefarmerbakery.com) M-SU 8am-8pm. Serves a hot dog and slice of pie $2.95. Breakfast sandwiches, salads, sandwiches. Credit card minimum $10.

	✗	**Doughboy's Pizza** 570-421-1900. (www.doughboysoftheponos.com) M-Th 11am-11pm, F-Sa 11am-11pm, Su 11am-9pm.			
	🖈🚗⌨	**Edge of the Woods Outfitters** 570-421-6681. (www.edgeofthewoodsoutfitters.com/theshop.html) Full line of gear, carries a large selection of hiker trail food, backpacking meals, ultralight back pack gear, and footwear. Alcohol and coleman by the ounce. Shuttles from Little Gap to Bear Mtn by advance reservation only. Open 7 days, Memorial - Labor Day. Mail drops: (FedEx/UPS only) 110 Main St, Delaware Water Gap, PA 18327. USPS will be held at the post office.			
	🖈🚗	**Water Gap Adventures** 570-424-8533. (www.adventuresport.com) Apr-Oct.			

Delaware Water Gap, PA

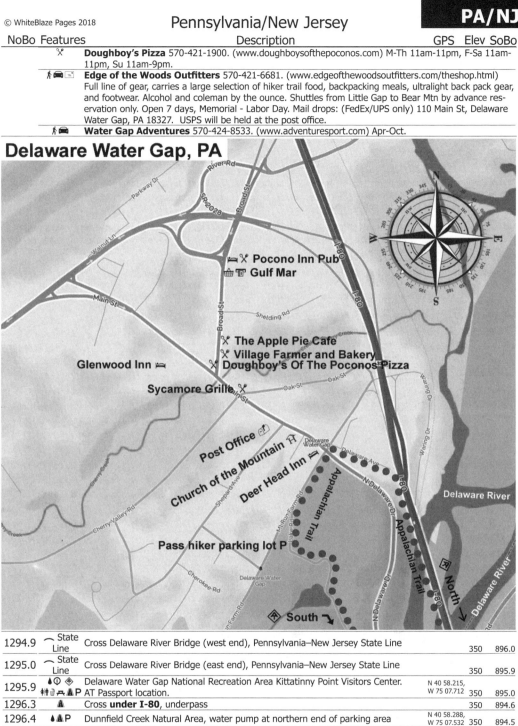

1294.9	⌒ State Line	Cross Delaware River Bridge (west end), Pennsylvania–New Jersey State Line		350	896.0
1295.0	⌒ State Line	Cross Delaware River Bridge (east end), Pennsylvania–New Jersey State Line		350	895.9
1295.9	⛲⏲◈ 🖈♨⛺⚠P	Delaware Water Gap National Recreation Area Kittatinny Point Visitors Center. AT Passport location.	N 40 58.215, W 75 07.712	350	895.0
1296.3	⚠	Cross **under I-80**, underpass		350	894.6
1296.4	⛲⚠P	Dunnfield Creek Natural Area, water pump at northern end of parking area	N 40 58.288, W 75 07.532	350	894.5
1296.8	⛲Y	Blue blazed Blue Dot Trail leads (1.8) east to the summit of Mt. Tammany overlooking Delaware Water Gap. Green blazed Dunnfield Hollow Trail to Dunnfield, Creek Falls, (0.25E) to water.		350	894.1
1297.9	⛲Y	Red blazed Holly Springs Trail (0.2E) to water. Yellow blazed Beulah Trail west.		950	893.0
1298.9	⛲Y⛺🚿	Blue blazed Douglas Trail to Backpacker campsite. (1.7) west to tenting, water and shower		1300	892.0
1299.5	⛺	Pass Backpacker Site, no water. Blue blaze Douglas Trail west.		1353	891.4
1300.1	⛲	Sunfish Pond, glacial pond, **NO CAMPING**		1382	890.8

NoBo	Features	Description	GPS	Elev	SoBo
1300.4	♦	Outlet stream of Sunfish Pond. Unmarked Sunfish Drainage Trail to the west.		1387	890.5
1300.8	Y	Turquoise Trail to the east.		1445	890.1
1300.9	♦Y	Orange blazed Garvey Spring Trail west and leads 600 feet to spring.		1400	890.0
1301.8	♦	Cross brook.		1454	889.1
1302.5	⊤	Power line.		1568	888.4
1302.6	📷	Large pile of rocks, views on both sides of trail.		1579	888.3
1303.0	♦Y	Blue on White, Kaiser Road Trail leads east (0.3) to spring.		1445	887.9
1303.3	YP	Blue on White, Kaiser Road Trail leads west (1.5) to Old Mine Road and parking.to		1419	887.6
1303.7	📷	Open rocks, view.		1480	887.2
1304.6	⋀	Open area to east can be used for camping.		1325	886.3
1305.2	♦⋀P ★★★★★	Cross **Camp Road**. Just south of road crossing trail crosses Yards Creek water source and red blazed Coppermines Trail on west side of AT. **AMC Mohican Outdoor Center**		1150	885.7
	♦Y⌂⋀ ◈✕🏠⛉ ⊕▭	(0.3W) **Mohican Outdoor Center** 908-362-5670. (www.outdoors.org/lodging/mohican) AT Passport location. Thru-hiker rates $30 PP bunkroom includes electricity, showers, full kitchen and access to WiFi typically. Tenting with access to showers, bear boxes, and WiFi $10 PP, price subject to change, call ahead and inquire. Towel and Shower for non-guests are $5 PP. Sheets and Towels available for rent at varying rates. Campfires only in designated areas. Water available at the lodge or at spigot near the garage across the street. Coleman, alcohol by the ounce as well as camp supplies, MREs, trekking poles, raingear, etc. The Mohican Outdoor Center Deli is open and we are ready to satiate your Hiker Hunger! We have soup, sandwiches, ice cream, breakfast all day AND an exclusive Hiker Hunger menu with high calorie meal options, simply ask at the front desk. Welcome center and camp store hours April- October Su-Th 8am-7pm, F 8am-9pm, Sa 8am-8pm.Our off-season hours are Nov-Apr 9am-5pm. Mail drops: 50 Camp Mohican Rd, Blairstown, NJ 07825.			
1307.6	⋀🔥	Catfish Fire Tower, 360 degree views.	N 41 02.855, W 74 58.347	1565	883.3
1307.9	⋀	Intersects with fire tower road.		1485	883.0
1308.2	♦⋀	Rattlesnake Spring 50 feet west, dirt road.		1260	882.7
1308.6	⋀♦🚙⋀ P(6)	Cross **Millbrook–Blairstown Road/County Road 602**, (1.1W) to water, park overnight at your own risk.	N 41 03.564, W 74 57.808	1260	882.3
1309.1	⌒	Cross bridge over outlet of beaver pond.		1258	881.8
1309.4	⊤📷	Powerline, view.		1451	881.5
1309.5	Y📷	Side trail east leads to viewpoint.		1463	881.4
1310.3	Y	Red and white blaze trail descends east over private property to Camp No-Bo-Bo-Sco (boy scout camp).		1458	880.6
1310.9	⋀	Intersects with dirt road.		1486	880.0
1312.2	⋀📷	Unmarked woods road leads east 125 feet to view.		1457	878.7
1312.5	⋀P(8)	Blue **Mountain Lakes Road (Flatbrookville-Stillwater Road)**	N 41 05.387, W 74 54.689	1350	878.4
1313.8		Pass swamp to east of trail.		1407	877.1
1314.3	♦Y📷P	Crater Lake Trail leads east 150 feet to view overlooking Crater Lake, (0.3E) to water	N 41 06.563, W 74 53.514	1560	876.6
1314.6	Y	Hemlock Pond Trail west (0.4) to Hemlock Pond.		1470	876.3
1315.4	♦Y⛏	Buttermilk Falls Trail leads west descending to Buttermilk Falls, (1.5) west on trail to water, dependable.		1560	875.5
1316.4	Y	Unmarked trail to west leads to view from slanted rock slabs.		1499	874.5
1316.9	♦⌒Y	Cross stream on logs. Just north of stream is a blue blazed trail east to water.		1291	874.0
1317.3	⋀⋀📷	Rattlesnake Mountain summit, open ledges		1492	873.6
1317.6	♦	Cross stream on rocks.		1405	873.3
1318.1	⋀	Intersects with dirt road.		1483	872.8
1318.8	📷	Reach crest of ridge with good views.		1441	872.1
1319.5	♦Y⌐(8) ☾🎒	900 feet west to **Brink Shelter**, water (spring) is located across the road 100 yards northeast of the shelter, privy, bear box. 61.6◄44.9◄31.2◄►6.6►12.4►15.0	N 41 09.192, W 74 50.292	1110	871.4

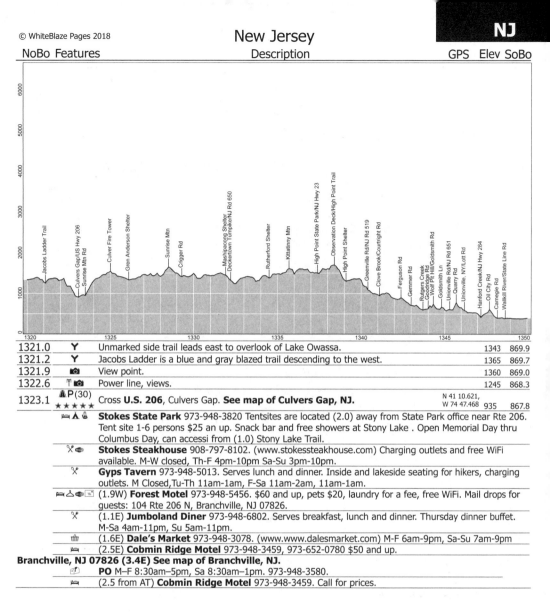

NoBo	Features	Description	GPS	Elev	SoBo
1321.0	Y	Unmarked side trail leads east to overlook of Lake Owassa.		1343	869.9
1321.2	Y	Jacobs Ladder is a blue and gray blazed trail descending to the west.		1365	869.7
1321.9	📷	View point.		1360	869.0
1322.6	⊤📷	Power line, views.		1245	868.3
1323.1	▲P(30) ★★★★★	Cross **U.S. 206**, Culvers Gap. **See map of Culvers Gap, NJ.**	N 41 10.621, W 74 47.468	935	867.8
	🛏⛺🚿	**Stokes State Park** 973-948-3820 Tentsites are located (2.0) away from State Park office near Rte 206. Tent site 1-6 persons $25 an up. Snack bar and free showers at Stony Lake . Open Memorial Day thru Columbus Day, can accessi from (1.0) Stony Lake Trail.			
	✕⛽	**Stokes Steakhouse** 908-797-8102. (www.stokessteakhouse.com) Charging outlets and free WiFi available. M-W closed, Th-F 4pm-10pm Sa-Su 3pm-10pm.			
	✕	**Gyps Tavern** 973-948-5013. Serves lunch and dinner. Inside and lakeside seating for hikers, charging outlets. M Closed,Tu-Th 11am-1am, F-Sa 11am-2am, 11am-1am.			
	🛏⛺⛽✉	(1.9W) **Forest Motel** 973-948-5456. $60 and up, pets $20, laundry for a fee, free WiFi. Mail drops for guests: 104 Rte 206 N, Branchville, NJ 07826.			
	✕	(1.1E) **Jumboland Diner** 973-948-6802. Serves breakfast, lunch and dinner. Thursday dinner buffet. M-Sa 4am-11pm, Su 5am-11pm.			
	🏦	(1.6E) **Dale's Market** 973-948-3078. (www.www.dalesmarket.com) M-F 6am-9pm, Sa-Su 7am-9pm			
	🛏	(2.5E) **Cobmin Ridge Motel** 973-948-3459, 973-652-0780 $50 and up.			
Branchville, NJ 07826 (3.4E) See map of Branchville, NJ.					
	✉	**PO** M–F 8:30am–5pm, Sa 8:30am–1pm. 973-948-3580.			
	🛏	(2.5 from AT) **Cobmin Ridge Motel** 973-948-3459. Call for prices.			

Culvers Gap, NJ

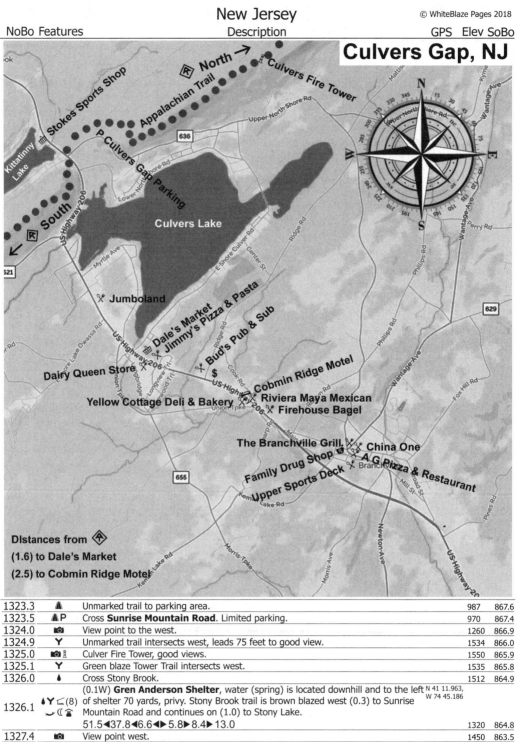

Distances from ®

(1.6) to Dale's Market

(2.5) to Cobmin Ridge Motel

NoBo	Features	Description	GPS	Elev	SoBo
1323.3	▲	Unmarked trail to parking area.		987	867.6
1323.5	▲P	Cross **Sunrise Mountain Road**. Limited parking.		970	867.4
1324.0	📷	View point to the west.		1260	866.9
1324.9	Y	Unmarked trail intersects west, leads 75 feet to good view.		1534	866.0
1325.0	📷	Culver Fire Tower, good views.		1550	865.9
1325.1	Y	Green blaze Tower Trail intersects west.		1535	865.8
1326.0	♦	Cross Stony Brook.		1512	864.9
1326.1	♦Y⌐(8) ⌐((🏠	(0.1W) **Gren Anderson Shelter**, water (spring) is located downhill and to the left of shelter 70 yards, privy. Stony Brook trail is brown blazed west (0.3) to Sunrise Mountain Road and continues on (1.0) to Stony Lake. 51.5◄37.8◄6.6◄►5.8►8.4►13.0	N 41 11.963, W 74 45.186 1320		864.8
1327.4	📷	View point west.		1450	863.5
1327.5	Y	Intersects with yellow blazed Tinsley Trail.		1476	863.4
1328.5	🚻▲📷 P(25)	Sunrise Mountain, picnic pavilion, panoramic views.	N 41 13.090, W 74 43.224 parking N 41 13.165, W 74 43.105	1653	862.4
1328.6	Y	Path leading to parking lot.		1617	862.3

NoBo	Features	Description	GPS	Elev	SoBo
1329.3	⚑	Cross **Crigger Road, dirt**		1400	861.6
1330.2	♦	Cross swamp outlet.		1407	860.7
1331.2	⚑	Trail joins woods road for 225 feet.		1484	859.7
1331.9	⚑⊏(8) ⌣《🐻	**Mashipacong Shelter**, NO WATER here, bear box. 43.6◄12.4◄5.8◄►2.6►7.2►19.6	N 41 15.130, W 74 41.183	1425	859.0
1332.1	⚑P(10)	Cross **Deckertown Turnpike**, paved	N 41 15.138, W 74 41.362	1320	858.8
1332.8	Y	Intersects with red on white blazes of Iris Trail.		1414	858.1
1333.2	Y📷	Clear strip of land, a buried pipeline. A trail east leads to view.		1417	857.7
1333.6	♦⌒	Cross stream on logs. Just north of stream is a blue blazed trail east to water.		1334	857.3
1334.0	⚑Y	Intersects with woods road and the red and white blazes of Iris Trail.		1370	856.9
1334.5	◊Y⚑ ⊏(6) ⌣《🐻📷	Dutch Rock with views. **(0.4E) Rutherford Shelter**, Spring 100 yards before shelter on connecting trail. Slow stream. Tenting, privy, bear box. 15.0◄8.4◄2.6◄►4.6►17.0►28.5	N 41 16.651, W 74 40.689	1345	856.4
1334.7	📷	View east.		1614	856.2
1339.7	📷	View west.		1584	851.2
1336.1	📷	View west over Sawmill Lake.		1590	854.8
1336.5	♦Y⚑	Blue Dot Trail, (0.4W) to tenting and water		1600	854.4
1337.3	Y	Trail intersection. Yellow blaze Mashipacong Trail west. Red and white Iris Trail east.		1552	853.6
1337.4	♦⚑ ★★★★★	Cross **N.J. 23; High Point State Park HQ**	N 41 18.156, W 74 40.068	1500	853.5
	♦⚑◈👫 P(20)✉	**High Point State Park Headquarters** 973-875-4800. AT Passport location. Office is open year round M-Su 9am-4pm. Bathrooms inside, water spigot outside. Overnight parking (0.25E).			
	🛏⛺- 🚗📶✉	**(1.5E) High Point Country Inn** 973-702-1860 $90 and up, pets $10. Laundry $7, free WiFi. Free pick-up and return to trail from NJ 23, longer shuttles for a fee. Mail drops for guests: 1328 NJ 23, Wantage, NJ 07461.			

Port Jervis, NY 12785 (4.4W)

NoBo	Features	Description	GPS	Elev	SoBo
	🛏📶🖥✉	**Days Inn** 845-856-6611 $80 and up, $10EAP, continental breakfast pets $25. Computer available for use, free WiFi. Mail drops for guests: 2247 Greenville Turnpike, Port Jervis, NY 12771.			
	✗	**Village Pizza** 973-293-3364. (www.villagepizzaitalianrestaurant.com) M-Sa 11am-11pm, Su 12-11pm.			
	🛒🗑	**Shop Rite Market** M-Su 6am-12am.			
	🗑	**Rite Aid** 845-856-8342. M-Sa 7am-10pm, Su 9am-8pm, Pharmacy M-F 8am-9pm, Sa 9am-6pm, Su 9am-5pm.			
		Medicine Shoppe 845-856-6681. M-F 9am-6pm, Sa 9am-1pm, Su closed.			
	✚	**Bon Secours Community Hospital** 845-858-7000. (www.bonsecourscommunityhosp.org)			
	🐾	**Tri-States Veterinary Medical** 845-856-1914. M-Tu 8am-5pm, W-Th 8am-7pm, F 8am-5pm, Sa 8am-2pm, Su closed.			
1338.4	Y📷⚑ 👫⚑	Observation Platform		1680	852.5
1338.6	Y📷⚑	Side Trail to High Point Monument intersects with red and green blazed Monument Trail.		1600	852.3
1339.1	♦Y⊏(8) 《🐻	**(0.1E) High Point Shelter**, streams on both sides of shelter are known to dry up at times, privy, bear box. 13.0◄7.2◄4.6◄►12.4►23.9►36.0	N 41 19.665, W 74 38.628	1280	851.8
1339.4	◊	Cross brook at head of ravine, unreliable.		1233	851.5
1340.4	🛏⚑P(5)	Cross **County Road 519**, paved, (2.5E) to lodging	N 41 19.759, W 74 38.595	1100	850.5
1341.1	♦	Cross two streams in area.		951	849.8
1341.2	⚑	Cross **Courtwright Road**, gravel		1000	849.7
1341.4		Follow blazes carefully in area along stone walls.		994	849.5
1341.9	♦	Pass pond to the west.		916	849.0
1342.2		Intersection of stone walls.		864	848.7
1342.3	♦⌒	Cross steam on bridge.		861	848.6
1342.4	⚑	Cross **Ferguson Road also known as Mt. Salem Road.**	N 41 19.292, W 74 36.991	900	848.5
1343.0	⚑P(2)	Cross **Gemmer Road**, paved	N 41 18.982, W 74 36.473	740	847.9
1343.1	♦⌒	Cross wooden bridge over brook.		727	847.8
1343.3	♦⌒	Cross stream over wooden bridge.		741	847.6
1343.7	♦	Cross two wooden brides over streams.		710	847.2
1344.0	⚑P(2)	Cross **Goodrich Road**, paved	N 41 18.895, W 74 36.148	610	846.9
1344.2	♦	Cross over concrete dam (outlet of pond).		700	846.7
1344.3		Reach crest of Wolf Pit Hill, open field.		741	846.6

NoBo	Features	Description	GPS	Elev	SoBo
1344.4	♦Y⅄⌐ ⊂⊆♣▲ ★★★★★	Cross **Goldsmith Road**, road leads (0.2) west to Jim Murray property, water, shelter, tenting, privy, shower.		660	846.5
	♦⊂⊆⅄▲ ♨▲	**Private cabin** open for the use of long distance hikers as it has been for nearly 20 years, tenting, well water, shower and privy. If you feel the need to change your brain chemistry this is probably not your stop but serious hikers welcome. No groups please.			
1344.5	▲	Cross **Goldsmith Lane**, gravel. Vernie Swamp (southern end)		600	846.4
1344.7		Vernie Swamp (northern end).		590	846.2
1344.8	▲	Cross **Goldsmith Lane**.		674	846.1
1345.1		Reach hilltop, overgrown fields with abandon apple orchards.		654	845.8
1345.3	▲P(3)	Cross **Unionville Road, county Road 651**	N 41 18.136, W 74 34.549	610	845.6
1345.4		Pass old quarry pit.		638	845.5
1345.5	▲P(5)	Cross **Quarry Road, paved**.	N 41 18.018, W 74 34.321	678	845.4
1346.2	▲ ★★★★★	Cross **Lott Road, also known as Jersey Avenue**	N 41 17.905, W 74 34.123	590	844.7

Unionville, NY. (0.7W)

	⌂	**PO** M-F 8am-11:30am & 1pm-5pm, Sa 9am-12pm. 845-726-353.			
	♦⅄♦♦	**Village Office** 845-726-3681. Check-in at office or at Horler's Store for overnight tenting.			
	✗☏	**Wit's End Tavern** 845-726-3956. (www.witsendtavern.com) Serves ribs, burgers, wings and more. ATM. M-Th 12pm-2am, F-Sa 12pm-4am, Su 12pm-2am.			
	⌐✗☏	**Horler's Store** 845-726-3210. M–Sa 6am–8pm, Su 7am–7pm. Has a short order grill open M-F 6:30am-3pm, Sa-Su 7am-1pm. ATM.			
	⛁☏	**End of the Line Grocery** 845-726-3228. Deli, ATM. M-Su 7am-7pm.			
	✗	**Annabel's Pizza** 845-726-9992 (www.annabelspizza.com) M-Sa 11am-10pm, Su 11am-9pm.			
1346.4		Intersects with abandon railroad grade.		611	844.5
1346.9		Intersects with abandon railroad grade.		602	844.0
1347.2	▲P(5) ★★★★★	Cross **N.J. 284**.	N 41 17.300, W 74 33.130	420	843.7

Unionville, NY. (0.7W) see NoBo mile 1346.2

1347.7	▲	Cross **Oil City Road**, paved		400	843.2
1348.3	♦⌐▲	Intersects with private road just north of a bridge over small stream.		442	842.6
1348.5	▲	Intersects with private road leading to private property of Carnegie Industries.		442	842.4
1348.7	▲⌐	Cross bridge over Wallkill River on **Oil City Road**.	N 41 17.264, W 74 32.053	410	842.2
1349.0	▲	Intersects with **Oil City Road**, Wallkill National Wildlife Preserve	N 41 17.119, W 74 31.853	410	841.9

1350.5	⅄▲	Intersects with Liberty Loop Trail, dirt road.		387	840.4
1351.0	▲	Intersects with **Lake Wallkill Road (Liberty Corners Road)**, paved		440	839.9
1351.5	♦⅄⅄ ⌐(6) ↩⊂⊆☂	(0.1W) **Pochuck Mountain Shelter**, water is available at a spigot on the north side of a vacant white house at the foot of Pochuck Mountain (0.5) south on Lake Wallkill Road(Liberty Corners Road), tenting, privy, bear box. 19.6◄17.0◄12.4◄►11.5►23.6►37.9	N 41 16.300, W 74 30.978	840	839.4

New Jersey

NoBo	Features	Description	GPS	Elev	SoBo
1351.7		Pochuck Mountain western ridge.		1200	839.2
1352.0	▲	Cross woods road.		975	838.9
1352.3	◙	Overlook at crest , views across Wallkill Valley to High Point.		1134	838.6
1352.5		Pass old stone foundation.		1078	838.4
1352.8	◊▲	Cross dirt road and slab, some possible water sources.		1114	838.1
1353.0	▲	Pochuck Mountain summit, side trail leads 40 feet west to view.		1194	837.9
1353.6	▲	Cross dirt road that leads to youth camp.		942	837.3
1353.8	◊	Cross stream.		846	837.1
1354.1	◊⌒	Cross bridge over stream.		741	836.8
1354.2	▲P (3) ★★★★★	Cross **County Road 565**, limited parking	N 41 14.897, W 74 28.866	720	836.7

Glenwood, NJ 07418 (1.1W)

⌂	**PO** M-F 7:30am–5pm. Sa 10am–2pm. 973-764-2616.	
⇌⊛☎▣	**Apple Valley Inn** 973-764-3735. (www.applevalleyinn.com) No pets. $145 and up, includes country breakfast, with stay also return to the trail to County Roads 517 & 565. Mail drop for guest: PO Box 302, Glenwood, NJ 07418.	
◊▲⌂✗	(1.0W) **Pochuck Valley Farms** Market & Deli 973-764-4732. (www.pochuckvalleyfarms.com) Serves breakfast and lunch. Water spigot outside. Ask about tenting. M–F 6am–6pm, Sa–Su 6am–5pm.	

1354.6	▲ ★★★★★	Intersects with **County Road 517**. Obey the No Parking signs on 517. Parking along 517 is very limited and cars parked in the No Parking zone have been ticketed.	N 41 14.139, W 74 28.828	440	835.2
1355.7	▲ ★★★★★	Intersects with **County Road 517**. Obey the No Parking signs on 517. Parking along 517 is very limited and cars parked in the No Parking zone have been ticketed.	N 41 14.139, W 74 28.828	440	835.2
1355.9	⌒	Cross 2,000 foot section of boardwalk over Pochuck Swamp.		410	835.0
1356.3	⌒	Cross 1,100 foot section of boardwalk over Pochuck Swamp.		410	834.6
1356.4	⌒	Cross suspension bridge over Pochuck Creek.		410	834.5
1356.5	⌒	Cross 850 foot section of boardwalk over Pochuck Swamp.		410	834.4
1356.6	⌒	Cross wooden bridge.		410	834.3
1357.0		Intersects Canal Road		410	833.9
1357.1	▲P	Intersects Canal Road	N 41 13.599, W 74 28.136	410	833.8
1357.3	◊⌒	Cross bridge over Wawayanda Creek.		434	833.6
1357.8	✗	Cross New York/Susquehanna and Western Railway tracks.		422	833.1
1358.0	▲P(8) ★★★★★	Cross **N.J. 94. See map of Vernon, NJ.**	N 41 13.162, W 74 27.311	450	832.9

⌂♦⛺☎	(0.1W) **Heaven Hill Farm** 973-764-5144. (www.heavenhillfarm.com) Has bakery items, vegetables, ice cream, picnic tables, ATM. M-F 9am–7pm, Su 9am-6pm.	
✗⛱	(0.2E) **Mitch's Roadside Grill Hot dog Stand** 973-715-2608. M-Su 11am-3pm Hot dogs, sodas, Italian Ice and potato knishe, picnic tables.	
⇌⚐⊛▣	(1.2E) **Appalachian Motel** 973-764-6070. (www.appalachianmotel.com) $70 and up $10EAP. Call for ride. Pets $20. Microwave, fridge, laundry $10. Mail drops for guests: 367 Route 94, Vernon, NJ 07462.	

Vernon, NJ 07462 (2.4E) See map of Vernon, NJ.

⌂	**PO** M-F 8:30am-5pm, Sa 9:30am-12:30pm. 973-764-9056.	
⛟⚐⛢	**Acme Market** 973-764-5350. Pharmacy, ATM. M-Sa 6am-12am, Su 6am-10pm.	
✗	**China Star, Dairy Queen, Burger King, Paesano Pizza, Ming's Asian Bistro**	
⚕	**Vernon Urgent Care** 973-209-2260. (1.0) mile beyond hostel, M–F 8am–8pm, Sa–Su 9am–5pm.	
🐕	**Vernon Vet Clinic** 973-764-3630. (www.vernonvet.com) M-Su by appointment.	

New Milford, NY (2.7W) See Mile 1361.1

Vernon, NJ

NoBo	Features	Description	GPS	Elev	SoBo
1358.4	📷	Cross old stone wall above overgrown field with views.		562	832.5
1359.0		Reach the south most point of Wawayanda Mountain.		1244	831.9
1359.3	Y 📷	Blue blaze trail west (0.1) to Pinwheel's Vista along the cliffs of Wawayanda Mountain.		1345	831.6
1359.4	📷	Wawayanda Mountain, trail register.		1340	831.5
1359.9	▲	Cross woods road.		1143	831.0
1360.3	♦⌒	Cross stream on footbridge.		989	830.6
1360.7	📷	Luthers Rock, limited views through trees.		1206	830.2
1361.1	▲P(2) ★★★★★	Cross **Barrett Road**, New Milford, NY.	N 41 12.881, W 74 25.247	1140	829.8

New Milford, NY 10959 (1.8W)

	🖅	(1.4W) on Barret Rd, then right (0.6) on NJ 94 to shoe store and **Post Office**. M-F 8:30am-12:30pm, Sa 9am-11:30am. 845-986-3557.			
	✗	**Mom's Home Style Deli** 845-988-9089. M-F 6am-3pm, Sa 7am-3pm, Su 8:30am-3pm.			
	■	**Sneakers to Boots** 845-986-0333 (www.sneakerstoboots.com) Carries some name brand hiker footwear, Merrell, Keen, Salomon, Oboz and Hi-Tec. M-F 10am-6pm, Sa 10am-5pm, Su 11am-2pm.			
1361.3		Cross drain.		1145	829.6
1361.4	▲	Intersects with woods road.		1203	829.5
1361.8	◊	Stream, unreliable.		1185	829.1
1362.2	♦⌒	Cross iron bridge over Double Kill, 1890's era bridge.		1046	828.7
1362.4	▲✗	Intersects with **Iron Mountain Road**. At intersection blue trail east (1.6) to restaurant and water at Wawayanda Lake. Follow blue blaze trail (1.2) and cross a paved road, continue (0.4) to Lake. From Memorial Weekend to Labor Day, visitors can swim 10–6. Restrooms, first-aid station, food concession (ice cream, burgers, soda), and boat rental.		1060	828.5
1362.5	▲	Cross woods road.		1195	828.4
1362.8	▲	Intersects with **Wawayanda Road**, dirt.		1150	828.1
1363.0	▲⌂(6) ☾☂	275 feet to **Wawayanda Shelter**, privy, water is available at the park office which can be reached by going north on the AT (0.1) and east (0.2) on Hoeferlin Trail. Privy, bear box. 28.5◄23.9◄11.5◄►12.1►26.4►31.7	N 41 12.131, W 74 23.910	1200	827.9
1363.2	♦Y▲P 👬🚻🛢	Cross woods road, Hoeferlin Trail leads (0.2) east to quarters of Wawayanda State Park.	N 41 11.886, W 74 23.850	1200	827.7
1363.3	⌒	Cross plank bridge over swamp outlet.		1114	827.6
1363.5	▲P(8) ★★★★★	Cross **Warwick Turnpike**, (2.7W) to long term resupply and restaurant.	N 41 12.094, W 74 23.483	1140	827.4

Warwick, NY (2.7W)

	🛒🍴	**Price Chopper** 845-987-6333. M-Su 24 hours; Pharmacy M-F 8am-8pm, Sa 9am-5pm, Su 9am-3pm.			
1363.7		South end of farm road on edge of field.		1194	827.2
1363.8		North end of edge of farm road along field.		1197	827.1
1364.0	♦	Cross brook.		1152	826.9
1364.2	▲	Cross old woods road.		1183	826.7
1364.8	◊	Cross logs on stream, unreliable.		1136	826.1
1364.9	▲P(4)	Intersects with **Long House Road (Brady Road)** for short distance.	N 41 11.736, W 74 22.292	1080	826.0
1365.2		Follow grassy woods road.		1154	825.7
1365.4	▲	Follow woods road for a short distance.		1155	825.5
1365.6	♦⌒	Cross wooden bridge over stream.		1160	825.3
1366.0	♦⌒	Cross log bridge over Long House Creek.		1085	824.9
1366.1	▲	Follows dirt road for a short distance.		1087	824.8
1366.3	▲	Cross two woods roads in a short distance.		1193	824.6
1366.4	♦	Cross stream on rocks.		1365	824.5
1366.6	📷	Rock ledge with view west.		1379	824.3
1366.8	Y	Yellow blazed Ernest Walter Trail leads east.		1368	824.1
1366.9	📷	View overlooking Surprise Lake and Sterling Ridge.		1393	824.0
1367.1	Y State Line	New Jersey–New York State Line State Line Trail; Hewitt, N.J.		1385	823.8
1367.2		Pass trail register.		1364	823.7
1367.5	📷	Prospect Rock, views over Greenwood Lake and south.		1433	823.4
1367.6	Y	Zig Zag trail leads west to Cascade Lake Park.		1402	823.3
1367.7	📷	Rock promontory west of trail.		1379	823.2
1368.5	♦	Cross Furnace Brook.		1135	822.4
1368.7	♦	Cross stream, seasonal.		1224	822.2
1368.8	📷	Rock outcrop with panoramic view south.		1328	822.1
1369.6	📷	Exposed rock outcrop, limited views		1273	821.3

NoBo	Features	Description	GPS	Elev	SoBo
1369.7	♦	Cross several small streams in the area.		1268	821.2
1370.1	♦	Cross Cascade Brook.		1246	820.8
1370.5	♦	Cross brook.		1173	820.4
1370.8	📷	Exposed rock outcrops with views of Greenwood Lake.		1280	820.1
1371.0	📷 ★★★★★	Vista Trail leads (0.8) east to the village of **Greenwood Lake, NY (0.8E)**.		1180	819.9
		Greenwood Lake, NY (0.8E) See note at NOBO mile 1373.1			
1372.2	♦	Cross brook.		1199	818.7
1372.6	⊤	Power line.		1159	818.3
1373.1	⚠P(12) ★★★★★	Cross **N.Y. 17A**	N 41 14.657, W 74 17.230	1180	817.8
	✗	**Hot Dog Plus** Korean War Army Veteran Bernard "Bud" Whitt is open seasonally Tu-Sa 10:30-3:30.			
	♦✗	**(0.3W) Bellvale Farms Creamery** 845-988-1818. (www.bellvalefarms.com) Ice cream. Water/electric charging station available outside.			

Bellvale, NY 10912 (1.6W)
- ✗   **Bellvale Market** 845-544-7700. (www.bellvalemarket.com) M-F 8am-7pm, Sa 8am-6pm, Su 8am-4pm.

Greenwood Lake, NY 10925 (2.0E) See map of Greenwood Lake, NY.
- ✉   **PO** M–F 8am–5pm, Sa 9am–12pm. 845-477-7328.
- 🛏⊗✗⛺   **Anton's on the Lake** 845-477-0010. (www.antonsonthelake.com)
- 🛏🖥☕🚗   Open year round.
- 🖥   No pets or smoking. Thru hiker rate, 2-night min, price per night: Su-Th $80S/D, F-Sa $125/up. Credit cards are accepted, rooms with whirlpool available, small laundry loads only, swimming, paddle boats and canoe. Free shuttles and slackpacking with stay, longer shuttles for fee. Mail for guests: (USPS) PO Box 1505 or (FedEx/UPS) 7 Waterstone Rd, Greenwood Lake, NY 10925.
- 🛏⊗⛽   **Lake Lodging** 845-477-0700, 845-705-2005. No Pets. Hiker rates, free WiFi, **no credit cards**.
- 🛏⊗✗⛽   **Breezy Point Inn** 845-477-8100. (www.breezypointinn.com) No pets, no smoking. $185 and up. Free
- ⊤🖥   WiFi, ATM. Serves lunch and dinner M-Su. Closed month of January. Mail drops for guests: (UPS/FedEx) 620 Jersey Ave, Greenwood Lake, NY 10925.
- ✗   **Country Kitchen, Ashley's Pizza, Sing Loong Kitchen, Subway**
- 🛒   **Country Grocery** 845-477-0100. M-F 8am-8pm, Sa 10am-7pm, Su 10am-6pm.
- 🧴   **CVS** M-Su 8am-9pm, **Pharmacy** M-F 8am-8pm, Sa 9am-6pm, Su 9am-5pm.
- 🔧   **True Value Hardware** 845-477-3327. M-Sa 8am-6pm, Su 9am-2pm.
- 🚗   **Greenwood Lake Taxi** 845-477-0314. (www.greenwoodlaketaxi.com)

Greenwood Lake, NJ

Vesuvius Brick Oven Pizza
Scoops Ice cream
Post Office
Subway
CVS
$
The Grill
Planet Pizza
Cumberland Farms
Jean Claudes Fine Cakes
Elks Lodge
Irish Whisper
Village Buzz Cafe
Sing Loong Kitchen
Murphy's Tavern & Restaurant
Public Library
True Value
4 Brothers Pizzeria & Deli
Doc's Pizza and Steaks
Country Grocery
The Helm
Anton's on the Lake
Waterstone Inn
Breezy Point Inn
Emerald Point Restaurant & Marina
Greenwood Lake

1373.7		Clearing for gas pipe line.		1216	817.2
1374.3	📷	Eastern Pinnacles, views to the east and south.		1294	816.6
1374.6	💧	Cross brook.		1026	816.3
1374.8	📷	Cat Rocks, 360 degree views. Blue blaze trail to the east bypasses this.		1080	816.1
1375.1	💧 Y Å (3) ⌂ (8) ⌇ ☾ ☎	600 feet west to **Wildcat Shelter**, water (spring) is located 75 yards downhill and left from the shelter, tenting, privy, bear box. 36.0◀23.6◀12.1◀▶14.3▶19.6▶22.8	N 41 16.101, W 74 16.098	1180	815.8
1375.3		Cross old stone wall and pass foundation to the west.		1201	815.6
1376.0	Y	Highlands Trail, teal diamond blazed leads west but runs with the AT north for (2.1) miles.		1127	814.9
1376.6	⛰P(2)	Cross **Lakes Road**, paved	N 41 16.420, W 74 15.252	680	814.3
1376.7	💧〰	Cross wooden bridge over Trout Brook.		643	814.2
1376.8	Y	Blue blaze trail leads east, avoiding two more crossings of Trout Brook during high water seasons, rejoining at Fitzgerald Falls.		662	814.1
1376.9	💧Y⚓	Fitzgerald Falls. Blue blaze bypass trail leads east after crossing the brook avoids two more crossings of Trout Brook during high water seasons.		800	814.0
1377.0	💧	Cross Trout Brook and tributary.		666	813.9
1377.3		Pass old stone walls and remains of abandon settlement.		965	813.6
1378.1	Y	Allis Trail leads (2.5) east and descends over One Cedar Mountain to N.Y. 17A.		1198	812.8
1378.9	📷	Mombasha High Point		1280	812.0
1379.6	⛰	Cross grassy woods road.		950	811.3

1380.1	⛰P(5)	Cross **West Mombasha Road**, paved. You might fit one car here to park.	N 41 16.205, W 74 12.896	980	810.8
1380.2	💧	Cross stream, outlet of Kloiber's Pond to the east, not visible.		931	810.7
1380.5	💧	Cross stream.		1021	810.4
1381.0	📷	Viewpoint from rock ledge near the summit of Buchanan Mountain.		1142	809.9
1381.4	💧	Cross four streams in the area.		877	809.5
1381.6	📷	View to the east.		1016	809.3
1381.8	⛰P	Cross **East Mombasha Road**, paved. Limited parking. Overnight parking prohibited.	N 41 16.018, W 74 11.615	840	809.1
1382.1	💧	Cross inlet of Little Dam Lake on stone.		719	808.8
1382.5		Cross Eastern end of Little Dam Lake		720	808.4
1383.2	⛰P(4)	Intersects with **Orange Turnpike** and follow for 250 feet.	N 41 16.140, W 74 10.828	780	807.7
1383.4	📷	Ridge of Arden Mountain, views west.		984	807.5
1383.5	📷	Reach secondary peak of Arden Mountain, views west.		1061	807.4
1383.9	⛰📷	Arden Mountain, Agony Grind, views west and north.		1180	807.0
1384.2	Y	Blue blaze trail east leads (0.4) to yellow blazed Indian Hill Loop Trail. Trail register near here.		1166	806.7
1384.3	Y✕	Sapphire Trail west leads (2.6) to Harriman station on Metro-North's Port Jervis Line which provides rail service to Hoboken and Penn Station.		1166	806.6
1384.6	📷	View above Agony Grind.		1083	806.3

NoBo	Features	Description	GPS	Elev	SoBo
1385.0	▲ ★★★★★	Cross **N.Y. 17**, Arden Valley Road		550	805.9

NY 17 Southfields, NY (2.1E)

	🏤	**PO** M–F 10am–12pm & 1pm–5pm, Sa 8:30am–11:30am. 845-351-2628.			
	🚌⊛⛺🖂	**Tuxedo Motel** 845-351-4747. (www.tuxedomotelinc.com) $54.50S, $59.50D, $10EAP. No pets, no cooking. Laundry. Accepts Visa, MC. Mail drops: 985 Route 17 South, Southfields, NY, 10975.			
	🏪	**Valero** (0.1W) of Post Office.			
	🚗	**Suffern's Deborah Taxi** 845-300-0332. Text is best or deborahtaxi@gmail.com Based out of Suffern, NY/Mahwah, NJ. Deborah Tapp. Shuttles from NJ to CT. (from Delaware Water Gap, Pa. to Hoyt Rd.)			
	Harriman, NY. (3.7W)	Lodging, restaurants.			
1385.2	▲	Cross over **I-87 N.Y. State Thruway**, overpass		560	805.7
1385.3	▲P(30) ★★★★★	Pass entrance to Elk Pen parking area.	N 41 15.921, W 74 09.210	587	805.6
1385.4	▲ ★★★★★	Intersects with **Arden Valley Road**.		680	805.5
	🚌P	**Harriman Shuttle** Runs Sa, Su and holidays will pickup here at 11:43 and Tiorati circle at 11:40. Connects to town of Southfields and Tuxedo Train Station. $5 per ride.			
1385.5	▲	Intersects with **Old Arden Road.**		628	805.4
1386.3	▲	Green Pond Mountain summit		1180	804.6
1386.5	▲	**Island Pond Road** briefly joins the AT.		988	804.4
1386.6	▲	Cross gravel road.		1006	804.3
1386.7	♦	Cross Island Pond Outlet		1350	804.2
1386.8	▲📷	Reach crest with view of Island Pond.		1309	804.1
1387.0	▲	**Crooked Pond Road**, and old woods road briefly joins the AT and crosses the inlet of Island Pond.		1073	803.9
1387.3	Y	Lemon Squeezer. Arden-Surebridge Trail (A-SB) leads east.		1150	803.6
1387.5	▲	Island Pond summit.		1303	803.4
1387.9	Y	Cross the Aqua-blazed Long Path Trail.		1160	803.0
1388.1	◊	Stream, unreliable.		1130	802.8
1388.4	▲	Surebridge Mountain		1200	802.5
1388.7	♦	Cross Surebridge Brook..		1103	802.2
1388.8	▲	**Surebridge Mine Road** joins the AT.		1197	802.1
1389.3	Y	Rampo-Dunderberg Trail (R-D) leads east, marked with red on white blazes.		1354	801.6
1389.4	♦Y⊏(8) ⌣((☂	350 feet east to **Fingerboard Shelter**, water (spring) is located downhill to left but is unreliable. 37.9◀26.4◀14.3◀▶5.3▶8.5▶40.7	N 41 15.799, W 74 06.243	1300	801.5
1390.0	▲	Fingerboard Mountain summit.		1374	800.9
1390.4		Pass round water tank.		1204	800.5
1390.5	♦▲⛲ ★★★★★	Cross **Arden Valley Road**, to Lake Tiorati Circle, (0.3W) to water and shower.		1196	800.4
	♦✕♨⛟ 🍴🚗⛵	(0.3E) **Lake Tiorati Beach** 845-429-8257. M-Su 9am-7pm, mid Jun thru mid Aug, Only open on weekends in spring and fall. Free showers, restrooms, trash cans, picnic tables, vending machine, swimming.			
1391.2	▲Y	Cross wide woods road diagonally to the left. Ramapo-Dunderberg Trail (R-D) east marked with red on white blazes.		1026	799.7
1391.7	📷	Reach high point with view through trees.		1182	799.2
1392.5	♦	Cross stream.		862	798.4
1392.7	▲	Cross **Seven Lakes Drive** diagonally to the left.		850	798.2
1393.9	Y	Cross over Bockey Swamp Brook between Goshen and Letterock Mountains. Ramapo-Dunderberg Trail (R-D) marked with red on white blazes.		1105	797.0
1394.7	◊▲⊏(8) ⌣📷	**William Brien Memorial Shelter**, Water is located at a unreliable spring-fed well 80 yards down blue blazed trail to right of shelter. Tenting. 31.7◀19.6◀5.3◀▶3.2▶35.4▶44.4	N 41 16.782, W 74 03.594	1070	796.2
1394.8		Cross rocky high point of Letterrock Mountain.		1143	796.1
1395.6	▲	Cross **Silvermine Road**, fire road.		913	795.3
1395.7	📷	Overlook with view of Silvermine Lake.		1060	795.2
1396.1	📷	South side of Black Mountain, views of Hudson River and Bew York City.		1175	794.8
1396.5	Y	Cross the 1779 Trail east.		822	794.4
1396.8	♦🚻☉🏧	Cross Palisade Interstate Parkway, divided highway, (0.4W) to water		680	794.1
1396.9	Y	Rampo-Dunderberg Trail (R-D) leads east, marked with red on white blazes.		685	794.0
1397.0	♦⌐	Cross Beechy Bottom Brook on wooden bridge.		660	793.9
1397.1	♦	Cross stream.		606	793.8
1397.3	▲	Cross **Beechy Bottom Road**, marked with blue on white plastic blazes as a bike path.		665	793.6

NoBo	Features	Description	GPS	Elev	SoBo
1397.9	Y ⊑(8) 📷	(0.6E) on Timp-Torne Trail to **West Mountain Shelter**. Views of Hudson River and NYC.	N 41 17.944, W 74 00.553		793.0
		22.8◄8.5◄3.2◄►32.2►41.2►49.0		1240	793.0
1398.2	📷	Flat rock on West Mountain near ledges with views.		1120	792.7
1398.5	Y	Timp-Torne Trail (T-T) west.			792.4
1398.6	📷	View on West Mountain looking at Bear Mountain and Hudson River.			792.3
1399.1	Y	Fawn Trail west, red blazed.			791.8
1399.3	▲	Follows woods road which is not a cross country ski trail.			791.6
1399.7	▲	Cross **Seven Lakes Drive**		610	791.2
1400.2	▲	Intersects with **Perkins Drive**, paved.		950	790.7
1400.7	▲	Intersects with wide road, now an abandon section of Perkins Memorial Drive.			790.2
1400.8	📷	View over West Mountain.			790.1
1401.1	Y 📷	Panoramic view west. Blue blaze trail leads (0.2) to another viewpoint.			789.8
1401.2	Y	Blue blaze (0.2) east to the summit of Bear Mountain.			789.7
1401.7	Y	Intersects with Major Welch Trail, red ring on white blazed.		1151	789.2
1402.1	📷 ⎾ P(99)	Bear Mountain, Perkins Tower	N 41 18.689, W 74 00.411	1305	788.8
1402.7	▲	Intersects with paved **scenic drive**.		1206	788.2
1402.9	▲	Intersects with paved **scenic drive**.		1152	788.0
1403.9	⌒📷	Cross 28 foot wooden bridge, view of Hudson River.		456	787.0
1404.1	◑P🚗	Passes by Bear Mountain Inn, Hessian Lake. See notes for Bear Mountain Inn under Fort Montgomery, NY.	N 41 18.781, W 73 59.339	155	786.8
1404.8	⊛ ★★★★★	Cross under U.S. 9W in tunnel, **Bear Mountain Museum and Zoo.**		124	786.1
	⊛ ◈	**Bear Mountain Museum and Zoo** AT Passport location. No pets allowed. If closed, or if you have a dog, use bypass. 845-786-2701 Open 10 am-4:30 pm; no charge for hiking through.			
1404.9	▲⌒📷 ★★★★★	Intersects with **U.S. 9W**, Bear Mountain Circle, Bear Mountain Bridge (south end), Hudson River **Bear Mountain, NY. See map of Bear Mountain/Fort Montgomery, NY.**		150	786.0

Fort Montgomery, NY 10922 (1.8W) See map of Fort Montgomery, NY.

🏠	**PO** M-F 8am-1pm & 2:30pm-5pm, Sa 9-am12pm, 845-446-8459	
🛏✕🖥⛛ ☎	**Bear Mountain Inn** 845-786-2731 $149 and up, includes continental breakfast, restaurant, computer available for use, free WiFi, ATM.	
🛏⛛	**Overlook Lodge** 845-786-2731 $149 and up, continental breakfast, pet rooms free WiFi.	
🛏⊛⛛▢	**Bear Mountain Bridge Motel** 845-446-2472. No pets. $75D, pickup and return to trail at park, zoo or bridge with stay, free WiFi. Accepts Visa, MC. Mail drops for guests: PO Box 554, Fort Montgomery, NY 10922.	
🛏△🖥⛛ ▢	**Holiday Inn Express** 845-446-4277. To make reservations, please call for rates and availability, walk-ins welcome also. Free Express Start Breakfast with stay. Coin laundry, indoor pool and sauna. Complimentary Wi-Fi and business center includes computer and printer for use. Mail drops for guests: 1106 Route 9 W, Fort Montgomery, NY 10922-0620.	
✕	**Foodies Pizza** 845-839-0383. M-Sa 11am-9pm, Su 12pm-9pm. Serves breakfast, lunch and dinner.	

Highland Falls, NY (3.8W)

🛏⛛	**Fairbridge Inn & Suites** 845-446-9400. $75 and up, includes continental breakfast. Pets $10.	
🏪	**My Town Marketplace** 845-446-3663.M-Sa 8am-9pm, Su 8am-6pm.	
✛	**Rite Aid** 845-446-3170. M-Su 8am-10pm, Pharmacy M-F 9am-9pm, Sa 9am-6pm, Su 9am-5pm.	
🖥	**Highland Falls Library** 845-446-3113. (www.highlandfallslibrary.org) M 10am-5pm, Tu 10am-7pm, W 10am-5pm, Th-F 10am-5pm, Sa 10am-2pm, Su closed.	

Bear Mtn/Fort Montgomery, NY

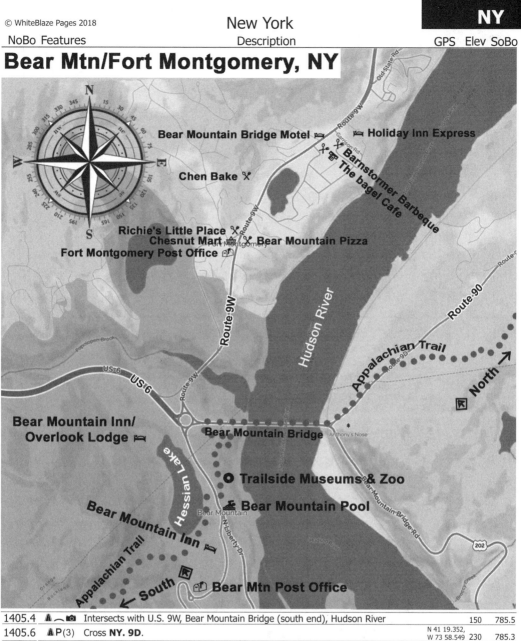

Bear Mountain Bridge Motel 🛏 Holiday Inn Express

Barnstormer Barbeque

The bagel Cafe

Chen Bake 🍴

Richie's Little Place 🍴

Chesnut Mart 🍴 Bear Mountain Pizza

Fort Montgomery Post Office 🏤

Route 9W

Hudson River

Appalachian Trail

Route 90

North

Bear Mountain Inn/
Overlook Lodge 🛏

US 6

Bear Mountain Bridge

Anthony's Nose

Hessian Lake

🔵 Trailside Museums & Zoo

🏊 Bear Mountain Pool

Bear Mountain Inn 🛏

Bear Mountain

Appalachian Trail

South

Bear Mtn Post Office 🏤

202

NoBo	Features	Description	GPS	Elev	SoBo
1405.4	🏕 ⛺ 📷	Intersects with U.S. 9W, Bear Mountain Bridge (south end), Hudson River		150	785.5
1405.6	🏕 P(3)	Cross **NY. 9D**.	N 41 19.352, W 73 58.549	230	785.3
1406.1	Y 📷	Camp Smith Trail to Anthony's Nose (0.5E) with view of Hudson River.		700	784.8
1406.3	🏕	Intersects with rocky dirt road.		786	784.6
1407.0	⬥	Cross brook.		551	783.9
1407.1	⬥ Y 🏕 ⛺	Intersects with dirt road ay a "Y" intersection. Blue blaze trail leads 100 feet east to Hemlock Springs Campsite, nearby spring. Do not camp in the area where blue blaze trail leaves the AT.		550	783.8
1407.3	🏕 P(4)	Intersects **South Mountain Pass Road** and follows the road for 250 feet.	N 41 19.786, W 73 57.141	460	783.6
1407.4		Trail register.		667	783.5
1408.2		High point near Canada Hill summit.		832	782.7
1408.3	Y	Osborn Loop Trail west.		787	782.6
1408.4	🏕	Unmarked woods road east.		864	782.5
1408.8	Y	Curry Pond Trail west, yellow blazed.		821	782.1
1409.6	Y	Blue blaze trail leads 100 feet to view over Hudson River and Bear Mountain Bridge.		931	781.3
1409.7	Y	Osborn Loop Trail west.		872	781.2

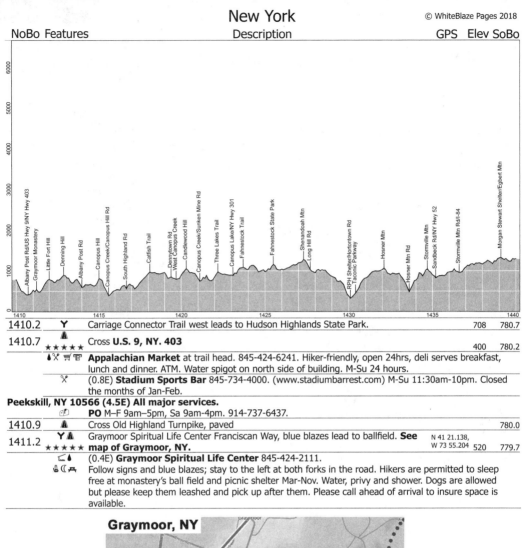

NoBo	Features	Description	GPS	Elev	SoBo
1410.2	Y ▲	Carriage Connector Trail west leads to Hudson Highlands State Park.		708	780.7
1410.7	★★★★★	Cross **U.S. 9, NY. 403**		400	780.2
	◑✕ 🛒 ☕	**Appalachian Market** at trail head. 845-424-6241. Hiker-friendly, open 24hrs, deli serves breakfast, lunch and dinner. ATM. Water spigot on north side of building. M-Su 24 hours.			
	✕	(0.8E) **Stadium Sports Bar** 845-734-4000. (www.stadiumbarrest.com) M-Su 11:30am-10pm. Closed the months of Jan-Feb.			

Peekskill, NY 10566 (4.5E) All major services.

	✉	**PO** M–F 9am–5pm, Sa 9am-4pm. 914-737-6437.			
1410.9	▲	Cross Old Highland Turnpike, paved			780.0
1411.2	Y ▲ ★★★★★	Graymoor Spiritual Life Center Franciscan Way, blue blazes lead to ballfield. **See map of Graymoor, NY.**	N 41 21.138, W 73 55.204	520	779.7
	⛺◑ 🛏☕🚿	(0.4E) **Graymoor Spiritual Life Center** 845-424-2111. Follow signs and blue blazes; stay to the left at both forks in the road. Hikers are permitted to sleep free at monastery's ball field and picnic shelter Mar-Nov. Water, privy and shower. Dogs are allowed but please keep them leashed and pick up after them. Please call ahead of arrival to insure space is available.			

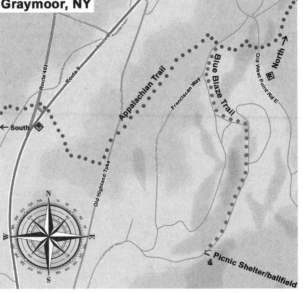

Graymoor, NY

NoBo	Features	Description	GPS	Elev	SoBo
1411.3	▲	Cross Old West Point Road		550	779.6
1411.4	▲	Pass private gravel road.		576	779.5
1412.0	Y	Short side trail marked with orange blazes leads east to a shrine on Graymoor Spiritual Life Center.		863	778.9
1412.8	▲	Intersects with woods road.		889	778.1
1412.9	▲ Y 📷	Follows woods road. Blue blaze side trail leads 650 feet west to good view of Hudson River.		960	778.0
1413.2	📷	(0.1W) Denning Hill, panoramic view south.		900	777.7
1414.0	▲ P(3)	Cross **Old Albany Post Road–Chapman Road**	N 41 22.741, W 73 53.753	607	776.9
1415.0	📷	View on top of Canompus Hill		820	775.9
1415.6	♦	Cross brook.		350	775.3
1415.7	▲ ★★★★★	Cross **Canopus Hill Road**.	N 41 23.181, W 73 52.635	420	775.2
	✗ 🍴 ☎	(1.6E) **Putnam Valley Market** 845-528-8626. (www.theputnamvalleymarket.com) (0.3E) on Campus Hill Road, (0.1E) on Canopus Hollow Road, (1.2W) on Sunset Hill Road. Pizza, hot food off the grill, ATM, open M-Sa 6am–9pm, Su 9am-7pm.			
1416.7	▲ P(2)	Cross **South Highland Road**	N 41 23.976, W 73 52.590	570	774.2
1417.1	📷	Rocky knob with limited views.		715	773.8
1417.3	▲	Intersects with old woods road.		665	773.6
1417.5	▲	Intersects with old woods road.		836	773.4
1417.8	▲	Intersects with old woods road.		980	773.1
1417.9	♦	Cross stream.		998	773.0
1418.2	Y	Catfish Loop Trail east, red blazed.		976	772.7
1418.9	📷	View east, limited.		1019	772.0
1419.4	♦ ▲ ▲ P(12)	Cross **Dennytown Road**, water faucet on building	N 41 25.244, W 73 52.132	860	771.5
1419.6	Y	Catfish Loop Trail east , red blazed.		862	771.3
1419.7	♦	Cross stream.		838	771.2
1420.3	📷	High point on ridge, views west.		1073	770.6
1421.0	▲	Cross **Sunk Mine Road**, leads west to blue blazed Three Lakes Trail.	N 41 25.842, W 73 50.993	800	769.9
1421.1	♦ ⌒	Cross bridge over stream.		823	769.8
1422.2	Y	Cross Three Lakes Trail.		1019	768.7
1422.4		Intersects with old mine-railway bed (south end).		1000	768.5
1423.1	▲ P(9) ★★★★★	**NY. 301** (south side), old mine-railway bed (north end), Canopus Lake.	N 41 27.179, W 73 50.216	920	767.8
	▲ ✗ 🍴 ♿	(1.0E) **Clarence Fahnestock State Park** 845-225-7207, 800-456-2267 Open mid-Apr to mid-Dec. Thru-hikers get one free night of camping. Concession at beach open wkends only Mem Day - June; open daily July - Labor Day. Hours M-Sa 9-5, Su 9-6.			
1423.2	▲	Intersects with **NY. 301 (south side)**		1009	767.7
1423.1	▲	Intersects with **NY. 301 (north side)**		1009	767.8
1423.4		Trail register.		1092	767.5
1423.7	Y	Fahnestock Trail west.		1118	767.2
1424.0	♦	Cross rocky stream.		1111	766.9
1425.1	♦	Cross stream.		1197	765.8
1425.4	📷	View south of Canopus Lake. Blue blazed trail leads east around lake and (0.5) to park campground.		1038	765.5
1425.5	Y	Side trails lead west to views of Catskills.		1149	765.4
1425.9	♦	Cross small stream.		1061	765.0
1426.1	▲	Intersects with woods road.		1055	764.8
1426.2		Ruins of stone building.		1086	764.7
1426.9	▲	Trail follows woods road, stone wall to east.		1185	764.0
1427.3	▲ 📷	Shenandoah Mountain summit, good views.		1282	763.6
1427.4	📷	Views to west.		1266	763.5
1427.7	▲ P(5)	Cross **Long Hill Road**	N 41 30.017, W 73 48.821	1100	763.2
1428.0	◊	Cross stream, unreliable.		991	762.9
1428.3	⟙	Power line.		993	762.6
1428.8	♦ Y ▲	Blue blaze trail leads (0.1) west to Shenandoah Tenting Area, water from pump.		900	762.1
1429.1	📷	Shenandoah Mountain high point with views through trees.		1060	761.8
1429.2	♦	Cross stream.		907	761.7
1429.8	♦	Cross stream.		875	761.1
1429.9	♦ ⌒	Cross bridge over brook.		837	761.0

NoBo		Features / Description	GPS	Elev	SoBo
1430.1	♦Y⋏ ⊏(6)◖ P(3) ★★★★★	Side trail to **RPH Shelter**, water is a hand pump, tenting, privy, trash can. 40.7◄35.4◄32.2◄►9.0►16.8►25.6 300 feet north to Hortontown Road.	Shelter N 41 30.869, W 73 47.548 Parking N 41 30.854, W 73 47.473	350	760.8
	✕	**Carlo's Pizza Express** 845-896-6500. (www.carlospizzaexpress.com) Pizza delivered after 4pm only. **Gian Bruno's** 845-227-9276. (www.gianbrunorestaurant.com) M closed, Tu-Su 12pm-3pm.			
1430.3	♦⌒	Cross bridge over brook.		480	760.6
1430.4	▲	Cross under **Taconic State Parkway**, underpass		650	760.5
1430.5	▲	Intersects with **Rockledge Road**.		540	760.4
1431.4	📷	Rocky viewpoint.		968	759.5
1431.7	♦	Cross small brook.		1077	759.2
1431.8	Y	Hosner Mountain Side Trail west.		1020	759.1
1432.0	📷	View, panoramic view of Hudson Highlands, Shawangunks, and Catskills at top of rocks.		1075	758.9
1432.3	Y	Hosner Mountain Side Trail west.		1074	758.6
1432.8	📷	Rocky area with views of Hudson River Valley and Fishkill Plains.		1000	758.1
1433.6	▲	Cross **Hosner Mountain Road**		500	757.3
1434.2	📷	Views of Hudson Valley.		1026	756.7
1434.4	Y	Old trail west.		989	756.5
1434.7	▲	Stormville Mountain summit.		1056	756.2
1435.2	▲P(4) ★★★★★	Cross **NY. 52**	N 41 32.469, W 73 43.963	800	755.7
	♦⌂✕⋏ ☎🍴	(0.4E) **Mountaintop Market Deli** 845-221-0928. ATM, pay phone inside, water from faucet on side of building and electric outlets for charging. Camping allowed. M-F 6am-8pm.			
	✕	**Danny's Pizzeria** 845-223-5888. pizza by the slice.			
Stormville, NY 12582 (1.9W)					
	✉	**PO** M-F 8:30am-5pm, Sa 9am-12pm. 845.226.2627.			
1436.2	Y	Blue blaze trail to parking area on NY. 52	N 41 32.469, W 73 43.963	893	754.7
1436.4	▲P(4)	Intersects with **Stormville Mountain Road (south end)**	N 41 32.694, W 73 43.051	999	754.5
1436.6	▲	Intersects with **Stormville Mountain Road (north end)**, **Mountain Top Road, and crosses over I-84**, overpass		950	754.3
1436.8	▲	Cross **Graplow Road**.		982	754.1
1438.5	♦	Cross brook.		1222	752.4
1438.8	📷	Ridgecrest with good views.		1278	752.1
1439.0	▲	Mt. Egbert summit		1329	751.9
1439.1	♦Y ⋏⊏(6)◖	75 feet east to **Morgan Stewart Shelter**, water is a well with a pump located downhill and in front of the shelter, tenting, privy. 44.4◄41.2◄9.0◄►7.8►16.6►20.6	N 41 33.874, W 73 41.506	1285	751.8
1439.4	Y📷	Side trail to view.		1327	751.5
1439.7	◊	Seasonal pond.		1313	751.2

NoBo	Features	Description	GPS	Elev	SoBo
1440.2	▲P(6)	Cross **Depot Hill Road**, near radio tower.	N 41 34.357, W 73 40.856	1230	750.7
1442.0	✕	Railroad tracks.		719	748.9
1442.1	▲P(3)	Cross **Old Route 55**, paved	N 41 35.271, W 73 39.690	750	748.8
1442.4	▲P(5) ★★★★★	Cross **N.Y. 55**, parking (0.1W)	N 41 35.384, W 73 39.551	720	748.5
	✕	(1.5W) **Pleasant Ridge Pizza** 845-724-3444. (www.pleasantridgepizzarestaurant.com) Serves lunch and dinner. Accepts major credit cards. M-Sa 10:30am-10pm, Su 11am-9pm.			
	✕	(1.5W) **A&A Italian Deli** 845-724-3400. M-F 6am-7pm, Sa 7am-6pm, Su 8am-3:30pm.			
	✇	(1.5W) **Total Care Pharmacy** 845-724-5757. M-F 9am-8pm, Sa 9am-3pm.			
	✕	(1.6W) **Great Wall** 845-724-5387.			

Poughquag, NY 12570 (3.1W)

	⌖	**PO** M–F 8:30am–1pm & 2pm-5pm, Sa 8:30am–12:30pm. 845-724-4763.			
	🛏⊛☕	**Pine Grove Motel** 845-724-5151.			
		No pets. $70S $75D. Free WiFi. Accepts Visa/MC/Disc.			
	✕	**Clove Valley Deli & Café** 845-227-1585.			
	✇	**Beekman Pharmacy** 845-724-3200. M-F 9am-8pm, Sa 9am-4pm, Su 10am-2pm.			
	🐾	**Beekman Animal Hospital** 845-724-8387. M-Tu closed, W 12pm-6pm, Th closed, F 8am-1pm, Sa-Su closed.			
1442.6	YP	Blue blaze west to parking area on NY. 55.	N 41 35.384, W 73 39.551		748.3
1442.7	Y	Beekman Uplands Trail west.			748.2
1443.4	♦	Cross stream.			747.5
1443.8	♦	Cross stream, outlet of Nuclear Lake. Nuclear Lake between 1958-72 was a facility licensed by the government to experiment with bomb-grade uranium and plutonium. It was cleaned up in 1972 and purchased by the National Park Service in 1979.		750	747.1
1443.9	Y	Nuclear Loop Trail east, yellow blazed.			747.0
1444.7	Y	Nuclear Loop Trail east, yellow blazed.			746.2
1445.0	◊	Cross stream, unreliable.			745.9
1445.1	Y	Beekman Uplands Trail west.			745.8
1446.1	▲	Cross **Penny Road**, dirt.			744.8
1446.6	📷	West Mountain, views		1200	744.3
1446.7	📷	Side trail leads 100 feet to rocky ledge with views.		1153	744.2
1446.9	◊▲⊏(6) ☾	(0.1E) **Telephone Pioneers Shelter** trail crosses stream, if dry go (0.7) north at the Champion residence, tenting, privy. 49.0◀16.8◀7.8◀▶8.8▶12.8▶21.2	N 41 36.256, W 73 37.158	910	744.0
1447.3	♦	Cross stream.		520	743.6
1447.6	⭘▲P(5) ★★★★★	Cross **County Road 20, West Dover Road, Dover Oak. See map of Pawling, NY.**	N 41 36.175, W 73 36.686	650	743.3

Pawling, NY 12564 (3.1E) See map of Pawling, NJ.

	⌖	**PO** M-F 8:30am-5pm. Sa 9am-12pm. 845-855-2669.			
	⅄⊛🍴⚓	**Edward R. Murrow Memorial Park** No pets. Town allows hikers to camp in the park for one night only. Located one mile from the center of town, restrooms, swimming.			
	✕	**Vinny's Deli** 845-855-1922. (www.vinnysdeliandcatering.com) M-Sa 8am-6pm, Su 9am-2pm.			
		Gaudino's Pizzeria 845-855-3200. M-Sa 11am-10pm, Su 12pm-8pm.			
		Mama Pizza II 845-855-9270. (www.mamapizzapawling.com) M closed, T-Su 11am-10pm.			
		Great Wall 845-855-9750. M-F 11am-10:30pm, Sa-Su 11am-11:30pm.			
		McGrath Restaurant 845-855-0800. (www.mcgrathstavern.com) Serves lunch and dinner. M 11:30am-9pm, Tu 4pm-9pm, W-Th 11:30am-9pm, F-Sa 11:30am-10pm, Su 11:30am-9pm.			
	🖵	**Pawling Free Library** M-12pm-5pm, Tu-TH 10am-8pm, F 12pm-5pm, Sa 10am-4pm, Su 12pm-4pm. Closed Sundays in July and August.			
	🚗	**Martin and Donna** 845-505-1671, 845-546-1832. Nights and weekends only. Shuttle range RPH Shelter to Kent, CT.			

Pawling, NY

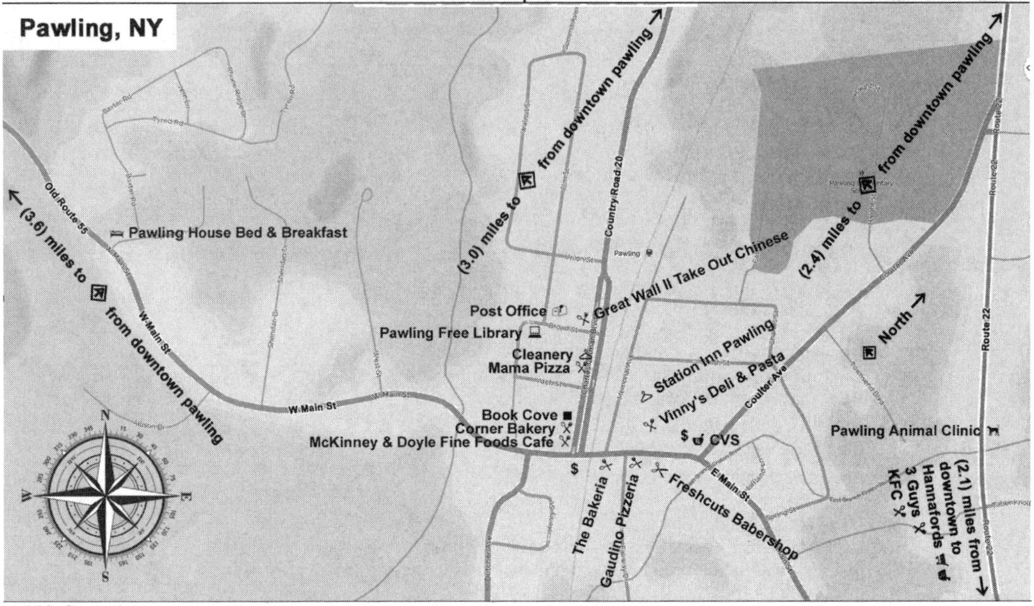

(map of Pawling, NY showing the following labels)

- (3.6) miles to / from downtown pawling — Old Route 55 — W.Main St
- Pawling House Bed & Breakfast
- (3.0) miles to / from downtown pawling — Country Road 20
- Great Wall II Take Out Chinese
- (2.4) miles to / from downtown pawling — Route 22
- Post Office
- Pawling Free Library
- Cleanery
- Mama Pizza
- Station Inn Pawling
- Vinny's Deli & Pasta
- Coulter Ave
- North
- Book Cove
- Corner Bakery
- McKinney & Doyle Fine Foods Cafe
- CVS
- Pawling Animal Clinic
- W.Main St
- E.Main St
- The Bakeria
- Gaudino Pizzeria
- Freshcuts Babershop
- (2.1) miles from downtown to Hannafords 3 Guys KFC

			GPS	Elev	SoBo
1449.6	♦	Cross Swamp River.		415	741.3
1449.9	▲	Intersects with dirt road west.		430	741.0
1450.0	♦♨♿✗ ▲P(15) ★★★★★	Cross **NY. 22**, Appalachian Trail Metro–North Train Platform	N 41 35.564, W 73 35.255	480	740.9
	◈♿⌂ ⚐♿▯	**Native Landscapes & Garden Center** 845-855-7050. (www.nativelandscaping.net) AT Passport location. M-Su 9-5, please do not loiter after hours. Owner Pete Muroski is hiker friendly. Free outside cold shower, $5 for indoor hot shower, charging outlet, use of restrooms. Drinks, snacks, freeze-dried meals and canister fuel sold at the garden center. Mail drops: 991 Route 22, Pawling, NY 12564.			
	✗⌂⚐▯	(0.6E) **Tony's Deli** 845-855-9540. (www.tonysdeli22.com) Short order grill, sandwiches, salads, soda machine outside. Ask about camping. M-F 3:30 am-12am, Sa 4am-12am, Su 5am-12am.			

Pawling, NY 12564 (2.5E) see mile 1447.6
Wingdale, NY 12594 (4W)

	✉	**PO** M-F 8:30am-12:30pm & 1:30pm-5pm, Sa 8am-12:30pm. 845-832-6147.			
	⌂♿⚐▯	**Dutchess Motor Lodge** 845-832-6400, 914-525-9276. (www.dutchessmotorlodge.com) $73 for single, A/C, Fridge, Guest laundry $7, Free WiFi. One pet room available. Ride for a fee when available. Mail drops for guests: 1512 Route 22, Wingdale, NY 12594.			
	🛒	**Wingdale Supermarket** 845-832-9361			
	✗	Many other restaurants. **Cousins Pizza** 845-832-6510. (www.cousinspizzawingdale.com) Acceptss Visa, Master Card & Discover. M-Sa 11am-10pm, Su 1pm-9pm. **Peking Kitchen** 845-832-9500. M-Th 10:30am-10pm, F-Sa 10:30am-10:30pm, Su 10:30am-10pm. **Dunkin Donuts** 845-832-6118. M-Su 24 hours. **Ben's Deli** 845-832-9460. M-Su 3am-9pm. **Big W BBQ** 845-832-6200. (www.theforkingpig.com) M-Tu closed, W-Th 12pm-8pm, F-Sa 12pm-9pm, Su 12pm-8pm.			
	🖳	**Dover Plains Library** 845-832-6605. M-F 10am-8pm, Sa closed, Su 10am-8pm.			
1450.2	▲	Cross **Hurds Corners Road**, paved		480	740.7
1450.4	♦	Cross stream.		473	740.5
1450.8	Y	Pawling Nature Preserve, blue blaze trail west, trail register		675	740.1
1451.8	Y	Pass terminus of Red Trail.		1010	739.1
1452.0	♦	Cross stream.		934	738.9
1452.3	♦Y	Cross stream. Yellow Trail in the area.		921	738.6
1452.7	Y	Intersection of Red Trail east and Green Trail west.		968	738.2
1453.6	Y	Yellow Trail east.		900	737.3
1455.3	▲	Cross **Leather Hill Road**, dirt road		750	735.6
1455.6	▲	Cross logging road, dirt		829	735.3

NoBo	Features	Description	GPS	Elev	SoBo
1455.7	♦▲⌐(6) ⌣⊂	**Wiley Shelter**, water is located at pump on trail (0.1) north of the shelter on the AT beyond tent platform, tenting, privy. 25.6◄16.6◄8.8◄►4.0►12.4►19.7	N 41 38.272, W 73 31.944	740	735.2
1455.8	♦	Pump, water source.		593	735.1
1455.9	▲P(5)	Cross **Duell Hollow Road**, paved	N 41 38.190, W 73 31.794	620	735.0
1456.2	♦⌒	Cross wooden bridge over Duel Hollow Brook.		567	734.7
1456.7	▲	Trail briefly follows old woods road.		417	734.2
1456.9	▲P(4) State Line	Cross **Hoyt Road**, New York–Connecticut State Line	N 41 38.463, W 73 31.211	400	734.0
1457.2	Y P(12)	Side trail west leads to CT. 55 and large parking area.	N 41 38.683, W 73 31.153	424	733.7
1457.4	♦	Cross brook, reliable.		445	733.5
1457.6	▲P(12) ★★★★★	Cross **CT. 55**, Gaylordsville, CT. 06755, (2.5E) Post Office, long term resupply, restaurant.	N 41 38.683, W 73 31.153	580	733.3

Gaylordsville, CT (2.9E)

		(2.4E) across bridge on route 55, (0.5) further on route 7 south to PO and diner.			
	⌂	**PO** M-F 8am-1pm & 2pm-5pm, Sa 8am-12pm. 860-354-9727.			
	✗	**Gaylordsville Diner** 860-210-1622. Servers breakfast, lunch and dinner.			
1458.7	◙	Top of Ten Mile Hill, views of Housatonic Valley		1000	732.2
1458.8	Y	Herrick Trail east.		948	732.1
1459.2	◊	Spring west, unreliable.		761	731.7
1459.4	▲	Cross dirt road.		584	731.5
1459.7	♦Y▲ ⌐(6) ⌣⊂📶	(0.1E) **Ten Mile River Shelter**, water is a hand pump 100 feet south and west of the shelter, tenting, privy, bear box. 20.6◄12.8◄4.0◄►8.4►15.7►25.7	N 41 39.912, W 73 30.583	290	731.2
1459.9	♦⌒▲	Cross Ten Mile River on footbridge, camping is in field south of the bridge.		280	731.0
1460.5	▲P(14) ★★★★★	Cross **Bulls Bridge Road**, Trail to Bulls Bridge Parking Area (0.2E)	N 41 40.522, W 73 30.624	450	730.4
	⌂ ☎	(0.5E) **Country Market** 860-619-8199. (www.cornwallcountrymarket.com) Deli, bakery, breakfast, fruit, ice cream, soda, ATM. M-F 6am-5pm, Sa-Su 7am-5pm.			
	✗	(0.5E) **Bulls Bridge Inn** 860-927-1000. (www.bullsbridge.com) M-Th 5am-9pm, F 5am-9:30pm, Sa-Su 12pm-9:30, Su 12-9pm. American foods, meals reasonable, bar.			
1461.0	▲	Intersects with **Schaghticoke Road**, Bulls Bridge Road to east.		372	729.9
1461.3	▲	Intersects with **Schaghticoke Road**.		320	729.6
1461.6	♦	Cross stream.		524	729.3
1462.8	◙	View.		1190	728.1
1463.0	▲	Skirts the west of Schaghticoke Mountain.		1331	727.9
1463.3	◊	Two seasonal springs in the area.		1282	727.6
1464.2	State Line	Connecticut–New York State Line		1250	726.7
1464.3	♦	Cross stream.		1193	726.6
1464.6	◙	Indian Rocks		1290	726.3
1465.0	◙	Open ledge with good views of Housatonic River.		1285	725.9
1465.2	♦⊂▲	Blue blaze west to Schaghticoke Mountain campsite, **NO FIRES**.		950	725.7
1466.6	◙	Reach high point with good views.		1403	724.3
1467.1	♦	Cross Thayer Brook.		900	723.8
1467.5	▲	Reach height of land on Mt. Algo.		1190	723.4
1468.1	♦Y▲ ⌐(6)⌣⊂	200 feet west to **Mt. Algo Shelter**, water is located on the blue blaze trail leading to shelter, 15 yards in front of shelter, tenting, privy. 21.2◄12.4◄8.4◄►7.3►17.3►28.6	N 41 43.899, W 73 29.802	655	722.8
1468.4	▲P(10) ★★★★★	Cross **CT. 341, Schaghticoke Road**.	N 41 43.863, W 73 29.439	350	722.5

Kent, CT 06757 (0.8E) See map of Kent, CT.

	⌂	**PO** M-F 8am-1pm & 2pm-5pm, Sa 8:30am-12:30pm. 860-927-3435.			
	⊨⊛✗⟲	**Fife 'n Drum Restaurant & Inn** 860-927-3509. (www.fifendrum.com)			
	▭	No pets.			
		Hiker room rates $140D +tax weekdays, $170D +tax weekends, $25EAP +tax. Front desk closed Tu, so make prior arrangements for Tu night stays.			
		Mail drops for guests: (USPS) PO Box 188 or (FedEx/UPS) 53 N Main Street, Kent, CT 06757.			
		Restaurant hours:			
		Lunch; M 11:30am-3pm, Tu closed, W-Sa 11:30am – 3pm, Su Brunch 11:30am-3pm			
		Dinner; M 5:30pm-9:30pm, Tu closed, W-Th 5:30pm-9:30pm, Fr-Sa 5:30pm-10pm, Su 3pm-8:30pm			
	⊨⟲🛏🛌	**Cooper Creek B&B** 860-927-4334.			
		(2.5) north of town on US 7.			
		Hiker rate M-Th $110D +tax. Weekend rates $145-200 +tax. Free WiFi. Shuttles to and from Kent with stay, slackpacking and longer shuttles for a fee.			

NoBo	Features	Description	GPS	Elev SoBo

Starbuck Inn 860-927-1788. (www.starbuckinn.com)
No pets.
$207D/up + tax, includes full breakfast and afternoon tea. Includes healthy breakfast made with local ingredients, it's different every day.
Free WiFi. Sometimes discounted mid-week, accepts credit cards.

Davis IGA (860) 927-4093. (www.davisiga.com) M-Sa 8am-7pm, Su 8am-6pm.

Backcountry Outfitters 860-927-3377. (www.bcoutfitters.com)
Fuel, fuel by the ounce.
Summer hours; M–Sa 9am–9pm, Su 10am–8pm.
Winter Hours; M W-Sa 9am-6pm, Tu closed, W-Sa 9am-6pm, Su 10am-5pm.
Sells stamps, ships Priority Mail. Fuel by the ounce, canisters, good selection of gear, free WiFi, ATM.

Laundromat 860-927-1144. (www.kentgreenlaundromat.com) M-Su 6am-11pm.

JP Gifford 860-592-0200. (www.jpgifford.com/kent) breakfast sandwiches, salads, bakery, coffee and supplies. M-Sa 6:30am-6pm, Su 7am-3pm.

Kent Pizza Garden 860-927-3733. (www.kentpizzagarden.com) M-Th 11am-1am, F-Sa 11am-2am, Su 11am-1am.
Panini Cafe & Gelateria 860-927-5083. M-Su 9:30am-5pm.
Shanghai 860-927-4809. M-Sa 11:30am-10pm, Su 12pm-9pm.
Chris's Hot Dog Cart

Kent Animal Clinic 8600927-1200.

Library 860.927.3761. (www.kentmemoriallibrary.org) M-F 10am-5:30pm, Sa 10am-4pm.

Kent, CT

| 1468.5 | | Cross Macedonia Brook on log bridge. | 363 | 722.4 |
| 1469.2 | | Ledge with view of Kent and Housatonic Valley. | 799 | 721.7 |

NoBo	Features	Description	GPS	Elev	SoBo
1471.1	◊	Cross Choggam Brook, dries up in the summer.		863	719.8
1471.2	▲	Cross **Skiff Mountain Road**, paved		850	719.7
1471.4	📷	View from ledge outcropping.		923	719.5
1471.9	📷	Caleb's Peak. Views of Housatonic River.		1160	719.0
1472.6	📷	Cross top of St. Johns Ledges.		900	718.3
1473.1	▲P	Intersects **River Road**		480	717.8
1473.7	♦	Cross mountain brook.		426	717.2
1474.1	▲	Terminus of town road running north along river from Kent.		384	716.8
1475.4	♦Y▲ ⊑(6)⌣⪍	79 yards east to **Stewart Hollow Brook Shelter**, water (Stony Brook) is located 0.4 mile north of the shelter on the AT, tenting, privy. **No fires permitted.** 19.7◄15.7◄7.3◄► 10.0► 21.3► 28.7	N 41 46.758, W 73 25.114	400	715.5
1475.8	♦▲⪍	Cross Stony Brook, campsites nearby, privy. **No fires permitted**.		440	715.1
1477.8	♦▲P(5)	Cross dirt **River Road** that parallels Housatonic River. Seasonal spring a few feet north of trail crossing.	N 41 48.342, W 73 23.700	460	713.1
1478.0	▲	Cross Dawn Hill Road, paved.		541	712.9
1478.6	◊Y▲⌄ ⪍⛺	Side trail 160 feet to Silver Hill Campsite, water pump, privy. **No fires permitted.**		1000	712.3
1479.4	📷	Lookout at north side of Sliver Hill.		1142	711.5
1479.5	◊▲P(12) ★★★★★	Cross **CT. 4**		700	711.4

Cornwall Bridge, CT (0.9E) See map of Cornwall Bridge, CT.

📬	**PO** M-F 8:30am-1pm & 2pm-5pm, Sa 9am-12pm. 860-672-6710.
🛏⛺△➡️	**Hitching Post Motel** 860-672-6219. (www.cthitchingpostmotel.us) $65/up weekdays, $85/up weekends. Pets $10, laundry $5, shuttles $2 per mile. Mail drops for guests: 45 Kent Road, Cornwall Bridge, CT 06754.
🛏 ◈△➡️	**The Amselhaus** 860-248-3155. (www.theamselhaus.com)
🖥	AT Passport location. Located behind carpet store, check-in at grey house next door to apartments. $85S, $100 for couple, $50 EAP. 2-3 bedroom apartments, includes laundry, satelite TV, local and long-distance phone. Rides available. Mail drops for guests: C/O Tyler, 6 River Road South, Cornwall Bridge, CT 06754.
🛏▲	**Housatonic Meadows State Park** 860-672-6772. Camping and Cabins 1.3 miles north of town on US 7. Open mid-May to Oct, registration at main cabin by gate. Campsite $17 for CT residents, $27 nonresidents, $3 walk-in fee for first night. Cabins $60 with 2 nights minimum, CT resident fees for cabins is $50 plus tax. No hammocks. No alcohol. Reservations can be made Memorial Day Through Labor Day by contacting ReserveAmerica.com or by calling 1-877-668-2267
🛏➡️🚗	**Cornwall Inn** 860-672-6884. (www.cornwallinn.com) (2.2) miles south on US 7. Su-Th $129D +tax, includes cont. breakfast. Weekends 10% hiker discount. Seasonal pool and hot tub. Free WiFi. Pet fee. Pickup and return to trail head and other shuttles for a fee. Mail drops with reservation.

© WhiteBlaze Pages 2018

Cornwall Country Market 860-619-8199. (www.cornwallcountrymarket.com)
AT Passport location. Hiker friendly, hot meals, breakfast, groceries, charging stations. M-F 6am-5pm, Sa-Su 7am-5pm.

Citgo 860-672-6786. M 6am-11pm, Tu-Sa 6am-10pm, Su 6am-9pm.

Cornwall Package Store 860-672-6645. (www.cornwallpackagestore.com)
AT Passport location.
Water available from spigot outside. Stop in to sign their register. M-Th 10am-7pm, F 10am-8pm Sa 11am-3pm, Su closed.

Housatonic Veterinary Care 860-672-4948. (www.housatonicveterinarycare.com) M-Tu 9am-5:30pm, W closed, Th-F 9am-5:30pm, Sa 9am-1pm, Su closed.

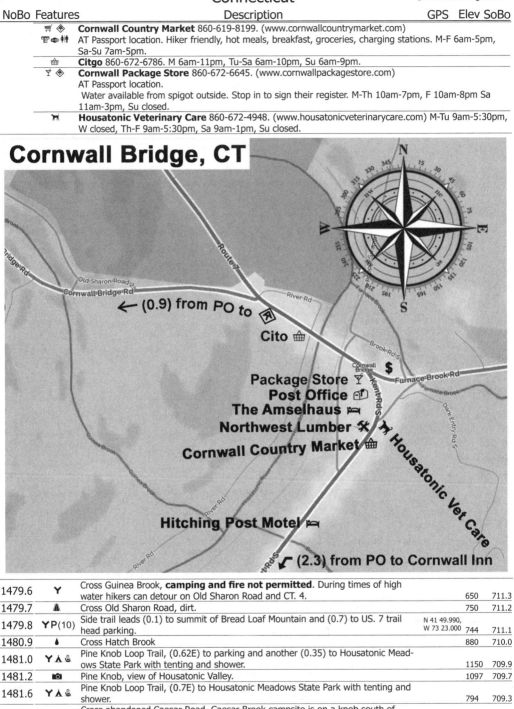

Cornwall Bridge, CT

← (0.9) from PO to Cito

Package Store
Post Office
The Amselhaus
Northwest Lumber
Cornwall Country Market

Hitching Post Motel

↙ (2.3) from PO to Cornwall Inn

1479.6	Y	Cross Guinea Brook, **camping and fire not permitted**. During times of high water hikers can detour on Old Sharon Road and CT. 4.		650	711.3
1479.7	▲	Cross Old Sharon Road, dirt.		750	711.2
1479.8	Y P(10)	Side trail leads (0.1) to summit of Bread Loaf Mountain and (0.7) to US. 7 trail head parking.	N 41 49.990, W 73 23.000	744	711.1
1480.9	♦	Cross Hatch Brook		880	710.0
1481.0	Y ⅄ &	Pine Knob Loop Trail, (0.62E) to parking and another (0.35) to Housatonic Meadows State Park with tenting and shower.		1150	709.9
1481.2	📷	Pine Knob, view of Housatonic Valley.		1097	709.7
1481.6	Y ⅄ &	Pine Knob Loop Trail, (0.7E) to Housatonic Meadows State Park with tenting and shower.		794	709.3
1482.0	♦⅄ℂ▲	Cross abandoned Caesar Road, Caesar Brook campsite is on a knob south of Caesar Brook, privy.		760	708.9
1483.4	▲	Cross abandoned Surdam Road.		874	707.5
1484.2	♦⌒	Cross Carse Brook on log bridge.		810	706.7
1484.3	▲P (3) ★★★★★	Cross **West Cornwall Road**, paved. See map of US 7/CT 112.	N 41 52.406, W 73 23.467	800	706.6
	⛺	**Bearded Woods B&D** One of a Kind Bunk & Dine, will pickup at trail heads between West Cornwall Road to Salisbury with stay. **See Notes at mile 1491.6**			

NoBo	Features	Description	GPS	Elev	SoBo

West Cornwall, CT 06796 (2.2E)

	⌂	**PO** M–F 8:30am–12pm & 2pm–4:30pm, Sa 9am–12pm. 860-672-6791.			
	✗	**Wandering Moose Café** 860-672-0178. (www.thewanderingmoosecafe.com)			
		Breakfast; M 6:30am-11am, Tu-F 6:30-11:30am, Sa 8am-11:30am, Su 8am-12pm.			
		Lunch; M none, T 11:30am-2pm, W-F 11:30am-2:30pm, Sa 11:30am-5:30pm, Su 12p,-5pm.			
		Dinner; M-Tu none, W-Th 5:30pm-8pm, F-Sa 5:30pm-9pm, Su 5pm-8pm.			

Sharon, CT 06069 (4.7W)

	⌂	**PO** M–F 9:30am–4:30pm, Sa 9:30am–12:30pm. 860-364-5306.			
	🛒	**Sharon Farm Market** 860-397-5161. M-Sa 8am-8pm, Su 8am-7pm.			
	✗	**Stacked Kitchen** 860-397-5001. M-Su 8:30am-4pm.			
	⚕	**Sharon Hospital** 860-364-4141. (www.sharonhospital.com)			
	✚	**Sharon Pharmacy** 860-364-5272. M-F 8am-6pm, Sa 8am-3pm, Su 8am-12pm.			
1485.4	▲Y⚑ ⌐(6)⌣《	95 yards west to **Pine Swamp Brook Shelter**, water is located on the blue-blazed trail, tenting, privy. 25.7◀17.3◀10.0◀▶ 11.3▶18.7▶19.9▶	N 41 52.898, W 73 23.526 1075		705.5
1486.3	▲	Cross **Mt. Easter Road**	1150		704.6
1486.6		Skirt the summit of Mt. Easter	1350		704.3
1487.7	▲	Cross brook, source of water for Sharon Mountain Campsite.	1271		703.2
1487.8	Y⚑	Side trail to Sharon Mountain campsite.	1200		703.1
1488.6	📷	Hang Glider View	1150		702.3
1489.4	📷	Several viewpoints along the ridge area.	1137		701.5
1490.6	▲Y⚑《📷	Side trail to Belter's campsite, privy.	770		700.3
1490.7	📷	Belter's Bump, scenic look.	721		700.2
1491.0	▲P	Cross **U.S. 7 (south end)**, CT. 112	N 41 55.855, W 73 21.859 520		699.9
1491.6	▲⌣▲⚏ P(12) ★★★★★	Cross **U.S. 7 (north end)**, Warren Turnpike, Housatonic River Bridge. **See map of US 7 /CT 112.**	N 41 55.957, W 73 21.806 500		699.3
	✗	(0.2E) **Mountainside Café restaurant** 860-824-1397. (www.mountainside.com/café) 860-824-7876, M–Su 7am-3pm. After crossing Housatonic River on US. 7 and just before the Trail turns left onto Warren Turnpike, cross bridge over railroad tracks, then continue (0.2) mile.			
	🏠◈◉🛏 ⌂⛺💻🚌 🖻	(3.6E) **Bearded Woods B&D** 860-480-2966. (www.beardedwoods.com) AT Passport location. No dogs. Relax and let your AT experience be fulfilled! Open May 1 thru August 1. Limited services may be available outside of those dates. Reservations recommended. Hudson & BIG Lu shuttle hikers to their home $45pp, includes shower with amenities, clean bunk with linens, communal laundry, loaner clothes, computer available for use, WIFI, Hearty Breakfast, rides to and from trail and local PO. Call or text Hudson for pickup from: West Cornwall Rd, Falls Village or Salisbury between 1pm-6pm. Pizza, ice cream, drinks, snacks and resupplies available for purchase. Free slackpacking between West Cornwall Rd and Salisbury with second night stay. Long distance shuttles anywhere for a fee. Cash or Credit Cards accepted via PayPal. Mail drops: P.O. Box 1068 Sharon, CT 06069-1068. Not a party place. Sorry No Pets or Walk-ins. **See Map**			

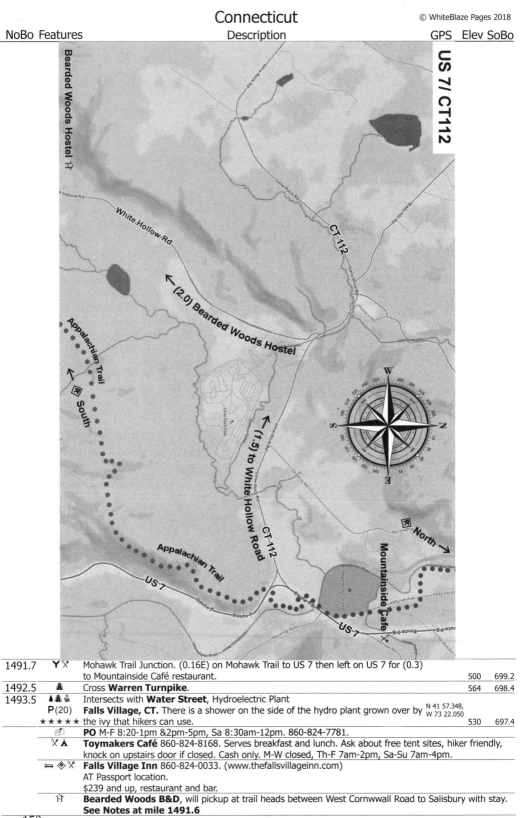

			GPS	Elev	SoBo
1491.7	Y ✗	Mohawk Trail Junction. (0.16E) on Mohawk Trail to US 7 then left on US 7 for (0.3) to Mountainside Café restaurant.		500	699.2
1492.5	▲	Cross **Warren Turnpike**.		564	698.4
1493.5	♦▲♨ P(20) ★★★★★	Intersects with **Water Street**, Hydroelectric Plant **Falls Village, CT.** There is a shower on the side of the hydro plant grown over by the ivy that hikers can use.	N 41 57.348, W 73 22.050	530	697.4
	◫	**PO** M-F 8:20-1pm &2pm-5pm, Sa 8:30am-12pm. 860-824-7781.			
	✗ ▲	**Toymakers Café** 860-824-8168. Serves breakfast and lunch. Ask about free tent sites, hiker friendly, knock on upstairs door if closed. Cash only. M-W closed, Th-F 7am-2pm, Sa-Su 7am-4pm.			
	⇌ ◈✗	**Falls Village Inn** 860-824-0033. (www.thefallsvillageinn.com) AT Passport location. $239 and up, restaurant and bar.			
	⌂	**Bearded Woods B&D**, will pickup at trail heads between West Cornwwall Road to Salisbury with stay. **See Notes at mile 1491.6**			

Falls Village, CT

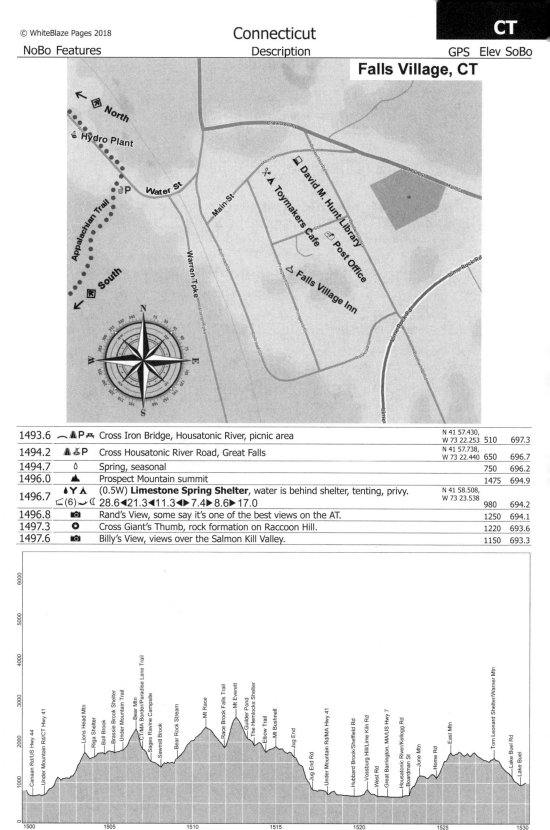

1493.6	⌒▲P⛱	Cross Iron Bridge, Housatonic River, picnic area	N 41 57.430, W 73 22.253	510	697.3
1494.2	▲♨P	Cross Housatonic River Road, Great Falls	N 41 57.738, W 73 22.440	650	696.7
1494.7	◊	Spring, seasonal		750	696.2
1496.0	▲	Prospect Mountain summit		1475	694.9
1496.7	♦Y人 ⌐(6)〰︎℃	(0.5W) **Limestone Spring Shelter**, water is behind shelter, tenting, privy. 28.6◀21.3◀11.3◀▶7.4▶8.6▶17.0	N 41 58.508, W 73 23.538	980	694.2
1496.8	📷	Rand's View, some say it's one of the best views on the AT.		1250	694.1
1497.3	◉	Cross Giant's Thumb, rock formation on Raccoon Hill.		1220	693.6
1497.6	📷	Billy's View, views over the Salmon Kill Valley.		1150	693.3

NoBo	Features	Description	GPS	Elev	SoBo
1500.4	▲	Intersects U.S. 44 (south end) **See map of Salisbury, CT**		700	690.5
1500.5	▲	Trail turns where U.S. 44 and Lower Cobble Road intersect.		678	690.4
1500.7	▲P(2)	Intersects with Lower Cobble Road.	N 41 59.395, W 73 25.140	685	690.2
1501.1	▲⦅P(4) ★★★★★	Cross CT. 41, Undermountain Road. **Salisbury, CT. See map of Salisbury, CT.**	N 41 59.647, W 73 25.593	720	689.8
	⌖✉	**PO** M-F 8:30am-1pm & 2pm-5pm, Sa 9am-12om. 860-435-5072.			
	⌂✉	**Maria McCabe** 860-435-0593 As of Dec 1017, Maria has had some setbacks and is not sure if she will be open for the 2018 season. Call in advance. Beds in home $35PP includes shower, use of living room, shuttle to coin laundry, cash only. Mail drops for guests: 4 Grove Street Salisbury, CT 06068.			
	⌂⛺🚗✉	**Vanessa Breton** 860-435-9577, 860-671-9832. Beds in home $40PP, pets $5, laundry $5. Shuttle range 100 miles. Mail drops for guests (fee for non-guests $5). Street address is 7 The Lock Up Rd, but send mail drops to PO Box: PO Box 131, Salisbury, CT 06068.			
	🛒✗	**LaBonne's Market** (www.labonnes.com) Grocery, deli, bakery, pizza. M–Sa 8am–7pm, Su 8am-6pm.			
	ⓘ♦♦🚻	**Town Hall** 860-435-5170 M-F 8:30-4 Hikers welcome to use bathrooms and phone (local calls only.			
	🖥	**Scoville Memorial Library** 860-435-2838. (www.scovillelibrary.org) M closed, Tu-W 10am-5pm, Th 10am-7pm, F 10am-5pm, Sa 10am-4pm, Su 1pm-4pm.			

Lakeville, CT (2.0 mi. south of Salisbury)

✗	**Boathouse** 860-435-2111. (www.theboathouseatlakeville.com) Sports bar and restaurant. M-Th 11am-9pm, F-Sa 11am-11pm, Su 11am-9pm.
	Mizza's Pizza 860-435-6266. (www.mizzas.com) M-Sa 11am-10:30pm Su 12pm-10:30pm.
⛺	**Washboard Laundromat** Located behind Mizza's Pizza.
⌂	**Bearded Woods B&D**, will pickup at trail heads between West Cornwwall Road to Salisbury with stay. **See Notes at mile 1491.6**

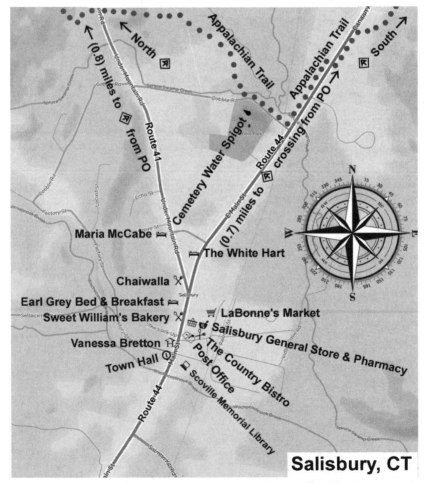

Salisbury, CT

NoBo	Features	Description	GPS	Elev	SoBo
1501.3	Y◑	Side trail leads 270 feet east to spring.		844	689.6
1501.8	Y	Side trail sometimes used by local motorcyclist.		1139	689.1
1502.6	◑	Cross small stream, dependable.		1281	688.3
1503.0	▲	Cross **old charcoal road**.		1698	687.9
1503.3	Y	Intersects with Lions Head Trail leads west.		1583	687.6
1503.4	Y	Blue blaze bypass trail intersects west.		1562	687.5
1502.5	📷	Lions Head summit and ridgeline of the Taconic Range with views of Sheffield and Salisbury.		1738	688.4
1503.6	📷	North outlook of Lions Head with views of Bear Mountain Mt. Greylock. Blue blaze bypass trail intersects to the west.		1626	687.3
1504.0	Y	Blue blaze trail leads west to private property.		1607	686.9
1504.1	◑Y▲ ⊏(6)⌒⟲ 📷	117 yards east to **Riga Shelter and Camping Area**, water (spring) is located on a blue blazed trail to the left of the clearing on the AT, tenting, privy. **No fires permitted**. Views. 28.7◄18.7◄7.4◄► 1.2►9.6►9.7►	N 42 00.938, W 73 26.126	1610	686.8
1504.7	◑▲	Cross Ball Brook. Ball Brook Group Campsite is south of the brook on east side of the trail. **No fires permitted**.		1650	686.2
1505.3	◑▲⊏(6) ⌒⟲	Cross Brassie Brook (south branch). 75 yards east to **Brassie Brook Shelter and Camping Area**, water (stream) is located on the AT 50 feet north of the side trail to the shelter, tenting, privy. Limited hammocking. **No fires permitted**. 19.9◄8.6◄1.2◄► 8.4►8.5►22.8	N 42 01.700, W 73 27.216	1705	685.6
1505.8	Y	Riga Junction, Trail intersects with Undermountain Trail leading east (1.1) to Paradise Lane Trail and group camping area, and (1.9) to CT. 91 which is one of the most popular trail heads in CT.		1820	685.1
1506.0	▲P(3)	Intersects with **Bear Mountain Road**, old charcoal road.		1920	684.9
1506.3	▲📷▯	Cross Bear Mountain summit, rock observation tower		2316	684.6
1507.0	Y▲ State Line	Connecticut–Massachusetts State Line. Paradise Lane Trail intersects above the ravine to the east. A good camping area is east the intersection of the AT.		1800	683.9
1507.5	◑▲⚱⚓	Sages Ravine Brook campsite, water falls.		1360	683.4
1508.1	◑	Sawmill Branch (Sages Ravine).		1340	682.8
1509.0	◑▲⟲	Laurel Ridge campsite (0.1) west, privy.		1750	681.9
1509.1	◑	Cross Bear Rock Stream		1548	681.8
1510.8	▲📷	Race Mountain summit, open ledges, views.		2365	680.1
1511.9	◑Y▲⟲🐻	Race Brook Falls Trail, (0.2E) to tenting, (0.4W) to water. Privy, bear box.		1950	679.0
1512.6	📷	Mt. Everett		2602	678.3
1513.2	▲	Cross summit road, **Mt. Evertt Road**.		2189	677.7
1513.3	⛽⟲▲ P(20)	Guilder Pond Picnic Area, day use only, privy.	N 42 06.420, W 73 26.151	2050	677.6
1513.4	Y	Side trail west to Guilder Pond, highest fresh water pond in MA.		2042	677.5
1513.7	◑Y⊏(10) ⟲	(0.1E) **The Hemlocks Shelter**, water is located on the blue blazed access trail, privy. 17.0◄9.6◄8.4◄► 0.1►14.4►19.7	N 42 06.594, W 73 25.740	1880	677.2
1513.8	◑Y▲(2) ⊏(4)⌒⟲	(0.1E) **Glen Brook Shelter**, water (stream) is located in front of and downhill from the shelter, 2 tent platforms and extensive tenting area, privy. 9.7◄8.5◄0.1◄► 14.3►19.6►21.4	N 42 06.668, W 73 25.698	1885	677.1
1514.4	Y ★★★★★	Elbow Trail leads (1.5E) to **MA. 41**.		1750	676.5
	🛏🍴📶	**Racebrook Lodge** 413-229-2916. (www.rblodge.com) Open year round. Call for rates, lowest during off season (Nov-May). M-Th $85-$160, F-Su $115-170. Free WiFi. Stay includes breakfast. Pets $25 per night. Accepts Visa, MC, Disc.			
1516.1	📷	Jug End summit, rocky with good views.		1750	674.8
1517.2	◑▲P(3)	Cross **Jug End Road (Curtiss Road)**, (0.25E) to spring.	N 42 08.664, W 73 25.896	890	673.7
1518.1	▲ ★★★★★	Cross **MA. 41, Undermountain Road**, ATC Kellogg Conservation Center		810	672.8

South Egremont, MA (1.2W)

	📬	**PO** M–F 8:15am–12pm & 12:30pm–4pm, Sa 9am–11:30am. 413-528-1571.			
	◑▲🚗📶	(0.1W) **ATC New England Regional Office** 413-528-8002. Located in Kellogg Conservation Center. Water from hose, picnic table, 2 charging outlets, fre WiFi, no camping or parking.			
	🍴🏪	**Egremont Market** 413-528-0075 Market & deli, ice cream, trail mix, sodas. M-Su 6:30am-7pm.(6pm in winter)			
	🍴	**Mom's Country Cafe** 413-528-2414. Servers breakfast and lunch, breakfast all day, free coffee refills, outdoor water spigot available, hikers welcome. M-Su 6:30am-3pm.			
1518.3	⌂	Cross bog bridges.		707	672.6

NoBo	Features	Description	GPS	Elev	SoBo
1518.5	▲	Trail follows old woods road along a narrow ridge.		791	672.4
1518.9	⌒	Cross bog bridges.		722	672.0
1519.7	⬤⌒	Cross Hubbard Brook on boardwalk and bridge.		675	671.2
1519.9	▲P(6)	Cross Sheffield–Egremont Road Shay's Rebellion Monument	N 42 08.826, W 73 23.202	700	671.0
1520.4	▲⬤	Lime Kiln Road is 100 yards east, where **two historical lime kilns** can be seen on the north side of the road.		814	670.5
1521.1	▲	Cross **West Road**.		694	669.8
1521.5	⌒	Cross long boardwalk across swamp.		664	669.4
1521.6	✕	Cross active railroad tracks of the Housatonic Railroad.		668	669.3
1521.7	▲ ★★★★★	Cross U.S. 7		700	669.2

Sheffield, MA (3.0E)

- ✉ **PO** M–F 9am–4:30pm, Sa 9am–12pm. 413-229-8772.
- 🏠▲⚲🚗 **Jess Treat** 860-248-5710. jesstrea@gmail.com
  $40PP or $55 shared bed, cash or paypal only. $15PP tenting includes shower. Stay includes pickup and return; ask about resupply stop and mail drops. Shower, breakfast, free WiFi. Clean private home, not a party place, reservations needed. $5 laundry, pets outside only. Convenience store and cafe and BBQ/Pizza restaurant in walking distance. Fee for shuttles.
- ▲⌂⚲ **Moon in the Pond Farm**
  413-229-3092(home) 413-446-3320(text/cell) dom@mooninthepond.org (www.mooninthepond.org) 816 Barnum St., Sheffield, MA 01257
  Dominic Palumbo offers exchange for farm work (minimum full day's work): organic farm meals, tentsite, shower, $2 laundry, insight into farming, farm work and food justice issues. Call ahead to reserve. Plan to arrive late afternoon for following work day. Pick up and drop off from: Salisbury, CT, Jug End Rd, MA 41, Shay's Rebellion, US Rte. 7, Home Rd. or Great Barrington.

Great Barrington, MA 01230 (3.0W) (all major services) See map of Great Barrington, MA.

- ✉ **PO** M–F 8:30am-4:30pm, Sa 8:30am-12:30pm. 413-528-3670.
- 🛏⊛☕ **Days Inn** 413-528-3150. No pets. Rates $89 and UP, includes continental breakfast, free WiFi, non-smoking rooms.
- 🛏⊛☕ **Mountain View Motel** 413-528-0250. (www.themountainviewmotel.com) No pets. Week days $69S $89D, $20EAP +tax. Microwave, fridge, free WiFi. Rides sometimes available.
- 🛏☕🖥 **Monument Mtn Motel** 413-528-3272. (www.monumentmountainmotel.com) weekdays $65S $75D. Free WiFi, outdoor pool. Mail drops for guests with reservations: 247 Stockbridge Rd, Rt 7, Great Barrington, MA 01230.
- 🛏⊛⚲🖥 **Fairfield Inn & Suites** 413-644-3200. No pets. Prices seasonal, call for pricing. Full breakfast, heated pool and hot tub. Mail drops for guests with advance reservations: 249 Stockbridge Rd, Rt 7, Great Barrington, MA 01230.
- 🛏⚲☕ **Travel Lodge** 413-528-2340 Su-Th $59-89D + tax, $10EAP, continental breakfast, coin laundry, free WiFi.
- ▲⊛♨ **Berkshire South Regional Community Center** 413-528-2810. (www.berkshiresouth.org) 15 Crissey Rd at north end of town.
  No Pets. No smoking, drugs, alcohol. Free tenting, check-in at front desk. $5PP for use of facilities ,showers, saunas, pool. Free dinner M 5pm-6pm, donations accepted.
- 🛒 **Guido's Organic produce**, 413-528-9255. (www.guidosfreshmarketplace.com) Cold juices, and more.
  Berkshire Co-op 413-528-9697. (www.berkshire.coop). M-Su 8am-8pm.
  Price Chopper 413-528-8415. M-Sa 6am-12am, Su 7am-12am; **Pharmacy** M-F 8am-8pm, Sa 9am-7pm, Su 9am-3pm.
  Big Y Foods 413-528-1314. M-F 7am-10pm, Sa 7am-10pm, Su 7am-9pm; **Pharmacy** 413-528-5460 M-F 9am-8pm, Sa 9am-5pm.
- ✕ **Aroma Bar & Grill** 413-528-3116, 413-528-3992. (www.aromabarandgrill.com) Lunch M-closed, Tu-Su 11:30am-3pm. Dinner M-Th 4:30pm-10pm, F-Su 4:30pm-10:30pm.
  Manhattan Pizza 413-528-2550. M-Th 11am-10pm, F-Sa 11am-11pm, Su 12pm-10pm.
  528 Café 413-528-2233. M-W 7am-4pm, Th-Su 7am-9pm.
  Four Brothers Pizza 413-528-9684. M-Su 10am-10pm.
  McDonalds 413-528-0434. M-Su 5am-11pm.
- ⚕ **Fairview Hospital** 413-528-0790. (www.berkshirehealthsystems.org/fairview) M-Su 24 hours.
- 🚗 **All Points Driving Service** 413-429-7397 Range from Salisbury to Dalton.

Great Barrington, MA

Barrington Brewery & Restaurant
Holiday Inn Express
Fairfield Inn & Suites
Aegean Breeze
The East
Monument Mountain Motel
Price Chopper
McDonald's
Dollar Tree
Travelodge
Shiro Sushi & Hibachi
Great Wall Chinese
US-7
Lantern House Motel
Marty And Jim's
Four Brothers Pizza Inn
Xicohtencatl Mexican
From here it is (3.4) to
MA-23
Great Barrington Pizza House
Allium Restaurant & Bar
Post Office
Rite Aid
Koi Chinese
Mountain View Motel
Bizen Gourmet Japanese
Restaurant and Sushi Bar
Mason Public Library
Fuel Coffee Shop
Patisserie Lenox
CVS
Days Inn
Berkshire Co-op Market
MA-23
from
Aroma Bar and Grill
Manhattan Pizza Co
(3.0) to
US-7
The Wainwright Inn Bed & Breakfast
Mountain Retreat Center

NoBo	Features	Description	GPS	Elev	SoBo
1521.8	⌒	Cross footbridge over drainage in middle of agricultural fields.		661	669.1
1522.6	⌒▲ P(6)	Cross **Housatonic River Bridge, Kellogg Road**	N 42 08.659, W 73 21.644	720	668.3
1523.0	▲	Cross **Boardman Street** near it's intersection with Kellogg Road.		694	667.9
1523.6		Cross rim of June Mountain.		1206	667.3
1524.3	◊	Cross intermittent brook.		1184	666.6
1524.6	▲P(5)	Cross **Home Road also known as Brush Hill Road.**	N 42 09.290, W 73 20.473	1150	666.3
1526.0	◊📷	Ridge at southern end of East Mountain, offers good views.		1800	664.9
1527.1	▲	Cross obscure woods road.		1681	663.8
1527.6	Y	Pass obscure trail junction.		1541	663.3
1528.1	◊Y▲ ⊆(10) ⌣☾☂	47 yards east to **Tom Leonard Shelter**, water (stream) is located (0.2) down a ravine on a blue blazed trail to the left of the shelter, campsite overlooking ravine north of shelter, privy, bear box, view.	N 42 09.893, W 73 18.351		662.8
	📷	22.8◀14.4◀14.3◀▶5.3▶7.1▶21.1		1540	662.8
1528.2	📷	Steep cliffs, view.		1616	662.7
1529.2	▲P(10) ★★★★★	Cross **Lake Buel Road**, paved.	N 42 10.482, W 73 17.638	1150	661.7
1529.6	▲	Cross dirt road.		1008	661.3
1529.7	⌒	Cross broken cement dam.		940	661.2

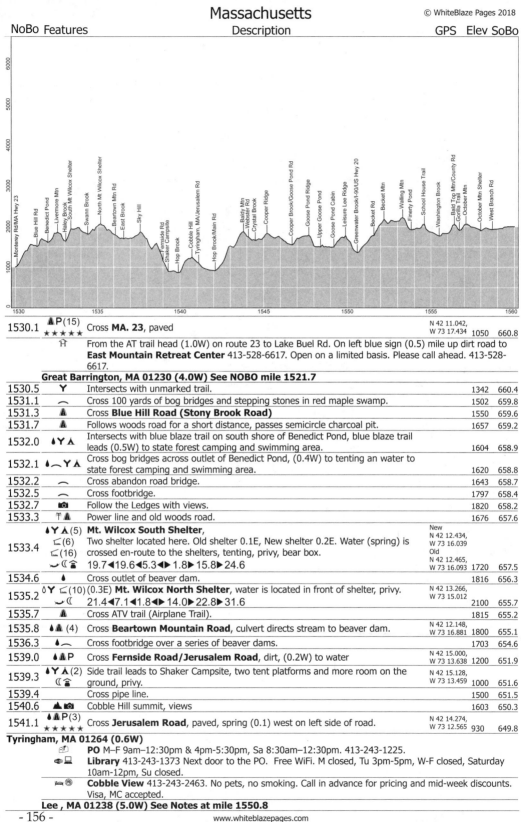

NoBo	Features	Description	GPS	Elev	SoBo
1530.1	⛰P(15) ★★★★★	Cross **MA. 23**, paved	N 42 11.042, W 73 17.434	1050	660.8
	⛺	From the AT trail head (1.0W) on route 23 to Lake Buel Rd. On left blue sign (0.5) mile up dirt road to **East Mountain Retreat Center** 413-528-6617. Open on a limited basis. Please call ahead. 413-528-6617.			
		Great Barrington, MA 01230 (4.0W) See NOBO mile 1521.7			
1530.5	Y	Intersects with unmarked trail.		1342	660.4
1531.1	⌒	Cross 100 yards of bog bridges and stepping stones in red maple swamp.		1502	659.8
1531.3	⛰	Cross **Blue Hill Road (Stony Brook Road)**		1550	659.6
1531.7	⛰	Follows woods road for a short distance, passes semicircle charcoal pit.		1657	659.2
1532.0	♦Y⛺	Intersects with blue blaze trail on south shore of Benedict Pond, blue blaze trail leads (0.5W) to state forest camping and swimming area.		1604	658.9
1532.1	♦⌒Y⛺	Cross bog bridges across outlet of Benedict Pond, (0.4W) to tenting an water to state forest camping and swimming area.		1620	658.8
1532.2	⌒	Cross abandon road bridge.		1643	658.7
1532.5	⌒	Cross footbridge.		1797	658.4
1532.7	📷	Follow the Ledges with views.		1820	658.2
1533.3	⛢⛰	Power line and old woods road.		1676	657.6
1533.4	♦Y⛺(5) ⌫(6) ⌫(16) ⌣☾☂	**Mt. Wilcox South Shelter,** Two shelter located here. Old shelter 0.1E, New shelter 0.2E. Water (spring) is crossed en-route to the shelters, tenting, privy, bear box. 19.7◀19.6◀5.3◀▶ 1.8▶15.8▶24.6	New N 42 12.434, W 73 16.039 Old N 42 12.465, W 73 16.093	1720	657.5
1534.6	♦	Cross outlet of beaver dam.		1816	656.3
1535.2	♦Y⌫(10) ⌣☾	(0.3E) **Mt. Wilcox North Shelter,** water is located in front of shelter, privy. 21.4◀7.1◀1.8◀▶ 14.0▶22.8▶31.6	N 42 13.266, W 73 15.012	2100	655.7
1535.7	⛰	Cross ATV trail (Airplane Trail).		1815	655.2
1535.8	♦⛰(4)	Cross **Beartown Mountain Road**, culvert directs stream to beaver dam.	N 42 12.148, W 73 16.881	1800	655.1
1536.3	♦⌒	Cross footbridge over a series of beaver dams.		1703	654.6
1539.0	♦⛰P	Cross **Fernside Road/Jerusalem Road**, dirt, (0.2W) to water	N 42 15.000, W 73 13.638	1200	651.9
1539.3	♦Y⛺(2) ☾☂	Side trail leads to Shaker Campsite, two tent platforms and more room on the ground, privy.	N 42 15.128, W 73 13.459	1000	651.6
1539.4	⌒	Cross pipe line.		1500	651.5
1540.6	⛰📷	Cobble Hill summit, views		1603	650.3
1541.1	♦⛰P(3) ★★★★★	Cross **Jerusalem Road**, paved, spring (0.1) west on left side of road.	N 42 14.274, W 73 12.565	930	649.8
		Tyringham, MA 01264 (0.6W)			
	📫	**PO** M–F 9am–12:30pm & 4pm-5:30pm, Sa 8:30am–12:30pm. 413-243-1225.			
	📖💻	**Library** 413-243-1373 Next door to the PO. Free WiFi. M closed, Tu 3pm-5pm, W-F closed, Saturday 10am-12pm, Su closed.			
	🏠⊛	**Cobble View** 413-243-2463. No pets, no smoking. Call in advance for pricing and mid-week discounts. Visa, MC accepted.			
		Lee , MA 01238 (5.0W) See Notes at mile 1550.8			

NoBo	Features	Description	GPS	Elev	SoBo
1541.2		Cross active cow pasture.		889	649.7
1541.4	◊	Cross intermitted brooks.		891	649.5
1541.5		Cross buried pipe line.		903	649.4
1542.1	⌒	Cross extensive boardwalk over wet fields.		956	648.8
1542.2	◊🛪P(5) ★★★★★	Cross **Tyringham Main Road**	N 42 14.118, W 73 11.664	930	648.7

Tyringham, MA 01264 (0.9W) See Notes at mile 1541.1
Lee , MA 01238 (5.3W) See Notes at mile 1550.8

NoBo	Features	Description	GPS	Elev	SoBo
1544.1	◊🛪P(2)	Cross **Webster Road**	N 42 15.153, W 73 10.737	1800	646.8
1544.7	Y📷	Unmarked trail gives view to Knee Deep Pond west.		1654	646.2
1545.6	◊Y	Unmarked side trail (0.1) leads west to spring.		1762	645.3
1546.5	🛪P(10)	Cross **Goose Pond Road**, gravel, parking (0.1E)	N 42 16.464, W 73 11.016	1650	644.4
1546.7	⌒	Telephone pole bridge over marsh of Cooper Brook beaver pond.		1570	644.2
1548.4	◊	Cross outlet of Upper Goose Pond.		1500	642.5
1548.9		Pass old Chimney and Plaque		1520	642.0
1549.2	Y ◊Y ✦▲ ⊏(14) ☾📷⚓⛵	Side trail (0.5) west to Upper Goose Pond Cabin. **(0.5W) Upper Goose Pond Cabin** Open daily May 13 - 22 Oct 2017. AT Passport location. Cabin offers bunks, fireplace, covered porch, tenting platforms, privy, bear box, AT Passport location, swimming and canoeing. During the summer, the resident volunteer caretaker brings water by canoe from a spring across the pond; otherwise, the pond is the water source. No fee is charged for staying at this site but donations are appreciated. **No Alcohol.** 21.1◀15.8◀14.0◀▶ 8.8▶ 17.6▶34.5	N 42 17.319, W 73 10.878	1480	641.7
1549.8	📷	Ridge overlooking I-90 and Upper Goose Pond Natural Area, register box. **No camping or fires allowed**.		1752	641.1
1550.4	⌒▲	Cross **I-90 MA**. Turnpike, pedestrian bridge		1400	640.5
1550.5	◊⌒○	Cross Greenwater Brook on high bridge over historical mill site on outlet stream.		1400	640.4
1550.8	🛪P(20) ★★★★★	Cross **U.S. 20**	N 42 17.576, W 73 09.684	1400	640.1
	◊ 🛏⊛☐	**(0.1E) Berkshire Lakeside Lodge** 413-243-9907. (www.berkshirelakesidelodge.com) No pets. Weekdays $65-95, weekends $100-160 2-person room, $10EAP. Includes continental breakfast, fridge. Hikers may get water. Mail drops (call ahead to arrange pickup): 3949 Jacob's Ladder Rd, Rt 10, Becket, MA 01223			

Lee, MA 01238 (5.0W) (all major services)

📪	**PO** M–F 8:30am–4:30pm, Sa 9am–12pm. 413-243-1392.		
🛏	Several hotels and motels but very expensive.		
🛒	**Price Chopper Supermarket** & Pharmacy 413-528-2408. M-Su 24 hour.		
✚	**Rite Aid** M-F 7am-9pm, Sa 7am-8pm, Su 8am-6pm; **Pharmacy** M-F 8am-8pm, Sa 9am-6pm, Su 9am-5pm.		
🐎	**Valley Veterinary Clinic** 413-243-2414. (www.valleyveterinaryservice.com) M-F 8am-5pm, Sa 8am-12pm, Su closed.		
⛲	**Lee Coin-Op Laundry** 413-243-0480.		

NoBo	Features	Description	GPS	Elev	SoBo
1550.9	YP	Trail leads west to parking area.	N 42 17.576, W 73 09.684	1407	640.0
1551.0	⟟	Power line.		1574	639.9
1551.6	🛪P	Cross **Tyne Road also known as Becket Road**. US. 20 is (0.9) west. MA 8 is (3.5) east. Very limited parking.	N 42 17.808, W 73 09.029	1750	639.3
1552.1	▲📷	Becket Mountain summit, concrete footing mark the location of the old fire tower, register box.		2180	638.8
1553.2		Overgrown Walling Mountain.		2220	637.7
1553.9	◊Y	South side of Finerty Pond, crosses an ATV trail.		1900	637.0
1554.1	◊	Skirt west side of Finerty Pond.		1928	636.8
1554.2	◊	Northwest side of Finerty Pond.		1947	636.7
1554.8		High point north of Finerty Pond		2070	636.1
1554.9	Y	School House Trail, ATV trail.		1991	636.0
1555.6	◊	Cross some streams in the area.		1799	635.3
1556.2	🛪P	Cross **County Road**, road leads (4.0) east to MA. 8.		1850	634.7
1556.4	⌒	Bald Top summit, overgrown		2040	634.5
1556.9	Y	Gorilla Trail, motorcycle/ATV trail.		1933	634.0
1558.0	◊▲⊏(12) ☾⌣🎒	15 yards west to **October Mountain Shelter**, water (stream) is located south of the shelter on the AT, tenting, privy, bear cables. 24.6◀22.8◀8.8◀▶ 8.8▶ 25.7▶ 32.3	N 42 21.292, W 73 09.270	1950	632.9
1558.7	🛪P	Cross **West Branch Road**. Beavers often plug culverts in this area.		1960	632.2

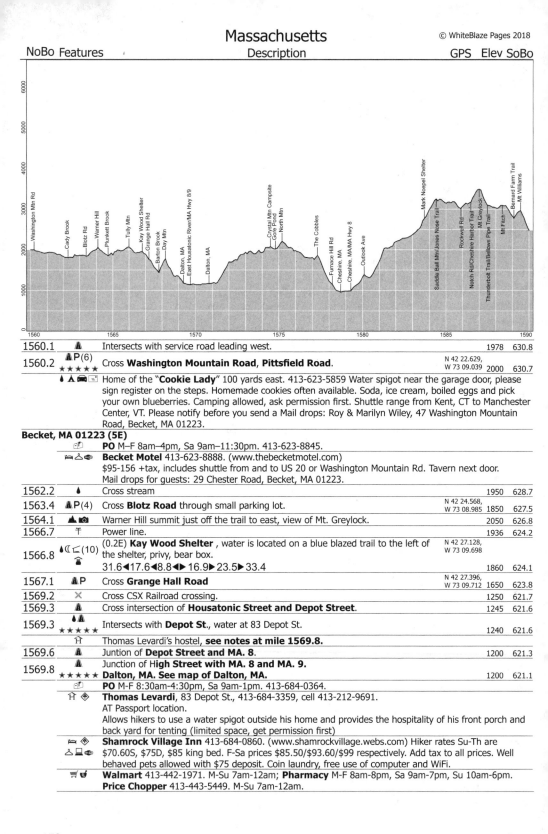

NoBo	Features	Description	GPS	Elev	SoBo
1560.1	▲	Intersects with service road leading west.		1978	630.8
1560.2	▲P(6) ★★★★★	Cross **Washington Mountain Road, Pittsfield Road**.	N 42 22.629, W 73 09.039	2000	630.7
	♦ ▲ �car 🖻	Home of the "**Cookie Lady**" 100 yards east. 413-623-5859 Water spigot near the garage door, please sign register on the steps. Homemade cookies often available. Soda, ice cream, boiled eggs and pick your own blueberries. Camping allowed, ask permission first. Shuttle range from Kent, CT to Manchester Center, VT. Please notify before you send a Mail drops: Roy & Marilyn Wiley, 47 Washington Mountain Road, Becket, MA 01223.			

Becket, MA 01223 (5E)

	🖃	**PO** M–F 8am–4pm, Sa 9am–11:30pm. 413-623-8845.			
	🛏 ▲ 🖵	**Becket Motel** 413-623-8888. (www.thebecketmotel.com) $95-156 +tax, includes shuttle from and to US 20 or Washington Mountain Rd. Tavern next door. Mail drops for guests: 29 Chester Road, Becket, MA 01223.			
1562.2	♦	Cross stream		1950	628.7
1563.4	▲P(4)	Cross **Blotz Road** through small parking lot.	N 42 24.568, W 73 08.985	1850	627.5
1564.1	▲ 🖾	Warner Hill summit just off the trail to east, view of Mt. Greylock.		2050	626.8
1566.7	ㅜ	Power line.		1936	624.2
1566.8	♦ℂ⊏(10) 🔋	(0.2E) **Kay Wood Shelter** , water is located on a blue blazed trail to the left of the shelter, privy, bear box.	N 42 27.128, W 73 09.698		
		31.6◄17.6◄8.8◄► 16.9►23.5►33.4		1860	624.1
1567.1	▲P	Cross **Grange Hall Road**	N 42 27.396, W 73 09.712	1650	623.8
1569.2	✕	Cross CSX Railroad crossing.		1250	621.7
1569.3	▲	Cross intersection of **Housatonic Street and Depot Street**.		1245	621.6
1569.3	♦▲ ★★★★★	Intersects with **Depot St.**, water at 83 Depot St.		1240	621.6
	🏠	Thomas Levardi's hostel, **see notes at mile 1569.8.**			
1569.6	▲	Junction of **Depot Street and MA. 8.**		1200	621.3
1569.8	▲ ★★★★★	Junction of **High Street with MA. 8 and MA. 9.** **Dalton, MA. See map of Dalton, MA.**		1200	621.1
	🖃	**PO** M-F 8:30am-4:30pm, Sa 9am-1pm. 413-684-0364.			
	🏠 ◈	**Thomas Levardi**, 83 Depot St., 413-684-3359, cell 413-212-9691. AT Passport location. Allows hikers to use a water spigot outside his home and provides the hospitality of his front porch and back yard for tenting (limited space, get permission first)			
	🛏 ◈ ▲ 🖵 🖵	**Shamrock Village Inn** 413-684-0860. (www.shamrockvillage.webs.com) Hiker rates Su-Th are $70.60S, $75D, $85 king bed. F-Sa prices $85.50/$93.60/$99 respectively. Add tax to all prices. Well behaved pets allowed with $75 deposit. Coin laundry, free use of computer and WiFi.			
	🛒 🥤	**Walmart** 413-442-1971. M-Su 7am-12am; **Pharmacy** M-F 8am-8pm, Sa 9am-7pm, Su 10am-6pm. **Price Chopper** 413-443-5449. M-Su 7am-12am.			

NoBo Features   Description   GPS   Elev SoBo

✗	**Angelina's Subs** 413-443-9875. (www.angelinassubshop.com) M-Su 8:30am-11pm.	
	Dalton Restaurant 413-684-0414. Serves breakfast, lunch and dinner. M-Th 6am-8pm, F-Sa 6am-8:30pm, Su 6am-12:30pm.	
✗	**SweetPea's Ice Cream Shop** 413-684-9799.	
	Serving 32 flavors of Hershey's ice cream, Hot Dogs, Pulled Pork and Chicken Sandwich, and a daily Lunch Special.	
	Summer hours; M-Th 12pm-9pm, F-Sa 12pm-10pm, Su 1pm-8pm.	
⌂	**Dalton Laundry** 413-684-9702. M-F 9am-5:30pm, Sa 8am-4:15pm, Su 10am-2pm.	
⚲	(0.7 from AT) **Dalton CRA** (www.daltoncra.org) 413-684-0260. Free Showers M-F 5am-8pm, Sa 7am-3:30pm, Su 9am-1pm.	
⚕	**O'Laughlin's Pharmacy** 413-684-0023.	
✗	**LP Adams** 413-684-0025. (www.lpadams.com) Coleman and denatured alcohol. M-F 6am-5pm, Sa 6am-1pm, Su closed.	

Pittsfield, MA Many stores and restaurants approx. (2.0W) from Dalton.

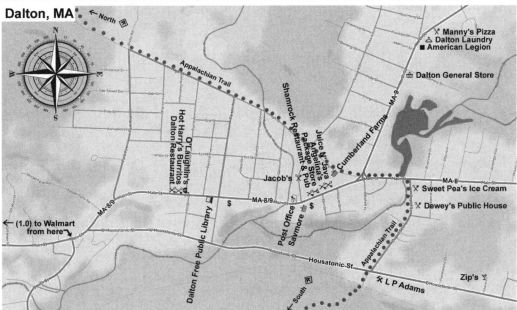

Dalton, MA

- ✗ Manny's Pizza
- ⌂ Dalton Laundry
- ■ American Legion
- 🏛 Dalton General Store
- Jacob's ✗
- ✗ Sweet Pea's Ice Cream
- ✗ Dewey's Public House
- ← (1.0) to Walmart from here
- ✗ L P Adams
- Zip's ✗

1570.7	🅰	Cross **Park Avenue**.		1169	620.2
1570.8	🅰P(6)	Cross parking lot on Gulf Road which becomes High Street, hiker kiosk.	N 42 28.903, W 73 10.693	1180	620.1
1574.1	⊤	Power line. Bears frequent here when berries are around.		1920	616.8
1574.5	♦Y⅄(5)☾	(0.2E) Crystal Mountain campsite, privy.		2100	616.4
1574.9	♦	Cross outlet of Gore Pond.		2050	616.0
1575.3	🅰	Cross logging road, dirt		2092	615.6
1577.4	📷	Blue blaze side tail to The Cobbles, series of white quartz ledges, good views.		1850	613.5
1578.2	🅰	Intersection of **Furnace Hill Road** with private driveway.		960	612.7
1578.4	🅰	Intersection of **Furnace Hill Road and East Main Street**.		964	612.5
1578.7	Y🚹🅰	Intersects with **Church St.**, Hoosic River, Ashuwillticook Rail Trail		950	612.2
1578.8	♦🅰 ★★★★★	Intersects with Church St., School St., hiker kiosk. Post office across the street. **Cheshire, MA. See map of Cheshire, MA.**		970	612.1
	⊠	**PO** M-F 7:30am-1pm & 2pm-4:30pm, Sa 8:30am-11:30am. 413-743-3184.			
	✗	**Diane's Twist** 413-743-9776. Limited hours, deli sandwiches, soda, ice cream.			
	🏛	**HD Reynolds** 413-743-9512. (www.reynoldslawnmower.com) General store, hiker snacks, Coleman fuel by the ounce. M-W 8a,-5pm, Th 8am-7pm, F 8am-5pm, Sa 8am-3pm, Su closed.			
	🅰🚹⟡	**St Marry of the Assumption Church** St. Mary of the Assumption in Cheshire will be offering limited services to hikers. Restroom facilities will be open from May 1st to October 1st from 9:00 a.m. until 7:00 p.m. each day. Tent camping on the east lawn is available. No indoor sleeping. No showers.			
	💻	**Cheshire Public Library** 413-743-4746. M 9am-3pm, Tu 10am-2pm & 5pm-8pm, W closed, Th 3pm-6pm, F-Su closed.			

Cheshire, MA

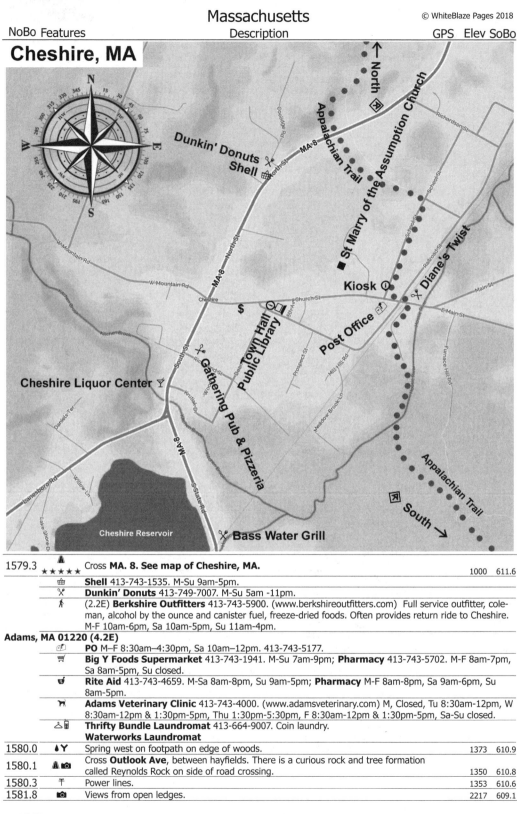

NoBo		Features / Description	GPS	SoBo
1579.3	★★★★★	Cross **MA. 8. See map of Cheshire, MA.**	1000	611.6
	🏠	**Shell** 413-743-1535. M-Su 9am-5pm.		
	✗	**Dunkin' Donuts** 413-749-7007. M-Su 5am -11pm.		
	⚲	(2.2E) **Berkshire Outfitters** 413-743-5900. (www.berkshireoutfitters.com) Full service outfitter, coleman, alcohol by the ounce and canister fuel, freeze-dried foods. Often provides return ride to Cheshire. M-F 10am-6pm, Sa 10am-5pm, Su 11am-4pm.		
Adams, MA 01220 (4.2E)				
	🖃	**PO** M–F 8:30am–4:30pm, Sa 10am–12pm. 413-743-5177.		
	🛒	**Big Y Foods Supermarket** 413-743-1941. M-Su 7am-9pm; **Pharmacy** 413-743-5702. M-F 8am-7pm, Sa 8am-5pm, Su closed.		
	⛟	**Rite Aid** 413-743-4659. M-Sa 8am-8pm, Su 9am-5pm; **Pharmacy** M-F 8am-8pm, Sa 9am-6pm, Su 8am-5pm.		
	🐕	**Adams Veterinary Clinic** 413-743-4000. (www.adamsveterinary.com) M, Closed, Tu 8:30am-12pm, W 8:30am-12pm & 1:30pm-5pm, Thu 1:30pm-5:30pm, F 8:30am-12pm & 1:30pm-5pm, Sa-Su closed.		
	🧺	**Thrifty Bundle Laundromat** 413-664-9007. Coin laundry.		
		Waterworks Laundromat		
1580.0	♦ Y	Spring west on footpath on edge of woods.	1373	610.9
1580.1	⚠ 📷	Cross **Outlook Ave**, between hayfields. There is a curious rock and tree formation called Reynolds Rock on side of road crossing.	1350	610.8
1580.3	⊤	Power lines.	1353	610.6
1581.8	📷	Views from open ledges.	2217	609.1

NoBo	Features	Description	GPS	Elev	SoBo
1582.8	⚑P(15)	Cross **Old Adams Road**		2350	608.1
1583.7	⛉Y⚑(2) ⊏(10)⊂	(0.2E) **Mark Noepel Shelter**, water (stream) is located on a blue blazed trail to the right of the shelter, tenting platforms, privy, fire pit. 34.5◄25.7◄16.9◄▶ 6.6▶ 16.5▶23.7▶	N 42 36.518, W 73 11.052	2750	607.2
1584.3	Y	Side trail to Jones Nose Trail intersects along the southern end of Saddle Ball Mountain.		3150	606.6
1585.9	⌇📷	View of Mt. Greylock just north of bog bridges.		3254	605.0
1586.5	⚑P	Meet **Rockwell Road** at hairpin turn in road. Gravel parking lot.	N 42 37.860, W 73 10.690	3290	604.4
1586.7	⚑Y	Intersection of **Rockwell Road** and Cheshire Harbor Trail, which descends eat.		3119	604.2
1586.8	Y	Intersection with Hopper Trail, descends west to Sperry Campground.		3132	604.1
1586.9	⚑P	Crosses the junction of **Notch, Rockwell, and Summits Roads**. Old water supply and pump house are on AT south of this junction. East of this junction is a gravel parking lot.	N 42 38.034, W 73 09.250	3177	604.0
1587.0	⛉▲🗼📷 ⚑P ★★★★★	Mt. Greylock summit, **Summit Road**, Bascom Lodge, War Memorial. Many parking spots.	N 42 38.235, W 73 09.956	3491	603.9
	⛺⛩✕⛲ ⊚	**Bascom Lodge** on summit of Mt Greylock, 413-743-1591. (www.bascomlodge.net) No smoking. Private rooms $125 and up, bunkroom $40PP. Bunkroom includes use of shower and continental breakfast. Shower and towel without stay $5, some snacks, restaurant serves breakfast, lunch and dinner, free WiFi. Open May 20-mid Oct 2017.			
1587.5	Y	Intersects with Thunderbolt Trail and Bellows Pipe Trail to the east and a shorter connecting trail to the Robinson Point Trail and Notch Road to the west, all within 100 yards of each.		3095	603.4
1588.3	📷	Unusual outcropping of milky quartz atop of Mt. Fitch.		3096	602.6
1589.1	Y	Four way junction with Bernard Farm Trail east.		2772	601.8
1589.3	▲📷	Mt. Williams summit, register box.		2951	601.6

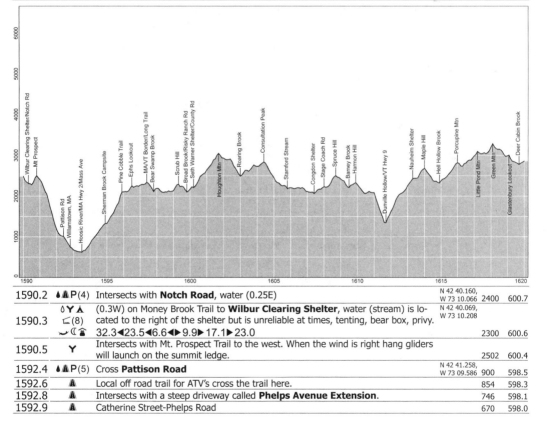

NoBo	Features	Description	GPS	Elev	SoBo
1590.2	⛉⚑P(4)	Intersects with **Notch Road**, water (0.25E)	N 42 40.160, W 73 10.066	2400	600.7
1590.3	⛉Y⚑ ⊏(8) ⌇⊂☂	(0.3W) on Money Brook Trail to **Wilbur Clearing Shelter**, water (stream) is located to the right of the shelter but is unreliable at times, tenting, bear box, privy. 32.3◄23.5◄6.6◄▶ 9.9▶ 17.1▶23.0	N 42 40.069, W 73 10.208	2300	600.6
1590.5	Y	Intersects with Mt. Prospect Trail to the west. When the wind is right hang gliders will launch on the summit ledge.		2502	600.4
1592.4	⛉⚑P(5)	Cross **Pattison Road**	N 42 41.258, W 73 09.586	900	598.5
1592.6	⚑	Local off road trail for ATV's cross the trail here.		854	598.3
1592.8	⚑	Intersects with a steep driveway called **Phelps Avenue Extension**.		746	598.1
1592.9	⚑	Catherine Street-Phelps Road		670	598.0

NoBo	Features	Description	GPS	Elev	SoBo
1593.3	**A P** ★★★★★	Cross intersection of **Phelps Avenue and MA. 2**	N 42 41.940, W 73 09.210	650	597.6
	P	**Greylock Community Center** 413-664-9020. Park on grass west of building and leave a note with name and vehicle License Plate in mailbox, donations accepted.			

Williamstown, MA 01267 (2.6W) See map of Williamstown (downtown and mid-town).

	🏤	**PO** M-F 8:30am-4:30pm, Sa 9am-12pm. 413-458-3707.			
	🛏⊗⚿⌨ 🍴🖥	**Willows Motel** 413-458-5768. (www.willowsmotel.com) No pets, no smoking. $79-149, includes continental breakfast, free pickup and return to trail with stay. Microwave, fridge. Laundry $6, outdoor pool, Computer available for use, free WiFi. Mail drops for guests: 480 Main Street, Williamstown, MA 01267.			
	🛏⚿⌨🍴 🖥	**Williamstown Motel** 413-458-5202. (www.williamstownmotel.com) $68 to 109 weekdays, $89 $169 weekends, includes continental breakfast, microwave, fridge. Laundry (they do for you) $8, computer available for use, free WiFi. Will pickup at Route MA 2. All major credit cards accepted. Mail drops for guests: 295 Main Street, Williamstown, MA 01267.			
	🛏⌨🍴🖥 ⟋	**Howard Johnson** 413-458-8158, Rates seasonal, continental breakfast, outdoor pool, BBQ grills, computer available for use, free WiFi. Mail drops free for guests (fee for non guests): 213 Main Street, Williamstown, MA 01267.			
	🛏🍴	**Maple Terrace** 413-458-9677. (www.mapleterrace.com) Prices seasonal, call for rates. Heated pool, all rooms non smoking.			
	🛏P	**River Bend Farm** 413-458-3121. (www.riverbendfarmbb.com) $120 includes breakfast. Free pickup and return to trail when available, short term parking for guests.			
	🛏✗⚿🍵 P	**Williams Inn** 413-458-9371. (www.williamsinn.com) $155 and up, includes continental breakfast, pool, hot tub, sauna. Non guests can pay $8 for use of shower, swim and sauna. ATM. Restaurant M-Su 5am-10pm. Short term parking $2 per day.			
	🛒⛟	**Stop & Shop** 413-664-8100. M0Sa 6am-12am, Su 7am-9pm; **Pharmacy** 413-664-8550. M-F 9am-9pm, Sa 9am-8pm, Su 9am-6pm.			
	🛒	**Wild Oats** 413-458-8060. (www.wildoats.coop) M-Sa 7am-8pm, Su 9am-8pm.			
	✗	**Desperado's** 4130458-2100. (www.mydesperados.net) M-Th 4pm-9pm, F-Sa 4pm,-10pm, Su 3pm-9pm.			
		Spice Root Indian Cuisine 413-458-5200. (www.spiceroot.com)Weekday Lunch Buffet - Served Tu-F 11:30pm 2:30pm ~ $10.95; Weekend Maharaja Brunch Buffet Served Sa: 11:30pm 2:30pm; Sunday: 12pm 3pm ~ $12.95. 10% hiker discount.			
		Water Street Grill 413-458-2175. (www.waterstgrill.com) Serves lunch and dinner. M-Su 11:30am-11pm.			
	⚓🖥	**Nature's Closet** 413-458-7909. (www.naturescloset.net) Clothing, footwear, canister fuel. M-Th 10am-6pm, F-Sa 10am-7pm, Su 10am-6pm.			
		Mail drops: 61 Spring St, Williamstown, MA 01267.			
	🖥	**Milne Public Library** 413-458-5369. (wwwmilnelibrary.org) M-Tu 10am-5:30pm, W 10-8, Th-F 10am-5:30pm, Sa 10am-4pm, Su closed.			

North Adams, MA 01247 (2.5E) See map of North Adams, MA.

	🏤	**PO** M-F 8:30am-4:30pm, Sa 10am-12pm. 413-664-4554.			
	🛏✗⚿🖥 🍴	**Holiday Inn** 413-663-6500. Summer rates $170 and up, Pool, hot tub; **Richmond Grill** on location.			
	🛒	**Big Y** 413-663-6549. M-F 7am-9pm, Sa-Su 7am-9pm.			
	🏛	**Family Dollar** M-Su 9am-9pm.			
	✗	**Subway, Brewhaha, McDonalds, Dunkin Donuts**			
	✗ ◈	**Papa John's Pizza** 413-663-7272. AT Passport.			
	⛟	**Rite aid** 413-663-5270. m-Sa 8am-8pm, Su 9am-6pm; **Pharmacy** M-F 8am-8pm, Sa 9am-6pm, Su 9am-5pm.			
		CVS 413-664-8712. M-Su 8am-9pm; **Pharmacy** M-F 8am-8pm, Sa 9am-6pm, Su 9am-5pm.			
	🐕	**Greylock Animal Hospital** 413-663-5365. (www.greylockanimalhospital.com) M-F 8am-8pm, Sa-Su 8am-4pm.			
	🚗	**David Ackerson** 413-346-1033, 413-652-9573. daveackerson@yahoo.com. Shuttles range from Bear Mtn Bridge to Hanover NH, and to and from area airports.			

Massachusetts

NoBo Features	Description	GPS Elev SoBo

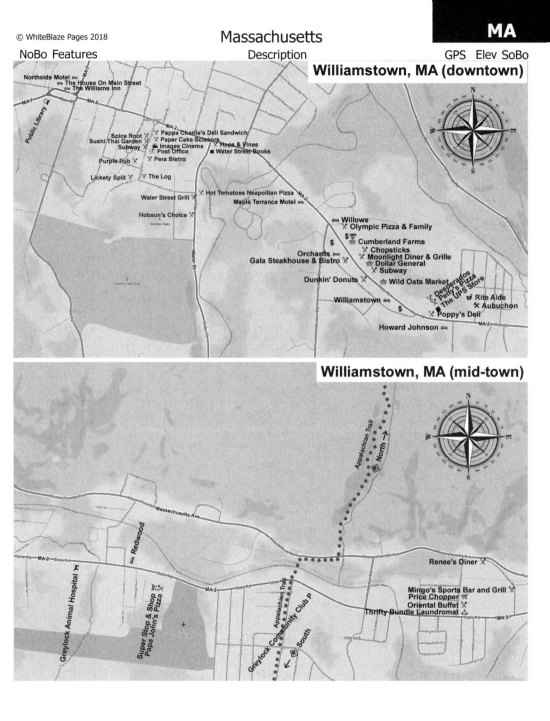

Williamstown, MA (downtown)

Northside Motel
The House On Main Street
The Williams Inn

Public Library

Spice Root
Sushi Thai Garden
Subway

Pappa Charlie's Deli Sandwich
Paper Cake Scissors
Images Cinema
Post Office

Hops & Vines
Water Street Books

Purple Pub

Pera Bistro

Lickety Split

The Log

Water Street Grill

Hot Tomatoes Neapolitan Pizza
Maple Terrance Motel

Hobson's Choice

Willows
Olympic Pizza & Family

Cumberland Farms
Chopsticks
Moonlight Diner & Grille
Dollar General
Subway

Orchards
Gala Steakhouse & Bistro

Dunkin' Donuts

Wild Oats Market

Desperados
Petty's Pizza
The UPS Store

Williamstown

Rite Aide
Aubuchon
Poppy's Deli

Howard Johnson

Williamstown, MA (mid-town)

Appalachian Trail
North

Massachusetts Ave.

Redwood

Greylock Animal Hospital

Super Stop & Shop
Papa John's Pizza

Appalachian Trail
Greylock Community Club P
South

Renee's Diner

Mingo's Sports Bar and Grill
Price Chopper
Oriental Buffet
Thrifty Bundle Laundromat

North Adams, MA

NoBo	Features	Description	GPS	Elev	SoBo
1593.5	✕	Cross footbridge across Boston & Maine Railroad and the Housic River.		648	597.4
1593.6	▲ ★★★★★	Cross **Massachusetts Avenue**.		666	597.3
	🛏⚐⬤🍴	(4.2W) **The Birches B&B** 413-458-8134. (www.birchesbb.com) $125D and up, includes breakfast. Swimming pond, laundry, free WiFi. Ask about slackpacking. Free pickup and return from Massachusetts Ave or MA 2 with stay, advance notice required. Two night min on weekends during the summer months. Located on 522 White Oaks Road.			
1593.7		Cross Sherman Brook twice, passing an old dam, spillway, this was all part of textile mills.		693	597.2
1593.9	⏚	Power line.		817	597.0
1594.9	♦Y⚑(3) ⌣ℂ	Side trail (south end) to (0.1) west to Sherman Brook Campsite to west. Pete's Spring is on east side of AT.		1371	596.0
1595.1	♦Y⚑(3) ⌣ℂ	Side trail (north end) to (0.1) west to Sherman Brook Campsite, privy.		1300	595.8
1595.7	Y	South end of Blue blaze bad weather trail intersects west.		1874	595.2
1595.9	Y📷	North end of Blue blaze bad weather trail intersects west. Views of Mt. Greylock.		2128	595.0
1596.0		Trail skirts north side of bog.		2130	594.9
1596.1	Y	Intersects with Pine Cobble Trail, a quartzite covered viewpoint is 200 feet south of Pine Cobble.		2010	594.8
1596.4	Y	Class of '98 Trail leads west to make a loop with Pine Cobble Trail.		2122	594.5
1596.6	📷	Eph's Lookout, a quartzite ridge with limited view.		2254	594.3
1596.9	▲	Abandon road descends west to Henderson Road in Williamstown.		2256	594.0
1597.4	State Line	Massachusetts–Vermont State Line, Long Trail (southern terminus), sign.		2330	593.5
1597.8	♦	Brook		2300	593.1
1600.2	◊Y⚑ ⌐(8)⌣ℂ	(0.2W) **Seth Warner Shelter**, water (brook) is located 150 yards to the left of the shelter but is known to go dry, tenting, privy. 33.4◀16.5◀9.9◀▶7.2▶13.1▶21.6	N 42 46.310, W 73 08.256	2180	590.7
1600.5	▲P(4)	Cross **County Road**. Getting to this road can be iffy in wet weather if you don't have a 4WD vehicle.	N 42 46.505, W 73 07.994	2290	590.4
1601.4	♦	Side trail east 100 feet to Ed's Spring.		2890	589.5
1601.7	📷	View of Mt. Greylock.			589.2
1601.9	📷	Ridgeline with views.		3025	589.0
1602.3	⏚	Power line.		2906	588.6
1603.0	♦📷	Follow along eastern shore of old beaver pond, view of Scrub Hill.		1516	587.9
1603.2	♦	Cross Roaring Branch at base of beaver dam.		2470	587.7
1603.4		Pass over knob.		2615	587.5
1603.7		Pass over knob.		2773	587.2
1604.4	▲	Consultation Peak summit, wooded.		2840	586.5
1605.4	▲	Cross woods road, leads (0.2) west to clearing on eastern shore of Sucker Pond.		2232	585.5

NoBo	Features	Description	GPS	Elev	SoBo
1605.8		Cross Sucker Pond outlet brook.		2180	585.1
1606.3		Pass old foundation, nineteenth century tavern.		2209	584.6
1606.5	⚠	Cross woods road.		2162	584.4
1606.8	♦	Stamford Stream		2040	584.1
1607.4	♦⚠⊏(8) ⌣℄	**Congdon Shelter**, water (brook) is located in front of the shelter, tenting, privy. 23.7◀17.1◀7.2◀▶ 5.9▶ 14.4▶ 18.7	N 42 50.883, W 73 06.624	2060	583.5
1608.0	⚠	Cross **Old Bennington-Heartwellville Road**, also known as Burgess/Old **Stage Road**.		2220	582.9
1608.1	♦	Cross small stream.		2268	582.8
1609.6	♦	Cross brook.		2262	581.3
1609.9	▲📷	Harmon Hill summit, views of Bennington		2325	581.0
1611.7	♦⌣▲ P(1) ★★★★★	Cross stream on bridge. Cross **VT. 9**, City Stream.	N 42 53.105, W 73 06.947	1360	579.2

VT 9 Bennington, VT (5.1W) See map of Bennington, VA.

    🏤 **PO** M-F 8am-5pm, Sa 9am-2pm. 802-442-2421.

  🛏♿🍴🚐 **Catamount Motel** 802-442-5977. (www.catamountmotel.com)
      🖥 1 Hiker $54 plus tax, 2 Hikers $65 plus tax. each extra person $5, laundry $4, $5 dog fee. Free WiFi. Free shuttle service. Credit cards accepted.
         Mail drops for guests: 500 South St. Route 7 Bennington VT 05201.

  🛏♿🖥🚐 **Autumn Inn Motel** 802-447-7625. (www.theautumninn.com) $60-99, microwave, fridge, laundry, 🚗🖥 free WiFi. Pickup or return to trail for $10 each way. Pets $10. Mail drops for guests: 924 Main Street, Bennington, VT 05201.

  🛏🖥🍴🖥 **Knotty Pine Motel** 802-442-5487. (www.knottypinemotel.com) 6.5 miles from the AT on VT 9, $89D and up, $8EAP up to 4. Includes continental breakfast, pets free, microwave, fridge, pool, computer available to use, free WiFi. Mail drops for guests: 130 Northside Drive, Bennington, VT 05201.

  🛏♿🖥🍴 **Best Western** 802-442-6311. $99 and up.

  🛏♿🖥🍴 **Hampton Inn** 802-440-9862. call for prices, seasonal rates, includes hot breakfast.

    🛒 **Spice & Nice Natural Foods** 802-442-8365. (www.spicenice.net) M-Sa 9am-5:30pm, Su 1am-4pm.

  🍴🛒 **Price Chopper** M-Su 24 hours; **Pharmacy** M-F 8am-8pm, Sa 9am-6pm, Su 9am-3pm. **Walmart** 802-447-1614. M-Su 6am-12am; **Pharmacy** M-F 8am-8pm, Sa 9am-8pm, Su 10am-6pm.

    ✗ **Lil' Britain** 802-442-2447. Fish & chips. M closed, Tu-Sa 11:30am-8pm, Su closed.

    ☤ **Express Care Walk-in Clinic** 802-440-4077. (www.svhealthcare.org) M-Su 8am to 6pm.

    🎞 **Cinema 7** 802-442-8170.

Bennington, VT

NoBo	Features	Description	GPS	Elev	SoBo
1613.0	🔺	Cross woods road.		2268	577.9
1613.2	🔺	Cross woods road.		2440	577.7
1613.3	♦Y⌐(8)☾	Cross brook, spur trail leads 100 yard to **Melville Nauheim Shelter**, water (stream) is located north of trail to shelter, privy. 23.0▶13.1▶5.9◀▶8.5▶12.8▶17.4	N 42 53.267, W 73 05.772	2330	577.6
1613.8	⊥	Power line.		2620	577.1
1614.0	🔺	Maple Hill summit, wooded.		2588	576.9
1614.6	♦	Cross stream.		2492	576.3
1614.9	♦	Cross Hell Hollow Brook is a rock hop, **camping is not permitted here**.		2350	576.0
1616.1	📷	Porcupine Lookout.		2815	574.8
1617.2	🔺	Little Pond summit.		3100	573.7
1617.5	📷	Little Pond Lookout, views		3060	573.4
1619.3	📷	Glastenbury Lookout, view west of Glastenbury Mountain and West Ridge.		2920	571.6
1619.8	🔺	Cross old woods road.		2877	571.1

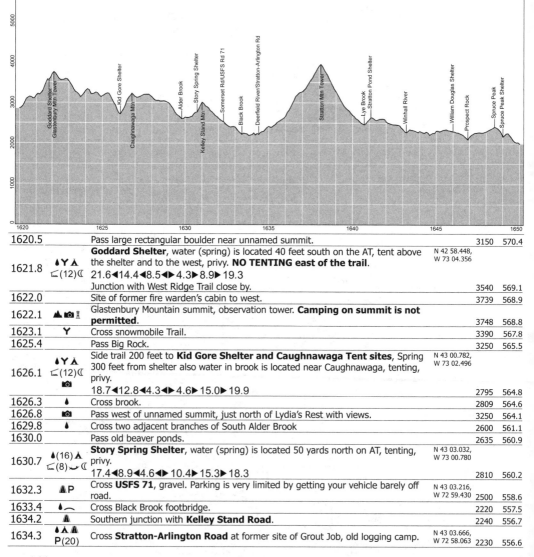

1620.5		Pass large rectangular boulder near unnamed summit.		3150	570.4
1621.8	♦Y⅄ ⌐(12)☾	**Goddard Shelter**, water (spring) is located 40 feet south on the AT, tent above the shelter and to the west, privy. **NO TENTING east of the trail**. 21.6◀14.4◀8.5◀▶4.3▶8.9▶19.3	N 42 58.448, W 73 04.356	3540	569.1
1622.0		Junction with West Ridge Trail close by. Site of former fire warden's cabin to west.		3739	568.9
1622.1	🔺📷🏠	Glastenbury Mountain summit, observation tower. **Camping on summit is not permitted**.		3748	568.8
1623.1	Y	Cross snowmobile Trail.		3390	567.8
1625.4		Pass Big Rock.		3250	565.5
1626.1	♦Y⅄ ⌐(12)☾ 📷	Side trail 200 feet to **Kid Gore Shelter and Caughnawaga Tent sites**, Spring 300 feet from shelter also water in brook is located near Caughnawaga, tenting, privy. 18.7◀12.8◀4.3◀▶4.6▶15.0▶19.9	N 43 00.782, W 73 02.496	2795	564.8
1626.3	♦	Cross brook.		2809	564.6
1626.8	📷	Pass west of unnamed summit, just north of Lydia's Rest with views.		3250	564.1
1629.8	♦	Cross two adjacent branches of South Alder Brook		2600	561.1
1630.0		Pass old beaver ponds.		2635	560.9
1630.7	♦(16)⅄ ⌐(8)⌣☾	**Story Spring Shelter**, water (spring) is located 50 yards north on AT, tenting, privy. 17.4◀8.9◀4.6◀▶10.4▶15.3▶18.3	N 43 03.032, W 73 00.780	2810	560.2
1632.3	🔺P	Cross **USFS 71**, gravel. Parking is very limited by getting your vehicle barely off road.	N 43 03.216, W 72 59.430	2500	558.6
1633.4	♦⌐	Cross Black Brook footbridge.		2220	557.5
1634.2	🔺	Southern junction with **Kelley Stand Road**.		2240	556.7
1634.3	♦🔺🔺 P(20)	Cross **Stratton-Arlington Road** at former site of Grout Job, old logging camp.	N 43 03.666, W 72 58.063	2230	556.6

NoBo	Features	Description	GPS	Elev	SoBo
1635.7	▲	Cross gravel road.		2520	555.2
1636.3	📷	Pass Vista.		3032	554.6
1637.0		Reach Col between Stratton and Little Stratton Mountains.		3467	553.9
1637.5	♦	Spring to west.		3816	553.4
1638.1	📷 🎋 ★★★★★	Stratton Mountain, fire tower, caretaker cabin, (0.8E) to gondola. **Camping is not permitted here**.		3936	552.8
	⛺ ✕	(1.0) side trail summit and gondola ride. **Stratton Mountain Resort** 802-297-4000. Gondola has limited days and hours of operation. Make sure you know it's in operation before you make the side trip. Restaurant on site, hotel rooms $89 and up.			
1638.3	♦	Spring to east.		3810	552.6
1640.1	▲	Cross gravel road.		3694	550.8
1640.7	♦⌒	Cross brook on bridge.		3145	550.2
1640.8		Pass beaver pond.		2862	550.1
1641.1	♦Y⌐(16) ☾$	Stratton Pond Trail leads 100 yards west to **Stratton Pond Shelter**, water, privy. Overnight/caretaker fee. **Camping is not permitted here at shelter, NO FIRES.** 19.3◀15.0◀10.4◀▶4.9▶7.9▶12.7	N 43 06.085, W 72 58.128	2565	549.8
1641.3	◊Y	Willis Ross Clearing at Stratton Pond and intermittent spring 25 feet north on trail, unreliable. Lye Brook Trail leads west to Bigelow Spring Pond Trail.		2583	549.6
1641.4	♦Y⅄	Stratton Pond. North Shore Trail leads (0.5) west to North Shore Tenting Area.		2555	549.5
1643.2	♦⌒	Cross Winhall River, footbridge.		2175	547.7
1646.0	♦Y⌐(10) ☽☾	Branch Pond Trail (0.5W) to **William B. Douglas Shelter**, water (spring) is located south of the shelter, privy. 19.9◀15.3◀4.9◀▶3.0▶7.8▶15.9 100 feet after the side trail to the shelter you Cross brook on AT.	N 43 08.670, W 72 59.484	2210	544.9
1646.9	♦📷▲	Junction with side trail to Prospect Rock and Old Rootville Road. 50 yards to Prospect Rock, views of Manchester and Mt. Equinox. Water is 150 feet west. No parking is permitted here.		2079	544.0
1648.6		Pass west of summit.		2300	542.3
1649.0	♦Y⅄(10) ⌐(16)☾	(0.1W) **Spruce Peak Shelter**, water (piped boxed spring) is located 100 feet to the right of the shelter, tenting, privy. 18.3◀7.9◀3.0◀▶4.8▶12.9▶17.6	N 43 10.716, W 72 59.742	2180	541.9
1649.4	📷	Side trail 100 yards west to Spruce Peak, views of Taconic Range and valley below.		2040	541.5

Elevation profile with labeled points: Manchester, VT/VT Hwy 11/30; Bromley Shelter; Bromley Mtn; Mad Tom Notch/USFS Rd 21; Styles Peak; Peru Peak; Peru Peak Shelter; Griffith Lake; Baker Peak; Lost Pond Shelter; Big Branch Shelter; Black Branch Brook/USFS Rd 10; LittleRock Pond Shelter; Homer Stone Brook; White Rocks Mtn; Greenwall Shelter; Bully Brook/Keewaydin Trail; Roaring Brook/VT Hwy 140; Bear Mtn

NoBo	Features	Description	GPS	Elev	SoBo
1651.3	♦	Cross small brook.		1770	539.6
1651.4	▲	Cross **abandon Old VT. 30** and bridge over stream.		1760	539.5
1651.8	♦▲ P(26) ★★★★★	Cross **VT. 11 & 30**	N 43 12.414, W 72 58.242	1840	539.1

Manchester Center, VT (5.4W) See map of Manchester, VT.

     ⛺🍴⛺🖥 (3.6W) **Red Sled Motel** 802-362-2161. (www.redsledmotel.com) Hiker friendly. $78. Laundry for a fee, swimming pool, trout pond. Ride to trail when available. Located (1.5E) of town. Mail drops for guests: 2066 Depot Street Manchester Center, VT, 05255.

🛏🐾🖥	**(3.4W) Econo Lodge** 802-362-3333, $88 and up, includes continental breakfast, microwave, fridge, outdoor pool. Pets $15. Mail drop for guests: 2187 Depot St, Manchester Center, VT 05255.	
✉	**PO** M-F 8:30am-4:30pm, Sa 9am-12pm. 802-362-3070.	
🖥	**Manchester Library** 802-362-2607 Open M-Th 10am-6pm, F-Sat 10am to 4pm.	
✗	**Cilantro Restaurant** 802-768-8141. (www.cilantrorestaurantvt.com) Burritos, ice cream, sodas. Summer hours; M-Sa 11am-9pm, Su 11:30am-3pm. Winter hours; M-Sa 11:30am-8pm, Su closed.	
✗	**Starbucks**	
🏠◈ 🏕🖥🐾	**Green Mountain House** 330-388-6478. (www.greenmountainhouse.net) AT Passport location. Jeff & Regina Taussig host hikers at their home. Open Jun 7 - Sep 15. Not a party place, no alcohol. Space is limited so reservations are essential. Clean bed with linens, shower, free laundry, WiFi, computer available for use, free WiFi, well equipped hiker kitchen. Private room for couples. Free breakfast supplies; make your own pancakes, eggs, cereal, coffee. Hikers with reservations get a ride to town, resupply, then call for pick-up. Check-in from 1pm to 7pm. Free morning shuttle back to the trail for guests. Credit cards accepted. $35+tax per person.	
🛏🐾🖥	**Sutton's Place** 802-362-1165. (www.suttonsplacevermont.com) $75and up, pets okay on porch. Accepts MC/Visa. USPS Mail drops for guests: (USPS) PO Box 142 or (UPS) 50 School St, Manchester Center, VT 05255.	
🛏⑧🐾	**Palmer House** 802-362-3600. (www.palmerhouse.com) No pets, Call for pricing, ask for hiker discount, stay includes continental breakfast, indoor and outdoor pool. golf course, tennis courts and trout pond (all equipment provided).	
🛏⑧🐾	**Carriage House** 802-362-1706. (www.carriagehousemotel.com) No pets. $58 and up for summer.	
🛒♻	**Price Chopper** 802-362-9896. M-Su 7am-8pm.	
✗ ◈	**Up For Breakfast** 802-362-4204. AT Passport location. Casual breakfast and brunch. M-F 7am-13:30 pm, Sa-Su 7am-1:30pm.	
✗	**Up For Breakfast, Thai Basil, Gringo Jack's, Manchester PizzaManchester Pizza, Subway, China City, McDonalds**	
✗ ◈	**Up For Breakfast**. AT Passport. 802-362-4204. M-F 7am-12:30PM, Sa-Su 7am-1:30pm.	
🥾◈🖥	**Mountain Goat Outfitter** 802-362-5159. (www.mountaingoat.com) AT Passport location. Full service outfitter, white gas, alcohol, by the ounce. canister fuel, footwear. M-Sa 10am-6pm, Su 10am-5pm. Mail drops: 4886 Main St, Manchester, VT 05255.	
♻	**Rite aid** 802-362-2230. M-Sa 8am-9pm, Su 8am-6pm. **Pharmacy**; M-F 9am-9pm, Sa 9am-6pm, Su 9am-5pm.	

Peru, VT (4.3E)

🛏⑧🏕🐾🖥	**(2.1E) The Lodge at Bromley** 802-824-6941. (www.lodgeatbromley.com) No pets. Call for pricing, $100 hiker rate, tavern with light menu, game room, ride to and from trail with stay. Mail for guests: (non-guests $5) 4216 VT 11, Peru, VT 05152.	
✗🏪	**(2.5E) Bromley Market** 802-824-4444. (www.bromleymarket.com) M-Su 7am-7pm.	
🛏🐾🖥	**(3.6E) Bromley View Inn** on VA 30, 802-297-1459. (www.bromleyviewinn.com) $99 and up, includes hot breakfast, shuttle to and from trail head at VT 11/30 with stay. Mail drops for guests: 522 VT 30, Bondville, VT 05340.	
✗🏪📱🐾	**(4.2E) JJ Hapgood General Store & Eatery** 802-824-4800. (www.jjhapgood.com) Located in Peru, next to PO. Restaurant serves breakfast, lunch and dinner, ATM. M-Su 7am-7pm, hours may differ on weekends.	

Manchester, VT

Vermont

NoBo	Features	Description	GPS	Elev	SoBo
1651.9	▲	Cross gravel road.		1856	539.0
1652.0	♦⌒	Cross brook on I-beam bridge.		1852	538.9
1652.1	⊤	Power line.		1859	538.8
1652.5	♦⌒	Cross Bromly Brook on bridge.		1043	538.4
1653.8	♦Y⅄(4) ⊏(12)☾	100 yards east to **Bromley Shelter**, water (brook) is located at the terminus of the spur trail, privy, tenting is (0.1) north on the AT see next entry.	N 43 14.370, W 72 56.232		537.1
		12.7◄7.8◄◄4.8◄▶8.1▶12.8▶14.3		2560	
1653.9	⅄(4)	Bromley Shelter tent platforms.		2685	537.0
1654.8	☾🗖	Bromley Mountain, ski patrol hut, **no tenting or fires** but it is okay to overnight in ski warming hut, **no smoking**, please keep hut clean so hikers can continue to use it.		3260	536.1
1657.3	▲P(10)	Cross **USFS 21**, Mad Tom Notch, gravel.	N 43 15.462, W 72 56.317	2446	533.6
1658.9	▲🗖	Rock outcrop on Styles Peak summit, views of Bromley Mountain.		3394	532.0
1660.6	▲	Peru Peak summit, wooded.		3429	530.3
1661.9	♦⅄⊏(10) ☾$	**Peru Peak Shelter**, water (brook) is located near the shelter, tenting, privy. Overnight/caretaker fee.	N 43 18.079, W 72 57.174		529.0
		15.9◄12.9◄8.1◄▶4.7▶6.2▶6.4▶		2605	
1662.0	⌒	Cross wooden bridge.		2619	528.9
1662.1	⌒	Cross wooden bridge.		2602	528.8
1662.2	♦	Eastern shore of Griffith Lake.		2600	528.7
1662.4	♦⅄	Pass west of Griffith Lake Tenting Area on slab. Griffith Lake.		2600	528.5
1662.6	♦Y	Griffith Lake (north end), junction with Old Job Trail. Griffith Lake Trail leads (2.0) west to USFS 58.		2600	528.3
1662.7	Y	Junction with Lake Trail.		2620	528.2
1663.5	▲	Cross old woods road.		2627	527.4
1663.6	▲	Cross old woods road.		2655	527.3
1664.5	Y	Baker Peak Trail west.		2760	526.4
1664.6	▲🗖	Baker Peak summit.		2850	526.3
1665.1		Reach height of land.		2664	525.8
1666.4	▲	Intersection with wide grassy fire road.		2278	524.5
1666.6	♦Y⅄(10) ⊏(6)⌣☾	100 feet west to **Lost Pond Shelter**, water is Stare Brook in a ravine below site, tenting, privy.	N 43 20.726, W 72 57.186		524.3
		17.6◄12.8◄4.7◄▶1.5▶1.7▶5.0		2150	
1668.1	♦Y⅄(12) ⊏(8)☾	(1.0E) on Old Job Trail to **Old Job Shelter**, water (Lake Brook) is source, tenting, privy.	N 43 21.244, W 72 55.734		522.8
		14.3◄6.2◄1.5◄▶0.2▶3.5▶8.3		1525	
1668.3	♦⅄(12) ⊏(8)☾	**Big Branch Shelter**, water (Big Branch) is located in front of the shelter, tenting, privy. This shelter is close to road and heavily used on weekends.	N 43 21.844, W 72 56.814		522.6
		6.4◄1.7◄0.2◄▶3.3▶8.1▶13.2		1460	
1669.5	♦▲	Intersects with **USFS 10, Danby–Landgrove Road (southern junction)**		1598	521.4
1669.6	♦⌒☾▲ P(25) ★★★★★	Intersects with **USFS 10, Danby–Landgrove Road (northern junction)**, bridge over Black Branch.	N 43 22.362, W 72 57.762	1521	521.3
	✉	**PO** M–F 7:15am–10:15am & 11:15am-2:15pm, Sa 7am–10:30am. 802-293-5105.			
	🏢	**Mt. Tabor Country Store** 802-293-5641. M-Sa 5am-8pm, Su 6am-7pm.			
	🏢	**Nichols Store & Deli** 802-293-5154. M-Su 6am-8pm.			
	🖥	**Silas Griffith Library** 802-293-5106. (www.slgriffithlibrary.wordpress.com) W 2pm-7pm, Sa 9am-12pm, one computer.			
1670.2	♦⌒	Cross Little Black Branch on I-beam bridge.		1686	520.7
1670.4	♦	Rock hop across Little Black Branch.		1740	520.5
1671.5	♦Y	Little Rock Pond (southern end), junction with Little Rock Pond Loop Trail which rejoins the AT mile 1670.8.		1880	519.4
1671.6	♦⅄(28) ⊏(8)☾$	100 feet east to **Little Rock Pond Shelter and Tenting Area**, Overnight fee. Water is located at the caretaker's platform, tenting, privy. Overnight/caretaker fee.	N 43 24.253, W 72 57.216		519.3
		5.0◄3.5◄3.3◄▶4.8▶9.9▶13.6▶		1920	
1671.7	♦	Spring, water for LRP Shelter		1854	519.2
1671.9	♦Y	Little Rock Pond (northern end), rejoins the AT at mile 1670.4. Junctions with Green Mountain Trail to Homer Stone Brook Trail.		1854	519.0
1672.0	⅄	Side trail leads east to camping with tent platforms.		1878	518.9

NoBo	Features	Description	GPS	Elev	SoBo
1672.7		Aldrichville clearing.		1914	518.2
1672.9	♦⌒	Cross Homer Stone Brook on footbridge.		1900	518.0
1673.1	⚠	Cross **South Wallingford-Wallingford Pond Road**, snowmobile trail.		1983	517.8
1675.1		West of White Rocks Mountain summit.		2680	515.8
1675.9	Y📷	Side trail to White Rocks Cliffs, (0.2W) vista		2400	515.0
1676.4	◊Y⊏(8)☾	(0.2E) **Greenwall Shelter**, water (spring) is located 200 yards along a trail behind the shelter and is known to go dry, privy.	N 43 26.425, W 72 55.746		514.5
		8.3◄8.1◄4.8◄►5.1►8.8►14.9		2025	
1677.1	Y	Junction with Keewaydin Trail.		1380	513.8
1677.2	♦	Cross Bully Brook.		1760	513.7
1677.8	⚠	Cross **Sugar Hill Road**, gravel, descends (0.5) west to VT. 140, passing White Rocks Road USFS 52.		1260	513.1
1677.9	♦⚠⌒ P(25) ★★★★★	Cross **VT. 140, Wallingford Gulf Road**, Roaring Brook, parking (0.2E)	N 43 27.414, W 72 55.962	1160	513.0

Wallingford, VT (2.8W)

	✉	**PO** M–F 8am–4:30pm, Sa 9am–12pm. 802-446-2140.			
	🏪	**Wallingford Country Store & Deli** 802-446-2352. Country store, deli and snack bar food. **Cumberland Farms**			
	✗	**Nail It Down Hardware** 802-446-2133			
	💻📶	**Gilbert Library** 802-446-2685. (www.ghlib.wordpress.com) Computer avaiable to use, free WiFI. M 10am-5pm, Tu closed, W 10am-8pm, Th-F 10am-5pm, Sa 9am-12pm, Su closed.			
1678.0	P	Pass trail head parking lot.	N 43 27.407, W 72 55.937	1195	512.9
1678.5	⚠	Cross abandon **Bear Mountain Road**.		1441	512.4
1678.9	Y📷	Side trail leads 300 feet west to Domed Ledges Vista.		1575	512.0

NoBo	Features	Description	GPS	Elev	SoBo
1680.0	▲	Bear Mountain summit.		2240	510.9
1680.6		Patch's Hollow at northern end of beaver pond.		1800	510.3
1681.2	⟙	Power line.		1645	509.7
1681.5	♦Y⚑(10) ⊏(8)⌣☾	200 feet east to **Minerva Hinchey Shelter**, water (spring) is located 150 feet south of shelter and follow "Wada" signs, tenting, privy.	N 43 29.267, W 72 55.500		509.4
		13.2◄9.9◄5.1◄►3.7►9.8►14.1		1605	
1682.1		Spring Lake Clearing.		1620	508.8
1682.2	⟙	Power line with airport beacons.		1658	508.7
1683.1	📷	Overlook.		1291	507.8
1683.2	📷	Overlook.		1516	507.7
1683.4	📷	Rutland Airport Lookout, views west of Taconic Range.		1478	507.5
1683.8	⚠	Cross **Knipes Road**, gravel, gated.		1108	507.0
1684.1	♦⌒ ✗⚠	Cross high suspension bridge over Mill River in Clarendon Gorge.		800	506.8
1684.2	P(14) ★★★★★	Cross **VT. 103, railroad tracks**	N 43 31.289, W 72 55.550	860	506.7

NoBo	Features	Description	GPS	Elev	SoBo
	🏠	(1.0W) **Loretta's Deli** 802-772-7638. Full Service Deli and meals to go. Fuel by the ounce, water filters. M–F 6am-7pm, Sa-Su 10am-5pm.			
North Clarendon, VT 05759 (4.2W)					
	⏎	**PO** M–F 8am–1pm & 2pm–4:30pm, Sa 8am–10am. 802-773-7893.			
	🏠	**Mike's Country Store** 802-773-7100. M-F 10am-5pm, Sa 10am-2pm, Su closed.			
Rutland, VT (8W of VT 103) see NOBO mile 1701.9. See map of Rutland, VT (north/south)					
1684.3	⟙	Power line.		976	506.6
1684.5		Pass though boulder filled ravine.		1380	506.4
1684.6	Y 📷	Side trail 400 feet east to Clarendon Lookout, rock outcrop with views of VT. 103 and Rutland Airport.		1516	506.3
1685.2	♦Y⚔(20) ⊏(12) ⌣ ☾	(0.1E) **Clarendon Shelter**, water (stream) is located 50 feet east from the shelter, tenting, privy. 13.6◀8.8◀3.7◀▶6.1▶10.4▶12.9	N 43 31.412, W 72 54.786	1190	505.7
1685.3	♦	Cross brook.		1566	505.6
1685.7		Beacon Hill, airport beacon.		1740	505.2
1686.1	🛣	Cross **Lottery Road**, unpaved.		1720	504.8
1686.5	◊	Hermit Spring to east, unreliable.		1864	504.4
1686.8		Ridgecrest.		1947	504.1
1687.8	🛣P	Cross **Keiffer Road**, unpaved. Limited parking.	N 43 32.036, W 72 52.405	1533	503.1
1688.0	♦	Western bank of Cold River.		1403	502.9
1688.1	🛣P ★★★★★	Cross **Cold River Road**, paved. Limited parking.	N 43 32.262, W 72 52.335	1400	502.8
	🛒✗	(2.4E) W.E. **Pierce Groceries** 802-492-3326. (www.piercesstorevt.com). Bakery & Deli. M-Sa 7am-7pm, Su 8am-5pm.			
1688.9	♦	Cross Gould Brook, ford, can be **hazardous in high water.**		1480	502.0
1689.7	♦🛣 P(2)	Cross **Upper Cold River Road**, gravel road.	N 43 33.012, W 72 51.415	1630	501.2
1690.4	♦⌒🛣	Junction with **Clement Shelter Road**, Sargent Brook Bridge, gravel road.		1730	500.5
1690.8		Overgrown clearing and stone wall.		1802	500.1
1691.1	♦⌒	Cross Robinson Brook on bridge.		1919	499.8
1691.3	♦⚔⊏(10) ⌣☾	**Governor Clement Shelter**, water (stream) is located across the road and north of the shelter, tenting, privy. Shelter is located close to road. 14.9◀9.8◀6.1◀▶4.3▶6.8▶8.7	N 43 33.874, W 72 50.928	1900	499.6
1693.5	♦	Cross two small brooks in the area.		2040	497.4
1693.9	Y	Junction with Shrewsbury Peak Trail.		3500	497.0
1694.4		High point on Killington Ridge.		3719	496.5
1695.6	♦Y⚔(2) ⊏(12) ⌣☾📷 ★★★★★	**Cooper Lodge**, water, (spring) is located north of shelter on AT, privy, two tent platforms, privy. 14.1◀10.4◀4.3◀▶2.5▶4.4▶16.3	N 43 36.363, W 72 49.347	3900	495.3
	Y✗	(0.2E) **Killington Peak Lodge** 800-621-6867. Food service at the summit lodge, gondola ride ($25 round trip) to the ski resort below. Summer hours 10am-5pm. There is a new, safe, easy, and short trail to get from Cooper Lodge on Mount Killington and the gondola and cafe on the other side of the mountain. As of yet there are no signs. At the summit there are also no signs for how to get to the gondola. The new trail starts just beyond the privy. You pass the top of a ski run take a set of stairs to the gondola area.			
1695.8	Y	Junction with Bucklin Trail.		3770	495.1
1696.6		Height of land on Snowden Peak.		3449	494.3
1698.1	♦Y⊏(12) $	Jungle Junction. Sherburne Pass Trail (southern junction) leads (0.5) east to **Pico Camp**, water is located 45 yards north on the Sherburne Pass Trail, privy. If caretaker is present there is an overnight/caretaker fee. Pico Link trail leads (0.4) to Pico Peak summit and rejoins the AT north of Sheburne Pass (in VT). 12.9◀6.8◀2.5◀▶1.9▶13.8▶23.7	N 43 38.347, W 72 49.832	3480	492.8
1699.7	📷	Mendon Lookout.		2890	491.2
1700.0	◊Y☾ ⚔(1) ⊏(8)	(0.1W) **Churchill Scott Shelter**, water is located on spur trail downhill behind shelter, privy, tent sites. **NO FIRES.** 8.7◀4.4◀1.9◀▶11.9▶21.8▶34.1	N 43 38.693, W 72 51.203	2560	490.9
1699.2	♦	Cross brook.		2530	491.7
1701.9	♦🛣P(24) ★★★★★	Cross **U.S. 4**. See map of Killington, VT.	N 43 39.969, W 72 50.920	1880	489.0

(0.8E) **The Inn at Long Trail** 802-775-7181, 800-325-2540. (www.innatlongtrail.com) AT Passport location.

Ask about hiker rates, rooms include full breakfast. Limited pet rooms, reservations recommended on weekends. Overflow camping across street but there are no facilities. Coin laundry, outside water spigot. Closed mid-April through Memorial Day. **McGrath's Irish Pub**; serves lunch and dinner from 11:30am-9pm. Mail drops for guests: (FedEx/UPS) 709 US 4, Killington, VT 05751.

(1.4W) **Mendon Mountain View Lodge** 802-773-4311. (www.mendonmountainviewlodge.com) No pets. Hiker rate $70 and up, $15EAP. Breakfast $10. Heated pool, hot tub, sauna. Mail drops for guests: 5654 Route 4, Mendon, VT 05701.

Rutland, VT (8.5W from US 4 trail head) See map of Rutland, VT (north/south)

PO M-F 10am-2pm, Sa 8:30am-11:30pm. 802-773-0223.

Hikers Hostel at the Yellow Deli 802-683-9378, 802-775-9800. (www.hikershostel.org) AT Passport location.

No alcohol, no smoking

Run by a Twelve Tribes spiritual community. Donation or WFS. Kitchenette, coin laundry ($1 wash $1 dry). Free showers even without stay. Shuttles sometimes available by donation. Hostel open 24 hours. Stay includes breakfast and 15% off at deli and at **Simon the Tanner**; Outfitter, M- Th 10am-5pm, F 10am-3pm. Mail drops: Hiker Hostel, 23 Center Street, Rutland, VT 05701.

Mountain Travelers Outdoor Shop 802-775-0814. (www.mtntravelers.com) All gear, Coleman, alcohol by the ounce. M-Tu 10am-6pm, W closed, 10am-6pm, Su 12pm-5pm.

Walmart 802-773-0200. M-Su 7am-10pm; **Pharmacy** M-F 8am-8pm, Sa 9am-7pm, Su 10am-6pm. **Price Chopper** 802-438-6119. M-Su 6am-12am.

Rutland Food Co-op 802-773-0737. (www.rutlandcoop.com) M-Sa 9am-7pm, Su 10am-6pm.

Subway, Applebee's, Little Caesars

Beauchamps & O'Rourke Pharmacy 802-775-4321. (www.beauchamppharmacy.com) M-F 8am-6pm, Sa 9am-12pm, Su closed.

Rutland Veterinary 802-773-2779. (www.rutlandvet.com) M-F 7am-8pm, Sa-Su 7am-5pm.

Killington, VT 05751 (1.8E) from US 4, See **NOBO mile 1705.2**

Killington, VT

South ← | North →

Kent Pond

Gifford Woods State Park

Base Camp Outfitters

Greenbrier Inn   Deli At Killington Corners

Post Office

Killington Motel

Mountain Meadows Lodge

NoBo		Description	GPS	Elev	SoBo
1702.0	Y	Catamount Trail to west.		1939	488.9
1702.9	Y	Maine Junction at Willard Gap. Long Trail to Tucker Johnson Tenting Area (0.4W)	N 43 40.766, W 72 50.577	2250	488.0
1703.0	Y	Junction of Deer Leap Trail, rejoins the AT at 21.8/1.9.		2290	487.9
1703.8	Y	Sherburne Pass Trail, to **Inn at Long Trail** (0.5E) **See notes at mile 1701.9.**		2440	487.1
1704.1	Y	Side trail leads 500 feet east to Bens Balcony, views of Killington and Pico Peaks.		2443	486.8
1704.9	Y ★★★★★	Kent Brook Trail Junction, upper camping area of Gifford Woods State Park.		1700	486.0
		The AT passes thru **Gifford Woods State Park** 802-775-5354. AT Passport location. Shelters, discounted tent sites for AT hikers in special hiker section, coin operated showers, water spigot. Open Memorial Day-Columbus Day. Fills quickly in fall.			
1705.2	P(24) ★★★★★	Cross **VT. 100. See map of Killington, VT.**	N 43 40.437, W 72 48.545	1660	485.7

Killington, VT 05751 (0.6E from VT 100, 1.8E from US 4)

PO M-F 6:30am (window pickup only), 8:30am-11am & 12pm-4:30pm. Sa 8:30-12, 802-775-4247.

NoBo		Description	GPS	Elev	SoBo
	🚶⊡	**Base Camp Outfitters** 802-775-0166. Full service outfitter, alcohol by the ounce and canister fuel. Also accessible by side trail from Mountain Meadows Lodge. Summer hours M-Su 10am-5pm. Mail drops: 2363 Route 4, Killington VT 05751.			
	🏛	**Killington Deli & Marketplace** 802-775-1599. (www.killingtondeli.com)			
	🛏⊛🍴	**Greenbrier Inn** 802-775-1575. (www.greenbriervt.com) No pets. Ask about the 15% hiker discount. Fridge, free WiFi.			
	🛏🖥🍴	**Killington Motel** 802-773-9535. (www.killingtonmotel.com) No smoking rooms. Call for pricing and ask for hiker rate, includes continental breakfast, pool, fridge, free WiFi.			
	✗⚐	**JAX Food & Games** 802-422-5334. (www.jaxfoodandgames.com) Eat and have a drink while your doing your laundry. M-Su 3pm-2am. Located (0.8) south on US 4 on Killington Rd.			
1705.3	◐〰	Cross Kent Brook on footbridge.		1580	485.6
1705.4	◐Y ★★★★★	Kent Pond, shore. Trail to Base camp Outfitters.		1621	485.5
	🛏⊛◈✗ ⚐🖥⊛🍴 P⊡	**Mountain Meadows Lodge** 802-775-1010. (www.mountainmeadowslodge.com) AT Passport location. No pets inside. Rooms $69D, single room sometimes available for $59. Meals and lodging are not available most weekends & during events. Okay to charge phones, but please do not loiter when events are being held at the lodge. Occasional work for stay. Lunch or dinner $10. Hot tub, sauna, game room, laundry, computer available to use, free WiFi, and canoe for guests. Parking for section hiking guests. Ask about tenting. Mail drops free, even for non-guests: 285 Thundering Brook Rd, Killington, VT 05751.			
1705.9	Y⚑	Junction with **Thundering Brook Road (southern junction)**.		1450	485.0
1707.1	⚑	Junction with **Thunderinging Brook Road (northern junction)**, gravel.		1280	483.8
1707.3	Y⚓	Side trail leads 200 feet west on boardwalk to Thundering Falls.		1226	483.6
1707.5	📷	Views from boardwalk of Ottauquechee floodplain.		1224	483.4
1707.6	⚑P(6)	Cross **River Road**.	N 43 40.840, W 72 46.935	1214	483.3
1708.4	📷	Vista of Ottauquechee River Valley.		2136	482.5
1708.9		Summit of unnamed hill.		2523	482.0
1709.4	⟙	Power line.		2334	481.5
1709.7	⚑	Cross woods road.		2374	481.2

NoBo		Description	GPS	Elev	SoBo
1710.0	⛰	Cross unnamed summit.		2600	480.9
1710.8		Northern shoulder of Quimby Mountain.		2550	480.1
1711.9	◐YⒶ ⌂(6)⌣((	(0.1E) **Stony Brook Shelter**, water (brook) is located 100 yards north of shelter on AT, tenting, privy. 16.3◀13.8◀11.9◀▶9.9▶22.2▶31.0	N 43 41.507, W 72 43.836	1760	479.0
1712.1		Aluminum ladder on steep ledge.		1793	478.8
1712.7	◐⚑P(4)	Cross Mink Brook or Stony Brook a few times, **Stony Brook Road**.	N 43 41.476, W 72 43.211	2000	478.2
1714.1		Reach height of land.		2260	476.8
1714.6		Small pond in sag known locally as the Continental Divide.		2198	476.3
1715.0	⚑	Cross logging road.		2176	475.9
1715.1	◊	Cross intermittent brook.		2073	475.8

NoBo	Features	Description	GPS	Elev	SoBo
1715.9		West of Bull Hill.		2445	475.0
1716.1	▲	Cross logging road.		2464	474.8
1716.6	▲P(8)	Cross **Chateauguay Road**, gravel.	N 43 41.368, W 72 40.429	2000	474.3
1717.0	♦	Cross brook.		2248	473.9
1717.5	◊	Cross intermittent brook.		2670	473.4
1717.7	📷	Lakota Lake Lookout, view of Lakota Lake below and White Mountains. Thius lookout is now overgrown.		2640	473.2
1719.4	Y📷🗒	(0.2W) to private cabin and observation deck, owners permit its use as a viewpoint for hikers, **no fires**.		2320	471.5
1720.2	▲	Junction with **Lookout Farm Road**.		2297	470.7
1720.3	▲	Juntion with **King Cabin Road (southern junction)**.	N 43 40.126, W 72 38.150	2262	470.6
1720.5	▲P(6)	Junction with **King Cabin Road (northern junction)**.	N 43 40.904, W 72 39.377	2249	470.4
1721.1	📷	Don's Rock on The Pinnacle, view of Killington and Pico Peaks.		2494	469.8
1721.2		Reach height of land on Sawyer Hill.		2537	469.7
1721.8	♦Y⅄ ⌐(6)☾	(0.2W) **Winturri Shelter**, water (spring) is located to the right of the shelter, tenting, privy. 23.7◄21.8◄9.9◄► 12.3►21.1►28.4	N 43 39.731, W 72 37.356	1910	469.1
1722.6	▲	Cross old woods road.		1794	468.3
1722.8	Y📷	On crest of ridge side trail leads east view of North Bridgewater.		1805	468.1
1723.4	▲	Cross old woods road.		1630	467.5
1724.2	📷	Ridge with views of Mt. Ascutney.		1525	466.7
1724.4	📷	Bald hilltop with panoramic views.		1488	466.5
1725.4		Clearing with wooden stile that crosses electric fence.		967	465.5
1725.6	♦⌂▲ P(10) ★★★★★	Cross **VT. 12**, Gulf Stream Bridge **Woodstock, VT. (4.2E)**	N 43 39.313, W 72 33.974	882	465.3
	🏠	(0.2W) **On The Edge Farm** 802-457-4510. (www.ontheedgefarm.com) Mid-May to Labor Day M-Su 10am-5:30pm otherwise off season M 10am-5pm, Tu-W closed, Th-Su 10am-5pm. Local goods, pies, fruit, ice cream, smoked meats and cheese, cold drinks.			

Woodstock, VT 05091 (4.2E)

	✉	**PO** M-F 8:30am-5pm, Sa 9am-12pm. 802-457-1323.			
	🛏🍴	**Shire Woodstock** 802-457-2211. (www.shirewoodstock.com) Call for pricing, free WiFi. This is a tourist town.			
	🛏🍴	**Braeside Motel** 802-457-1366. (www.braesidemotel.com) $98-$168, fridge, free WiFi.			
	✗	**Pizza Che** 508-765-5979. (www.pizzachefsouthbridge.com) M-W 11am-10pm, Th-Sa 11am-11pm, Su 12pm-10pm.			
	🏠	**Cumberland Farms, Gillingham & Sons** 802-457-2100. (www.gillinghams.com) M-Sa 8:30am-6:30pm Su 10am-5pm.			
	⚕	**Woodstock Pharmacy** 770-926-6478. M-F 9am-6pm, Sa 9:30am-1:30pm, Su closed.			
	🐾	**Woodstock Veterinary Hospital** 860) 974-1802. M-9am-7pm, Tu-W 9am-6pm, Th 9am-7pm, F 9am-6pm, Sa-Su 9am-2pm.			
	💻	**Norman Williams Public Library** 802-457-2295. (www.normanwilliams.org) M-F 10am-6pm, Sa 10am-4pm, Su closed.			
1726.3		Cross corner of hilltop field.		1265	464.6
1726.7		Dana Hill, tree covered.		1530	464.2
1727.8	♦⌂▲ P(3) ★★★★★	Cross **Woodstock Stage Road** and Barnard Brook on footbridge.	N 43 40.313, W 72 33.226	820	463.1

South Pomfret, VT 05067 (1.0E)

	✉	**PO** M-F 10am-2pm, Sa 8:30am-11:30am. 802-457-1147, located inside of Teago's General Store.			
	🏠	**Teago's General Store** 802-457-1626. Homemade soups, salads, sandwiches, ice cream. M-Sa 7am-6pm, Su 8am-4pm.			
1728.3		Cross notch between Totman Hill and Breakneck Hill.		1192	462.6
1728.5	♦	Cross brook.		1285	462.4
1728.6	▲	Cross **Totman Hill Road**, dirt road.		1010	462.3
1729.3	♦⌂▲	Cross **Bartlett Brook Road**, gravel, footbridge, brook.	N 43 40.815, W 72 31.630	1050	461.6
1730.0	♦▲P(4)	Cross **Pomfret–South Pomfret Road**, Pomfret Brook		980	460.9
1730.5	📷	Hilltop field with view.		1515	460.4
1730.7	Y	Four way junction with old AT.		1544	460.2
1730.8	▲	Follow old town road.		1525	460.1
1730.9	Y◊	Side trail leads 50 feet east uphill to spring, unreliable.		1503	460.0
1731.3	▲	DuPuis Hill summit.		1630	459.6
1731.8	▲P🏠 ★★★★★	Cross **Cloudland Road**. Limited parking.	N 43 41.203, W 72 30.010	1370	459.1

NoBo	Features	Description	GPS	Elev	SoBo
	♦🏠	(0.2W) **Cloudland Farm Market** 802-457-2599. (www.cloudlandfarm.com) Family run farm. Mid-June-mid-Oct: Closed Sun thru Tues., Open We'd. 10-3 & Thurs. - Sat. 10-5. Rest of the year: Closed Sun. thru Wed., Open Thurs. 10-3 and Fri. & Sat. 10-5. Hikers are always welcome to fill up on tap water via an outdoor spigot. Soda, ice cream, cheeses and crackers, their own beef jerky, pickles, t-shirts, hats, soaps and balms. Occasionally have granola and sandwiches. Family run farm.			
1732.6	⊤	Power line.		1485	458.3
1733.8	▲	Cross woods road on top of Thistle Hill, wooded.		1800	457.1
1734.1	♦Y⅄ ⊑(8)⌣《	(0.1E) **Thistle Hill Shelter**, water (stream) is located near the shelter, tenting, privy. 34.1◄22.2◄12.3◄►8.8►16.1►25.6	N 43 41.710, W 72 28.548	1480	456.8
1734.8	♦	Cross brook.		1596	456.1
1734.9	📷	Open field called Arms Hill, views.		1609	456.0
1735.4	📷	Open field with views.		1416	455.5
1735.6	▲P(3)	Cross **Joe Ranger Road**, gravel, by small pond with stone dam.	N 43 42.318, W 72 27.748	1280	455.3
1736.2	▲	Bunker Hill summit, wooded.		1466	454.7
1736.3	▲	Cross old town road by a cemetery.		1412	454.6
1736.5	📷	Hilltop pastures with views.		1418	454.4
1736.6	▲	Cross old farm road.		1161	454.3
1737.9	📷	Hilltop field with views of White River Valley.		1005	453.0
1738.6	▲	Cross **Quechee - West Hartford Road**.		461	452.3
1738.8	▲	Juntion with **Promfret Road** on west bank of White River.		474	452.1
1738.9	♦⌒⅄P ★★★★★	Junction with **VT. 14 (eastern end)**, Patriots Bridge over White River.	N 43 42.743, W 72 25.055	390	452.0
	🚗	**Big Yellow Taxi** 802-281-8294. Covers Woodstock, Norwich, Hanover, Lebanon and White River Junction.			
1739.3	▲	Junction with **VT. 14 (western end)**.		390	451.6
1739.4	▲	Stetson Road joins to the east.		430	451.5
1739.5	▲P(3)	Junction with **Podunk Road at Tigertown Road**.	N 43 43.244, W 72 24.793	540	451.4

1740.3	▲P(3)	Cross **Podunk Road (northern junction)**	N 43 43.104, W 72 24.012	860	450.6
1740.4	♦	Cross Podunk Brook.		860	450.5
1740.6	▲	Cross logging road.		897	450.3
1740.9	▲	Cross logging road.		994	450.0
1741.2	♦	Cross East Fork of Podunk Brook and a logging road.		1100	449.7
1741.3	▲	Cross logging road.		1109	449.6
1742.4		Wooded shoulder of Griggs Mountain.		1570	448.5
1742.7	◊	Cross small stream, seasonal.		1572	448.2
1742.9	◊Y⅄(10) ⊑(8)⌣《	(0.1E) **Happy Hill Shelter**, water (brook) is located near the shelter but known to go dry, tenting privy. 31.0◄21.1◄8.8◄►7.3►16.8►22.5	N 43 43.432, W 72 21.942	1460	448.0
1743.1	Y	Junction with William Tucker Trail.		1320	447.8

NoBo	Features	Description	GPS	Elev	SoBo
1744.5	▲	Cross **Newton Lane**.		1145	446.4
1745.4		Skirt east side of Mosley Hill.		1180	445.5
1745.8	�	Power line.		1166	445.1
1745.9	◆	Cross stream.		1195	445.0
1746.4	▲	Intersects with Elm Street Trail head.		750	444.5
1746.7	▲	Cross **Hopson Road**.		606	444.2
1746.9	◆	Cross Bloody Brook.		567	444.0
1747.2	▲ ★★★★★	Junction of **Elm Street and U.S. 5**. **Norwich, VT.**		537	443.7

📮✗🖥🚐 **Norwich Inn** 802-649-1143. (www.norwichinn.com) $189 and up, 2 pet rooms available, no smoking,
🖥 reservations recommended. Computer available to use, free WiFi.
Mail drops for guests: PO Box 908, Norwich, VT 04055, or FedEx to 325 Main St.
Murdocks Ale House Serves diiner M-Su, serves breakfast and lunch W–Su.

🛒 (0.1W) on Main St. **Dan & Whits General Store** 802-649-1602. (www.danandwhitsonline.com) M-Su
7am-9pm. Hikers get free day old sandwiches when available. Small gear items, canister fuel, batteries,
ponchos, hardware and grocery.

🖥🚐 **Norwich Library** 802-649-1184. (www.norwichlibrary.org) M 1am-8pm, Tu-W-F 10am-5:30pm, Th
10am-8pm, F 10am-5:30pm, Sa 10am-3pm, Su 12pm-4pm.

1747.8	▲	**I-91 passes over VT. 10A**, AT on sidewalk.		450	443.1
1748.2	▲ State Line	Connecticut River, Vermont–New Hampshire State Line		380	442.7
1748.7	▲P(24) ★★★★★	**NH. 10, Intersection of North Main and East Wheelock streets**. Dartmouth **College. See map of Hanover, NH.**	N 43 42.242, W 72 17.907 520		442.2

📪 **PO** M-F 8:30am-5pm, Sa 8:30am-12pm, Sat pick-up available until 3pm. 603-643-4544.

ⓘ **Hanover Friends of the AT** produce a brochure with complete list of hiker services. Brochures can be
found at the DOC, PO, libraries, Co-op.

ⓘ🖥🚐 **Dartmouth Outing Club** (DOC) 603-646-2428. (www.outdoors.dartmouth.edu) Offer room for pack
storage in Robinson Hall and in Howe Library cannot be left overnight, it is an unsecured area. Not available during Dartmouth orientation (mid Aug - mid Sept). Both places have computers for free internet
use.

P Overnight parking on Wheelock Street Lot A, see map. No parking near Connecticut River Bridge.

📪⚒🚐🖥 **Sunset Motor Inn** 603-298-8721. (www.sunsetinnnh.com) M-Su 8-11. Call ahead for availability, Ask
for hiker discount. Will shuttle when bus is not running, free laundry before 6pm, free WiFi, quiet after
10pm, $15 pet fee. Mail drops for guest only: 305 N Main Street, West Lebanon, NH 03874.

📪✗ **Hanover Inn** 603-643-4300. (www.hanoverinn.com) $249 and up, discount sometimes available. Very
pricey.

✗ **Everything But Anchovies** 603-643-6135. (www.ebas.com) full menu and beer, daily specials. Pizza
buffet Tuesday night $7.95. M-Su 11am-2:10am.
Allen St. Deli 603-643-2245. M-Su 7am-4om. One free bagel for thru-hikers.
Jewel of India Buffet 603-643-2217. (www.jewelofindiahanover.com) M-Sa Lunch 11:30am-2:30pm,
Dinner 4:30pm-10pm. Sunday brunch 11:30am-2:30pm, dinner 2:20pm-10pm.
C&C Pizza 603643-2966. (www.candapizza.net) M-Th 11am-11pm, F-Sa 11am-12pm, Sun 11am-11pm.

🏪✗ **Stinson's Village Store Deli & Catering** 603-643-6086. Deli sandwich, soda & small bag of chips. $5
hiker lunch special. M-Su 8am-12am.

🛒🚐 **Hanover Food Co-op** 603-643-2667. Deli and food bar. Please use member #7000 at check out to help
fund AT related initiatives. M-Su 7am-8pm.

♿⚒🚐 **Richard W. Black Recreation Center** 603-643-5315. M 9am-5pm, Tu-F 9am-6pm, Sa 10am-6pm, Su
closed. Shower with towel and soap $3, laundry with soap $2, must finish before 4:30pm.

🚶🖥 **Zimmerman's** 603-643-6863. Canister fuel, Aquamira, outdoor clothing. Mail drops: 63 Main St, Hanover, NH 03756.

🖥 **Howe Library** 603-643-4120. (www.howelibrary.org) M-Th 10am-8pm, F 10am-6pm, Sa 10am-5pm, Su
1pm-5pm.

✗ **Hanover Hardware** 603-643-2308. Coleman, alcohol by the ounce. M-F 8am-5:30pm, Sa 9am-5pm,
Su 9:30am-2:30pm.

🐕 **Hanover Veterinary** 603-643-3313. (www.hvcvets.com) M-F 8am-5:30pm, Sa 8am-12pm, Su closed.

Lebanon & West Lebanon, NH (5.0E)

📪🚐🖥 **Days Inn** 603-448-5070, 4 mi. south of the Co-op on Route 120 on free bus route. Call for priving,
includes continental breakfast, free WiFi, pets $20.

🚶 **EMS** 603-298-7716. M-F 8am-8pm, Sa 8am-5pm, Su closed.
LL Bean 603-298-6975. M-F 9am-8pm, Sa 9am-5pm, Sun closed.

🛒 **Shaw's** 603-298-0388. M-Sa 7am-10pm, Su 7am-9pm.

Hanover, NH

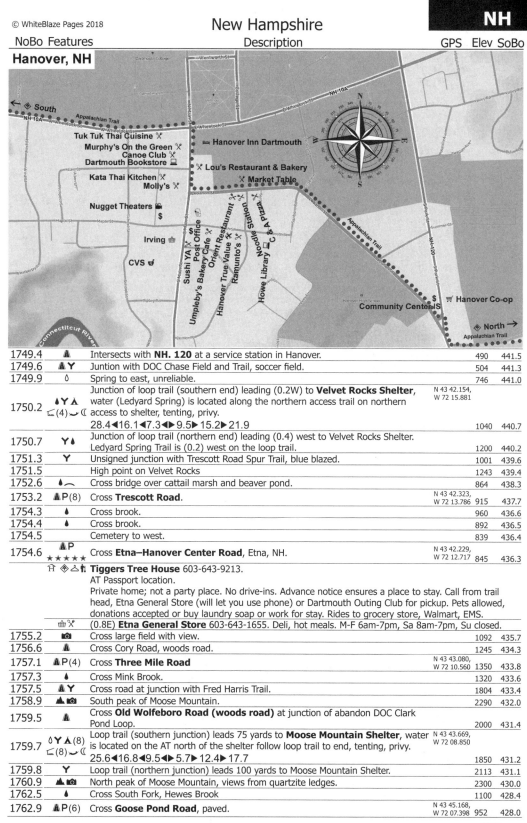

1749.4	⛰	Intersects with **NH. 120** at a service station in Hanover.		490	441.5
1749.6	⛰Y	Juntion with DOC Chase Field and Trail, soccer field.		504	441.3
1749.9	◊	Spring to east, unreliable.		746	441.0
1750.2	◊Y⛺ ⊏(4)↺《	Junction of loop trail (southern end) leading (0.2W) to **Velvet Rocks Shelter**, water (Ledyard Spring) is located along the northern access trail on northern access to shelter, tenting, privy. 28.4◀16.1◀7.3◀▶9.5▶15.2▶21.9	N 43 42.154, W 72 15.881	1040	440.7
1750.7	Y◊	Junction of loop trail (northern end) leading (0.4) west to Velvet Rocks Shelter. Ledyard Spring Trail is (0.2) west on the loop trail.		1200	440.2
1751.3	Y	Unsigned junction with Trescott Road Spur Trail, blue blazed.		1001	439.6
1751.5		High point on Velvet Rocks		1243	439.4
1752.6	◊〜	Cross bridge over cattail marsh and beaver pond.		864	438.3
1753.2	⛰P(8)	Cross **Trescott Road**.	N 43 42.323, W 72 13.786	915	437.7
1754.3	◊	Cross brook.		960	436.6
1754.4	◊	Cross brook.		892	436.5
1754.5		Cemetery to west.		839	436.4
1754.6	⛰P ★★★★★	Cross **Etna–Hanover Center Road**, Etna, NH.	N 43 42.229, W 72 12.717	845	436.3
	🏠◈⛺🍴	**Tiggers Tree House** 603-643-9213. AT Passport location. Private home; not a party place. No drive-ins. Advance notice ensures a place to stay. Call from trail head, Etna General Store (will let you use phone) or Dartmouth Outing Club for pickup. Pets allowed, donations accepted or buy laundry soap or work for stay. Rides to grocery store, Walmart, EMS.			
	🏪✕	(0.8E) **Etna General Store** 603-643-1655. Deli, hot meals. M-F 6am-7pm, Sa 8am-7pm, Su closed.			
1755.2	📷	Cross large field with view.		1092	435.7
1756.6	⛰	Cross Cory Road, woods road.		1245	434.3
1757.1	⛰P(4)	Cross **Three Mile Road**	N 43 43.080, W 72 10.560	1350	433.8
1757.3	◊	Cross Mink Brook.		1320	433.6
1757.5	⛰Y	Cross road at junction with Fred Harris Trail.		1804	433.4
1758.9	▲📷	South peak of Moose Mountain.		2290	432.0
1759.5	⛰	Cross **Old Wolfeboro Road (woods road)** at junction of abandon DOC Clark Pond Loop.		2000	431.4
1759.7	◊Y⛺(8) ⊏(8)↺《	Loop trail (southern junction) leads 75 yards to **Moose Mountain Shelter**, water is located on the AT north of the shelter follow loop trail to end, tenting, privy. 25.6◀16.8◀9.5◀▶5.7▶12.4▶17.7	N 43 43.669, W 72 08.850	1850	431.2
1759.8	Y	Loop trail (northern junction) leads 100 yards to Moose Mountain Shelter.		2113	431.1
1760.9	▲📷	North peak of Moose Mountain, views from quartzite ledges.		2300	430.0
1762.5	◊	Cross South Fork, Hewes Brook		1100	428.4
1762.9	⛰P(6)	Cross **Goose Pond Road**, paved.	N 43 45.168, W 72 07.398	952	428.0

NoBo	Features	Description	GPS	Elev	SoBo
1763.2	◖⌒	Cross beaver pond on dam.		918	427.7
1763.8	▲	Cross snowmobile trail.		1160	427.1
1764.6		Reach height of land on Holts Ledge.		2100	426.3
1764.9	📷	Side trail (0.1) east to Holts Ledge, view, peregrine falcon rookery		1930	426.0
1765.2	◊	Cross small intermittent brook.		1586	425.7
1765.4	◖Y▲ ⊏(8)⌣◖	(0.2W) **Trapper John Shelter**, water (brook) is located 15 yards to the left of the shelter, tenting, privy. 22.5◀15.2◀5.7◀▶6.7▶12.0▶27.5	N 43 46.982, W 72 06.720 1345		425.5
1765.6	▲	Cross ski area access road.		1508	425.3
1766.3	▲P(5) ★★★★	Cross **Dartmouth Skiway, Lyme–Dorchester Road**.	Area 1 N 43 47.550, W 72 06.167 Area 2 N 43 47.437, W 72 06.073	880	424.6

Lyme Center, NH 03769 (1.3W)
| | 📮 | **PO** M–F 8am–10am, Sa 8am–11:30am. 603-795-4037. | | | |

Lyme, NH 03768 (3.2W)
	📮	**PO** M–F 7:45am–12pm & 1:30am–5:15pm, Sa 7:45am–12pm. 603-795-4421.			
	✕📱	**Stella's Italian Kitchen & Market** 603-795-4302. (www.stellaslyme.com) Market is open M closed, Tu–Th 1am-9pm, F-Sa 10am-10pm, Su 10am-9pm. Dining Room is open for lunch Mon closed, Tu-Su 11am-5pm, dinner T-Th 5pm-9pm, F-Sa 5pm-10pm, Sun 10am-9pm.			
	🚪🖥🍴⊡	**Dowd's Country Inn B&B** 603-795-4712 (www.dowdscountryinn.com) Call in advance and let them know you are a hiker. Pickup and return to trail head is available. Rates change depending on the season mid week starting at $100 and up. Includes full breakfast and afternoon tea. Pets $15, allowed in some rooms. Computer available to use, free WiFi. Mail drops for guests: 9 Main Street, Lyme, NH 03768.			
	🧺✕🍴	(3.3W) **Lyme Country Store** 603-795-2213. (www.lymecountrystore.com) Local products, fresh cut meats, deli salads, homemade baked goods, ice cream, produce, deli. M-Su 6am-8pm. They do not take mail drop but they do offer shipping Shipping UPS and FEDEX.			
	🐕	(2.8W) **Lyme Veterinary Hospital** 603-795-2747. (www.lymevethospital.com) Loated on High St, hospital is 50 yards on the left. M-F 8am-5pm, Sa 8am-12pm, Su closed.			
1767.6	◖	Northwest side of Winslow Ledge, cross stream is shallow gorge.		1232	423.3
1768.0	▲	Junction of old road at granite AT marker.		1216	422.9
1768.2	◖	Cross Grant Brook		1090	422.7
1768.3	◖▲P(5)	Cross **Lyme–Dorchester Road**	N 43 47.822, W 72 06.295	1100	422.6
1769.1	📷	Pass numerous quartzite ledge outcrops in this area along Lambert Ridge while passing in and out of the woods.		2039	421.8

1770.1	📷	North end of Lamberts Ridge, view of summit.		2252	420.8
1770.6	◖	Cross stream.		2392	420.3
1771.5	Y	Smarts Mountain Ranger Trail leads east.		2848	419.4
1772.0	◊▲(4)🏚	Side trail leads 500 feet east to Smarts Mountain Tent site. Intermittent spring north on trail, unreliable.		3200	418.9

NoBo	Features	Description	GPS	Elev	SoBo
1772.1	◊ ⌒(12) ◖🄾	50 yards west to **Smarts Mountain Fire Warden's Cabin**, water (Mike Murphy Spring) is located (0.2) north of cabin on blue blazed Daniel Doan Trail, privy. Abandon fire tower with panoramic views. Southern end of J Trail.	N 43 49.517, W 72 02.268		
		21.9◄12.4◄6.7◄▶5.3▶20.8▶27.9		3230	418.8
1772.3	Y	Junction to the east with abandon DOC Clark Pond Loop.		3237	418.6
1775.9	◊	Cross South Jacob's Brook on rocks.		1450	415.0
1776.0	◊	Cross South Jacob's Brooks.		1538	414.9
1776.6	🄾	Eastman Ledges, rocky		2010	414.3
1777.1	⚠◊	Cross old logging road and North Branch of Jacob's Brook.		1900	413.8
1777.4	◊Y⚑(2) ⌒(8)⏎◖	Cross a branch of North Jacob's Brook. Just south is a side trail that leads (0.3E) to **Hexacuba Shelter**, water (stream) is located at the blue blaze junction to the shelter, tenting, privy.	N 43 52.438, W 72 01.740		
		17.7▶12.0▶5.3◄▶15.5▶22.6▶31.6		1980	413.5
1778.8	Y🄾	Mt. Cube (south summit), Cross Rivendell Trail Junction.		2909	412.1
1779.0	Y🄾	Side trail leads (0.3) west to Mt. Cube (north summit).		2911	411.9
1779.8		Stone chair west.		2276	411.1
1780.5	◊	Ford Brackett Brook, ford		1400	410.4
1781.8	⚠	Cross logging road, gravel.		1287	409.1
1782.3	⚠P(8) ★★★★★	Cross **N.H. 25A**.	N 43 54.082, W 71 59.033	900	408.6
	⚑	(1.9W) **Mount Cube Farm** 603-353-4111. Open year-round, pets welcome. Maple syrup products. Store is not manned, but caretaker makes frequent stops. Hikers may tent outside or may be allowed to stay in the sugar house. Sometimes more is offered.			

Wentworth, NH 03282 (4.5E) on NH 25A, then right (0.2) on NH 25

	⊠	(4.7E) **PO** M–F 7am–11am & 2:45pm–4:45pm, Sa 7:15am–12pm. 603-764-9444.			
	🛒🅱	(4.9E) **Shawnee's General Store** 603-764-5553. M-Su 5am-8pm.			
1782.4		Edge of swampy area.		1043	408.5
1783.9	⚠P (3) ★★★★★	Cross **Cape Moonshine Road**	N 43 54.960, W 71 57.869	1400	407.0
	⚑ ◈⚐	(1.4E) **Dancing Bones Intentional Community** 802-440-1612. (www.dancingbones.net) AT Passport location. Offers tenting, hot outdoor showers, outdoor kitchen, composting toilets. This is a residential community, please be respectful when using shared facilities. Smoking is permitted in designated areas. Pets are welcome on a case by case basis. Sometimes offer rides into town.			
1784.5	◊Y⚑(2)◖	Side trail 100 yards east to Ore Hill campsite, water is 150 yards south of campsite, privy.		1720	406.4
1784.8		Height of land on Sentinel Mountain.		1925	406.1
1785.1	◊	Spring on side trail to east.		1800	405.8
1785.4	⚠	Cross woods road.		1525	405.5
1785.8	◊	Cross small stream.		1686	405.1
1786.1		Beaver pond to east.		1650	404.8
1786.8		High point on Ore Hill.		1850	404.1
1787.1	⚠P(10) ★★★★★	Cross **N.H. 25C**, Ore Hill Brook.	N 43 57.225, W 71 56.687	1550	403.8

Warren, NH 03279 (4.0E)

	⊠	**PO** M-F 7:30am-9:30am & 3pm-5pm, Sa 7:30am-12pm. 603-764-5733.			
	✗	**Calamity Jane's Restaurant** 603-764-5288. Serves breakfast, lunch and dinner. M 6am-2pm, Tu closed, W-Th 6am-2pm, F 6am-8pm, Sa 6am-11pm, Su 8am-2pm. Serves breakfast and lunch M, W-Su. Serves dinner F-Sa.			
		Green House Food & Spirits 603-764-5708. (www.greenhousenh.com) M-W closed, Th-F 3pm-11pm, Sa 12pm-10pm, Su 12pm-8pm. Open mic Thursdays, band on Fridays.			
	✗ ◈⚐	**Moose Scoops** 603-764-9134. (www.moosescoopsicecream.com) AT Passport location. Open seasonally, see web site for hours. Hard & soft ice cream, soda, coffee, t-shirts and souvenirs. Free WiFi.			
	🛒	**Tedeschi Food Shop** 603-764-9002. Grocery with produce, deli with sandwiches & pizza, deli closes 7pm Su-Th, 8pm F-Sa. Store hours M-Su 5am-11pm.			
	⚒	**Laundry** M-Su 8:30am-8:30pm.			
	🖥⚐	**Joseph Patch Library** 603-764-9072. M 9am-1pm, Tu 1pm-5pm, W 3pm-7pm, Sa 10am-1pm, Su closed.			
1789.6	⚠🄾	Mt. Mist summit.		2200	401.3
1789.7	🄾	Vita east overlooking Wachipauka Pond.		2000	401.2
1789.8	◊Y	Junction with Webster Slide Trail		1650	401.1
1790.0	◊	Hairy Root Spring		1600	400.9
1790.1	◊	Wachipauka Pond		1493	400.8
1790.9	⚠	North summit of Wyatt Hill.		1700	400.0

NoBo	Features	Description	GPS	Elev	SoBo
1792.0	♦⚠ P(20) ★★★★★	**NH. 25**, Ford Oliverian Brook, ford, road bypass if high water.	N 43 59.392, W 71 53.959	1000	398.9

NH 25 Glencliff, NH (0.25E)

	🏤	**PO** M-F 12pm-2pm, Sa 7am-1pm. 603-989-5154.			
	🏠⚠◈ ⛺👣🛏🚐 🍴🚗🖥	**Hikers Welcome Hostel** 603-989-0040. Hikerswelcome@yahoo.com (www.hikerswelcome.com) Owned by Alyson, and John "Packrat" Robblee (AT'94, PCT'99, CDT'06) AT Passport location. Opens middle to late May to Oct 1. Bunk ($25) and camping ($18.50) includes shower. Shower only with towel $3, laundry $3 wash, $3 dry. Snacks, sodas, pizza, and ice cream. All hikers (even non-guests) are welcome to hang out and enjoy huge DVD library, computer available for use, free WiFi. Slackpacking over Moosilauke, etc. and shuttles (5 miles to resupply in Warren). Coleman, alcohol by the ounce. Tools to help with gear repair, and selection of used gear available, particularly winter wear. Pet Friendly. Both guests and non-guests are welcome to send mail drops (USPS/FedEx/UPS): C/O Hikers Welcome Hostel, 1396 NH Rt 25, PO Box 25, Glencliff, NH 03238.			

Warren, NH (5.0E) See NOBO mile 1787.1

NoBo	Features	Description	GPS	Elev	SoBo
1792.9	♦⌇(8)☾	Loop trail leads (0.1W) to **Jeffers Brook Shelter**, water (Jeffers Brook) is located in front of the shelter, privy.	N 43 59.793, W 71 53.364	1393	398.0
		27.5◀20.8◀15.5◀▶7.1▶16.1▶20.1			
1793.0	♦Y	Side trail leads 40 yards to cascades on Jeffers Brook in Oliverian Notch.		1383	397.9
1793.1	Y	Junction of loop trail leading 70 yards west to Jeffers Brook Shelter.		1350	397.8
1793.3	⚠Y	Junction of **Long Pond Road** and Town Line Trail.		1330	397.6
1793.5	⚠	Cross **USFS 19, Long Pond Road**		1330	397.4
1793.8	⚠P ★★★★★	Cross **High Street**.	N 43 59.888, W 71 52.939	1480	397.1
1794.1	♦	Cross brook.		1634	396.8
1794.2	Y	Junction with Hurricane Trail.		1680	396.7
1794.8	♦	Cross stream.		2322	396.1
1796.8	⚠Y	Junction with Glencliff Trail and spur trail to Mt. Moosilauke (south peak)		4460	394.1
1797.1	📷	Middle peak of Mt. Moosilauke, side trail leads 50 feet with views of ravine.		4500	393.8
1797.5		Tree line on Mt. Moosilauke.		4600	393.4
1797.7	Y📷	Mt. Moosilauke (north peak), Gorge Brook Trail descends (2.6) east to DOT Ravine Lodge.		4802	393.2
1798.1	Y	Junction with Benton Trail.		4550	392.8
1799.6	Y	Junction with Asquam Ridge Trail		4050	391.3

NoBo	Features	Description	GPS	Elev	SoBo
1800.0	♦⚠(2) ⌇(8)☾📷	80 yards west to **Beaver Brook Shelter and campsite**, water (Beaver Brook) is located on the spur trail leading to the shelter, tenting, privy. Nice view of Franconia Ridge	N 44 01.978, W 71 48.708	3750	390.9
		27.9◀22.6◀7.1◀▶9.0▶13.0▶28.1			
1800.4	♦	Beaver Brook Cascades		3000	390.5
1801.3	♦⌐	Cross Beaver Brook on bridge.		1890	389.6
1801.4	♦⌐	Cross Beaver Brook on bridge.		1880	389.5

NoBo	Features	Description	GPS	Elev	SoBo
1801.5	▲P(25) ★★★★★	Cross **NH. 112**; Kinsman Notch.	N 44 02.396, W 71 47.518	1870	389.4
	🏛	**(0.5E) Lost River Gorge & Boulder Caves** 603-745-8031. (www.lostrivergorge.com) Open early May-late Oct. Tourist attraction. Gift store with microwave and microwavable food, snacks, coffee, soda.			
	▲⚑⚒☂ 🖃	**(3.0E) Lost River Valley Campground** 603-745-8321, 800-370-5678. (www.lostriver.com) primitive camp sites $22, pets allowed but not in cabins, cabin $65 and up. Showers, coin laundry, open mid-May to Columbus Day, quiet hours 10pm-8am. Mail drops for guests: 951 Lost River Rd, North Woodstock, NH 03262.			
	🚗⊛⚙	**(16E) Wise Way Wellness Center** 603-726-7600. Open May- Oct. No smoking or pets. $89 for 1-2 persons per cabin, includes light breakfast. Cabin is 10 miles south of Lincoln in Thornton NH. Rustic cabin with no TV or phone but does have pool, mini-fridge and grill. Bathroom and shower inside adjacent building. Licensed Massage Therapist on-site. Additional services: sauna and outdoor Epsom salt bath. No pick up / drop off service. Cash, checks or PayPal.			
		North Woodstock, NH (5E), Lincoln, NH (6E) See Notes at miles 1817.8			
1802.1	Y	Junction with Dilly Trail descends over rough terrain (0.5) to Lost River Gorge and Boulder Caves on NH. 112.		2650	388.8
1802.4		Cross summit of knob, wooded.		2750	388.5
1804.8	Y	Junction with Gordon Pond Trail.		2700	386.1
1805.4	♦	Cross small brook, reliable.		3100	385.5
1806.0	▲	Mt. Wolf (western summit).		3360	384.9
1806.1	▲Y📷	Mt. Wolf (East Peak), Side trail leads 60 yards east to outlook.		3478	384.8
1806.9	Y	Side trail descends 20 yards east to edge of bog, known as Falling Water Pond with views of South Kinsman Mountains.		3200	384.0
1808.0	Y	Junction with Reel Brook Trail.		2600	382.9
1808.5	☨	Power line.		2625	382.4
1809.0	♦▲(4) ⊏(8) ⌣☾☂	75 feet west to **Eliza Brook Shelter and campsite**, water (Eliza Brook), 3 single tent pads and one double, privy, bear box. 31.6◀16.1◀9.0◀▶4.0▶19.1▶24.6	N 44 06.047, W 71 44.544	2400	381.9
1809.3	▲	Junction with logging road, grass cover.		2650	381.6
1809.5	♦	Cascades west of trail.		2760	381.4
1810.1	♦	Cross headwaters to Eliza Brook.		2880	380.8
1810.4	⌒	East of Harrington Pond, bog bridges.		3400	380.5
1810.5	♦	Cross brook.		3425	380.4
1811.4		An exposed knob on South Kinsman Mountain		4300	379.5
1811.5	📷	15 yards west of north knob of South Kinsman Mountain		4358	379.4
1812.0		Col between South and North Kinsman Mountains.		4050	378.9
1812.4	▲	North Kinsman Mountain summit.		4293	378.5
1812.8	Y	Junction with Mt. Kinsman Trail.		3900	378.1
1813.0	♦▲(4) ⊏(12) ⌣☾☂$ ★★★★★	Kinsman Pond Trail loop trail (south) leads (0.1) east to **AMC Kinsman Pond Shelter and campsite**, water, (Kinsman Pond) treat pond water, 2 single and 2 double tent platforms, privy, bear box. Overnight/caretaker fee. Kinsman Pond Trail loop trail rejoins AT 2.0/14.3. 20.1◀13.0◀4.0◀▶15.1▶20.6▶29.6	N 44 08.215, W 71 43.944	3750	377.9

The **Appalachian Mountain Club** (AMC) 603-466-2727 operates huts in the Whites, with bunk space for 30-90 people. There is no road access, no heat, and no showers. They use alternative energy sources and composting toilets. Overnight stays vary in price during the weekday and more on weekends, discounts for AMC members. Reservations recommended. Includes a bunk, dinner and breakfast. Work for stay is available to the first 2 thru-hikers; 4 at Lakes of the Clouds Hut and more at the croo's discretion. Work for stay hikers get floor space for sleeping and feast on leftovers. Do not count on hut stays without reservations, and camping is not allowed near most of the huts.

🚗 **AMC Hiker Shuttle** 603-466-2727 Schedule of stops and time are on line at (www.outdoors.org/lodging/lodging-shuttle.cfm) Operates June-mid Sept daily, and weekends and holidays through mid Oct. Stops in Lincoln, at Franconia Notch, Crawford Notch, Highland Center, Pinkham Notch, and in Gorham; $23 for non AMC members, $19 for AMV members. Walk-ins on a space available basis ONLY, RESERVATIONS ARE STRONGLY RECOMMENDED.

NoBo	Features	Description	GPS	Elev	SoBo
1814.9	♦Y◈ ☾🚗	**AMC Lonesome Lake Hut**, junction of Around-Lonesome Lake Trail. **Lonesome Lake Hut** is a AT Passport location.	N 44 08.308, W 71 42.222	2760	376.0
1815.0	♦Y	Southern edge of Lonesome Lake, junction with Fishin' Jimmy Trail, **No Camping permitted here.**		2740	375.9
1815.8	Y	Junction with Kinsman Pond Trail (north)		2294	375.1
1816.3	♦Y	Junction with Basin–Cascade Trail, Cross Cascade Brook, ford		2084	374.6
1817.4	♦	Cross Whitehouse Brook		1610	373.5
1817.6	Y	Junction with Pemi Trail.		1520	373.3

NoBo	Features	Description	GPS	Elev	SoBo
1817.7	▲	Pass under **I-93, US. 3 (south side)**.		1450	373.2
1817.8	▲ Y ★★★★★	Pass under **I-93, U.S. 3 (north side)**, Franconia Notch, Pemigawasset River, Franconia Notch paved bike path east to Liberty Springs hiker parking and shuttle; and beyond to The Flume Visitor center; west to Lafayette Place campground.	N 44 05.992, W 71 40.938	1450	373.1
	✗🍴❄☐	(0.7E) **Flume Visitor Center** 603-745-8391. Has a cafeteria, serves pastries, hamburgers, hot dogs, pizza remainder of the day. Restrooms, payphone. May–late Oct, M-Su 9am–5pm, Mail drops: Flume Gorge, 850 Daniel Webster Hwy, Lincoln, NH 03251.			
	▲⊛🏠👤🚻 ☐	(2.1W) **Lafayette Place Campground** 603-823-9513. Open mid May-Columbus Day. No pets. Tent sites $25, limited store, quiet time 10pm. Mail drops: Franconia State Park, Lafayette Campground, Franconia, NH 03580.			
	🛏⊛☐	(1.2E) **Profile Motel & Cottages** 603-745-2759. (www.profilemotel.com) Call for prices. Microwave, fridge, free WiFi, A/C.			
	🛏⊛👤🚻 ☐	(3.0E) **Mt. Liberty Motel** 603-745-3600. (www.mtlibertylodging.com) Open May-Oct. No pets or smoking. Prices increase during tourist season. $69 and up for off season, microwave, fridge, laundry, free WiFi, includes pickup and return from to trail heads at Kinsman, Franconia Notch and town shuttle. Laundry $5. CC accepted. Mail drops for guests: 10 Liberty Road, Lincoln, NH 03251.			
	🚗	**AMC Hiker Shuttle, See Notes at mile 1813.0**			

North Woodstock, NH (4.8E) of Franconia Notch. See map of North Woodstock/Lincoln, NH.

	✉	**PO** M-F 9:30am-12:30pm & 1:30pm-4:30pm, Sa 9am-12pm. 603-745-8134.			
	🏠⊛👤 🖥🛏🚗☐	**The Notch Hostel** 603-348-1483 (www.notchhostel.com) AT Passport location. Ideally situated for slackpack between Kinsman & Franconia Notch. Reserve by website, text, or call. Bunk in large, white farmhouse on NH 112 (Lost River Rd). 1.0 W of North Woodstock, 2.0 W of Lincoln. $33PP includes bunk, linens, towel, shower, group laundry service, coffee/tea, make-ur-own pancakes, WiFi, computer, guest kitchen, fridge & large yard. Check-in 4-9p, (earlier ok with text/call: follow welcome sheet if no one home). Beer & wine OK in moderation. No liquor. Small store: ice cream, pizza, snacks, soda, & fuel. Rental bikes $5/day. Shuttles run June 1 - Oct. 1, Su - Th for guests with reservations. For shuttle, send same-day text confirmation with reservation name, pick-up time and location. Town and Trailhead shuttles depart from hostel 7am, 10am, 3pm, 6pm. Kinsman Notch (NH 112) Pickup +5min, Flume Visitors Center Pickup +25min, Town +40min. Maildrops: C/O The Notch Hostel, 324 Lost River Rd. North Woodstock, NH 03262.			
	🛏✗⊛	**Woodstock Inn** 603-745-3951, 800-321-3985. (www.woodstockinnnh.com) Ask about 10% thru-hikers discount, prices are seasonal, includes full breakfast, free WiFi. Pet rooms available. Woodstock Station restaurant, outdoor bar, and a micro-brewery.			
	🛏👤⊛	**Autumn Breeze** 603-745-8549. (www.autumnbreezemotel.com) Open year round. $60 hiker rate includes kitchenette, laundry, free WiFi, shuttle to and from trail head. One pet room. Shuttle to town if available. Credit cards accepted.			
	🛏⊛☐☐	**The Carriage Motel** 603-745-2416. (www.carriagemotel.com) No pets. $69 and up, game room, pool, grills, free WiFi. Mail drops: PO Box 198, 180 Main St, North Woodstock, NH 03262.			
	🛒✗🍴	**Wayne's Market** 603-745-8819. (www.lincolnwoodstockmarket.com) Open year round. Deli, meats, cheap sandwiches, ATM. M-Su 5am-10pm.			
	🏠	**Fadden's General Store & Maple Sugarhouse** 603-745-8371. (www.nhmaplesyrup.com) Open year-round. Maple sugar products, ice cream, fudge and more. M-Su 9am-5pm.			

Lincoln, NH (5.8S of Franconia Notch) See map of North Woodstock/Lincoln, NH.

	✉	**PO** M-F 8am-5pm, Sa 8am-12pm. 603-745-8133.			
	🏠⊛	**Chet's One Step at a Time** 603-745-8196.			
	👤🚻☐	AT Passport location.			
	🛒🍴	**Price Chopper** M-Su 24 hours.			
	🏃	**Lahout's Summit Shop** 603-745-2882. (www.lahouts.com) Full service outfitter, packs, coleman, alcohol by the ounce, canister fuel, freeze dried foods. Located at 165 Main St. in the plaza next to Subway. M-F 9:30am-5:30pm, Sa 9am-5:30pm, Su 9am-5pm.			
	🖥	**Chat Room Coffee House & Books** 603-745-2626. (www.chatroomcoffeehouse.com) M-Sa 10-6, Su closed.			
	👤	**Homerun Laundromat** 603-620-8497. Coin operated. M-Su 24 hours.			
	🚗	**AMC Hiker Shuttle, See Notes at mile 1813.0**			

Franconia, NH 03580 (11W of Franconia notch)

	✉	**PO** M-F 8:30am-1pm & 2pm-5pm, Sa 9am-12pm. 603-823-5611.			
	🛏👤⊛☐- 🚗☐	**Gale River Motel** 603-823-5655, 800-255-7989. (www.galerivermotel.com) Open year round. $50–$200, pets with approval, laundry wash $1, dry $1, Coleman by the ounce. Free pickup and return to Franconia Notch trail heads with stay, longer shuttles for a fee. Credit cards accepted. Mail drops (fee for non-guest): 1 Main Street, Franconia, NH 03580.			
	🛒	**Mac's Market** 603-823-7795. M-Su 7am-8pm.			
	🏠✗	**Franconia Village Store** 603-823-7782. Convenience Store and deli. M-Sa 6am-9pm, Su 6:30am-7pm.			
	🖥⊛	**Abbie Greenleaf Library** 603-823-8424. (www.abbielibrary.org) Free WiFi. M-Tu 2pm-6pm, W 10am-12pm & 2pm-6pm, Th-F 2pm-5pm, Sa 10am-1pm, Su closed.			

(6.9) miles from
Woodstock PO to

North Woodstock/Lincoln, NH

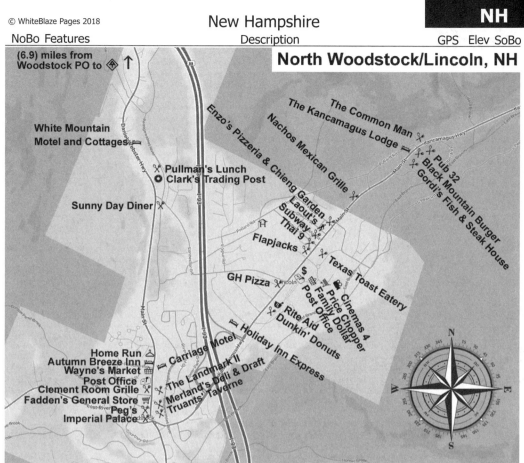

NoBo		Description	GPS	Elev	SoBo
1818.4	Y	Side trail to Flume Side Trail		1800	372.5
1818.9	⬥	Cross brook.		2050	372.0
1819.2	⚠	Junction of old logging road (northern).		1350	371.7
1820.4	⬥⚑(10)⌣	10 yards east to AMC Liberty Springs Tent site, 7 single and 3 double tent platforms, accommodates 44.		3870	370.5
1820.7	Y📷	Junction of Liberty Spring Trail and Franconia Ridge Trail, (0.3) to Mt. Liberty summit.		4260	370.2
1822.5	▲Y📷	Little Haystack Mountain summit, Falling Waters Trail, above tree line for next 2.5 miles north on Franconia Ridge		4800	368.4
1823.2	▲📷	Mt. Lincoln summit		5089	367.7
1823.7		Unnamed hump.		5020	367.2
1824.2	⬥Y▲⌂ ◈◖📷	Mt. Lafayette summit, Greenleaf Trail. (1.0W) on Greenleaf Trail to **AMC Greenleaf Hut** AT Passport location.	N 44 09.624, W 71 39.620	5260	366.7
1824.6	▲	North peak of Mt. Lafayette.		5000	366.3
1825.0	Y	Tree line and junction with Skookumchuck Trail, above tree line for the next 2.5 miles south on Franconia Ridge.		4680	365.9
1827.2	⬥	Garfield Pond east.		3860	363.7
1827.7	▲	Side trail leads 50 yards east to Mt. Garfield summit		4500	363.2
1827.9	Y	Garfield Trail		4180	363.0
1828.1	⬥Y⚑(7) ⌐(12) ⌣◖🎒$	(0.1W) **AMC Garfield Ridge Shelter and campsite**, water (spring) at the junction to the campsite, two single and five double tent platforms, privy, bear box. Overnight/caretaker fee. 28.1◀19.1◀15.1◀▶5.5▶14.5▶56.5	N 44 11.441, W 71 36.502	3900	362.8
1828.6	Y	Franconia Brook Trail leads (2.2) east to 13 Falls Tent site with nine tent pads, accommodates 36, bear box, water on site.		3420	362.3
1829.9	📷	Ledgy knob with view.		3420	361.0

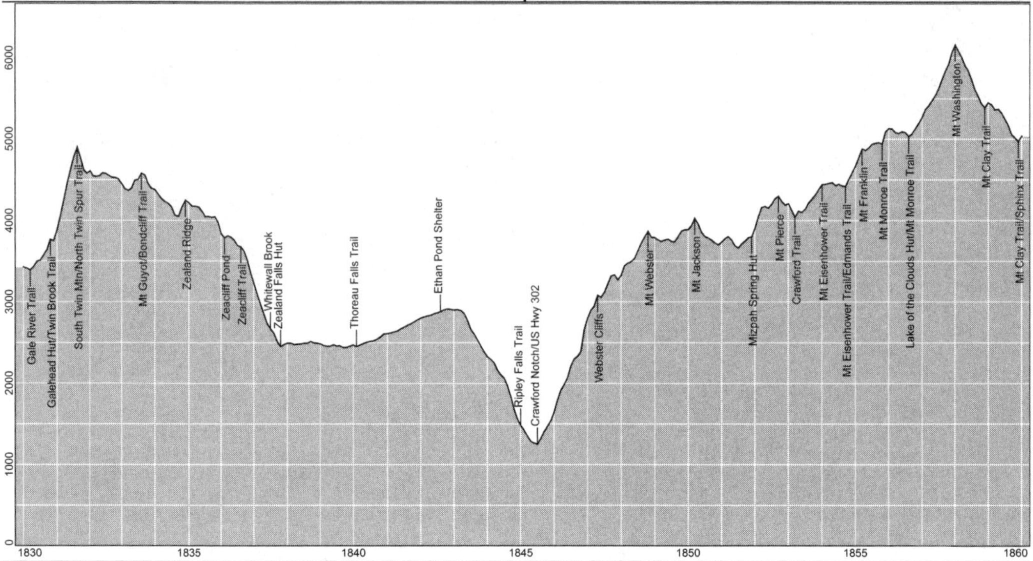

NoBo	Features	Description	GPS	Elev	SoBo
1830.2	Y	Gale River Trail		3390	360.7
1830.8	♦Y� ◈℄	Joins the Garfield Trail. Frost Trail leads 40 yards east to **AMC Galehead Hut**. Twin Brook Trail. AT Passport location.	N 44 11.278, W 71 34.134	3780	360.1
1831.6	▲Y	South Twin Mountain summit and junction with North Twin Spur.		4902	359.3
1832.5	📷	Ledgy hump with views of South Twin Mountain and Guyot and Carrigain Mountains.		4550	358.4
1833.6	♦Y⚠(6) ℄(12) ⌣℄🐻$	Mt. Guyot summit. 100 yards south of summit is junction with Bondcliff Trail leading (0.8) east to **AMC Guyot Shelter and campsite**, water (spring) is located at the campsite, four single and two double tent platforms will accommodate 18, privy, bear box. Overnight/caretaker fee. 24.6◄20.6◄5.5◄▶9.0▶51.0▶57.1	N 44 09.658, W 71 32.136	4580	357.3
1834.9	▲	Side trail leads (0.1) west to Zealand Mountain summit		4250	356.0
1836.1	♦Y	Side trail leads (0.1) east to Zeacliff Pond.		3800	354.8
1836.5	Y	Junction with Zeacliff Trail (south), rejoins the AT again (2.8) north.		3700	354.4
1836.6	Y📷	100 yard side loop trail east to spectacular lookout edge of Zeacliff.		3700	354.3
1837.7	♦Y	Junction with Lend-a-Hand Trail. Whitewall Brook is crossed twice in this area.		2750	353.2
1837.8	♦🚿�◈ ℄📷	**AMC Zealand Falls Hut** AT Passport location.	N 44 11.748, W 71 29.667	2630	353.1
1837.9	Y🚿	Side trail east leads to Zealand Falls.		2600	353.0
1838.0	Y	Junction with Zealand Trail (south), former railroad bed.		2460	352.9
1839.3	Y	Junction with Zeacliff Trail (north)		2448	351.6
1839.6	Y	East side of trail shows slide and scarred slopes of Whitewall Mountain.		2450	351.3
1840.1	Y	Junction with Thoreau Falls Trail. **Camping is not permitted here.**		2460	350.8
1840.3	♦⌒	Cross North Fork on wooden bridge.		2490	350.6
1840.6	Y	Shoal Pond Trail. (0.8) east to water		2500	350.3
1840.8	♦	Cross brook.		2520	350.1
1842.6	♦⚠(5) ℄(10) ⌣℄🐻$	250 yards west to **AMC Ethan Pond Shelter and campsite**, Caretaker on site. Overnight fee. Water (brook) is inlet brook to the pond, three single and two double tent platforms, privy, bear box. Overnight/caretaker fee. 29.6◄14.5◄9.0◄▶42.0▶48.1▶61.8	N 44 10.631, W 71 25.607	2860	348.3
1843.1		Height of land.		2900	347.8
1843.6	Y	Willey Range Trail		2680	347.3
1843.9	Y	Kedron Flume Trail		2450	347.0
1845.0	Y	Junction with Arethusa–Ripley Falls Trail.		1600	345.9
1845.2	✕▲ P(10)	Cross Railroad Tracks, Junction with Willey House Station Road. For parking go all the way up Willey House Station Road.	N 44 10.251, W 71 23.283	1440	345.7
1845.5	▲�car P(10) ★★★★★	Cross **U.S. 302**, Crawford Notch, Presidential Range. See previous entry for parking.		1275	345.4
	✕📱	(1.0W) **Willey House** 603-271-3556. Memorial Day-Columbus Day. Snack bar. M-Su 9:30am-5pm.			

NoBo	Features	Description	GPS	Elev	SoBo
	▲🍴⌂	**(1.8E) Dry River Campground** 603-374-2272. (www.nhstateparks.com/crawford.html) Open May-late Oct. Tent sites $25. Pets allowed, coin laundry and showers. Quiet time 10pm-8am.			
	⇔🏠⊛✗ 🏪🔌📠	**(3.5W) AMC Highland Center** 603-278-4453. (www.outdoors.org) No pets, no smoking. Rates in summer during tourist season and during holidays. Call ahead for prices. AMC members get a discount. AMC Shuttle stops daily mid-Jun thru Columbus Day, after this time it only stops on weekends and holidays. Restaurant serves breakfast, lunch and dinner. Store carries snacks, sodas, canister fuel and some clothing. Mail drops (include ETA): Route 302, Bretton Woods, NH 03574.			
	⇔▲🏪	**(3.3E) Crawford Notch General Store & Campground** 603-374-2779 (www.crawfordnotch.com) Open mid May-mid Oct. Cabins $75-95, tent sites, space for two tents $30. 9% lodging tax. Store carries hiker foods, ice cream and beer.			
	🚗	**AMC Hiker Shuttle, See Notes at mile 1813.0**			
1845.6	⌢	Cross Saco River, footbridge		1350	345.3
1845.7	♦Y	Junction with Saco River Trail (southern)		1350	345.2
1845.8	Y	Junction Saco River Trail (northern)		1400	345.1
1847.3	📷	Webster Cliffs, view.		3025	343.6
1847.9	📷	View from ledge looks down at state park buildings.		3506	343.0
1848.8	▲📷	Mt. Webster summit		3910	342.1
1848.9	Y	Junction with Webster Branch and Webster Jackson Trail.		3820	342.0
1850.2	▲📷	Mt. Jackson summit.		4052	340.7
1851.8	Y	Mizpah Cutoff to the west.		3816	339.1
1851.9	♦Y◈ ▲(7) ⌣🏠 ⇔✗	Junction with Mt. Clinton Trail. **AMC Mizpah Spring Hut, AMC Nauman Tent site**, 5 single and 2 double tent platforms accommodate 30, privy, bear box, water from stream. **Mizpah Hut** is a AT Passport location.	N 44 13.160, W 71 22.206 3800		339.0
1852.7	▲📷	Mt. Pierce (Mt. Clinton) summit, above tree line for the next 12.7 miles north		4312	338.2
1853.6	♦	Spring. Join or leave Webster Cliff Trail or the Crawford Path.		4350	337.3
1853.5	♦	Cross small stream in Col.		4226	337.4
1854.0	Y	Junction of Mt. Eisenhower Loop (south) which leads (0.4) west to Mt. Eisenhower summit and rejoins the AT (0.5) north.		4425	336.9
1854.4	Y📷	Mt. Eisenhower Loop (north), Edmonds Path		4475	336.5
1854.8	Y	Junction with Mt. Eisenhower Trail.		4423	336.1
1854.9	♦	Spring		4480	336.0
1855.5	📷	West of summit of Mt. Franklin		5004	335.4
1855.6	Y	Unmarked path leads 130 yards east to summit of Mt. Franklin.		4972	335.3
1855.8		Junction with Mt. Monroe Loop Trail (southern), leads (0.4) west to Mt. Monroe summit.		5077	335.1
1856.5	Y📷	Junction with Mt. Monroe Loop Trail (northern), leads (0.4) west to Mt. Monroe summit.		5075	334.4
1856.6	♦◈⌇ ★★★★★ ⇔🏠♦⌇🍴	**AMC Lakes of the Clouds Hut**, "The Dungeon". AT Passport location. Lodging and Work For Stay Also "**The Dungeon**," a bunkroom available for 6 thru-hikers for $10PP with access to hut restroom and the common area. When the hut is closed, The Dungeon serves as an emergency shelter.	N 44 15.528, W 71 19.137 5125		334.3
1856.7	Y	Junction with Tuckerman Crossover and Camel Trail, which leads (0.7) east to Davis Path.		5125	334.2
1857.4	Y	Junction with Davis Path is 35 yards south on the AT. Junction with Westside Trail which rejoins the AT (1.5) north. Westside Trail (south).		5625	333.5
1857.8	Y	Gulfside Trail to the west.		6150	333.1
1858.0	▲📷✗- 🚹📷♦P ★★★★★	Mt. Washington summit, Mt. Washington Auto Road. Juntion with Tuckerman Ravine Trail leads (2.0) east to **AMC Hermit Lake Shelter**, Pinkham Notch at NH. 16. Many parking spots at the top. **Mt. Washington, NH.**	N 44 16.180, W 71 18.124 6288		332.9
	📬	**PO** M-S 10am-4pm. For outgoing mail only. Do not send mail drops here.			
	✗🏪🚹♦🛁▲	**Sherman Adams Building** 603-466-3347. M-Su 8am-6pm mid-May thru Columbus Day. Snack bar M-Su 9am-6pm.			
1858.2	Y	Junction with Trinity Heights Connector.		6100	332.7
1858.3	✗	Cross Cog Railroad Tracks.		6090	332.6
1858.4	Y	Great Gulf Trail leads east.		5925	332.5
1858.9	Y	Junction with Westside Trail (northern).		5500	332.0
1859.0	Y	Junction with Mt. Clay Loop Trail (southern), leads (0.7) east to Mt. Clay summit.		5400	331.9
1859.3	Y	Junction with Jewell Trail.		5400	331.6
1859.8	♦	Loop trail to west to Greenough Spring, reliable.		5100	331.1
1859.9	Y	Sphinx Col, Junction with Mt. Clay Loop Trail (northern), leads (0.5) east to Mt. Clay summit.		5025	331.0

NoBo	Features	Description	GPS	Elev	SoBo

NoBo	Features	Description	GPS	Elev	SoBo
1860.0	Y	Junction with Sphinx Trail.		4975	330.9
1860.5	Y	Junction with Cornice Trail and cross Monticello Lawn, a grassy plateau.		5325	330.4
1860.6	Y	Junction with Mt. Jefferson Loop (southern), leads (0.3) west to Mt. Jefferson summit.		5396	330.3
1861.0	Y	Junction with Six Husbands Trail.		5325	329.9
1861.3	Y	Junction with Mt. Jefferson Loop (north).		5125	329.6
1861.5	♦Y	Edmands Col, Randolph Path leads (0.2) west to reliable Spaulding Spring and continues (1.1) to The Perch Shelter.		4938	329.4
1862.2	♦Y ⅄(4) ⌂(8)⌔⊆	Junction with Israel Ridge Path leads to (0.9W) **RMC The Perch Shelter and campsite**, 4 tent pads accommodate 16, privy. **no fires permitted here.**	N 44 19.470, W 71 18.660	5475	328.7
1862.3	◊	Peabody Spring west, unreliable.		5220	328.6
1862.7	Y	Junction with Israel Ridge Path (northern).		5211	328.2
1862.8	Y	Thunderstorm Junction, Trail (1.1W) to **RMC Crag camp Cabin**; Lowe's Path to Mt. Adams and (1.2W) **RMC Gray Knob Cabin**		5490	328.1
1863.3	Y	Junction with Air Line Trail (southern) leads (0.5) to Mt. Adams summit.		5125	327.6
1863.4	Y	Junction with Air Line Trail (northern).		5125	327.5
1863.7	♦⅄ ◈⌻	**AMC Madison Spring Hut** AT Passport location. Valley Way Trail (0.6) west to tent site.	N 44 19.667, W 71 17.991	4825	327.2
1845.5	♦⅄	(0.6W) USFS Valley Way Tent site		3900	345.4
1864.2	◙Y	Mt. Madison and junction of Watson Path west.		5366	326.7
1864.4	Y	Junction with Howker Ridge Trail.		5100	326.5
1864.7	Y	Osgood Junction, Parapet Trail east; Daniel Webster Scout Trail west.		4822	326.2
1865.4		Osgood Ridge, above tree line for the next 12.7 miles south		4300	325.5
1866.7	♦Y⅄⌔ ⊆	Junction with Osgood Trail at USFS Osgood campsite, privy.	N 44 18.515, W 71 15.307	2540	324.2
1867.3	♦Y	Junction with Osgood Cutoff at the Bluff. Great Gulf Trail		2450	323.6
1867.4	♦Y	Junction with Madison Gulf Trail, West Branch of the Peabody River		2300	323.5
1867.5	Y	Junction with Great Gulf Trail (north)		2290	323.4
1869.4	◙	Side trail leads 200 yards to Low's Bald Spot, rock dome.		2875	321.5
1869.6	⚠P	Cross Mt. Washington Auto Road	N 44 16.887, W 71 15.184	2675	321.3
1869.7	Y	Junction with Raymond Path.		2625	321.2
1870.5	Y	Junction with George's Gorge Trail.		2525	320.4
1871.0	Y	Junction with Crew Cutoff Trail.		2075	319.9
1871.5	⚠P ★★★★★	Cross **N.H. 16**, Pinkham Notch, Pinkham Notch Visitor center, AMC Joe Dodge Lodge. Many parking spots.	N 44 15.425, W 71 15.147	2050	319.4

⌂✕♦♦ ♨⌂⛺ ☐✉

Pinkham Notch Visitor Center & Joe Dodge Lodge 603-466-2721. (www.outdoors.org) Open year-round. No pets. Rates in summer during tourist season and during holidays. Call ahead for prices. AMC members get a discount. Meals available to non guests; AYCE breakfast 6:30am-9am daily, food to order for lunch, family style dinner Sat-Thurs 6pm, Friday dinner buffet. Coin-op shower available 24 hours, $2 towel rental. Vending machines, coleman, alcohol by the ounce, canister fuel, free WiFi. Shuttle 7:30am daily. Accepts credit cards. Mail drops: AMC Visitor Center, C/O Front Desk, 361 Rte. 16, Gorham, NH 03581.

NoBo	Features	Description	GPS	Elev	SoBo
	🚐	**AMC Hiker Shuttle, See Notes at mile 1813.0**			
		Gorham, NH (10.7W from Pinkham Notch) See map of Gorham, NH at mile 1892.4.			
1871.6	Y	Junction with Square Ledge Trail.		2020	319.3
1872.4	Y ⚓	Junction with Lost Pond Trail. Glen Ellis Falls (0.1) east on Whitecat Ridge Trail.		1990	318.5
1873.2	📷	Open Ledge, Sarge's Crag, views.		3000	317.7
1873.5	♦	Side path west to signed spring.		3250	317.4
1873.8	📷	Steep ledge with views of ravine and Mt. Washington.		3500	317.1
1874.2	▲	Cross just yards west of Wildcat Mountain Peak E.		4046	316.7
1874.4		Wildcat Mountain Ski Area Gondola.		4020	316.5
1874.5	📷 ⌂	Wildcat Mountain, Peak D		4020	316.4
1874.8		Wildcat Col.		3770	316.1
1875.6	📷	Wildcat Mountain, Peak C		4298	315.3
1876.0		Wildcat Mountain, Peak B		4330	314.9
1876.5	📷	Wildcat Mountain, Peak A, views down into Carter Notch.		4442	314.4
1877.2	Y	Junction with Wildcat Ridge Trail.		3388	313.7
1877.4	♦Y🚐 ◈ ☾	Junction with Nineteen Mile Brook Trail which leads (0.2) east to (0.2E) **AMC Carter Notch Hut** into Carter Notch. AT Passport location.	N 44 15.558, W 71 11.725	3350	313.5
1877.8	📷	View into Carter Notch.		4000	313.1
1878.1	♦Y	60 yards west to good spring.		4300	312.8
1878.6	▲ Y📷	Carter Dome summit and junction with Rainbow Trail.		4832	312.3
1879.0	Y	Black Angel Trail		4600	311.9
1879.4	▲📷	Mt. Hight summit.		4675	311.5
1880.0	♦Y	Zeta Pass and junction with Carter Dome Trail junction. **No camping permitted here**.		3890	310.9
1880.8	▲	South Carter Mountain summit, wooded.		4458	310.1
1882.1	▲	Middle Carter Mountain summit, wooded.		4610	308.8
1882.4	📷	Open ledges of Mt. Lethe.		4584	308.5
1882.7	Y	Junction with North Carter Trail.		4500	308.2
1882.9	▲📷	North Carter Mountain summit, wooded.		4539	308.0
1884.6	♦Y⛺(5) ⌐(12) ⌣☾🔒$	(0.2W) **AMC Imp Shelter and campsite**, water (stream) is located near shelter, four single and one double tent pads, privy. Overnight/caretaker fee. tent platform, bear box. 56.5◄51.0◄42.0◄►6.1►19.8►25.0	N 44 19.739, W 71 09.007	3250	306.3
1885.3	Y	Junction with Stony Brook Trail which descends (3.6) west to NH. 16, Moriah Brook Trail.		3127	305.6
1886.7	Y	Junction with Carter Moriah Trail to Mt. Moriah Mountain summit.		4000	304.2
1887.9	📷	East of Middle Moriah summit.		3640	303.0
1888.1	Y	Junction with Kenduskeag Trail.		3300	302.8
1889.2	♦	Cross Rattle River		1700	301.7

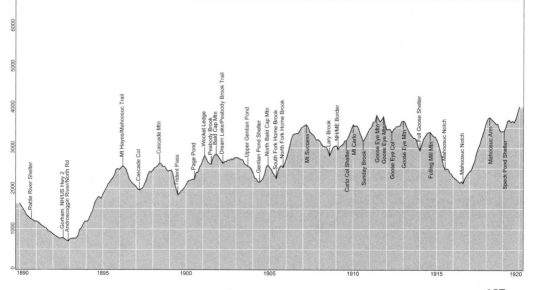

NoBo	Features	Description	GPS	Elev SoBo
1890.3		Cross East Rattle River, **difficult in high water**.		1500 300.6
1890.7	◗▲⌐(8) ⌣(	**Rattle River Shelter and campsite**, water (Rattle River), tenting, privy. 57.1▶48.1▶6.1◀▶13.7▶18.9▶23.3	N 44 22.802, W 71 06.449	1260 300.2
1892.4	◗▲P(12) ★★★★★	Cross **U.S. 2 (southern end)**. **See Map of Gorham, NH.**	N 44 24.064, W 71 06.561	780 298.5

⌂ ✗ ⚅⏦ **Rattle River Lodge & Hostel** 603-466-5049 (rattleriverhostel.com)
▣➤P▱ Open year round. Online booking available. Located on the AT.
Clean B&B style rooms, some private rooms starting at $75 with fresh linens & towels. Thru hiker bunk rate $35PP includes breakfast, laundry, loaner clothes, showers, fast WiFi, free resupply shuttle to Walmart. Sodas, ice cream, Mr. Pizza delivery available for guests & non-guests. Town shuttles for guests $2. Free morning shuttle to Post Office and gas station at 8:30am. Bus pickup and drop off available. Late bus pickup fees may apply. Long distance shuttles avail $2 mile one way. Section hike planning assistance. 21 Mile slackpack free with 2 night stay (Pinkham Notch to US 2). Pickup at Pinkham Notch available at 8am, noon, and 5pm for $5PP, ($20 for unscheduled pickup) based on availability. Parking available for section hikers. Authorized Sierra Madre Research hammock outfitter.
Mail drops free for guests and $5 for nonguests. Label side of box with last name and eta. Mail: 592 State Route 2, Shelburne, NH 03581.

⌂▲◈ (1.7W) **White Birches Camping Park** 603-466-2022. (www.whitebirchescamping.com)
⛺⚅➤▱ AT Passport location.
Open May-Oct. Bunks $15, tent sites $13PP, laundry, pool, air hockey, pool table, pets allowed, coleman, alcohol by the ounce and canister fuel, free WiFi. Free shuttle to and from trail head and town with stay. Credit cards accepted.
Mail drops for guests ($5 fee for nonguest): 218 US 2, Shelburne, NH 03581.

➤✗▢⏦ (2.6W) **Town & Country Inn and Resort** 603-466-3315. (www.townandcountryinn.com)
Open year round. $64.00 to $155.00 seasonal, pets $25.00 daily fee, complimentary WiFi, microwave oven and fridge.
Breakfast and dinner served daily, lounge with entertainment. Indoor heated pool, Jacuzzi, Sauna, steam room and fully equipped health club.

Gorham, NH 03581 (3.5W from U.S. 2 Trail head). See map of Gorham, NH.
✉ **PO** M-F 8:30am-5pm, Sa 8:30am-12pm. 603-466-2182. ID required; all packages should include your legal name.

➤⌂▲◈ **Libby House Inn & The Barn Hikers Hostel** 603-466-2271. (www.libbyhouseinn.webs.com)
⑧⚅⏦ AT Passport location.
▣➤▱ Open year-round. No pets. Bunks $22, tenting $15PP, B&B rooms available. Hot country breakfast available. Fast, free pickup and return to Route 2 trail head for guests. Shuttle from Pinkham Notch free with 2 night stay to facilitate slackpacking. Shuttle to Walmart. Clean beds with linens, full kitchen with cookware and refrigerator, lounge with big screen TV, free WiFi. Laundry $5. Visa MC accepted.
Mail drops free for guests, $15 fee for non-guests: 55 Main Street, Gorham, NH 03581.

➤⌂◈⑧ **Hiker's Paradise at Colonial Fort Inn** 603-466-2732. (www.hikersparadise.com)
✗⚅⏦➾ AT Passport location.
No pets. Bunks $24 (includes tax) with linen, tub and shower, kitchen, free WiFi. Private rooms available. Coin laundry for guests.
Coleman, alcohol by the ounce. Free shuttle with stay to and from Route 2, other limited shuttles. Credit cards accepted. Smoking only on outside porch. No mail drops.

➤⚅⏦ **Royalty Inn** 603-466-3312. (www.royaltyinn.com) Hiker rate $89 weekday, $99 weekend depending on the season. Pet fee $20. Indoor and outdoor pool, jucuzzi, sauna, A/C, laundry, free WiFi. Vending machines.

➤⚅⏦▱ **Top Notch Inn** 603-466-5496. (www.topnotchinn.com)
Open May-mid Oct. Call for pricing. Guest laundry, limited shuttles, pool, hot tub, laundry, free WiFi, well behaved dogs under 50 lbs okay, no smoking. Credit cards accepted. 10% local restaurant discount.
Mail drops for guests and non guests: 265 Main St, Gorham, NH 03581.

➤⏦ **Northern Peaks Motor Inn** 603-466-2288. (www.northernpeaksmotorinn.com)
$70/up + tax, pets $5, A/C, free WiFi, no smoking. Hikers welcome. Accepts Master, Visa, Discover and American express card.

➤⏦ **Gorham Motor Inn** 603-466-3381 $58-$158 Open May-Oct.
🥾🛒 **Gorham Hardware & Sports** 603-466-2312. (www.nhhockeyshop.com) Clothing, hiking poles, water treatment, hiking food, cold weather clothes, white gas, alcohol by the ounce snd canisters. Accepts Visa MC Disc. M-F 8am-5:30pm, Sa 8am-4pm, Su 8am-1pm. Close Su after Columbus Day.

🚗 **AMC Hiker Shuttle, See Notes at mile 1811.9**
🛒💊 (6.7W) **Walmart** 603-752-4621. M-Su 7am-10pm; **Pharmacy** M-F 8am-8pm, Sa 9am-7pm, Su 10am-6pm.

Berlin, NH (10.1W) from U.S. 2 trail head)
⚕ **Androscoggin Valley Hospital** 603-752-2200.

© WhiteBlaze Pages 2018

New Hampshire/Maine

NH/ME

NoBo Features

Description

GPS Elev SoBo

Gorham, NH

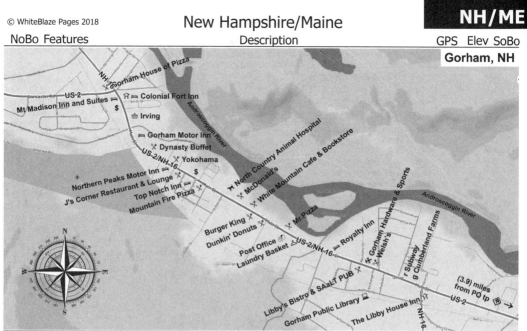

NoBo	Features	Description	GPS	Elev	SoBo
1892.6	⚠	Cross **U.S. 2 (northern end)**.		780	298.3
1892.7	✕	Intersects with **North Road, Cross railroad tracks**.		755	298.2
1892.9	⚠	Cross Androscoggin River on Leadmine Bridge at power plant, North Road.	N 44 24.384, W 71 07.008	750	298.0
1893.1	⚠	Junction with **North Road**		760	297.8
1893.4	◊⚠P(4)	Junction with **Hogan Road**, unpaved	N 44 24.245, W 71 07.213	800	297.5
1894.1	◊	Cross Brook.		1350	296.8
1896.2	Y📷	Mt. Hayes, Mahoosuc Trail		2555	294.7
1896.5	Y	Junction with Centennial Trail and Mahoosuc Trail below Mt. Hayes.		2550	294.4
1897.2	◊	Water in Col between Cascade Mountain and Mt. Hayes.		1960	293.7
1897.6	📷	Good views on large steep open rock slabs and ledges.		2631	293.3
1898.4	▲	Cascade Mountain summit, wooded.		2631	292.5
1899.5	◊▲(4) ⌣☾☂	Side tail leads (0.1) west to Trident Col Tent site, water at spring 50 yards from campsite, 4 tent sites accommodates 16, privy, bear box.		2020	291.4
1900.5	◊	Trident Pass, pass south of Page Pond over outlet.		2240	290.4
1901.1	📷	View 50 yards west on Wockett Ledge, shoulder of Bald Cap.		2780	289.8
1901.8	◊	Cross Upper Branch of Peabody Brook.		2750	289.1
1902.2	◊Y	Cross Dream Lake inlet brook, Junction with Peabody Brook Trail leads to Dryad Falls Trail.		2610	288.7
1903.7	◊	Northwestern shore of Moss Pond.		2630	287.2
1904.0	◊	Southwest shore of Upper Gentian Pond.		2530	286.9
1904.4	◊Y▲(4) ⌐(12) ⌣☾☂	Junction of Austin Brook Trail leads (0.2E) **Gentian Pond Shelter and campsite**, water is the inlet brook of Gentian Pond, three single and one double tent platforms accommodate 16, privy, bear box. 61.8◄19.8◄13.7◄►5.2►9.6►14.7	N 44 27.110, W 71 04.163	2166	286.5
1905.8	◊	Cross small brook.		2500	285.1
1907.2	▲	Mt. Success summit, alpine meadows on north side.		3565	283.7
1907.8	Y📷	Junction with Success Trail.		3170	283.1
1909.1	State Line	New Hampshire–Maine State Line		2972	281.8
1909.6	◊Y▲ ⌐(8) ⌣☾☂	Junction with Carlo Col Trail leads to (0.3W) **Carlo Col Shelter and campsite**, water (spring) is located left of the lean-to, two single and one double tent platforms, privy, bear box. 25.0◄18.9◄5.2◄►4.4►9.5►16.4	N 44 29.321, W 71 00.970	2945	281.3
1910.0	📷	Mt. Carlo summit, 360 degree views.		3565	280.9
1910.6		Sag between Mt. Carlo and West Peak of Goose Eye Mtn.		3165	280.3
1911.4	📷	Goose Eye Trail to Goose Eye Mountain (West Peak), (0.1W) to summit		3854	279.5
1911.7	Y	Junction with south fork of Wright Trail.		3659	279.2
1911.8	▲📷	Goose Eye Mountain summit (East Peak)		3794	279.1
1911.9	Y	Junction of north fork of Wright Trail.		3466	279.0
1913.0	📷	Goose Eye Mountain (North Peak)		3675	277.9
1913.4		Tree line on North Peak of Goose Eye Mtn.		3320	277.5

NoBo	Features	Description	GPS	Elev	SoBo
1914.0	♦⛺ ⌂(12) ⌣(☾☂	300 feet east to **Full Goose Shelter and camps**, water (stream) is located behind shelter, three single and one double tent platforms, privy, bear box. 23.3◄9.6◄4.4◄►5.1►12.0►15.5	N 44 31.506, W 70 58.884	3030	276.9
1914.5	▲	Fulling Mill Mountain (South Peak)		3395	276.4
1914.6		Tree line of South Peak of Goose Eye Mtn.		3400	276.3
1915.5	Y	Mahoosuc Notch Trail, Mahoosuc Notch (west end)		2400	275.4
1916.6	♦⛺	Mahoosuc Notch (east end), Bull Branch		2150	274.4
1917.1	♦	Cross brook, Mahoosuc Notch Two.		2593	273.8
1918.2	Y	Mahoosuc Arm Summit, Joe May Cut-off Trail Jct		3765	272.7
1918.8		Cross Speck Pond Brook, outlet of Speck Pond		3430	272.1
1919.1	♦Y⛺ ⌂(8)(☾☂$	Junction with Speck Pond Trail. **AMC Speck Pond Shelter and campsite**, NO FIRES. Water (spring) is located (0.1) west on the blue blazed trail behind the caretaker's yurt, three single and three double tent platforms, bear box. Overnight/caretaker fee. Speck Pond is the highest body of water in Maine. 14.7◄9.5◄5.1◄►6.9►10.4►20.9	N 44 33.879, W 70 58.416	3500	271.8
1919.7	♦	Sag with intermittent spring.		3855	271.2
1919.8	Y🎒📷	Junction with Old Speck Trail and Grafton Loop Trail, (0.3E) to observation tower		3985	271.1

NoBo	Features	Description	GPS	Elev	SoBo
1920.0		Top of an old slide now overgrown with brush.		4017	270.9
1922.2	📷	Several knobs on the north shoulder of Old Speck.		3718	268.7
1922.5	Y	Junction with Eyebrow Trail, upper junction		2480	268.4
1922.6	♦	Cross brook, last water for the next 3.5 miles south		2500	268.3
1923.4	♦	Cross small brook		1760	267.5
1923.6	Y	Junction with Eyebrow Trail, lower junction		1530	267.3
1923.7	(☾🔥⛺ P(50) ★★★★★	Cross **ME. 26**, Grafton Notch.	N 44 35.388, W 70 56.806	1495	267.2

⛺🏠⛺🍴 ⊕🚿🛏 (12.8E) **Stony Brook Camping** 207-824-2836. (www.stonybrookrec.com) tent site $28, lean-to $33. Will shuttle from Grafton Notch for a fee. Pool, miniature golf, zip line, rec room, campstore, shower, laundry, free WiFi, swimming. Location: (12.2E) on Hwy 26, then left (0.6) miles on Route 2. Mail drops for guests: 42 Powell Place, Hanover, ME 04237.

Bethel, ME 04217 (17.9E) Directions: (12.2E) to Rt 2, right (5.7) miles on Rt 2.

📮   **PO** M-F 9am-4pm, Sa 10am-12:30pm. 207-824-2668.

🛏🏠- 🛏⊕🖥   **Chapman Inn** 207-824-2657. (www.chapmaninn.com) Bunk space $35 includes shower and full breakfast, $25 without breakfast. Rooms $69 and up, include breakfast. Kitchen privileges, $6 laundry, free WiFi. Mail drops for guests: PO Box 1067, Bethel, ME 04217.

⛺🛏⊕   **Bethel Outdoor Adventure** 207-824-4224. (www.betheloutdooradventure.com) $22 campsites, walking distance of Bethel. Laundry, free WiFi. Will shuttle to and from Grafton Notch tail head $45 group each way (one way).

🍴   **Pat's Pizza** 207-824-3637. M-F 11am-9pm.

NoBo	Features	Description	GPS	Elev	SoBo
	✗	**Sudbury Inn Restaurant & Pub**, 207-824-2174. (www.thesudburyinn.com) $89 and up, higher depending on the season, includes a full country breakfast. Restaurant is Thurs-Sat 5:30-9 and Pub is Daily 11:30am-9:30pm.			
	🍴	**Bethel Shop N Save** 207-824-2121. (www.bethelfoodliner.com) M-Th 8am-8pm, F-Sa 8am-9pm, Su 8am-7pm.			
	🏃 ◈	**True North Adventureware** 207-824-2201. (www.truenorthadventureware.com) AT Passport location. M-Th 10am-6pm, F-Sa 9am-6pm, Su 10am-5pm. Full service outdoor store, clothing, gear and footwear. Trekking pole repair, warranty sock replacement, Coleman, alcohol by the ounce and canisters, freeze dried foods, WiFi.			
	🐾	**Bethel Animal Hospital** 207-824-2212. (www.bethelanimalhospital.com) M-Th 8am-6pm, F 8am-5pm, Sa 8am-12pm, Su closed.			
1923.8	Y	Junction with Table Rock Trail (lower junction).		1556	267.1
1924.1		Bottom of steep slope.		1841	266.8
1924.5	Y📷	Junction with Table Rock Trail, upper junction, views at Table Rock.		2125	266.4
1926.0	♦Y⚑(4) ⊏(8)⌣☾	(0.1E) **Baldpate Lean-to**, water (stream) next to lean-to, 4 tent sites, privy. 16.4◄12.0◄6.9◄▶3.5▶14.0▶26.8	N 44 35.907, W 70 54.697	2645	264.9
1926.8	📷	Baldpate Mountain (West Peak)		3662	264.1
1927.4		Bottom of sag between East and West Peaks of Baldpate Mountain.		3471	263.5
1927.7	Y📷	Baldpate Mountain (East Peak), Grafton Loop Trail Junction		3812	263.3
1928.2		Little Baldpate Mountain		3442	262.7
1928.3		Tree line on north side of Little Baldpate Mountain.		3303	262.6
1929.5	♦⚑(5) ⊏(6)⌣☾	**Frye Notch Lean-to**, water (Frye Brook) is located in front of the lean-to, 5 tent sites, privy. 15.5◄10.4◄3.5◄▶10.5▶23.3▶31.6	N 44 37.663, W 70 54.048	2280	261.4
1930.0		Surplus Mountain, highpoint on NE ridge		2875	260.9
1931.4		Sharp turn in trail on north east ridge of Surplus Mountain.		2554	259.5
1933.0		South rim of Dunn Notch.		1615	257.9
1933.2	♦Y♨	Dunn Notch and Falls on side trail (0.2) west. West Branch Ellis River, ford.		1350	257.7
1933.9	♦	Cross small brook.		1435	257.0
1934.0	Y⚑⚑ P(6) ★★★★★	Junction with Cascade Trail. Cross **East B Hill Road**, not an ATC approved camping spot.	N 44 40.103, W 70 53.589	1485	256.9

East B Hill Rd Andover, ME 04216 (8.0E). See map of Andover, ME.

✉	**PO** M-F 9:15am-12pm & 1pm-4:15pm, Sa 9am-12pm. 207-392-4571.	
🏠🛏◈	**Pine Ellis Lodging** 207-392-4161. (www.pineellislodging.com)	
🍴⛺🖥	AT Passport location. Host Ilene Trainor.	
🍴🍴🚐🖥	No pets. Bunks $25PP, private rooms $45S, $60D, $75 triple. Stays include kitchen privileges, laundry and morning coffee, computer avaialble to use, free WiFi. Trail head pickup for a fee, call in advance, slackpack Grafton Notch to Rangeley, and shuttles to nearby towns, airport and bus station. Multi-day slackpacking packages for groups. Resupply of trail snacks and meals, coleman, denatured by the ounce, canister fuel. Mail drops for guests: (USPS) PO Box 12 or (UPS) 20 Pine Street, Andover. ME 04216.	
🛏⚑	**Paul's AT Camp for Hikers Stay** in a rustic cabin for $60 for 4. Located 3 miles from Andover. Stay includes, water, electricty in the cabin and shower house, one round trip shuttle from the hostel. "Great for families and friends meeting up with hikers". Contact Pine Ellis for more information.	
🍴✗🍵	**Andover General Store** 207-392-4172. Food to order off grill, pizza, ice cream. M-Sa 5am-8pm, Su 6am-8pm, in summer month they close at 9pm.	
🍴✗	**Mills Market** 207-392-3062. groceries, deli meats and cheese. Friday Pizza Special 16" one topping pizza and any 2 liter soda for $9.99. M-Th 5am-9pm, F-Sa 5am-10pm, Su 5am-9pm.	
✗ ◈ 🚐⚑🖥	**Little Red Hen** 207-392-2253. (www.littleredhendiner.com) AT Passport location. Mexican buffet Thursday night, prime rib & baby back ribs and other specials Friday night, Italian buffet Saturday night. Ask about tenting. Laundry & shower facility available $5 each, free WiFi. M closed, Tu 6:30am-2pm, W 6:30am-2pm, Th 6:30am-2pm & 5pm-8pm, F 6:30am-8pm, Sa - 6:30am-8pm, Su - 7am-2pm. Mail drops: 28 south Main Street, Andover. ME 04216.	
🖥	**Andover Public Library** 207-392-4841. (www.andover.lib.me.us) M closed, Tu-W 1pm-4:30pm, Th 1pm-4:30pm & 6pm-8pm, Sa 1pm-4:30pm, Su closed.	
■	**Donna Gifford** massage therapist, 207-357-5686. Call for rates. Free pickup at Hostel and return to Hostels in Andover.	
🏠◈🖥🚐	**The Cabin** 207-392-1333. (www.thecabininmaine.com) Located (2.8) from Andover. AT Passport location. Alumni hikers welcome; by reservation only. Hiker kitchen, laundry, computer available for use, free WiFi.	

Andover, ME

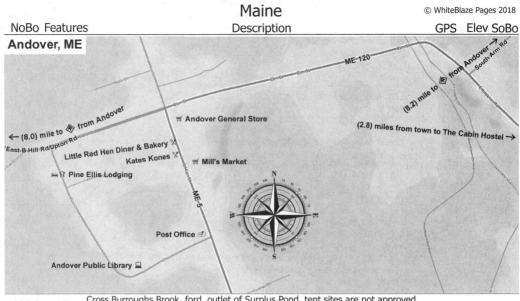

NoBo	Features	Description	GPS	Elev	SoBo
1935.8	♦⚑	Cross Burroughs Brook, ford, outlet of Surplus Pond, tent sites are not approved camping spots.		2050	255.1
1935.9	⚑	Cross gravel logging road		2050	255.0
1937.8		Southern shoulder of Wyman Mountain.		2381	253.1
1938.7		Wyman Mountain (north peak)		2945	252.2
1939.6	♦	Cross small brook.		2869	251.3
1940.0	♦⚑⊑(6) ⌣((📷	**Hall Mountain Lean-to**, water (spring) is located south of the lean-to on the AT, tent sites available, privy. Trail to view behind shelter. 20.9◄14.0◄10.5◄►12.8►21.1►32.3	N 44 42.050, W 70 49.506	2635	250.9
1941.3	♦	Cross small brook just below cascade.		1196	249.6
1941.4	♦	Sawyer Notch, cross Sawyer Brook, ford		1095	249.5
1942.3		Moody Mountain		2440	248.6
1943.0		Saddle between Sawyer and Moody Mountain.		2229	247.9
1943.4	♦	Cross small brook.		2266	247.5
1943.6		North shoulder of Sawyer Mountain.		2136	247.3
1944.1	♦⚑P(6) ★★★★★	Cross Black Brook and **South Arm Road**, ford, campsite.	N 44 43.291, W 70 47.148	1410	246.8
	Andover, ME. (8.2E) See NOBO mile 1934.0 See map of Andover, ME.				
1944.7	📷	Views of Black Brook Notch below.		2401	246.2
1946.4		Base of western slope of Sawyer Mountain.		2742	244.5
1946.9	▲📷	Old Blue Mountain summit		3600	244.0
1947.3		Base of northern slope of Old Blue Mountain.		3215	243.6
1948.4		Reach Col. with old growth.		3051	242.5

NoBo	Features	Description	GPS	Elev	SoBo
1950.1	♦Y	Junction with Bemis Stream Trail.		3350	240.8
1951.1		Bemis Mountain (West Peak)		3592	239.8
1951.2	▲	Bemis Mountain East Peak		3532	239.7
1952.4	▲	Bemis Mountain Third Peak.		3115	238.5
1952.8	◊ ▲(4) ⊏(8) ⏝ ⊄	(0.1E) **Bemis Mountain Lean-to**, water small (spring) is located to left of lean-to, 4 tent sites, privy.	N 44 48.615, W 70 45.354		
		26.8◄23.3◄12.8◄► 8.3► 19.5►28.4		2790	238.1
1954.3		Bemis Range (Second Peak), open ledges		2915	236.6
1955.2	▲	Bemis Mountain First Peak.		2604	235.7
1955.7	🔾	Knob on east ends of Bemis Range.		2608	235.2
1955.9		Tree line at north end of series of knobs.		2358	235.0
1956.3	♦	Small spring.		1747	234.6
1956.4	♦▲▲ P(3)	Cross gravel road, former rail bed, not an ATC approved camping spot.	N 44 50.080, W 70 43.454	1550	234.5
1956.6	♦	Cross Bemis Stream, ford		1495	234.3
1957.4	🔾▲ P(30) ★★★★★	Cross **ME. 17**, view of Mooselookmeguntic Lake. Parking at the scenic overlook.	N 44 50.259, W 70 42.610	2200	233.5

Oquossoc, ME (10.8W)

🖂	**PO** M–F 8am–10am & 2:15pm–4:15pm, Sa 9am–12pm. 207-864-3685.
🏪🏧	**Oquossoc Grocery** (207-864-3662. (www.oquossocgrocery.com) Deli, bakery, coleman fuel. M-Th 6am-8pm, F-Sa 6am-9pm, Su 6am-8pm.
✗	**Gingerbread House** (207-864-3602. (www.gingerbreadhouserestaurant.net) Breakfast 7am-11am, lunch 11:30am-3pm, dinner 5pm-9pm. Pub menu available 3pm-9pm. Sunday Breakfast until 11:30am. Ice cream available all day.
	Four Seasons Café 207-864-2020. M-Su 10:30am–10pm. Serves lunch and dinner.

NoBo	Features	Description	GPS	Elev	SoBo
1958.2		Spruce Mountain		2530	232.7
1959.0	♦	North shore of Moxie Pond		2400	231.9
1960.1	🔾	Bates Ledge. View south over Long Pond.		2713	230.8
1960.8	♦⬳	Northeastern shore of Long Pond, sandy beach		2330	230.1
1961.1	◊ ▲(1) ⊏(8) ⏝⊄⬳	78 yards west to **Sabbath Day Pond Lean-to**, water (piped spring) is located near pond in front of lean-to, 1 tent platform and tent sites available, privy. Sandy beach (0.3) south on AT, swimming.	N 44 50.457, W 70 39.723		
		31.6◄21.1◄8.3◄► 11.2►20.1►28.1		2390	229.8
1961.6		Cross Houghton Fire Road		2300	229.3
1962.8	⟙	Power line.		2788	228.1
1963.3		Unnamed high point.		2938	227.6
1965.7	♦▲⏝⊄	Little Swift River Pond, tent sites available, privy.		2460	225.2
1966.9	♦	Cross Chandler Mill Stream, outlet of boreal bog		2150	224.0
1968.4	♦	Skirt western shore of South Pond.		2174	222.5
1969.4	🔾	View at top of steep slope.		1986	221.5

| 1970.5 | ▲P(20) ★★★★★ | Cross **ME. Route 4**. | N 44 53.228, W 70 32.465 | 1700 | 220.4 |

⛺🏕🍴🚐   (0.3W) **The Hiker Hut** 207-897-8984, 207-670-8095. hikerhut@gmail.com.
🖪 $25PP includes bunk with mattress, pillows, shuttles into Rangeley. Extra meals $7, laundry $3. Private couples hut $50. Quiet, restful sanctuary along the Sandy River. Massage therapist on hand. Shuttles and slackpacking available, small resupply shop with snacks and fuel.
Mail drops: ($5 non-guest fee): C/O Steve Lynch 2 Pine Rd. Sandy River Plantation, ME 04970.

Rangeley, ME (9.0W). See map of Rangeley, ME.
✉   **PO** M-F 9:30am-12:30pm & 1:30pm-4:15pm, Sa 9:30am-12pm. 207-864-2233.

🛏🏕◈Ⓢ **Fieldstone Cottages** 207-670-5507
🚐🍴P🖪 AT Passport location.
No Pets. New location and new name, same owners as the former Farmhouse Inn. Located right at the edge of town. Not a party place. Features a hiker bunkroom for $35PP, includes shower with towel and return to Route 4 trail head.
Nice clean facility with lounge area. Free WiFi. Private Cabin rentals available.
Rides back to trail head without stay $10PP depending on availability.
Ask about slackpacking options.
Mail drops for guests: 2342 Main St. Rangeley, Maine, 04970.

🛏🚐🖪 **Town & Lake Motel** 207-864-3755. (www.rangeleytownandlake.com) Ask about hiker rate. Plus, $10.00 a person over two people. Pets $10. Canoes for guest use.
Mail drops for guests: PO Box 47, Rangeley, ME 04970.

🛏◈✕🚐 **Rangeley Inn & Tavern** 207-864-3341. (www.therangeleyinn.com)
Rates start at $150 in summer, $125 in fall (after Oct 20). Complimentary breakfast. Direct booking discount, kayaks/canoe, free wifi, free calls to US and Canada.

🛏✕🚐 **Rangeley Saddleback Inn** 207-864-3434. (www.rangeleysaddlebackinn.com) $120 and up, prices very depending on the season, includes continental breakfast, pets $10 includes . Ride to and from trail head are sometimes available.

🛏🚐 **North Country Inn B&B** 207-864-2440 (www.northcountrybb.com) info@northcountrybb.com $99-149 includes full breakfast, specials mid-week and off-season. Multi-night discount.

🍴✕ **Moose Loop Cafe** 207-864-3000. (www.rangeleysmooseloop.com) Café, Deli, bakery and rental. M-Su 9am-5pm.

✕ **Sarge's Sports Pub & Grub** 207-864-5616. Serves lunch and dinner also has a bar. M-Su 11am-1pm. Entertainment on weekends, outdoor deck. 2454 Main St.

✕ **Moose Alley** 207-864-9955. (www.moosealleymaine.com) Bowling, billiards, darts, dance floor, food.

🛒🍴 **IGA Supermarket** 207-864-5089. (www.rangeleyiga.com) ATM. Summer hours M-Su 7am-9pm. Winter hours M-Su 7am-8pm.

🚶◈ **Ecopelagicon** 207-864-2771. (www.ecopelagicon.com)
🍴🚐🖪 AT Passport location.
Good selection of hiking gear & accessories. Fuel (canister, alcohol & white gas by the oz.) freeze dried foods, snacks, water purification, Leki poles & warranty work, Darn Tough, Superfeet, Osprey & Big Agnes gear, first aid, rain gear and lots more. Free charging station, WIFI, water fill-up. Ask about shuttles.
Mail drops: USPS- PO Box 899, UPS/FedEx- 7 Pond Street, Rangeley, ME 04970.

🚶 **Alpine Shop** 207-864-3741. (www.alpineshoprangeley.com) Clothing and some hiking gear, fuel by the ounce. M-Th 9am-5pm, F-Sa 9am-6pm, Su 10am-5pm.

🚶 **Back Woods** 207-864-2335 Clothing, some gear. M-Sa 9am-5pm, Su 10am-4pm.

🚿 **Rangeley Family Medicine** 207-864-3303. (www.rangeleychc.org) Location: 42 Dallas Hill Road. $5 shower, towel provided. M-Th 5am-8pm, F 5am-7:30pm, Sa-Su 8-2.

Rangeley, ME

(8.1) miles from downtown to 🔆 ↘
🛒 Rangeley IGA

NoBo	Features	Description	GPS	Elev	SoBo
1970.6	♦⌒	Cross Sandy River on footbridge.		1595	220.3
1971.1	⚠	Cross gravel road.		1750	219.8
1971.7	⚠	Cross old logging road.		2011	219.2
1972.0	♦	Cross brook.		2102	218.9
1972.3	♦🅰(5) ⊏(8)⌣☾	200 yards east to **Piazza Rock Lean-to**, water (stream) that passes through campsite, 5 tent platforms, privy (two seater). 32.3◄19.5◄11.2◄►8.9►16.9►35.5	N 44 54.253, W 70 31.798	2080	218.6
1972.5	Y	Side trail leads to some small boulder caves.		2163	218.4
1973.2	♦	Skirt Ethel Pond		2200	217.7
1973.6	♦	Cross Saddleback Stream		2350	217.3
1973.7		Cross bog known ad Mud Pond.		2729	217.2
1974.2	♦	Cross Moose and Deer Pond Outlet near Eddy Pond, last water for the next 6 miles north		2616	216.7
1974.4	⚠	Cross gravel logging road, gravel		2625	216.5
1975.2		Tree line on south slope of Saddleback Mountain, above tree line for the next 2.9 miles north		3700	215.7
1976.2	▲📷	Saddleback Mountain summit		4120	214.7
1976.8		Sag between Saddleback Mountain and The Horn.		3565	214.1
1977.8	▲📷	The Horn summit		4041	213.1
1978.1		Tree line, above tree line for the next 2.9 miles south		3620	212.8
1978.5	♦🅰(8)☾	Redington Stream campsite, (0.2W) to water, 8 tent sites, privy.		3170	212.4
1979.3		Base of Saddleback Junior.		3094	211.6
1979.8	▲	Saddleback Junior, open summit.		3655	211.1

Elevation profile with labeled features (left to right): Poplar Ridge Shelter, Orbeton Brook/Redington Rd, Sluice Brook, Perham Stream, Lone Mtn, Mt Abraham Trail, Spaulding Mtn Shelter, Spaulding Mtn, AT Completion Plaque, Sugarloaf Mtn Trail, Carrabassett River/Caribou Valley Rd, Crocker Cirque Campsite, Crocker Mtn, Crocker Col, Crocker Mtn, Stratton, ME/ME Hwy 16/27, Stratton Brook Rd, Cranberry Stream, Cranberry Pond/Bigelow Trail, Cranberry Mtn, Horns Pond Shelter, South Horn Mtn, Bigelow Horn Col.

NoBo	Features	Description	GPS	Elev	SoBo
1980.2	♦	Cross brook, last water for the next 6 miles south		3200	210.7
1981.2	◊ ⚑ ⊏ (6) ☾ 🄫 📷	53 yards west to **Poplar Ridge Lean-to**, water (brook) is located in front of lean-to, tent sites available, privy. 28.4◄20.1◄8.9◄► 8.0► 26.6► 36.8	N 44 58.204, W 70 26.757	2920	209.7
1981.4	📷	Open ledges of Poplar Ridge.		3120	209.5
1983.9	♦	Cross Orbeton Stream, ford		1550	207.0
1984.0	⛟	Cross gravel road, old rail bed; north bound turn East 100 ft. to re-enter woods		1650	206.9
1984.7	♦	Cross Sluice Brook		2145	206.2
1985.4	⛟	Cross logging road.		2300	205.5
1985.9	♦⚑P(3)	Cross logging road, Perham Stream nearby	N 44 58.496, W 70 22.512	2300	205.0
1987.0	⛰	Lone Mountain summit, wooded.		3280	203.9
1988.1	Y📷	Junction with Mt. Abraham Trail. (1.7E) to summit and view		3184	202.8
1989.2	◊⚑⊏(8) ☾	150 feet west to **Spaulding Mountain Lean-to**, water small (spring) is located to right of lean-to, tent sites available, privy. 28.1◄16.9◄8.0◄► 18.6► 28.8► 36.5	N 44 59.746, W 70 20.484	3140	201.7
1990.0	Y⛰📷	Northwestern shoulder of Spaulding Mountain, side trail (0.1) east to summit.		4010	200.9
1990.7	⊙	**Bronze plaque**, 1937 completion of the final two miles of the AT.		3500	200.2
1992.1	Y📷	Junction with Sugarloaf Mountain Trail, Maine's third-highest peak, (0.3E) to summit		3540	198.8
1992.7	♦	Cross small brook.		3612	198.2
1993.5	📷	Open rim of deep ravine, 500 foot drop. Good views.		3219	197.4
1993.9		Base of northwest slope of Sugarloaf Mountain.		2457	197.0
1994.3	♦	Cross South Branch Carrabassett River, ford		2100	196.6
1994.4	♦⚑⚑ P(10)	Cross **Caribou Valley Road**, gravel, not an ATC approved camping spot.	N 45 02.377, W 70 20.680	2220	196.5
1995.4	♦Y⚑☾	(0.2E) Crocker Cirque campsite, stream, tent platform and tent sites available, privy.		2710	195.5
1996.5	📷	South Crocker Mountain, 150 feet west to summit		4040	194.4
1997.0		Saddle between North and South Peaks of Crocker Mountain.			193.9
1997.5	⛰	North Crocker Mountain, wooded summit		4228	193.4
1997.8	📷	Views of the Bigelow Range and Stratton.		3749	193.1
1998.5	♦	Cross small stream.		3300	192.4
2000.6	♦	Cross small stream, in stand of large white birch trees.		2500	190.3
2002.7	⚑P(20) ★★★★★	Cross **ME. 27**.	N 45 06.137, W 70 21.351	1450	188.2
	🛒	(2E) **Mountainside Grocers** 207-237-2248. M-Su 7:30am–8pm.			

Stratton, ME 04982 (5.0W)

     📪   **PO** M-F 8:30am-1pm & 1:30pm-4pm, Sa 8:30am-11am. 207-246-6461.

Maine

NoBo Features		Description	GPS	Elev	SoBo
	⇐ ⊓ ◈ 💻☕🛏P 🔳	**Stratton Motel** 207-246-4171 (www.thestrattonmotel.com) AT Passport location. $30 bunk, $70 private room. Shuttle from trail head $5PP (when available). The same owners as the former Farmhouse Inn of Rangeley (now known as Fieldstone Cottages). Canister fuel and fuel by the ounce, computer available for use, free WiFi. Parking avaibale. Shuttle range Gorham NH to Monson and to airports, train, bus and car rental hubs in Portland, Bangor, Farmington, Augusta and Waterville. Mail drops: PO Box 284, Stratton, ME 04982; FedEx & UPS 162 Main St., Stratton, ME 04982.			
	⇐ ◈ ✕ ☕🍽🔳	**White Wolf Inn & Restaurant** 207-246-2922. (www.thewhitewolfinn.com) AT Passport location. Hiker rate $59 mid-week, $65 weekends and holidays, $10EAP. Pets $15, free WiFi, ATM. **Restaurant**: M 11am-8:30pm, Tu closed, W 4am-8:30pm, Th-Su 11am-8:30pm. Serves lunch and din- ner, breakfast on weekends. Home of the 8oz Wolf Burger; Fish Fry Friday. Visa, M/C accepted $20 min. Mail drops for guests (non-guest fee): Main Street, PO Box 590, Stratton, ME 04982.			
	⇐ ☕🔳	**Spillover Motel** 207-246-6571. (www.spillovermaine.com) $89 and up, pets $15, includes continental breakfast. Full kitchen for use by guests, gas grill free WiFi. Mail drops for guests: PO Box 427, Stratton, ME 04982.			
	⇐ ✕	**Stratton Plaza Hotel** 207-246-2000. (www.strattonplazahotel.com) Dining, some rooms. Tuesday: Pitcher and Pizza $10. M closed, Tu-Sa 11am-1am, Su closed.			
	🛒 🍽	**Fotter's Market** 207-246-2401. (www.fottersmarket.com) M-Th 8am-7pm, F-Sa 8am-8pm, Su 9am- 5pm. Coleman, alcohol by the ounce, ATM.			
	🛒✕☕🍽	**Flagstaff General Store** 207-246-2300. Deli, hot coffee, snacks, subs, pizza, salads, fried foods, canis- ter fuel, free WiFi, ATM. M-F 6am-9pm, Sa 7am-9pm, Su 7am-7pm.			
	💻 ☕	**Stratton Public Library** 207-246-4401. (www.stratton.lib.me.us) M 10am-5pm Tu 1pm-5pm, W 10am- 5pm Th 1pm-5pm, F 10am-5pm, Sa 9am-1pm, Su closed. WiFi.			
2003.5	⚠P(10)	Cross **Stratton Brook Pond Road**.	N 45 06.708, W 70 20.962	1250	187.4
2003.6	⚠	Cross logging road, gravel.		1290	187.3
2003.7	⬦〰	Cross Stratton Brook on footbridge		1230	187.2
2004.3	⚠	Cross tote road.		1356	186.6
2004.6	⬦⚠(3) 〰☾	Cranberry Stream campsite, 3 tent sites available, privy.		1350	186.3
2005.9	⬦Y	Junction with Bigelow Range Trail, Cranberry Pond (0.2W)		2400	185.0
2006.0		Slab cave system.		2246	184.9
2006.8	Y	Side trail to views of Sugarloaf and Crooker Mountains.		2957	184.1
2007.0	📷	Views of Bigelow, Sugarloaf, Horns, and Crooker Mountains.		3278	183.9
2007.5	Y	Side trail to overlook of Horns Pond.		3278	183.4
2007.6	Y	Junction with Horns Pond Trail leads (3.9) to Stratton Brook Pond Road.		3200	183.3
2007.8	⬦⚠⌐(16) 〰☾	52 yards east to **Horns Pond Lean-to's**, two lean-to's, water is located north of the lean-tos or Horns Pond, tent sites available, privy. Caretaker, no fee. 35.5◄26.6◄18.6◄▶ 10.2▶ 17.9▶ 27.9	N 45 08.633, W 70 19.783	3160	183.1
2008.1	⬦	Box spring		3400	182.8
2008.2	Y	Side Trail to North Horn, (0.2W) to summit		3792	182.7
2008.3	⛰📷	South Horn summit		3831	182.6

NoBo	Features	Description	GPS	Elev	SoBo

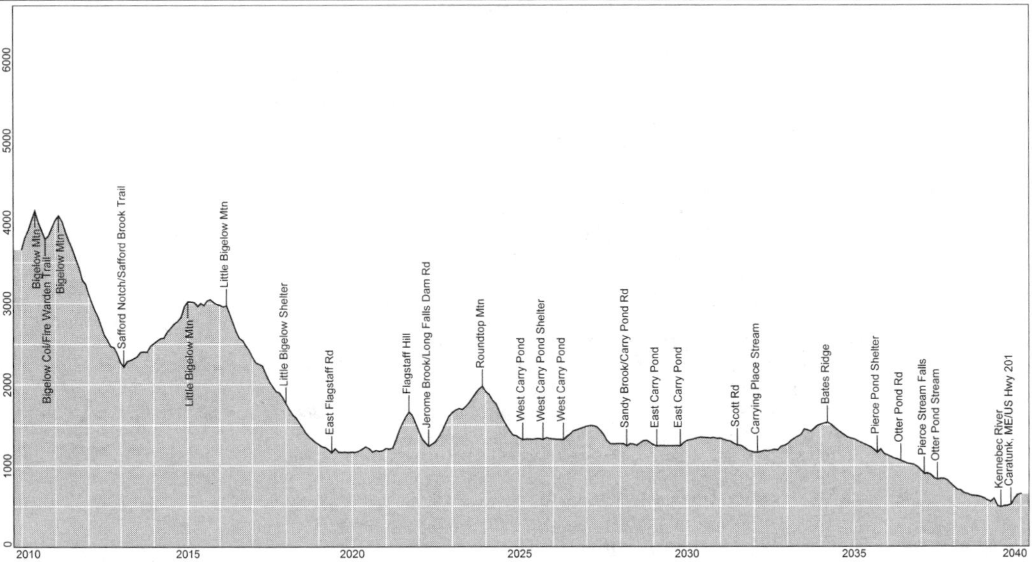

NoBo	Features	Description	GPS	Elev	SoBo
2010.4		Bigelow Mountain (West Peak), 260 degree views.		4145	180.5
2010.7	Y (6)	Bigelow Col, Fire Warden's Trail, Avery Memorial campsite, 6 tent platforms available, privy.		3850	180.2
2010.9		Spring		3900	180.0
2011.1		Bigelow Mountain, Avery Peak		4090	179.8
2011.9	Y	Side trail to Old Man's Head.		3187	179.0
2013.0	Y	Junction with Safford Brook Trail leading (2.2) to East Flagstaff Road and (0.3) more to Flagstaff Lake.		2260	177.9
2013.1	(2)	(0.3E) Safford Notch and campsite, 2 tent platforms and tent sites available, privy.		2230	177.8
2014.9		Little Bigelow Mountain (west end)		3035	176.0
2016.3		Little Bigelow Mountain (east end)		3040	174.6
2018.0	(2) (8)	(0.1W) **Little Bigelow Lean-to**, water (spring) is located 50 yards in front of the lean-to, 2 tent platforms and tent sites available, privy. Swimming in "the Tubs" along the side trail. 36.8◄28.8◄10.2◄►7.7►17.7►27.4	N 45 08.347, W 70 11.496	1760	172.9
2019.4	P	Cross **East Flagstaff Road**, 80 yards east to parking	N 45 08.077, W 70 10.282	1200	171.5
		Mountain Village Farm B&B 207-265-2030. (www.mountainvillageinn.com) Room rates range from $99 to $140 double occupancy with private bath and full breakfast included. Round trip shuttle $50 for up to four hikers. Pets welcome. Bed & Breakfast on an organic farm; ask about work for stay. Town center within walking distance has grocery, laundry and restaurants. Slackpack the Bigelows (Stratton to East Flagstaff Rd, either direction) $50 per car load. Mail drops: PO Box 216, Kingfield, ME 04947."			
2019.5	★★★★★	Cross **Bog Brook Road**, Flagstaff Lake, inlet. (0.2W) to Lake		1150	171.4
	Kingfield, ME (25.7E) see NOBO mile 2019.4				
2020.5	(9)	Campsites, privy.		1210	170.4
2022.2	P(10) ★★★★★	Cross **Long Falls Dam Road**.	N 45 09.363, W 70 09.264	1225	168.7
	Kingfield, ME (27.0E) see NOBO mile 2019.4				
2022.3		Cross Jerome Brook.		1300	168.6
2022.6		Cross logging road, gravel		1400	168.3
2023.9		Northern side of Roundtop Mountain		1760	167.0
2024.7		Cross brook.		1604	166.2
2025.0		South west corner of West Carry Pond (west side)		1320	165.9
2025.7	(2) (8)	72 yards east to **West Carry Pond Lean-to**, water (spring house) is located to the left of the lean-to or West Carry Pond, tent sites available, privy. Swimming in pond. 36.5◄17.9◄7.7◄►10.0►19.7►28.7	N 45 09.478, W 70 05.984	1340	165.2
2026.4	Y	West Carry Pond (east side), side trail west to Arnold Point Beach on Arnold Trail		1320	164.5

NoBo	Features	Description	GPS	Elev	SoBo
2027.9	⌒	Arnold Swamp, many bog bridges		1255	163.0
2028.1	⚑	Intersection with **Long Pond Road**.		1250	162.8
2028.3	⬧⌒⚑	Cross Sandy Stream and **Middle Carry Pond Road**, bridge		1229	162.6
2029.1	⚑	Cross East Carry Pond Logging Road, gravel		1250	161.8
2029.3	⬧	Western shore of East Carry Pond.		1237	161.6
2029.8	⬧	Northeast shore of East Carry Pond.		1256	161.1
2031.5	⚑	Cross **Scott Road**, main logging road		1300	159.4
2032.2	⬧	North Branch of Carrying Place Stream, ford		1200	158.7
2032.7	⬧	Spring.		1220	158.2
2034.2		Saddle in Bates Ridge.		1526	156.7
2035.7	⬧⚑⛺⌂(6) ⌣☾	67 yards west to **Pierce Pond Lean-to**, water (Pierce Pond), tenting, privy. 27.9◀17.7◀10.0◀▶ 9.7▶ 18.7▶ 22.8	N 45 14.420, W 70 03.360	1150	155.2
2035.8	Y ★★★★★	Side trail leads (0.3) to Harrison's Camps.		1162	155.1
	⇌✗	**Harrison's Pierce Pond Camps** 207-672-3625, 207-612-8184. (www.harrisonspiercepondcamps.com) May-Nov, 7 days. Bed, shower, and 12-pancake breakfast $40. For breakfast only, ($9-12 served 7am), **reserve a seat the day befor**e. Cash only, no reservations for overnight stay. Okay to get water at camp and dispose of trash. Shortest route to camp is west from the north end of blue-blaze shelter loop trail.			
2035.9	⬧⌒	Cross Wooden Dam, outlet of Pierce Pond		1120	155.0
2036.0	Y⛄	Side trail at top of waterfall.		1145	154.9
2036.1	Y	Trail to Harrison's Pierce Pond camps (0.1E)		1100	154.8
2036.4	⚑P	Cross **Otter Pond Road**, gravel	N 45 14.331, W 70 02.780	1080	154.5
2036.9	Y⛄	Side trail leads (0.1) east to top of waterfall.		1042	154.0
2037.1	⬧Y⛄	Side trail leads (0.1) east to pool at base of waterfalls, Pierce Pond Stream.		850	153.8
2037.5	⬧⌒	Cross Otter Pond Stream, bridge		900	153.4
2038.1	📷⛄	Ledge overlooking several high waterfalls.		785	152.8
2039.4	⬧ ★★★★★	Cross Kennebec River, ferry **See Schedule below**		490	151.5

> The ferry is free for hikers during open hours through the funding support of ATC, ALDHA and the dam operator. Management of the ferry is by ATC and MATC.
> Operated by Greg Caruso of Maine Guide Service, LLC.
> His contact is 207-858-3627, gcaruso@myfairpoint.net.
> **The Kennebec Ferry schedule for 2018** is:
> 25 May - 30 June, 9 am–11 am
> 1 July - 30 September, 9 am–2 p.m
> 1 October - 8 October, 9:00 am – 11:00 am
> Off hours, hikers can schedule a crossing for $50, 207-858-3627.

	◼	**Cheryl Anderson** 207-672-3997 Pivately run for fee ferry service.			
2039.7	⚑P(20) ★★★★★	Cross **U.S. 201**.	N 45 14.301, W 69 59.769	520	151.2

US 201 Caratunk, ME (0.3E)

	✉	**PO** M-F 2pm-4pm, Sa 7:30am-11:15am, 207-672-3416 Post office accepts debit cards with limited cash.			
	⇌◈ 🏪🚗🖥	**Caratunk House** (150 yds from AT) 207-672-4349. AT Passport location. Open 1 June and closed 30 Sept. A full service hiker B&B with a resupply store, "One Braid's" family style breakfasts. Ask about shuttles. Mail drops: 218 Main St Caratunk Maine 04925 or PO Box 98.			
	⇌⌂◈✗ 🍴⛄⛺🖥 ⛟🖥	**(1.4E) The Sterling Inn** 207-672-3333. maineskeptsecret@yahoo.com (www.mainesterlinginn.com) Open year-round. AT Passport location. Bunk room $30, private $45S, $64D (shared bed) $108/4, all rates includes sales tax, breakfast buffet, shower and laundry. Multi-night discount, pets welcome. Resupply, showers ($2.50) and laundry ($5) available even if you are not staying, computer available for use, free WiFi, long distance phone. **Caratunk Country Store**; resupply has everything a hiker needs, including fuel by the ounce, canister fuel, batteries and candy bars, ice cream, sodas, and cook yourself options and more. Free shuttle to and from trail head, Post Office and nearby restaurants with stay. Credit and debit cards accepted. Physical address: 1041 Route 201. Mail drops to (also free for non-guests): PO Box 129, Caratunk Maine 04925. Coordinates: N 45 13.146, W 69 59.253			

The Forks, ME (2.0W)

	🛏🏠🅰️🅑	(2.0W) **Northern Outdoors** 800-765-7238. (www.northernoutdoors.com)		
	✗🍴🅑🛁⛵	No pets in campground.		
	💻📷📠	Hikers welcome, free shuttle (it coincides with ferry schedule), use resort facilities with or without stay; hikers receive 30% lodging discount; prices vary, call for rates. Coin laundry, giant hot tub, swimming pool, computer available for use, free WiFi, ATM, food & craft beer in Kennebec River Brewpub. Mail drops: C/O Northern Outdoors, 1771 Route 201, The Forks, ME 04985.		
	🏠🅰️◈	(4.0W) **Three Rivers Trading Post** 207-663-2104. (www.threeriverswhitewater.com)		
	✗🏠📷🍴 📠	Bunks, tenting and restaurant open May-mid Sept. Store open year-round carries variety of packaged food, beer & wine. Bunk $25PP, tenting $12PP, free WiFi, ATM. Rafting trips by reservation. Boatman's Bar & Grill open M-Su 4pm-1am. Mail drops: 2265 US Route 201, The Forks, ME 04985.		
	🏬	(7.6W) **Berry's General Store** 207-663-4461. Open year round. M-Su 5am-7pm, open till 8pm in summer.		

2041.8	🅰️	Sharp turn in trail at tote road.		848	149.1
2042.4	💧	Cross Holly Brook		900	148.5
2043.1	💧	Cross Holly Brook tributary.		1076	147.8
2043.8	🅰️	Cross **Hangtown Road**, gravel logging road. (1.0) east to Pleasant Pond settlement and (3.2) further to Caratunk.		1240	147.1
2044.3	💧	Cross Holly Brook.		1339	146.6
2045.0	🅰️	Cross **Boise—Cascade Logging Road**. (1.4) east to Pleasant Pond settlement and (3.2) further to Caratunk.		1400	145.9
2045.1	🅰️P(10)	Trail head parking area on logging road.	N 45 16.295, W 69 55.411	1462	145.8
2045.4	💧🅰️⛺(6) ⛵🍴	100 yards east to **Pleasant Pond Lean-to**, water small (brook) is located on the path to the lean-to or pond, tent sites available, privy. Beach (0.2) on side trail beyond lean-to. 27.4◀19.7◀9.7◀▶9.0▶13.1▶22.0	N 45 16.274, W 69 55.004	1320	145.5
2045.6	💧Y🍴	Side trail leads (0.2) east to Pleasant Pond Beach, sand beach.		1360	145.3
2046.7	🅰️📷	Pleasant Pond Mountain summit. Signs of old fire tower still visible on summit.		2477	144.2
2051.1	💧	Cross brook.		1098	139.8
2051.5	🕇	Power line.		1010	139.4
2051.6	🅰️P(4)	Junction with road near **Moxie Pond (south end), Joe's Hole, Troutdale Road**.	N 45 14.979, W 69 49.860	970	139.3
2051.7	💧	Cross Baker Stream, ford.		1010	139.2
2052.1	🕇	Power line.		1027	138.8
2052.8	💧	Cross Joe's Hole Brook.		1240	138.1
2054.2	💧🅰️⛵	Cross Bald Mountain Brook, Bald Mountain Brook campsite, tent sites available.		1200	136.7
2054.4	💧🅰️⛺(8) ⛵	(0.1E) **Bald Mountain Brook Lean-to**, water (Bald Mountain Brook) is located in front of lean-to, tent sites available, privy. 28.7◀18.7◀9.0◀▶4.1▶13.0▶25.0	N 45 15.516, W 69 47.967	1280	136.5
2054.5	🅰️P(4)	Cross gravel road.	N 45 15.548, W 69 47.911	1367	136.4
2055.8	Y	Summit bypass trail, recommended in bad weather.		2250	135.1

NoBo	Features	Description	GPS	Elev	SoBo
2056.4	▲📷	Moxie Bald Mountain summit, 360 degree views.		2629	134.5
2056.7	Y	Summit bypass trail, recommended in bad weather.		2490	134.2
2057.4	Y📷	Side trail leads (0.7) west to Moxie Bald Mountain summit.		2320	133.5
2058.5	♦▲⌐(6) ⌣((	100 feet east to **Moxie Bald Lean-to**, water (stream) is located near by or Moxie Bald Pond, tent sites available, privy. 22.8◄13.1◄4.1◄►8.9►20.9►28.3	N 45 16.241, W 69 44.723 1220		132.4
2060.0	▲	Cross gravel road.		1290	130.9
2060.6	♦	Cross Bald Mountain Stream, outlet of Bald Mountain Pond, ford.		1213	130.3
2062.5	▲P(6)	Cross **Bald Mountain Stream Road**, gravel.	N 45 16.580, W 69 41.394	1100	128.4
2064.0	▲	Cross Marble Brook and "Jeep Road".		990	126.9
2064.3	♦	Ford confluence of West Branch Piscataquis River.		900	126.6
2067.4	♦▲⌐(8) ⌣((	(0.1E) **Horseshoe Canyon Lean-to**, water (spring) is located at the AT junction or the river in front of and below the lean-to, tent sites available, privy. 22.0◄13.0◄8.9◄►12.0►19.4►24.1	N 45 16.968, W 69 37.657 880		123.5
2067.5	♦Y	(0.1E) Horseshoe Canyon Lean-to, see notes above. Spring at trail junction.		859	123.4
2069.7	♦	Ford East Branch Piscataquis River, 50 feet wide and usually knee deep but during high water it can be difficult to cross.		650	121.2

2070.0		Cross Old Bangor and Aroostook Railroad bed, bed no longer has rails.		800	120.9
2070.1	▲P(6)	Cross **Shirley—Blanchard Road**, paved.	N 45 17.087, W 69 35.206	880	120.8
2071.6	▲	Cross logging road.		970	119.3
2073.1	Y▲P(6) ★★★★★	Side trail leads (0.3) east to parking area on north side of Lake Hebron. Not an ATC approved camping spot	N 45 17.412, W 69 31.083	900	117.8

Monson ME (1.7W) to the left when coming off blue blaze trail. **See NOBO mileage 2076.4.**

2074.2		East side of Buck Hill.		1390	116.7
2075.0	Y	Side trail leads (0.1) west to Doughty Ponds, two ponds.		1240	115.9
2076.4	▲P(20) ★★★★★	Cross **ME. 15**.	N 45 19.866, W 69 32.125	1215	114.5

Monson, ME (3.6E). See map of Monson, ME.

- ☒ **PO** M-F 9:15am-12:15pm & 1:15pm-4:15pm, Sa 7:30am-11am. 207-997-3975.
- 🛏🏠▲ **Shaw's Lodging** 207-997-3597. shawshikerhostel@gmail.com (www.shawshikerhostel.com)
- ◈✕♨⛺ AT Passport location.
- 💻🛒🍴🚗 Open Mid-May through Oct.
- ☒ Bunks $25, private room $50S $60D, $12 tenting. Free pickup and return at Pleasant Street and Route 6 trail heads with stay. $9 breakfast, $5 laundry, $5 shower without stay and towel, computer available for use, free WiFi. Food drops.

  Licensed and insured slackpacking and shuttles for all over Maine. Gear supplies include coleman and alcohol by the ounce, canister fuel, Aquamira, freeze dried and packaged food. Gear repair and shake-downs available. Credit cards accepted.

  Mail drops for guests (nonguests $5): PO Box 72 or 17 Pleasant St, Monson, ME 04464.

Lakeshore House Lodging & Pub 207-997-7069, 207-343-5033. (www.thelakeshorehouse.com) AT Passport location.

Bunkroom $25PP cash or $32.40PP with credit card. Private rooms $45S/$60D w/shared bath. Microwaves, fridge, coffee maker available for hiker. Ask about work for stay. Well behaved dogs okay. Reservations appreciated, packs out by 10:30am; full check-out/vacate by noon please, unless otherwise arranged. Free pickup and return from route 6 trail head for guests only, only till 11am for return, loaner clothing, loaner laptop available for use, free WiFi, kayaks, paddleboat, swimming, ATM. Laundry $5 and shower $5 available to non-guests. Pub hours: M closed, Tu-Sa 12pm-9pm, Su 12pm-9pm, bar open later. House quiet by 10pm and NO BINGE DRINKING, social drinking okay. Shaw's guests welcome for breakfast. Accepts credit cards. Parking $1 per day.

Mail drops for guests (non-guests $5): PO Box 215, C/O Lakeshore House, Monson, ME 04464 or UPS/FedEx (no Sat delivery): 9 Tenney Hill Rd.

Charlie Anderson 207-965-5678, 207-997-7069 Statewide shuttles, slackpack, food drops, call for prices.

Monson General Store Deli & Grocery 207-997-3800. Features foods grown locally and local artisan products. DELI offers delicious freshly made items to eat in or take out. In addition to sandwiches, choose from a daily selection of salads, baked goods and other treats.

A.E. Robinson's 207-997-3700. Convenience store, Country Cafe Deli inside serves burgers, pizza, breakfast. M-Su 4am-10pm.

Spring Creek Bar-B-Q 207-997-7025. (www.springcreekbar-b-qmaine.com) M-W closed, Th-Sa 11am-8pm, Sunday 11am-6pm.

The Monson Appalachian Trail Visitor Center monsonvisitorcenter@appalachiantrail.org (www.facebook.com/monsonatvisitorcenter).

AT Passport location.

Open 7 days a week, June 6 through October 14, from 8am-11am and 1pm-5pm (hours subject to adjustment). The Visitor Center is a critical source of information for long distance hikers, short term backpackers and day hikers on the trail in Maine. Northbound long distance hikers should stop in to make plans for entering and staying in Baxter State Park, climbing Katahdin and leaving the Trail. There will also be a small retail operation with souvenirs, maps and t-shirts available.

In the process of moving, this is subject to change.

Greenville, ME 04485 (10.4W from ME 15)

Kineo View Motor Lodge 207-695-4470. (www.kineoview.com) $79 and up-$99D, $10EAP includes continental breakfast, microwave, fridge. From trail head (7.6) north on route 5 and right turn on Overlook Drive (0.4) up drive to Lodge.

Kelly's Landing 207-695-4438. (www.kellysatmoosehead.com) M-Su 7am-9pm, Su offers AYCE breakfast.

Dairy Bar ice cream

Harris Drug Store 207-695-2921. Family owned and operated pharmacy serving the Moosehead Lake region since 1896. Also featuring an old fashioned soda fountain ,dining counter inside. M-Sa 8am-5:30pm, Su 9am-1pm.

Indian Hill Trading Post & Supermarket 207-695-2104. (www.indianhill.com) M-Su 8am-8pm.

Jamos Pizza 207-695-2201. Pizza, sandwiches, take out, breakfast sandwiches, ice, groceries, Ben & Jerry's Ice Cream, beer and wine, local information. M-Th 5am-9pm, F-Sa 5am-10pm, Su 6am-9pm.

Northwoods Outfitters 207-695-3288. (www.maineoutfitter.com) Full service outfitter with fuel by the ounce and canister fuel. Expresso bar, pastries, computer available for use, free WiFi. M-Su 8am-5pm.

Charles Dean Memorial Hospital 207-695-5200. (www.cadean.org)

More restaurants, stores, banks and ATM in town

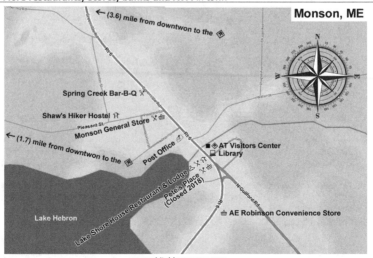

Monson, ME

← (3.6) mile from downtwon to the

Spring Creek Bar-B-Q

Shaw's Hiker Hostel

Monson General Store

Pleasant St.

← (1.7) mile from downtwon to the

Post Office

AT Visitors Center

Library

Lake Shore House Restaurant & Lodge

Pete's Place (Closed 2018)

N. Guilford Rd.

AE Robinson Convenience Store

Lake Hebron

NoBo	Features	Description	GPS	Elev	SoBo
2076.5	♦	Cross Goodell Brook, Spectacle Pond Outlet		1163	114.4
2077.3	⚠	Cross **Old Stage Road**. Was once a stagecoach road to Greenville in the 1800's.		1295	113.6
2077.6	♦	South shore of Bell Pond .		1278	113.3
2077.7	ⵢ	Power line.		1337	113.2
2078.0	📷	Open ledges on ridge.		1438	112.9
2078.3	♦	Side trail leads to Lily Pond.		1130	112.6
2079.4	♦⚞⊏(6)⏝⊀	**Leeman Brook Lean-to**, water (stream) is located in front of lean-to, tenting, privy. 25.0◀20.9◀12.0◀▶7.4▶12.1▶16.1	N 45 21.096, W 69 29.921	1060	111.5
2080.2	♦	Cross stream from North Pond		1000	110.7
2080.6	⚠	Cross **North Pond Tote Road**		1100	110.3
2081.6		Skirt Mud Pond.		1057	109.3
2081.9		Rim of Bear Pond Ledges		1200	109.0
2082.7	♦	Cross James Brook.		950	108.2
2082.9	⚠	Cross gravel haul road.		1000	108.0
2083.0	♦⚒📷	Little Wilson Falls, 60 ft. high. One of the highest falls on the AT.		850	107.9
2083.2	♦⚞⏝	Ford Little Wilson Stream, ford, not an ATC approved camping spot.		750	107.7
2083.5		Cross 200 yard beaver dam.		929	107.4
2083.6	⚠	Follow gravel road for 100 yds.		900	107.3
2084.1	📷	High point along (0.5) long slate ridge.		1152	106.8
2085.1		Deep rock gully.		806	105.8
2085.5	⚠	Cross **Big Wilson Tote Road**.		620	105.4
2085.6	♦	Cross Thompson Brook.		620	105.3
2086.1	♦	Ford Big Wilson Stream.		600	104.8
2086.4	✕	Cross Montreal, Maine & Atlantic Railroad Tracks		850	104.5
2086.8	♦⚞⊏(6)⏝⊀	42 yards west to **Wilson Valley Lean-to**, water small (spring) is located in front of the lean-to on the opposite side of the AT, tenting, privy. 28.3◀19.4◀7.4◀▶4.7▶8.7▶15.6	N 45 23.878, W 69 27.606	1000	104.1
2087.4		Cross old winter logging road.		1190	103.5
2088.0	📷	Open ledges with views east and of Barren Mountain.		1278	102.9
2088.3	📷	Cross 150 yard rocky slope.		967	102.6
2089.6		Base of ridge.		681	101.3
2090.0	♦	Cross Wilber Brook.		660	100.9
2090.1	♦⚒	Cross Vaughn Stream, top of 20 ft. waterfall		670	100.8
2090.6	⚠	Bodfish Farm–Long Pond tote road.		650	100.3
2090.7	♦	Ford Long Pond Stream, usually knee deep.		620	100.2
2091.4	♦Υ⚒	Side Trail to Slugundy Gorge and Falls		870	99.5
2091.5	♦⚞⊏(8)⏝⊀	67 yards east to **Long Pond Stream Lean-to**, water from small spring, tenting, privy. 24.1◀12.1◀4.7◀▶4.0▶10.9▶20.8	N 45 25.269, W 69 24.612	930	99.4
2091.6	ΥP(6)	Side trail east leads to parking area off Bodfish Valley Road.	N 45 24.818, W 69 25.014	1006	99.3
2092.6	Υ📷	Side trail leads 250 feet to top of Barren Slide with good views.		2024	98.3
2092.8	📷	Barren Ledges with very good views of Bodfish Intervale, Lake Onawa and Borestone Mountain.		2022	98.1
2093.8		Base of Barren Mountain.		1942	97.1
2094.6	⛰📷	Barren Mountain summit, remnants of old fire tower		2670	96.3
2095.5	♦Υ⚞⊏(6)⏝⊀	(0.4E) **Cloud Pond Lean-to**, water small (stream) is located to the left of the lean-to, tenting, privy. 16.1◀8.7◀4.0◀▶6.9▶16.8▶24.0	N 45 25.088, W 69 21.229	2420	95.4
2096.9	♦	Cross small stream.		1981	94.0
2097.2		Bog between Fourth and Barren Mountain.		2188	93.7
2097.6	⛰📷	Fourth Mountain summit, wooded.		2383	93.3
2098.4	◊	Cross stream at bottom of sag, unreliable.		1844	92.5
2099.6	Υ	Junction of unnamed trail.		2076	91.3

NoBo	Features	Description	GPS	Elev	SoBo
2100.1	📷	Third Mountain, Monument Cliff.		2061	90.8
2100.7	♦▲Y	Cross tote road and outlet stream. Side trail leads (0.2) east to West Chairback Pond.		1770	90.2
2102.0	📷	Ledge near Columbus Mountain summit.		2325	88.9
2102.4	♦▲⊑(6) ⌣℃	9 yards east to **Chairback Gap Lean-to**, water small (spring) is located downhill and north of the lean-to 25 yards and is known to go dry, tenting, privy. 15.6◀10.9◀6.9◀▶9.9▶17.1▶20.7	N 45 27.189, W 69 15.743	2000	88.5
2102.9	▲📷	Chairback Mountain summit, views of West Branch, Pleasant River Valley and White Cap Range.		2219	88.0
2103.3	📷	Semi open Ledges, views		2000	87.6
2105.1	Y📷	Side trail leads (0.2) west to Chairback Pond. Views of Chairback and Columbus Mountain.		1630	85.8
2105.6	♦	Cross small stream and spring.		1250	85.3
2106.3	▲	Cross **Katahdin Iron Works Road**		750	84.6
2106.8	♦YP(20)	Ford West Branch Pleasant River. Parking (0.2E)	N 45 28.632, W 69 17.106	680	84.1
2107.0	YP	Side trail leads east to Pugwash Pond, Pleasant River campsites, and (0.7) to Hay Brook Parking Area.		680	83.9
2107.1		Side trail leads 200 feet to The Hermitage. **No camping permitted here**.		695	83.8
2108.1	♦Y	Junction with Gulf Hagas Loop Trail.		950	82.8
2108.8	♦Y	Junction with Gulf Hagas Cut-off Loop Trail leads (1.0) west joining up with Gulf Hagas Loop Trail.		1050	82.1
2112.3	♦▲⊑(6) ℃	Cross Gulf Hagas Brook. 30 yards west to **Carl A. Newhall Lean-to**, water (Gulf Hagas Brook) is located south of shelter, tenting, privy. 20.8◀16.8◀9.9◀▶7.2▶10.8▶18.9	N 45 31.866, W 69 18.907	1860	78.6
2113.2	▲	Gulf Hagas Mountain summit.		2683	77.7
2114.1	♦⅄	Sidney Tappan campsite, (0.2) east to spring, tent sites available.		2425	76.8
2114.8	▲	West Peak summit		3178	76.1
2116.4	▲	Hay Mountain summit, wooded.		3244	74.5
2117.0	Y	Junction with White Brook Trail.		3125	73.9
2118.1	▲📷	White Cap Mountain summit, view of Katahdin.		3654	72.8
2119.1	📷	Side trail with lookout of Logon Brook Ravine.			71.8
2119.5	♦▲⊑(6) ℃	**Logan Brook Lean-to**, water (Logan Brook) is located behind the lean-to and cascades are farther upstream, tenting, privy. 24.0◀17.1◀7.2◀▶3.6▶11.7▶23.1	N 45 33.668, W 69 14.124	2480	71.4
2121.1	▲P	Cross **West Branch Ponds Road**, gravel	N 45 34.726, W 69 13.488	1650	69.8
2121.6	♦	Cross B Inlet Brook.		1438	69.3
2123.1	♦▲⊑(6) ℃	**East Branch Lean-to**, water (Pleasant River) is located in front of lean-to, tenting, privy. 20.7◀10.8◀3.6◀▶8.1▶19.5▶23.8	N 45 35.805, W 69 11.894	1225	67.8
2123.4	♦	Ford East Branch Pleasant River.		1200	67.5

NoBo	Features	Description	GPS	Elev	SoBo
2124.0	📷	View of White Cap Range.		1625	66.9
2125.0	💧	Cross Mountain View Pond outlet stream.		1597	65.9
2125.3	💧	Side trail east to spring.		1580	65.6
2125.8		Saddle between Big and Little Boardman Mountain.		1405	65.1
2126.6	Y📷	Little Boardman Mountain, 300 feet to summit		2017	64.3
2128.0	⚠️P(4)	Cross **Kokadjo-B Pond Road**, gravel	N 45 36.993, W 69 7.835	1380	62.9
2128.2	💧	Between two sand beaches on south shore of Crawford Pond. **No camping permitted here**.		1230	62.7
2128.9	💧	Cross Crawford Pond outlet. **No camping permitted here**.		1240	62.0

Cooper Falls Shelter • Church Pond • Jo Mary Rd • Cooper Pond • Mud Pond • Jo Mary Lake • Antlers Campsite • Jo Mary Lake • Potaywadjo Ridge • Potaywadjo Shelter • Pemadumcook Lake • Deer Brook • White House Landing • Tumbledown Dick Stream • Nahmakanta Shelter • Nahmakanta Lake • Prentiss Brook • Wadleigh Stream Shelter • Nesuntabunt Mtn • Crescent Pond • Crescent Pond • Pollywog Stream

2131.2	💧🏕️⛺(6) ➰《 ♨️⛴️	42 yards east to **Cooper Brook Falls Lean-to**, water (Cooper Brook) is located in front of lean-to, tenting, privy across trail and up hill. Water Falls in front of lean-to. Swimming hole in front of lean-to.	N 45 38.427, W 69 05.246		
		18.9◀11.7◀8.1◀▶ 11.4▶15.7▶21.5		880	59.7
2131.4	💧	Cross Cooper Brook tributary.		833	59.5
2134.2	📷	Views of Church Pond can bee seen through trees.		681	56.7
2134.9	💧🏕️⛺ P(10) ★★★★★	Cross **Jo-Mary Road**, gravel.	N 45 39.040, W 69 01.841	625	56.0
	⛺➰♨️⛺	(9.0E) **Jo-Mary Campground** 207-723-8117. Open mid May - Mid Sep. Two person minimun, campsites $7 per person. ME residents $12. Pets welcome, coin operated showers and laundry.			
2136.2	💧Y	Side trail leads (0.2) east to Cooper Pond.		600	54.7
2137.5	🏕️	Cross gravel logging road, snowmobile bridge over Cooper Brook nearby.		520	53.4
2137.8	💧➰	Cross over east end of Mud Brook, Mud Pond Outlet on bridge		508	53.1
2138.4	🏕️	Cross logging road.		565	52.5
2139.1	💧🏕️➰《	Side trail leads 100 yards to Antlers campsite, tent sites available, privy.		500	51.8
2140.3	💧	Cross brook. Treat water do to beaver activity.		574	50.6
2140.6	📷	Side trail leads (0.75) west to Potaywadjo Ridge with good views.		588	50.3
2140.8	💧⛴️	Side trail leads 100 feet to Lower Jo-Mary Lake, sand beach, good swimming.		580	50.1
2142.6	💧🏕️⛺(8) ➰《	31 yards west to **Potaywadjo Spring Lean-to**, water (Potaywadjo Spring) is located to the right of the lean-to, tent sites available, privy.	N 45 42.390, W 69 00.450		
		23.1◀19.5◀11.4◀▶ 4.3▶10.1▶18.2		710	48.3
2143.1	💧➰	Cross Twitchell Brook, bridge		590	47.8
2143.2	💧📷	Side trail leads 75 feet to shore of Pemadumcook Lake, views of Katahdin.		580	47.7
2144.4	💧	Cross Deer Brook.		588	46.5
2145.3	🏕️	Cross gravel logging road.		580	45.6
2145.4	Y ★★★★★	Cross Mahar Tote Logging Road, Blue-blazed trail 0.2E **White House Landing** pickup.		580	45.5

NoBo	Features	Description	GPS	Elev	SoBo
	⛺🍴🏠⬥	**White House Landing** 207-745-5116. Open May 15. Reservation recommended but not required. 1 night minimum for pickup and return to trail head area, arrival dates flexible. Bunk $35PP, semi-private $45S, $85D. Shower, towel, pillow case included; linens extra. AYCE breakfast. Dinner menu includes burgers, pizza and more. Can charge cell phones for a fee. Free use of canoes. Credit cards accepted. Mail drops for guests only: PO Box 1, Millinocket, ME 04462. Allow 10 days for drop to PO box.			
2145.5	◊	Cross branch of Nahmakanta Stream.		580	45.4
2146.4	◊	Cross Tumbledown Dick Stream.		590	44.5
2146.9	◊▲(6) ⌐(8)↝(	400 feet west to **Nahmakanta Stream Lean-to**, water from the stream, 6 tent sites available. 23.8◄15.7◄4.3◄►5.8►13.9►25.4		600	44.0
2148.4	Y	Junction with Tumble Down Dick Trail.		625	42.5
2149.5	◊	Wood Rat's Spring		740	41.4
2149.8	▲	Cross gravel road.		749	41.1
2150.1	◊▲ P(6)	Cross gravel road. Nahmakanta Lake (south end).	N 45 44.155, W 69 06.218	650	40.8
2151.0	◊	Cross Prentiss Brook.		590	39.9
2151.6	◊	Gravel beach on lake shore.		668	39.3
2152.3	◊ Y	Side trail leads 50 feet west to Sand Beach, east to spring		595	38.6
2152.6	◊	Cross Wadleigh Stream.		680	38.3
2152.7	◊▲⌐(6) ↝(	40 yards west to **Wadleigh Stream Lean-to**, water (spring) is located on the beach, tenting, privy. 21.5◄10.1◄5.8◄►8.1►19.6►33.0	N 45 44.840, W 69 08.712	685	38.2
2153.4		Unusual rock formation with rock roof.		964	37.5
2154.6	▲Y📷	Nesuntabunt Mountain summit, side trail leads 250 feet to ledge overlooking Nesuntabunt Lake and views of Katahdin.		1520	36.3
2155.8	▲	Cross logging road.		1010	35.1
2156.4	◊	Crescent Pond (east end)		1014	34.5
2157.0	◊	Crescent Pond (west end)		980	33.9
2157.1	Y	Side trail leads to bottom of Pollywog Gorge.		1021	33.8
2157.4	📷	Side trail leads 150 feet to Pollywog Gorge, good view of gorge.		1050	33.5
2158.4	◊↝▲ P(6)	Cross Pollywog Stream on logging road bridge.	N 45 46.775, W 69 10.336	682	32.5
2159.1	📷	Flume in gorge, remains of old logging dam		1000	31.8

2160.4	◊	Cross Murphy Pond Outlet Stream.		1020	30.5
2160.8	◊▲⌐(6) ↝(	**Rainbow Stream Lean-to**, water (Rainbow Stream) is located in front of lean-to, tenting and hammocking, privy. 18.2◄13.9◄8.1◄►11.5►24.9	N 45 47.945, W 69 10.260	1020	30.1
2161.0	◊	Cross stream, Rainbow Deadwaters (south end).		1060	29.9
2162.6	◊	Cross stream, Rainbow Deadwaters (north end).		1086	28.3

NoBo	Features	Description	GPS	Elev	SoBo
2162.8	◑📷	Rainbow Lake (west end), dam on side trail with Katahdin view		1080	28.1
2164.6	◑𝗔(2)☾	Rainbow Spring campsite, spring west 150 feet, 2 tent sites available, privy.		1100	26.3
2166.1	Y	Unmarked side trail.		1140	24.8
2166.3	Y	Side trail leads (0.75) east to Rainbow Mountain summit.		1100	24.6
2168.0	◑	Rainbow Lake (east end)		980	22.9
2168.1	Y	Side trail leads (0.1) east to Little Beaver and (0.4) further to Big Beaver Ponds.		1100	22.8
2169.8	📷	Rainbow Ledges, open ledges with views of Katahdin.		1517	21.1
2172.3	◑𝗔⊏(6) ☾	**Hurd Brook Lean-to**, water (Hurd Brook), tenting, privy. 25.4◄19.6◄11.5◄►13.4	N 45 49.112, W 69 01.140	710	18.6
2173.0	◑	Small spring.		740	17.9
2175.2		Pass through extensive cedar bog.		625	15.7
2175.6	ⒶＡ	Junction with **Golden Road (Greenville-Millinocket Road)**		600	15.3
2175.8	⌒📷ＡP ★★★★★	Parking area located between Abol Bridge and trail head. Many many parking spots. Cross Abol Bridge over West Branch of Penobscot River, junction with International A.T., Abol Bridge campground and Store **Millinocket, ME. (19.6E).**	N 45 50.112, W 68 58.158	588	15.1

	🛏𝗔✗🍴 ⚓⛺🏪	**Abol Bridge Campground & Store** 207-447-5803. (www.mainewoodsresorts.com Open summer (May-Sept), Campsites $25pp includes breakfast buffet. Bunk cabin $75 for 2, $25 each additional sleeps up to 6. Store hours M-Su 7am-7pm. Full store with subs, sodas, ice cream, long-term resupply. Coin laundry. Free showers, non-guests $5. Satellite Pay phone available. Visa/MC accepted.
	✗▭	**The Northern Restaurant,** full service restaurant with full bar onsite open mid june to end of sept 11am-7pm. Mail drops: $10 mail drop fee, call before sending and send well in advance: P.O. Box 536 Millinocket, ME 04462.
	𝗔	**Abol Pines** $8 ME residents $4, self register tent sites and shelters. Located across the street from Abol Bridge Store.
	🐕	**Connie McManus** 207-723-6795, 207-731-3111 Privately run kennel service; pickup and drop off at Abol Bridge.

Millinocket, ME 04462 (19.6E) from Abol Bridge. See map of Millinocket, ME.

	⌂◈⊛⚐	**The Appalachian Trail Lodge** 207-723-4321. (www.appalachiantraillodge.com)
	💻☎⚓🍴	AT Passport location.
	🚗P▭	No pets. Bunkroom $25, private room $55, family suite $95D $10EAP. Showers for non guests $5. Coin laundry. Computer available for use, free WiFi. Free daily shuttle from Baxter State Park from Sept 1-Oct 24, between 3:30pm–4:30pm. Licensed and insured shuttle service for hire to and from bus in Medway, into 100-Mile Wilderness or Monson, food drops. Slackpack in 100-Mile Wilderness, other shuttles by arrangement, free parking. Southbound special: pickup in Medway, bed in bunkroom, breakfast at AT Cafe, and shuttle to Katahdin Stream Campground. $70 per person, by reservation. Mail drops for guests only: 33 Penobscot Avenue, Millinocket, ME 04462. **Ole Man's Gear Shop** Full line of gear; ULA & Hyperlite packs, bags, fuel, stoves, poles. No clothing or shoes.
	🏃	
	✗◈	**The Appalachian Trail Café** 207-723-6720. AT Passport location. Serves breakfast, lunch and dinner. M-Su 5am-2pm.
	🛏⊛✗ ⛽▭	**Katahdin Cabins** 207-723-6305. (www.katahdincabins.com) Skip & Nicole Mohoff run eco-friendly cabins with continental breakfast, TV, DVD, microwave, fridge. $65 up to 3 persons, $85 up to 5. Cafe on site with coffee and baked goods. No smoking. Gas grill, bikes free for use, community room. Accepts Credit cards cash and checks. Mail drops for guests: 181 Medway Rd, Millinocket, ME 04462.
	🛏☀▭	**Parks Edge Inn** 207-447-4321, 207-227-2692. Rooms for guests ranging from $65 to $150. Larges capacity rooms sleep 6-8. All rooms have kitchen, bath, TV, DVD players, free WiFi. Mail drops for guests with reservations: 19 Central St, Millinocket, ME 04462.
	🛏✗⛽▭	**Pamola Motor Lodge** 800-575-9746. (http://www.pamolalodge.com) $69 and up $10EAP up to 4, prices very depending on season, includes continental breakfast, A/C, free WiFi. Pets $10. Restaurant on site.
	🛏⛽⚓	**Baxter Park Inn** 207-723-9777. (www.baxterparkinn.com) $99 and up, prices very depending on season, $10EAP, pets $25, sauna, pool, free WiFi.
	🛏⛽▭	**Ice Fish Inn** 207-723-9999. (www.icefishinn.com) $115 and up, prices very dependingon the season, includes full hot breakfast ($15 off with out breakfast). Mail drops for guests: PO Box 136, Millinocket, ME 04462.
	🛏✗⛽	**Hotel Terrace & Ruthie's Restaurant** 207-723-4545. $64.95S, $74.95D, free WiFi. Ruthie's; serves breakfast lunch and dinner.

🛏⛺📠📶 **Katahdin Inn** 207-723-4555. (www.katahdininnandsuites.com)
Room rates starting from $84.99/night for two people, includes continental breakfast, indoor heated pool, hot tub, computer available to use, free WiFi, coin laundry, pool tables.

⛺♨⛺🛁 **Wilderness Edge Campground** 207-447-8485. (www.wildernessedgecampground.com)
📠P   Open May 15-Oct 15 (weather permitting)
Tent sites $14pp, free showers. Pool (Memorial Day thru Labor Day). Fuel canisters. Shuttle Service available for a fee. Coin operated laundry- $1.50 each for wash and dry, soap available at store for $1.00 Free Wifi at office. Camp Store bug repellant, soap, toothbrushes, drinks, candy, ice cream, map, souvenirs, etc. RV sites $34.95 for 2 adults. RV sites have water/electric hookups, Dump station on site. Dump station privilege for non-campers $10Free parking for guests of Hikers. Arrangements can be made ahead of time to meet hikers when they exit the 100 mile wilderness or summit Katahdin to get them to the bus depot in East Millinocket.

✗   **Sawmill Grill** 207-447-6996. (www.sawmillbargrill.com) M closed, Open Tu-Sun 11am-11pm in summer. Pizza, spaghetti sandwiches, burgers.

🍸◈   **LanMan's Lounge**
AT Passport location.
28 Hill St. Lounge with TV, restroom; pack storage $5.

🚗   **Maine Quest Adventures** 207-447-5011. (www.mainequestadventures.com)
Will shuttle and pick up anywhere, Medway bus station, Katahdin Stream, Abol Bridge, 100 Mile Wilderness, he means anywhere. Also does Food Drops for by arrangement.

🚗   **Bull Moose Taxi** 207-447-8079. Medway to Millinocket $18, Millinocket to KSC $57. Fares are per ride, $1 EAP up to 4 persons. Covers all of Maine. M-Su 6am-2am.

Millinocket, ME

NoBo		Feature	GPS	SoBo
2175.9	⛰	Junction of **Golden Road and Old State Road**	600	15.0
2176.2	⛰	Junction of gravel and paved roads.	600	14.7
2176.4	Y	Ski trail leads (1.0) east to Abol Pond on old road.	611	14.5
2176.5	♦Y〰	Abol Stream Trail, Abol Stream, Baxter Park Boundary, bridge, ski trail	620	14.4
2176.7	Y	BSP Hiker Kiosk, registration for "The Birches campsite"; Abol Pond & Blueberry Ledges trails	620	14.2
2176.9	♦〰	Katahdin Stream, bridge	620	14.0
2177.0	Y	Foss and Knowlton Ponds Trail	630	13.9
2177.4	♦	Cross small brook.	618	13.5
2177.7	♦〰	Cross Foss and Knowlton Brook on bog bridge.	625	13.2
2179.9	♦Y	Pine Point. Side trail east is high water bypass trail.	640	11.0
2180.3	♦	Ford Lower Fork Nesowadnehunk Stream.	630	10.6
2181.3	♦	Ford Upper Fork Nesowadnehunk Stream.	800	9.6
2181.4		Upstream ledges.	778	9.5
2181.7	♦	Big ledge above Rocky Rips	850	9.2
2182.1	♦Y🛁📷	Side trail leads west 150 feet to Big Niagara Falls.	850	8.8
2182.3	♦	Side trail leads 150 feet east to spring.	990	8.6
2182.4	Y🛁	Side trail leads 150 feet west to Toll Dam and Little Niagara Falls.	1030	8.5
2183.2	Y☾	Junction with Daicey Pond Nature Trail.	1090	7.7

Maine

NoBo	Features	Description	GPS	Elev	SoBo
2183.3		Daicey Pond Campground and Ranger Station.		1114	7.6
2183.4	⛺P	Daicey Pond campground Road, side trail leads to Sentinel Mountain.	N 45 52.945, W 68 1.904	1100	7.5
2183.9	Y	Junction with Tracy and Elbow Ponds Trail.		1100	7.0
2184.4	♦	Junction with Grassy Pond Trail.		800	6.5
2184.6	♦⌒	Cross Elbow Pond on bridge.		1103	6.3
2184.7	♦⌒	Cross Tracy Pond on bridge, views of O-J-I and Doubletop Mountains.		1092	6.2
2184.9	⛺P	**Perimeter Road** (south end), tote road.	N 45 53.446, W 68 0.566	1101	6.0
2185.6	⛺	**Perimeter Road** (north end), tote road.		1070	5.3
2185.7	♦⛺ ⌂(12) ⛺P ★★★★★	Katahdin Stream campground, Ranger Station; (0.24E) **The Birches campsite**, Overnight fee. Advance reservations 33.0◄24.9◄13.4◄►	N 45 53.231, W 68 59.991	1070	5.2
		Millinocket, ME 04462 (24.8E) from Katahdin Stream Campground. See NoBo mile 2175.8. See map of Millinocket, ME.			
2186.7	Y	Junction with The Owl Trail.		1570	4.2
2186.8	♦⌒	Cross Katahdin Stream on footbridge.		1500	4.1
2186.9	♦⚠📷	Side trail leads 50 feet west to Katahdin Stream Falls.		1550	4.0
2187.8	◊	Cross small brook, unreliable.		2721	3.1
2188.4		"The Cave", small slab cave		4500	2.5
2188.5	📷	Hunt Spur, tree line at base of "The Boulders"		3400	2.4
2189.3	📷	Gateway to Tablelands		4600	1.6
2189.9	♦	Thoreau Spring		4627	1.0
2190.9	📷	Katahdin, Baxter Peak, sign, plaque, cairn.		5268	0.0

Manufactures

AntiGravity Gear	910-794-3308	www.antigravitygear.com
Arc 'Teryx	866-458-BIRD	www.arcteryx.com
Asics	800-678-9435	www.asicsamerica.com/footwear/
Asolo/Lowe Alpine	603-448-8827, ext. 105	www.asolo.com
	800-490-4502	
Backcountry	800-953-5499	www.backcountry.com/
Big Agnes	877-554-8975	www.bigagnes.com
Black Diamond Equipment	877-554-8975	www.blackdiamondequipment.com/
Camelbak	877-404-7673	www.camelbak.com
Campmor	800-226-7667	www.campmor.com
Camp Trails	800-345-7622	www.camptrails.eu/
Cascade Designs/ MSR/Therm-a-Rest/Platypus	800-531-9531	www.cascadedesigns.com
Cedar Tree (packa)	276-780-2354	www.thepacka.com
Columbia	800-622-6953	www.columbia.com
Danner	877-432-6637	www.danner.com
Eastern Mountain Sports(EMS)	888-463-6367	www.ems.com
Elemental horizons	919-280-5402	www.elementalhorizons.com/
Etowah Outfitters	770-975-7829	www.etowahoutfittersultralightbackpackinggear.com/
Eureka	888-6EUREKA	www.eurekacampingctr.com
Ex Officio	800-644-7303	www.exofficio.com
Feathered Friends	206-292-2210	www.featheredfriends.com
Frogg Toggs	800-349-1835	www.froggtoggs.com
Garmin	800-800-1020	ww.garmin.com
Garmont	800-943-4453	www.garmont.com/en
Gossamer Gear	512-374-0133	www.gossamergear.com
Golite	888-546-5483	www.golite.com/
Gossamer gear	512-374-0133	www.gossamergear.com/
Granite Gear	218-834-6157	www.granitegear.com
Gregory Mountain Products	877-477-4292	www.gregorypacks.com
	800-521-1698	
Hi-Tec US	209-545-1111	www.hi-tec.com/us/
Hyperlite Mountain Gear	800-464-9208	www.hyperlitemountaingear.com
Inoveight	508-480-8856	www.inov-8.com/
Jacks 'R' Better	757-643-8908	www.jacksrbetter.com
Jansport	800-552-6776	www.jansport.com/
Katadyn/PUR	800-755-6701	www.katadyn.com

Keen	866-676-5336	www.keenfootwear.com/
	866-349-7225	
Kelty Pack, Inc.	800-535-3589	www.kelty.com
Leki	800-255-9982, ext 150	www.leki.com
Lightheart Gear		www.lightheartgear.com/
L.L.Bean	800-441-5713	www.llbean.com
Lowe Alpine Systems	303-926-7228	www.lowealpine.com
Marmot	888-357-3262	www.marmot.com
Merrell	800-288-3124	www.merrell.com
Mont-bell	303-449-5331	www.montbell.com
Montrail	855-698-7245	www.montrail.com
Moonbow Gear	603-744-2264	www.moonbowgear.com
Mountain Hardwear	877-927-5649	www.mountainhardwear.com
Mountain Laurel	540-588-1721	www.mountainlaureldesigns.com/
Mountainsmith	800-426-4075, ext. 2	www.mountainsmith.com
MSR	800-531-9531	www.cascadedesigns.com/msr
Mystery Ranch	406-585-1428	www.mysteryranch.com/
NEMO Equipment	800-997-9301	www.nemoequipment.com/
New Balance	800-595-9138	www.newbalance.com/
The North Face	855-500-8639	www.thenorthface.com
Osprey	866-284-7830	cs@ospreypacks.com
Outdoor Research	888-467-4327	www.outdoorresearch.com
Patagonia	800-638-6464	www.patagonia.com
Peak 1/Coleman	800-835-3278	www.coleman.com/
Petzl	877-807-3805	www.petzl.com
Photon	877-584-6898	www.photonlight.com
Platypus	800-531-9531	www.platy.com/
Primus	888-546-2267	www.primusstoves.com
Princeton Tec	609-298-9331	www.princetontec.com
REI	800-426-4840	www.rei.com
Royal Robbins	800-587-9044	www.royalrobbins.com
Salomon	800-654-2668	www.salomonsports.com
Sierra Designs	800-736-8592	www.sierradesigns.com
Sierra Trading Post	800-713-4534	www.sierratradingpost.com
Six Moon Designs	503-430-2303	www.sixmoondesigns.com
Slumberjack	800-233-6283	www.slumberjack.com
Speer Hammocks	252-619-8292	www.tttrailgear.com
SOTO Outdoors	503-314-5119	www.sotooutdoors.com
Speer Hammocks	252-619-8292	www.tttrailgear.com/
Spot	866-651-7768	www.findmespot.com/en/
	855-258-0900	
Suunto	800-543-9124	www.suunto.com
Tarptent by Henry Shires	650-587-1548	www.tarptent.com
Teva/Deckers Corporation	800-367-8382	www.teva.com
The Underwear Guys/Warm Stuff	570-573-0209	www.theunderwearguys.com/www.warmstuff.com
ULA-Equipment	435-753-5191	www.ula-equipment.com
Vasque	800-224-4453	www.vasque.com
Western Mountaineering	408-287-8944	www.westernmountaineering.com
ZZManufacturing (Zipztove)	800-594-9046	www.zzstove.com

Planning and Preparation

Planning

Planning and preparing for hiking the Appalachian Trail curtails a lot. Every person is different. Some want to hike with the lightest gear they can find. Some are warm weather people and want to carry gear that will keep them warmer than others. Other want to dehydrate their own food, others will mail drop food to themselves or buy food along the way. Then there is the dilemma of what tent should you take or should you take a hammock. There is a lot to planning and hiking on the Appalachian Trail. I could go on and on and on about this but each person is different. You can ask and research some of this on web sites like www.whiteblaze.net.

I think the most important part of hiking on the Appalachian Trail is the mental preparation which is discussed next.

Mental Preparation

I have offered my opinion to prospective thru hikers for years, explaining that the trail is more mental than physical. Kyle Rohrig talks about mental preparedness in his book titled "Hear the Challenge... Hike the Appalachian Trail". I have paraphrased a portion of it and I believe his explanation is real good.

Completing an Appalachian Trail thru-hike is a major undertaking.

For completing a thru-hike (completing the whole trail in a calendar year) it is usually about 10% physical and 90% mental. You've got the gear, you've got the money, but do you have the mental toughness/strength and tenacity needed to achieve your goal? Once you get out there you can be sure to expect pain, misery, discomfort, and suffering within a wide range of varying degrees (do not let this scare or intimidate you). Some of your gear, as well as how much money you brought will sometimes play a part in how little or how much of this you endure (in some areas). In other areas, nothing will save you from some of the more unpleasant experiences of the Appalachian Trail. When these unpleasant experiences occur, what will you do? Will you break and quit? Or will you rise to the occasion, bend with your circumstances and adapt accordingly to any and all obstacles as you encounter them? Yes, your mind, attitude, and outlook will be the deciding factor on whether you complete your epic endeavor or not.

Mental Toughness "Mental Toughness" is something you're going to need a great deal of when it comes to completing your thru-hike. In its most basic definition, mental toughness is the voice in the back of your head that tells you "keep going, don't give up, you can't quit now." While out on the trail, you're going to have A LOT of internal dialogue with yourself, possibly more than you've ever had in your entire life. The big question is... what will the tone of that internal dialogue be? Will it be mostly negative or positive? Will you be trying to talk yourself "into quitting" or "out of quitting?" Will you be counting the reasons to "stay on" trail, or reasons to "get off" trail? Your internal dialogue while on the trail will play a huge part in your mental state; in turn, directly influencing your chances of victory.

Besides the internal dialogue that you will be having with yourself nearly every solitary second spent out there, you will have a large amount of other factors that will evoke responses from your mental/emotional state. One of the greatest markers of mental toughness is the ability to control your emotions. Not "control" so much in the sense of repressing them, but in understanding them. If you're not in control of your emotions, then they're in control of you. Being able to realize and understand why you feel a certain way, but still be able to make rational decisions despite how you may feel is HUGE. I cannot emphasize that point enough. So many people make snap/impulse decisions based on how they feel at the present moment; they seldom stop to think, "Why do I really feel this way?" or "Is this really the best thing to do at this exact moment?"

This sort of mental toughness comes into play when you're thinking about quitting. There are many things that will make you question your decision to thru-hike and possibly consider quitting; things like physical pain, misery, suffering brought on by the elements, missing home, missing loved ones, missed expectations, becoming bored, or thoughts of, "I'll never make it." Thoughts are strong, but feelings are stronger. Your feelings of discomfort, boredom, or pain in the present moment can mislead your thoughts into making irrational decisions that have long term consequences/effects. You can lie to yourself with your thoughts, but your feelings will always be true, yet less in your control. This is why being able to understand and control your feelings to a certain extent is so important. You need to be able to use your thoughts clearly when your temporary feelings of the present moment may be clouding your judgment. To put it in better perspective; pain, misery, depression, discomfort, etc. are all "feelings" that can very rapidly lead to low morale and the decision to quit. There's no getting around the fact that you will experience these feelings at some point during your journey, if not many times throughout. Once these feelings arise, they're going to be accompanied by thoughts - the voice inside your head that interprets those feelings. Are your thoughts going to feed into the negative aspects of your feelings, subsequently initiating a downward spiral? Or will you keep a focused, level headed handle on your thoughts... understand and accept your feelings for whatever they may be, then use them to get through whatever outward or inward obstacle you may be facing? Don't let your thoughts defeat you on account of your feelings. Pain, misery, bad weather, tough terrain; none of it lasts forever - so don't make a decision that does. Remember, "This too shall pass."

When you've gone out there to attempt a thru-hike, it's safe to say that you "wanted it" pretty badly. At some point in your life you decided you wanted to hike over 2,000 miles and accomplish one of the great feats and adventures our planet has to offer. However, in order to seize that goal, you'll have to want it more than anything else in the world, before and during the endeavor. You know that deep inside yourself, completing the Appalachian Trail is what you want. So, what is the only thing (besides injury and running out of money) that can possibly stop you from achieving your desire of a completed thru-hike? The answer is YOU. You are the only one who can stop yourself from reaching your goal. Completing an Appalachian Trail thru-hike is as simple as not quitting. Don't quit, no matter what, and your dream is as good as realized.

So, let us delve deeper into things that make people quit, as well as why someone would make the decision to quit. The most blatant explanation for quitting in almost any circumstance would undoubtedly be "rationalization." We humans are rational creatures, and we can rationalize just about anything in order to make it make sense to us, or seem like the right thing to do. You can rationalize positive things, as well as negative things. If you put your mind to it, you can rationalize pretty much any decision you could ever make to seem like the right or wrong decision. It all depends on whichever one you "feel" is more beneficial to you at the present moment. Pain and suffering (feelings!) do funny things to the human brain. It can cause you to rationalize decisions you "think" you really want to make, when in fact you really don't. Rationalization is so powerful that when you're under stress and pain, you can actually convince yourself that finishing your Appalachian thru-hike is something you never truly wanted. Maybe this is true, but more often than not, you're only fooling yourself. You don't decide to hike over 2,000 miles and not have really wanted it at some point. When do most people realize they rationalized a lie to themselves when they decided quitting was the best decision to make (at whatever time they decided to make it)? That moment of regret is when they realize they deceived themselves. They made a decision in the heat of the moment that they didn't actually believe in, and then regretted it very shortly afterward. Once they're away from the pain and suffering of the moment, and able to think clearly, they realize, "What was I thinking? I really did want to complete this adventure! Why did I talk myself out of it and quit!?" Mental toughness will help you to avoid rationalizing "heat of the moment" decisions you will later regret. It is the ability to look past your present suffering to realize you will most likely regret any decisions to quit, thus deterring you from quitting; this ability is part of what demonstrates an aspect of your mental toughness.

Portions taken from - Hear the Challenge, Hike the Appalachian Trail

By

Kyle S. Rohrig

Keeping a journal during your hike or thru hike

If you are thinking about keeping a journal during your hike, I highly recommend it. Keeping a journal is something that you will never regret and will greatly appreciate later on in life. As the days and years go by after the conclusion of your hike your memories get a little vague and fuzzy on how events happened and what took place during your hike. Time has a way of making us forget things. Keeping a journal of some type will allow you to go back and recapture all those memories and feelings that you experienced. Your journal is a souvenir to your future self. You will be able to look back and smile and laugh when you reread it, a truly priceless gift. It will also anchor you to where you were at a given point in time, on and off the trail during your hike.

I find myself going back and looking at my journals to see where I was on a certain date during my hike and end up reading through the entire day's entry. It brings my mind back to the places I was and sometimes just reading that journal entry reminds me of things I forgot to include. The journal was such a great gift to myself.

Getting into the habit of writing it down

Start your journal before your hike. Try to get yourself in the habit before you start your hike by doing a journal entry daily. This will help you get into the routine of keeping a journal. During your hike, you can write in it any time you want, as the thought or the occurrence happens or whenever the moment strikes you. Remember this is your journal; write in it when you want or as much as you want. (I did mine at the end of the day before I went to bed, that was what worked best for me.). I also stopped at times during my hike and wrote notes in it to remind me of things to write.

Finding the time during your hike

Find the time to write in your journal is the most important tip of all. If you do not get into the routine of writing in your journal regularly, you will find yourself skipping a day here and a day there. Next thing you know you will be skipping a whole week. Try to commit or program yourself to write to it daily, or do some form of regular writing. You should not make writing in your journal a chore; rather make it something you want to do. Find a way to make it enjoyable. A journal can be a helpful way to wind down at the day's end, especially if it's a comfortable place for you. Use your camera to take lots of pictures of something to help you remember what went on during the day or what your thoughts were at that time.

Don't fuss about grammar, spelling, or other imperfections. You need to write it down while it is still fresh in your memory. You can always go back and fix the grammar and spelling later. Wanting to erase errors while working through the day's events and your thoughts and ideas can hamper your flow. Pretend you are with a group of friends that were not with you during the day and you are telling them all the details and events of what went on during that day. Write in your journal anything you want. Doodles are totally acceptable. Lyrics to songs, poems, book excerpts, anything goes. Remember this is your journal, write whatever you want.

Always remember to date your entries and your location!

Notes for using any cell phone

I know hikers that used cell phones for their journals. They worked well for them but the biggest complaint from them was their batteries were always going dead. When you're not using your phone either turn off the phone or place it into airplane mode. Putting it into airplane mode will turn your phone off from trying to find cell phone towers. That is the biggest battery drain your phone will experience when you are hiking. When your phone is on it is constantly looking for a cell phone tower to lock onto and if it is not locked onto a tower it will continue to look for one until it finds one. Roaming is the biggest battery drain your phone will most likely experience. This is the reason to either turn it off or place it in airplane mode when not using it. Off is most likely better.

Date:

Date:

Date:

Date:

Date:

Date:

Date:

Date:

Notes/Numbers/Contacts/Passports

Date:

Date:

Date:

Date:

Date:

Date:

Date:

Date:

Date:

Date:

Date:

Date:

Date:

Date:

Date:

Date: